Return to

IXIL

Return to
IXIL

MAYA SOCIETY in an
EIGHTEENTH-CENTURY
YUCATEC TOWN

Mark Christensen
and **Matthew Restall**

University Press of Colorado
Louisville

© 2019 by University Press of Colorado

Published by University Press of Colorado
245 Century Circle, Suite 202
Louisville, Colorado 80027

 ASSOCIATION of UNIVERSITY PRESSES   The University Press of Colorado is a proud member of
the Association of University Presses.

The University Press of Colorado is a cooperative publishing enterprise supported, in part, by Adams
State University, Colorado State University, Fort Lewis College, Metropolitan State University of
Denver, University of Colorado, University of Northern Colorado, University of Wyoming, Utah
State University, and Western Colorado University.

∞ This paper meets the requirements of the ANSI/NISO Z39.48–1992 (Permanence of Paper).

ISBN: 978-1-60732-921-3 (cloth)
ISBN: 978-1-60732-922-0 (ebook)
DOI: https://doi.org/10.5876/9781607329220

Library of Congress Cataloging-in-Publication Data

Names: Christensen, Mark Z., author. | Restall, Matthew, 1964– author.
Title: Return to Ixil : Maya society in an eighteenth-century Yucatec town / Mark Christensen and
    Matthew Restall.
Description: Louisville : University Press of Colorado, [2019] | Includes bibliographical references
    and index.
Identifiers: LCCN 2019018475 | ISBN 9781607329213 (cloth) | ISBN 9781607329220 (ebook)
Subjects: LCSH: Mayas—History—18th century—Sources. | Mayas—Social conditions—18th
    century—Sources. | Indians of Mexico—Mexico—Yucatán (State)—History—18th
    century—Sources. | Indians of Mexico—Mexico—Yucatán (State)—Social conditions—18th
    century—Sources. | Wills—Mexico—Yucatán (State) | Ixil (Mexico)—History. | Ixil (Mexico)—
    Social life and customs.
Classification: LCC F1435 .C574 2019 | DDC 972/.6—dc23
LC record available at https://lccn.loc.gov/2019018475

Cover photograph by Matthew Restall

To our penultimates

Grant, little buddy through it all,

and

Lucy, who makes the world a better place

Contents

Figures

Tables and Text Boxes

TABLES

TEXT BOXES

Acknowledgments

MATTHEW RESTALL: Mark Christensen is first author on this volume, not just by alphabetic logic, but because it is in multiple and profound ways *his* book and *his* work. Without his discovery of the second batch of wills (explained in the introduction), his infectious enthusiasm for translating and analyzing them, and his tireless commitment to a transparent presentation of that work, *Return to Ixil* would not even have existed in my imagination, let alone in print. It has been a joyful privilege to work with him, and the fact that Mark was my doctoral student adds an additional layer of pleasure and pride. I would like to acknowledge the late James Lockhart, my own doctoral advisor, for introducing me to indigenous wills many decades ago; and Susan Kellogg, my first collaborator in thinking and writing about wills made by indigenous peoples of the early Americas. And I would like to thank Victoria Bricker, who decades ago gave me access—despite the fact that I was someone else's lowly graduate student—to the Tekanto wills, and spent hours with me in New Orleans discussing the language of Maya testaments and related topics. It was thus a true honor when, many years later when I was editor of *Ethnohistory*, she sought to publish in that journal her own articles based in part on Ixil's wills (see Bricker and Hill 2009; Bricker 2015). Finally, I thank Amara Solari, my ever-constant touchstone on all professional and personal matters, who proved particularly helpful with this project because she just happens to read colonial-period Yucatec Maya extremely well, to understand colonial-era Maya religion far better than I do, and to live with me.

MARK CHRISTENSEN: When I first arrived at Penn State in 2006 as Matthew Restall's graduate student, I could not have imagined a better mentor. True, his unparalleled knowledge and skill in working with colonial texts guided my own research in invaluable ways. Yet most inspiring was his encouragement. As any scholar and author will attest, often what really is needed is someone to listen to your ideas and then encourage their fruition with genuine enthusiasm. Matthew has never failed in this regard, and I am incredibly grateful. I am proud to be his perpetual student. I would also like to thank Rebecca Horn, who first introduced me to testaments and the New Philology, as well as John Chuchiak, who has always been so very generous with his assistance and sharing of his deep knowledge of colonial Yucatan. The firsthand knowledge of David Bolles has likewise proved immensely beneficial, and I am grateful. Ixil has occupied much of my spare time over the past decade, and my loving wife, Natalie, has been nothing but gracious in her support and understanding. Although my job as a historian has me so often immersed in the past, she and my children help bring me back to the present they make so enjoyable.

CHRISTENSEN AND RESTALL: We would like to thank Jessica d'Arbonne, formerly at the University Press of Colorado, for her support and encouragement, and her successor, Charlotte Steinhardt; without either of them, this book would not be what it is and probably not even exist. Alison Tartt handled a tricky copyediting task with great skill and aplomb. We are also grateful to Samantha Billing and Kate Godfrey, who while doctoral students at Penn State played crucial roles as editorial assistants to this project; thanks especially to Sam's efficiency and understanding of the project, the book was finished sooner and in better shape. Samantha Davis likewise provided important assistance as a research assistant in the compilation of data from the wills, and we thank her too. The thoughtful and astute comments of two anonymous readers also strengthened and improved the book, and we are very grateful. Finally, we acknowledge the generous publication subventions from the College of Family, Home and Social Sciences at Brigham Young University and from the College of Liberal Arts at the Pennsylvania State University.

Return to
IXIL

Introduction

Finding Testaments

MATTHEW RESTALL: In the spring of 1990, I was hunting in Merida, Yucatan, for documents written in Maya during the colonial centuries. With the naïve doggedness of a graduate student in my mid-twenties, I went from archives to libraries, from professors' offices to priests' anterooms, convinced that there were hidden stashes of Maya land records, testaments, and even a few Books of Chilam Balam. The latter—quasi-notarial compilations of knowledge descended from the famous and (mostly) destroyed codices of the pre-Columbian Maya—were not to be found in desk drawers in Merida.[1] But in a local school library a teacher told me there was a Maya manuscript in red ink gathering dust on a back shelf.

The manuscript was indeed in Yucatec and in red. But it had been typed on an old typewriter and, as best as I could make out, consisted of erotic poetry (whether bad or good, I was not qualified to judge). My hopes, raised momentarily so high, were dashed again. Then I noticed that at the bottom of the pile of loose papers was a bundle of folios tied with old twine. The ink was black, handwritten, in Maya. The first page was badly faded, but the rest were perfectly legible. Having already spent time with the Testaments of Tekanto—at that point, the only extant corpus of wills from a single colonial Maya town[2]—I instantly recognized that these were wills, colonial-era wills. Before my eyes was a treasure trove of information about a network of Maya families who two centuries earlier had lived, loved, squabbled, and died in a small town not far from where I was sitting.

DOI: 10.5876/9781607329220.c000

The wills numbered sixty-five in total, all from the *cah* (sociopolitical unit for the Maya, plural *cahob*) of Ixil, situated fifteen miles (as the crow flies) northeast of Merida, and all dating from 1765 to 1768. Providing a glimpse into the material and spiritual world of Ixil's residents during that sliver of time, the testaments offered rare details into everyday late-colonial Maya life. Although I was convinced that more such collections remained to be discovered, I knew that these surviving testaments of Ixil were sufficiently rare to warrant publication. I had also given a copy of my index and transcriptions of the wills to a venerable Merida scholar, who held a press conference to announce "his" discovery—complete with a show-and-tell of the original wills and "his" transcriptions—weeks after I had returned to the United States. In retrospect, his betrayal was harmless (and after all, as a Yucateco, he probably regarded the wills as part of his cultural heritage, not mine), but at the time it prompted in me a sense of urgency; in 1995 a small California press published my transcriptions and translations of the wills, as *Life and Death in a Maya Community: The Ixil Testaments of the 1760s*, with minimal analysis. (That venerable scholar is long deceased, by the way, and that small press defunct.)[3]

The summer after the book came out, I returned to Ixil to donate a copy to the town. I feared the gesture might be a little patronizing and presumptuous (who was I to tell the people of Ixil about their ancestors?), but a local official (whose surname was Pech) put me at ease by laughing at me and asking why I had wasted my time on such a project. He then walked me over to the school, where the teacher accepted the book (figure 0.1); she was as bemused as Señor Pech but very gracious, and I was grateful to them for humoring me so generously.

MARK CHRISTENSEN: In the summer of 2007, I found myself in a small, upstairs room in Merida's cathedral, accompanied by dozens of old cardboard boxes softened from the malfunctioning air conditioner's failed attempts to drive away the smothering humidity and bursting with colonial documents that also showed the effects of the Yucatan's unforgiving climate. I was in the Archivo Histórico de la Arquidiócesis de Yucatán, searching for any ecclesiastical text written in Maya. Of course, the nun who accompanied me into the room assured me that no such documents existed, a statement the director of the archive, the late Monsignor José F. Camargo Sosa, delivered to me personally (the same priest had told Restall the same thing seventeen years earlier). Yet any Latin American scholar who has spent time in archives knows the potential rewards awaiting those who graciously, but stubbornly, must "see for themselves."

After days spent rummaging through myriad colonial documents, I had already discovered a handful of religiously oriented Maya texts. Then, after several weeks, I found a collection of bound Maya documents at the bottom of a box titled "*Oficios*."

FIGURE O.I. The schoolteacher of Ixil receiving a copy of *Life and Death in a Maya Community*, 1996. (Photograph by Matthew Restall)

The word "*oraciones*" was penciled on the top of the first document, but after closer inspection it became apparent that the documents were not prayers but testaments.[4] Monsignor Camargo Sosa graciously allowed me to digitally photograph the corpus, enabling me to return home to the United States to examine the documents.

Numbering thirty-eight in total, the testaments and codicils largely covered a span of one year—from January to December 1748—but, interestingly, none of the testators had declared their town of residence, thus making the testaments' origin a mystery. However, after closer inspection, Restall recognized the name of the *batab* and some individuals on the *cabildo*, or town council, as the same as those found in his later corpus of Ixil testaments. A quick comparison confirmed that the 1748 corpus of testaments originated in the *cah* of Ixil. The two sets of wills were almost certainly surviving pieces of the fat book of wills maintained during the colonial period for centuries by the notaries of Ixil. This fact presented us with a unique situation. We now had Maya testaments that detailed aspects of the material and spiritual lives of Ixil's native residents for over forty years.

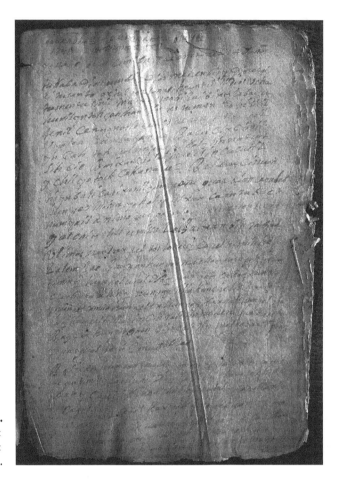

FIGURE 0.2.
Example of a last
will and testament
from Ixil (A1).

Whereas similar—and admittedly larger—corpora of testaments exist in Nahuatl, until now the Yucatan had been without a Maya equivalent.[5] In my doctoral dissertation, later published as *Nahua and Maya Catholicisms* (Christensen 2013), I made use of both sets of corpora from Ixil. However, Restall and I had planned immediately to combine the two sets into a single corpus and publish a larger social history of the town. This book is a result of that protracted effort, set in motion over a decade ago.

CHRISTENSEN AND RESTALL: The combined corpus consists of 102 testaments written between 1738 and 1779 and maintained by the *cabildo* (figure 0.2). Within this collection of testaments, a third are from 1748, a third from 1766, and a quarter from

TABLE 0.1. Number of Ixil wills and codicils by corpus and year

	1738	1748	1755	1760	1765	1766	1767	1768	1769	1773	1777	1779	Total
Christensen (A) corpus		34	1	3									38
Restall (B) corpus					5	34	24	2		1	2		68
Individual wills (C)	1								1			1	3
Total													109

Note: The letters *A*, *B*, and *C* are our designations for each corpus; see appendices A and B.

Sources: AHAY, "Oficios, 1748–1749, 1801–1884," vol. 1, "Peten Itza"; CAIHY and Restall (1995); ANEY (see appendix B for details).

1767 (table 0.1). The collection also includes three additional Ixil testaments discovered outside the two corpora. Inserted among the two bodies of testaments are seven codicils mostly discussing the affairs and receipts of bequeathed items from various wills (figure 0.3). Aside from their other insights, these codicils offer a possible explanation as to why bound corpora of Ixil testaments have been found in various archives. During the colonial period, the testaments of Ixil were preserved by the town's *cabildo* in a bound collection.[6] Yet when legal disputes over bequeathed items arose, large sections of testaments were removed and relocated to settle the disputes.

In many ways, and as hinted in the title of this book, this expanded corpus of testaments allows us to return to Ixil with new perspectives and insights. The return illustrates how many of the core elements of Maya society that Restall uncovered for the town in the 1760s likewise existed in 1748. Patterns of inheritance, wealth distribution, nobility, and status all persist throughout the forty years of testaments, albeit with some change over the decades. The expanded corpus allows for more detailed discussion of such topics.

However, our return likewise boasts many new discoveries regarding Ixil and its inhabitants, facilitated not only by the 1748 testaments, but also through an extensive search in the archives for any accompanying documentation shedding further light on obscure issues revealed in the wills. As a result, our return reveals the role of Ixil in the defense of the Yucatan Peninsula against pirates; new details on the role of its native government and the religious workings of the town; and intimate particulars surrounding family and everyday life in Ixil. In the end, this book employs newly discovered testaments and documents not only to update our understanding of Ixil but also to make exciting new contributions to current historiographical conversations—a return trip that is, we trust, worthwhile.

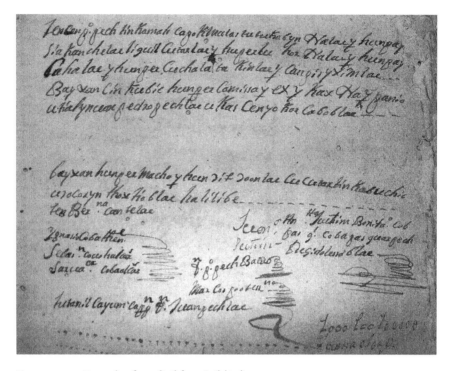

FIGURE 0.3. Example of a codicil from Ixil (A2).

THE HISTORIOGRAPHY OF INDIGENOUS TESTAMENTS AND THIS BOOK

The last will and testament stands alone in its ability to reveal detailed insights into the lives of the rich and poor, male and female; its formulaic religious preamble provides information on the religious exposure and experience of the town and scribe; the names within provide clues into genealogies, social networks of trust, and communal politics; even the deaths recorded allude to the presence of epidemics and/or famines. Put simply, there is a reason scholars continually return to the last will and testament as an invaluable source to the past; those studying the indigenous cultures of the colonial Americas are no exception.[7] In many instances, certain people and places would simply not exist in the historical record, or the subsequent histories it inspires, without the last will and testament. And Ixil is a perfect example.

Excluding last wills and testaments, the archival footprint of Ixil is limited in details. Indeed, without the wills, the town would hardly ever appear in the historical narrative. The town shows up in a few census records and in a few reports and travel accounts. Even the Chilam Balam of Ixil—produced in the town itself and portrayed proudly on its town sign (figures 0.5 and 2.6)—is little referenced and known compared with others more popular, such as the Chilam Balam books from Kaua, Tizimin, and Chumayel.[8] Hence the importance of this corpus of last wills and testaments from Ixil. These documents, although emerging from death, breathe life into this otherwise ignored Maya town.

Other colonial towns in New Spain have seen similar acts of historical resurrection. S. L. Cline and Miguel León-Portilla (1984) placed a spotlight on the Nahua town of Culhuacan with their publication of sixty-five Nahuatl testaments. Philip Thompson's 1978 dissertation and 1999 publication employed the Testaments of Tekanto to produce an insightful social history of the town. As mentioned, Restall initially focused on Ixil and its testaments in 1995, and others such as Stephanie Wood (1991) and Caterina Pizzigoni (2007) would do the same for the Nahua region of Toluca.[9] In most of these works the testaments and their transcription and translation take center stage, oftentimes accompanied by brief, yet insightful, commentary. Recently, however, scholars have begun to use testaments as the backbone of illustrative social histories that place emphasis on the everyday life of the town rather than its testaments. The works of Pizzigoni (2012) and Miriam Melton-Villanueva (2016) provide apt examples.

The present work attempts a marriage between both historiographical trends. The book follows the more recent pattern of reconstructing the social history of a colonial town through its testaments and additional documentation. Indeed, rather than presenting the testaments with their translations and a few comments, the chapters of this book convey new and detailed descriptions of various aspects of life in Ixil so that, to the extent possible, a better portrait of the everyday life of families in the town emerges. This portrait of quotidian life is placed within the larger context of colonial life in Yucatan to better understand the similarities and differences evident in Ixil. That said, the testaments themselves are valuable documents, essential in illustrating this portrait of Ixil, and this book includes frequent references and callouts to their transcription and translation provided for interested readers in full in our appendix B.

ORGANIZATION OF THE BOOK

Each of the book's chapters engages a different aspect of colonial life in Ixil. Although the work, on occasion, employs insights and commentaries found in Restall's original 1995 publication, the overwhelming majority of the content in each chapter reflects revised and updated interpretations of family life in Ixil. That said, the 1995 publication contains valuable observations on the wills themselves, and we refer readers to the earlier work for additional insights.

Chapter 1 identifies the Maya notaries of Ixil and their role in composing the town's testaments themselves. Often overlooked as mere scribes parroting the dictates of their superiors, notaries played an important role in shaping the material and spiritual lives of those dying in Ixil. The chapter employs the expanded corpus to provide an innovative comparison of notarial styles and preferences that better distinguishes between the contributions of the notary and those of the testator himself or herself.

Chapter 2 exposes in new ways the role of Ixil in the defense of the Yucatan from pirate attacks. The military titles adorning the names of a few nobles in their testaments reflects the presence of a militia in Ixil and the role of the Maya in staffing the nearby coastal watchtower, and the chapter employs a wide array of documents to reconstruct the town's contribution to the defense of the town and the colony. While contributing to the burgeoning scholarship on native militias in Yucatan, this chapter also illustrates how those who defended the town likewise served as its governors. Through an examination of the *cabildo* signatures included in every will within the corpus, the chapter provides an uncommonly clear view of which family lineages maintained their noble positions within the *cah* through its local governance.

Chapter 3 examines the economy of Ixil and its participants. The chapter exposes the connection between noble lineages and wealth while detailing patterns of gender ownership and the means and modes of production in Ixil compared over spatial and temporal lines. Importantly, the chapter exposes the large population of Ixil families claiming nobility—an image that sharply contradicts the assumption of a small noble minority.

Chapter 4 addresses religious life in Ixil through a triangulation of three types of source materials: the religious formula, vocabulary, and items in testaments; religious texts found in the Chilam Balam of Ixil; and ecclesiastical reports and records. All combine to provide a clearer image of God in Ixil and the role of the Maya and ecclesiastics in creating such an image.

Finally, chapter 5 uncovers the intimate familial relationships betrayed by the wills. The chapter provides deeper understandings of inheritance patterns, genealogical connections throughout the decades covered by the wills, and marriage patterns that reveal the frequent practice of endogamy among the Pech lineage. Two appendices follow the conclusion, providing an overview of the Ixil corpus and its relation to other archival documents (appendix A) and our transcriptions of the original Maya documents and our translations of them into English (appendix B), whichprovide additional details and scholarly fodder.

IXIL, THEN AND NOW

As it was back then, Ixil is now a small Maya town, or *cah*, located in the north-west of the Yucatan Peninsula in what was the Ceh Pech region—the network of *cahob* dominated by the Pech lineage, or *chibal* (plural, *chibalob*), for an uncertain number of centuries prior to the arrival of Spaniards in the early sixteenth cen-tury.[10] Although archaeologists have not surveyed Ixil and its neighbors (as far as we know), it is clear from the town's layout and its surviving mounds of ancient masonry that colonial-era Ixil evolved from precolonial Ixil. Its ancient plaza remained in the same location, while the church was built upon an existing plat-form, using stones from what were presumably pyramidal and temple structures (figures 0.4–0.9). Centuries of repurposing such structures have left overgrown masonry mounds immediately behind the church (on what was once the same plat-form) and beside it, marking one end of the large original plaza. In addition to the two surviving mounds, a third, far larger mound—facing the plaza and across from the church—lasted until 1940, when it was destroyed by the town's government under a mayor named Lorenzo Poot. Ixil baker and local historian Juan Francisco Orilla Canche lamented that such "destruction benefited nobody and removed one of Ixil's attractions, from which one could very nicely watch the baseball [played in the plaza] and enjoy the breeze from the sea [nine miles away]."[11]

An eighteenth-century document written in Yucatec Maya and known as the Title of Yaxkukul records Ixil's first appearance in colonial history, albeit retro-actively. The document is an ex post facto attempt to record the aid Macan Pech and his town Yaxkukul provided to the Spanish conquistadors—a common tactic employed by many indigenous towns and nobles throughout New Spain to encour-age favor with, and petition benefits from, the new regime. Macan Pech's assistance included tribute payments, and the document records how he and other Maya nobles "were the first to pay tribute to the foreigners."[12] Included among these other Maya nobles was Ah Dzulub Pech of Ixil.

In general, towns located on the *camino real*, or the main road connecting Campeche and Merida, experienced greater Spanish contact, and Ixil's location on the other side of Merida and away from that main road allowed it some degree of anonymity. Nonetheless, in 1549 the conquistador Julián Doncel was recorded as the *encomendero* of Ixil, which supplied him with six *fanegas* of salt and three *arro-bas* of fish in annual tribute.[13] These items reflect the fact that Ixil's northernmost lands extended to the ocean and lagoons important in the production of salt—a practice long predating the arrival of the Spaniards. Moreover, reports indicate that in 1686 Ixil was among those towns contracted to provide maize to Merida, a common condition given the growing urban population of the region's most popu-lous city.[14] Like many Yucatecan towns on the frontier of Spanish colonialism, Ixil

FIGURE 0.4. Ixil's colonial-era church and plaza, 2009. (Photograph by Matthew Restall)

FIGURE 0.5. Ixil's colonial church and its modern town sign (*letras turísticas*), painted by Óscar Ek and erected in the plaza in August 2018. This photo was taken a week after the sign was unveiled. (Photograph by Matthew Restall)

FIGURE 0.6. One of the precolonial mounds, unrestored and mostly obscured by trees, behind Ixil's colonial-era church, 2009. (Photograph by Matthew Restall)

FIGURE 0.7. A view from near the top of the precolonial mound shown in fig. 0.6, looking toward the church, 2018. (Photograph by Matthew Restall)

FIGURE 0.8. The view from the mound shown in figs. 0.6 and 0.7, looking across to a second, smaller precolonial mound, 2018. The smaller mound likely marked one corner of the ancient plaza on which the colonial church was built. (Photograph by Matthew Restall)

would remain an *encomienda* throughout the colonial period despite the Crown's attempts to end the practice in 1542.[15]

As for its religious status, or its position within the church's jurisdictional structure, Ixil's modest size prevented it from ever making head-town or *cabecera* status, and instead it remained throughout the colonial period a subject town, a *sujeto* and *visita*, to various other, larger towns. As early as 1582, Ixil appeared as a *visita* to the town of Conkal.[16] Later, in 1609, Ixil was recorded as a *visita* to nearby Mococha and its few resident ecclesiastics (there were three in 1808) until early in the eighteenth century when it became reassigned back to the *cabecera* of Conkal.[17] Indeed, although Ixil appears as a *visita* of Mococha in 1700, various reports from 1721 to 1803 list Conkal as the *cabecera* of Ixil.[18]

For example, in his summary included in a 1785 *visita* report, the curate of Conkal, fray Francisco Sánchez y Gálvez, identified the towns in his *doctrina*. A *doctrina* consisted of a *cabecera*, or head town where the priests typically resided, and its constituent *visitas*, or smaller towns that ecclesiastics would visit on occasion. Sánchez

FIGURE 0.9. A view of the second, smaller mound seen in fig. 0.8, with Ixil's church beyond it, 2009. (Photograph by Matthew Restall)

y Gálvez placed Conkal as the center of the *doctrina* with Chicxulub, Cholul, Sicpach, Ixil, and Chablekal as its *visitas*. In the end, the reasons for Ixil's reassignments between Mococha and Conkal are unknown, but such were not wholly uncommon as populations changed and jurisdictions of *doctrinas* were reevaluated.

Regarding population, in 1700 Ixil had a tributary population of 729, down to 715 in 1721.[19] Moreover, in his 1785 summary report, Sánchez y Gálvez paints an image of a parish once beautiful and great but which in the recent past largely consisted of towns with dilapidated and forgotten buildings. Sánchez y Gálvez blames this on the "epidemics and horrible famines that in the past had come to this our province" and claims that the parish is just beginning to recover. For evidence of the devastation, he comments that in 1769 tribute included 300 *mantas* (a blanket or measure of cotton cloth).[20] Yet by the following year "the calamity that again was suffered which, in truth, should forever be remembered in our annals" reduced the tribute quota to a little more than 100 *mantas*. According to the priest, many Maya abandoned the towns and fled into the wild during the "lamentable epidemic," but then returned, and by 1785, the collected *mantas* increased to 242.[21]

Ixil's modest size and small, fluctuating population in the late eighteenth century may help explain why today there appear to be few, if any, stone houses that date from the colonial period. Orilla Canche reports the local belief that "the large houses that are on the plaza" date from the nineteenth century.[22] A few of them show signs of having colonial-era bones, with lower walls built from repurposed precolonial masonry, but much or all of what is clearly visible does indeed reflect renovations of the nineteenth and twentieth centuries. We might thus reasonably imagine that in the eighteenth century the vast majority of Ixil's buildings, including those around the plaza, were wattle-thatch structures on stone foundations.

Like the corpora of testaments from Cacalchen and Tekanto, Ixil's testaments correspond to periods of epidemic and famine reported by colonial officials and even the Maya themselves.[23] In their insightful study concerning the topic, Victoria Bricker and Rebecca Hill employ both death records and wills to illustrate the intimate relationship between testament composition and periods of famine and disease.[24] Indeed, the Ixil corpus of 1765–67 correlates with, and reflects the impact of, the famine of 1765–68. Locusts in 1765 and a hurricane in 1766 accompanied by more locusts destroyed crops, leading to widespread hunger and starvation that affected young and old alike. The wills themselves contain examples of this tragedy. For example, in 1766 Diego Chan (B14) left a parcel of land to his grandson, Gabriel Tec. Yet Gabriel had little time to enjoy his inheritance, as just six days later he himself was dictating his will (B15). Moreover, the terse will of Nicolás Chan (B60) in 1767 provided a brief but specific reference to Nicolás Chan's condition—he was *sot*, "dropsied, swollen-bellied." The term recalls modern photo images of malnourished children in famine-ravaged countries, and in a moment what was the mundane business of dying in a Maya community is now tragedy brought to life.

The wills in the 1748 corpus could relate to the 1747 El Niño that caused droughts due to the cooler temperatures in the Atlantic Ocean and the subsequent fewer hurricanes in the summer and fall. The drought seemed to last only a year, and Tekanto fared better than Ixil, losing forty residents in 1747 but only seven in 1748.[25] Whether the 1748 deaths in Ixil corresponded to the El Niño is uncertain, yet likely. More certain is the heightened loss of life during that year, generating thirty-four testaments and thereby matching 1766 as the two years producing the most wills.

Children are among the testators, and comparative analysis of the two sets of wills paints a revealing and poignant picture. The hardships of 1748 forced many parents to bury their children, and the children to compose statements bequeathing any future inheritance they are to receive from their parents to others—29 percent of testators in 1748 made such a request of expected inheritances. The full corpus of wills also contains examples of young children passing, at times before a proper testament could be drawn up. For example, the will of Joseph Couoh (B16) contains simply a religious preamble with no property bequeathed. Opaque on its own, when compared with the death's entry in the parish records, additional details emerge, including the fact that Joseph was nine years old and died on January 3,

1766. Two days after his death, his grief-stricken parents had a will composed that included the proper requests for a mass to speed the soul of their young child through purgatory.[26]

One of Ixil's most significant roles during the colonial period, at least potentially, concerned defense. From the late sixteenth century into the turn of the eighteenth century, pirates were an all too frequent reality for those in the port cities of the Caribbean, and their presence threatened larger metropolises like Merida. Contrary to popular belief, Spain lacked a standing army in New Spain and would not begin to provide such until the 1760s. Thus, the defense of colonial Yucatan largely fell to local militias consisting of free and enslaved black men, mixed-race *mulatos* or *pardos*, and Mayas.[27] The colonial government required towns situated on or near the coast, such as Ixil, to staff a militia and defend important roads and coastal watchtowers, or *vigias*. The *vigia de Yxil* (watchtower of Ixil) appeared in various colonial maps of the coastline illustrating both the watchtower's importance and its connection to Ixil. Indeed, an eighteenth-century map detailing the depths and contours of Scorpion Reef (figure 0.10)—located sixty miles north of Progresso on the northern coast of Yucatan—marks its location from Ixil's *vigía*. As will be seen in chapter 2, various noble families in Ixil acquired military titles such as "captain" and "*alférez*," for their service in the militia.

Today, although it is roughly twenty miles southeast of the port city of Progreso and fifteen miles northeast of Merida, Ixil's seeming proximity to these two pop-ular Yucatecan cities has not endowed it with much notoriety. Simply put, the vast majority of Yucatecans, not to mention American tourists, will never visit the town, although numerous high-end beach houses continue to appear along the picturesque coastline of the municipality. Yet this does not prevent Ixil from having a vibrant life of its own, with a particular local identity and set of cultural traditions—as reflected in the images painted on the *letras turísticas* erected in the plaza in 2018 (figure 0.5). The town celebrates the feast day of its patron saint, San Bernabé, with a variety of festivities—including a bullfight. Just as the ancient plaza has witnessed baseball games, beauty contests, reenactments of Caste War battles between "*blancos*" and "*indios*," and other Carnival celebrations, so has it hosted generations of bullfights. The wooden ring is placed within throwing distance of the church. The small, local bulls, soon worn down by torment and fear, are then butchered in the ring; as dusk descends on the ancient plaza and blood soaks into its soil, the people of Ixil crowd round to claim choice cuts of meat.[28]

Throughout the peninsula, Ixil is perhaps best known for its *cebollitas*, or small onions, depicted on two of the four letters of the new town sign. Ixil, reportedly, is the only town to grow the vegetable, and the unique soil around the town gives the onions their distinct sweetness. The industry is closely and proudly guarded by a

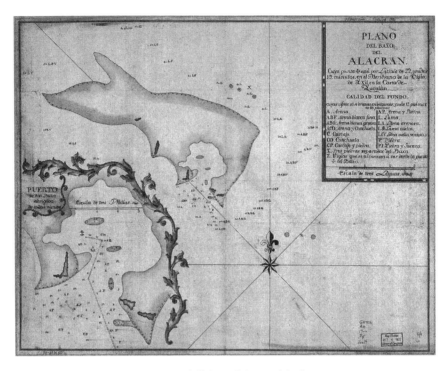

FIGURE O.10. Map of Scorpion Reef. ("Plano del Baxo del Alacran: cuya punta esta por latitud de 22. grados 19. minutos en el meridiano de la Vigia de Yxil en la costa de Yucatán," undated [17–?], Library of Congress, Geography and Map Division, G4752.A4 17-.P5)

handful of local families who fiercely defend its traditions and struggle against the frequent flooding that occurs.[29]

Ixil was for long a Maya town that was exposed to and involved in, but was not overrun by, Spanish society; it remains a town with deep Maya roots whose families—bearing the names of both their Maya and Spanish ancestors—continue to actively engage the outside world while continuing to maintain a highly local life, as they have for many centuries.

NOTES

1. For summary of the Books of Chilam Balam and their relationship to other colonial texts see Christensen (2016: 12–18).

2. By 1990, the original Tekanto documents had disappeared from the ANEY in Merida, where they had been found by Philip Thompson in the 1970s, but I was able to access

photocopies in private hands in the United States; Thompson's doctoral study of the wills had also been filed in 1978 and published as *Tekanto, A Maya Town in Colonial Yucatan* in 1999. By 2014, the Tekanto wills had been recovered and deposited in the AGEY. The other corpus of Yucatec Maya wills whose originals remain long lost, but which survive in the form of copies (in this case, photostats), is the semilegible set from Cacalchen, mentioned further below, but see Restall (1997: 435, detailed "Cacalchen" index entry; 1998b: 145–47).

3. The original 1765–68 wills are, to the best of our knowledge, now in CAIHY; hereafter we refer to them as the Restall corpus or the B corpus, also citing Restall (1995). The bulk of Restall's original analysis of the Ixil wills went into his 1992 doctoral dissertation, revised as 1997's *The Maya World* (also see 1998b).

4. Years later I noticed that Nancy Farriss commented in her *Maya Society* (1984: 450n44) on a collection of testaments misfiled in the AHAY and certainly the same collection I found.

5. The seventeenth-century wills from Cacalchen, mentioned above, survive only in barely legible photostats and are few in number; while the extant wills from Tekanto number 412, only a few go beyond testamentary formuli to make bequests or discuss other personal arrangements.

6. The identical holes on the top of each testament indicate that they were kept in a bound collection. The Christensen or A corpus originals are in AHAY, "Oficios, 1748–1749, 1801–1884," vol. 1. The individual wills or C corpus are in ANEY, 1819iv, fols. 19r, 19v, and 37r (note that the colonial-era volumes of ANEY, for some time stolen and lost, were recovered and are currently in the AGEY).

7. For a general overview of the historiography of examining wills, see Christensen and Truitt (2015: 5–7).

8. Although Caso Barrera (2011) does much to remedy the situation.

9. Other notable works of a broader spectrum include Martina Will de Chaparro's work on New Mexico (2007) and Gabriela Ramos's study of native testaments and conversion in Lima and Cuzco (2010).

10. Restall (1997: 14, 28, 64, 87–97, 149, 278–89; 1998a: ch. 6).

11. Orilla Canche (2005: 25). We are grateful to Tatiana Seijas for finding Orilla Canche's memoir and buying a copy from one of the members of Ixil's baker family. As historians of the Ceh Pech region, we would be thrilled if archaeologists were to survey and dig in Ixil. But it seems unlikely. The peninsula is peppered with over a hundred similar towns.

12. Restall (1998a: 112–13).

13. Roys (1957: 46); Quezada (2014: 134). For the eighteenth-century beneficiaries of Ixil's *encomienda* see García Bernal (1972: 72, 144). A colonial-era Spanish *arroba* was roughly 25 pounds (11.5 kilograms), and a *fanega* was typically 55 liters but varied greatly.

14. Patch (1993: 79). This contract continued into the eighteenth century.

15. García Bernal (1972: 144).

16. Hanks (2010: 44).

17. Carrillo y Ancona (1883: 56).

18. AGI, México, 1035; Patch (1993: 60); AHAY, Visitas Pastorales, 1803–4.

19. AGI, México, 1035; Cogolludo (1688: bk. 4, ch. 20, 237); Patch (1993: 60).

20. For an overview of the annual tribute that Mayas owed, see Farriss (1984: 41, table 1.1).

21. AHAY, Visitas Pastorales, 1782–85, Conkal.

22. Orilla Canche (2005: 8).

23. For an overview of such reports, see Farriss (1984: 61–62); Bricker and Hill (2009: 235–36); Hoggarth et al. (2017: 82–113).

24. Bricker and Hill (2009).

25. Ibid., 250.

26. For the death record of Joseph Couoh, see FS-MY, "registros parroquiales y diocesanos, 1543–1977," Conkal, San Francisco de Asís, Defunciones 1682–1802, image 220 of 452; parroquias Católicas, Yucatan.

27. For more on colonial militias see Vinson (2002); Restall (2009: 153–77, 239–42, 252–55).

28. As observed by Restall on San Bernabé's Day in 1990 and 1996.

29. José Tec Poot, an anthropologist and promoter of Maya culture native to Ixil and well known in the town, wrote a piece on the *cebollitas* for *Diario de Yucatán*.

1

Notaries and the Making of Testaments in Ixil

*Ten cen essno cin zic u hahil bicil amal mankinalob ychil no missa tin uuyah u xocol u
hunil u visita ah yum noh tzicbenil yum ahau caan hele u hahil en 23 de mayo de 1788
anios.*

I, who am the notary, put the truth here how on every occasion within the high
mass I heard (read out) the paper of the notification of the visit of the great priest,
the honorable bishop. Today, the truth, on May 23, 1788.

   —Juan Couoh, notary[1]

*En 6 de marzo de 1769 años Lay u kinil Cin kamic u takin Ca yum Animas sinquenta
y quarto pesos . . . y Uunpel libra U cibil tu tanil priostre y mayordomoob . . . Uay U
hahil yn frmo.*

March 6, 1769. On this day I received the money for the [*cofradía* of] Our Lord of
Souls, fifty-four *pesos* . . . and one pound of honeycomb. Before the administrator
and majordomos . . . Here is the truth, I sign.

   —Clemente Mukul, patron and notary[2]

*Teabo y Nobi 22 de 1803 anos Ca ti ɔoci yn canbal hoksic hunpel Libro fasion u kaba u
tial txocol Ca u sates ten yn yumob hemax bin ylic ua yan Kasite ten u ɔeɔil u Palilob
Uay ti Cah Teabo lae*

DOI: 10.5876/9781607329220.c001

Teabo, November 22, 1803, when I finished learning to bring forth (perform) a book called Passion in order for it to be read. That they may forgive me, my lords, who will see if there are errors, I who am the least of their servants. Here in this *cah* of Teabo.

—Baltasar Mutul, notary[3]

Documents are the foundational underpinnings of any historical work. Yet all too often we neglect those who wrote them—the scribes or notaries.[4] Particularly in New Spain, notaries can be overlooked as mere cogs in a larger notarial machine driven by Spanish colonialism. The preassigned rubrics they followed and the volume of documents they produced at the behest of others oftentimes seem to relegate them to a historical role of voiceless copyists. Seen in one light, the notaries above served as simple secretaries recording entries and following the dictates of their superiors. In another light, they shine as important members of the town leadership. These notaries were entrusted, as was Juan Couoh, to ensure adherence to the mandate that episcopal visits be announced prior to the bishop's arrival; they were distinguished, as was Clemente Mukul, who served first as notary to his *cofradía*, then patron, then *maestro* to the town; and they were erudite, as was Baltasar Mutul, who composed a Passion text for his town of Teabo. As Kathryn Burns demonstrated for notaries in Peru, writing was indeed connected to power.[5]

With regard to testaments, the notary's role was to record the testator's final spiritual and material bequests according to an established rubric. In one light, testament making in Ixil was the mundane, inconsequential task of a copyist. In another, it was the privileged responsibility of the few literate Maya that governed, and one that had profound social and religious impact on its inhabitants. Thus, this chapter begins this book's ethnohistorical study of Ixil's testaments by first examining their authors. Specifically, the chapter examines the notaries' rotation, status, and individual contributions to the testaments themselves along with those of the testators. In so doing, it gives each of the various notaries a distinguishable voice and recognizes their distinct preferences that further illustrate their importance in Ixil and its social and religious life.

THE NOTARY IN IXIL

The Spanish success in establishing a colonial system in New Spain relied in large part on Spaniards' custom of building upon preexisting structures, both physically and politically. Particularly in the Yucatan, Spaniards never even came close to outnumbering the indigenous population, and so a system of indirect rule and local governance was essential. Prior to the arrival of the Spaniards, the Maya employed a socially stratified hierarchy of governors and rulers taken from the nobility to oversee their religious and political affairs.[6] Thus, every Maya community having *pueblo* status quickly adapted to the Spanish-style town council, or *cabildo*, introduced in the colonial period. It included the position of *escribano*, scribe or notary.

The Maya sculpted and shaped the colonial position of notary to resemble more its prehispanic predecessor, the *ah dzib*, or "he who writes." In some cases, the prehispanic *ah dzib* stepped directly into the position of notary, taking with him his knowledge of Maya hieroglyphs.[7] Yet in all cases the Maya notary held a position of prestige elevated above that of his Spanish counterpart. Spanish practice held the notary at the lowest position in the hierarchy of the *cabildo*; the Maya ranked it as slightly below if not equal to that of the town's political leader, the *batab* (plural, *batabob*). John Chuchiak noted that despite Spanish notarial law stating that the notary's signature should be the final one on any document, Maya *batabob* and notaries continually signed the document together "either before the other officials of the *cabildo*, or in the center of the page, with the lesser officials' signatures off to the right- and left-hand sides."[8] The wills from Ixil confirm this tendency, as seen in figure 1.1.

The early Franciscans in Yucatan established schools for the sons of the Maya elite to train the province's future leaders. From these schools emerged the *maestros* and notaries—the only two positions requiring literacy and the only two salaried positions in the community.[9] *Maestros* served as religious caretakers of a Maya town tasked, among other things, with the instruction of Catholic doctrine.[10] Notaries composed a wide range of documents, including petitions, *registros* (notarial books) of all types, wills, bills of sale, complaints, receipts, and other local communal documents. For many of these tasks, notaries collected fees in addition to their salary, ranging from two to four *reales* for a will and one to two *reales* for a signature.[11]

Often, the notary held the responsibility of maintaining the town's written archive, both official and unofficial. Native notaries frequently composed the numerous and mundane ecclesiastical records that the priest was required to maintain. Two examples, of many, concern the towns of Chicxulub and Ixil, where Maya notaries penned baptismal records that friars subsequently signed. The Chicxulub record (figure 1.2) reads as follows:

En el 7 de Abril de 1783 a.s Bautice y puse los Santos olios a Juana yja lixitima
de Paspar taCu y de Manuela bas Cahnal Uai ti Cah Chicxulub lae Padrino D.n
Domingo Zapata

fr. Franc.ᶜᵒ Sanchez[12]

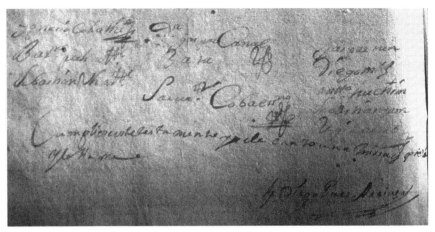

FIGURE 1.1. *Cabildo* signature, Ixil, 1748 (A14).

On the 7th of April, 1783, I baptized and placed the holy oils upon Juana, legitimate daughter of Gaspar Tacu and Manuela Bas, residents here in this town of Chicxulub. Don Domingo Zapata, godfather.

—Fray Francisco Sanchez (rubric)

The Ixil record (figure 1.3) reads as follows:

Baixan tu kamah Caput sihil huntu[l] xibil pal ydalgo cahnal Yxil sihi tu kinil Sabado en 30 de Disiembre [1797] u mehen Mateo Pech y al M.a Josefa Pech cahnalob Yxil u kila cabil u yume Luis Pech y Franca Pech u kila cabil u na franco Pech y Dominga Pech u Padrinoe Lucas Yam y Micaela chan u Kaba lay pala Josef M.a u ah okotbae u yum San Josef in pixnal yum padre Fuentes tu betah lay oc ha lae.

(Left-hand margin) *Jose M^aaria Ydalgo*[13]   *Fr. Fuentes*

Likewise, one noble boy, resident of Ixil, received baptism; born on Saturday, December 30, [1797], the son of Mateo Pech and the child of María Josepha Pech, residents of Ixil. The lineage of the father is Luis Pech and Francisca Pech; the lineage of the mother is Francisco Pech and Dominga Pech; the names of the godparents for this child, Joseph María, are Lucas Yam and Micaela Chan; his advocate is the lord San Joseph; my blessed lord Padre Fuentes performed this baptism.

(Left-hand margin) Joseph María, noble   Fr. Fuentes (rubric)

The spelling, orthography, and use of Yucatec Maya in both entries betray native notaries who would have composed documents for an ecclesiastic to sign later—in a similar fashion to wills.[14]

FIGURE 1.2. Baptismal record by a Maya notary, Chicxulub, 1783. (FS-MY, "registros parroquiales y diocesanos, 1543–1977," Ixil, San Bernabé, Bautismos 1782–1808, image 13 of 551)

FIGURE 1.3. Baptismal record by a Maya notary, Ixil, 1797. (FS-MY, "registros parroquiales y diocesanos, 1543–1977," Ixil, San Bernabé, Bautismos 1782–1808, image 352 of 551)

That the entries and verifying signatures of births, baptisms, marriages, and deaths often differed in both author and date of composition is made certain with a comparison of records. On January 4, 1766, both Isidro Pech and Antonia Coba died, the former in Conkal, the latter in Ixil. Yet both entries, done in separate hands and appearing in separate ledgers, bear the signature of fray Juan de Hoyos, the curate of Conkal, who simply verified and recorded that the event and accompanying rites occurred.[15] According to expectations confirmed by the 1722 ecclesiastical Yucatecan synod and those enforced by late eighteenth-century *visitas* (a bishop's pastoral visitation to a province), every *cabecera* was to maintain individual books containing, baptismal, confirmation, marriage, and death records for itself and its *visitas*.[16] Maya notaries would often compose such entries, which would later be signed by the Spanish curate.

With regard to Ixil, it is unclear why the Maya notary who penned the baptismal record for Joseph María Pech did so in Yucatec Maya. Indeed, it is strange that the baptismal ledger for Ixil from 1784 to 1799 was kept in Maya at all, whereas all other known Ixil ledgers and entries are in Spanish. Moreover, the Maya entry for Juana Tacu of Chicxulub states clearly that it was done in the town itself. It seems that on occasion, then, at least for Chicxulub and likely Ixil and perhaps others,

Maya notaries composed the ledgers locally in their towns for which Conkal was responsible. This, after all, is not unheard of, as unofficial death, birth, and marriage records appear penned by town notaries in various forbidden and locally preserved texts such as the Books of Chilam Balam and Maya Christian copybooks. In the end, and regardless of the location of the ledgers, the role of native notaries in composing such records is clear.

As mentioned, notaries could also be responsible for penning quasi-notarial documents—unofficial, unauthorized texts or texts composed outside the supervision of ecclesiastics and intended for a Maya audience. Indeed, the privileged duties of the notary for many Maya *cahob* included both official and unofficial tasks, as made evident by the many forbidden texts that ecclesiastic officials confiscated throughout the colonial period.[17] One example of a notary engaging in unofficial or quasi-notarial text production concerns the aforementioned 1803 copybook on the Passion of Christ from Teabo. The local native rulers of the town gave Baltasar Mutul the responsibility of composing the work, and he consequently signed his name at the end as *escribano*, complete with his particular rubric.[18]

The rubric itself is yet another distinction of status above that of other Maya positions. Spanish law decreed that a notary be issued a particular rubric to employ when signing his documents to prevent possible cases of forgery. Maya rubrics are, admittedly, not as lavish as their Spanish counterparts in the *escribano* business, often appearing as a series of loops or squiggles (figure 1.4)—although such a rubric would be perfectly respectable as used by a literate Spaniard who was neither a professional notary nor a high-ranking nobleman.

Regardless, the rubrics of Maya notaries distinguished their position above that of other members of the *cabildo*, with exception of the *batab*, who likewise could usually sign with a rubric (although not always) and who might have been a notary himself earlier in his career. As the colonial period progressed and the training of notaries increasingly became a communal responsibility fulfilled outside the monasteries, current notaries could handpick their successors, thus ensuring it as a position for elites only. Indeed, although Spaniards eventually appointed Maya commoners as governors in some towns, the position of notary largely continued to be a position for the native nobility.[19]

The Ixil testaments and codicils provide a unique insight in the *cah*'s rotation of notaries. To prevent conflicts, Spanish authorities theoretically prohibited the continuous holding of the office of notary among local indigenous men.[20] Yet in practice this was oftentimes ignored. Towns such as Cacalchen and Tekanto and the *cahob-barrios* (as Restall dubbed them) of Merida-Tiho—San Sebastián, Santiago, La Mejorada, Santa Ana, and San Cristóbal—illustrate a pattern of

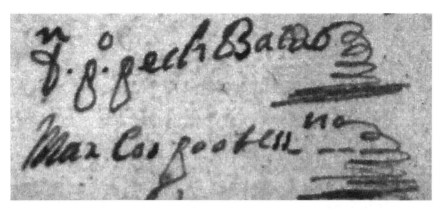

FIGURE 1.4. Rubrics of don Pedro Pech and Marcos Poot, *batab* and notary, Ixil, 1755 (A2).

semi-consistency with regard to the notary.[21] Here the notaries often resembled the *batab* or *maestro* and stayed in their position for extended amounts of time. Mateo Couoh served as notary in Tekanto for a striking nineteen consecutive years from 1683 to 1702.

Ixil's testaments, however, suggest that the town elected annually its notary in late November and that the position rotated among a select cache of individuals (table 1.1).[22] Despite the reappearance of regulars such as Marcos Poot and Pablo Tec, Ixil's consistent rotation of notaries is impressive for a town of its small size. It is possible that an Ixil notary occasionally held the position for a few consecutive years, as many of its testaments are dated years apart from each other, thus preventing a consistent, year-by-year glimpse. In reality, supply and demand along with famines, plagues, and death affected the rotational nature of the position for any town. However, the occasional run of sequential testaments suggests a trend, at least during the 1760s, of a strict annual rotation.

For example, the longest stretch of continuous years found in the extant wills occurs between 1765 and 1769. The notaries Marcos Poot and Pablo Tec passed the position back and forth from 1765 and 1768, with Alonso Cob, who took the position in 1769. Occasionally, the names of two notaries appear on a will, but this occurs in only two scenarios and both with Marcos Poot. The first scenario regards the months of December or January when the transition between notaries takes place. Perhaps the elected notary (re)familiarized and oriented the incoming notary by allowing him to compose a few testaments toward the end of the elected notary's tenure. This would allow, for example, the incoming notary, Marcos Poot, to pen various wills composed in late 1766 while including the name of the elected notary, Pablo Tec. Even with the names of both notaries appearing on the wills, a

TABLE 1.1. Notaries in Ixil (1738–1807)

	1738	1748	1755	1760	1765	1766	1767	1768	1769	1773	1777	1779	1786	1798	1807
Juan Cetz	X														
Salvador Coba		X													
Marcos Poot			X			X	X				X				
Joseph Cob				X	X										
Joseph Cob/ *Marcos Poot*					X										
Pablo Tec						X		X							
Pablo Tec / Marcos Poot						X									
Alonso Cob									X						
Diego Chim										X					
Domingo Itza												X			
José María Chim													X		
Estebán Yam														X	
Ysidro Cob															X

Note: This table builds on an earlier table in Restall (1997: appendix C). Italicized names are those serving as a substitute notary.

distinction is made. As the elected notary for that year, Tec always signs as *essno publico*, or public notary, while Poot signed simply as notary in 1766.[23]

The second scenario occurs with Poot appearing as *mahan kab*, literally "hired hand," or, in this case, substitute notary, in the tenure of the elected notary, Joseph Cob, at the end of 1765.[24] The testaments bearing Poot's name as *mahan kab* are all in his hand, and it seems that Cob's name appears only as a formality. Cob had previously served as notary in 1760 and would later become *batab* in 1773. Why Cob could not finish his elected year serving as notary is uncertain; perhaps he was battling illness. Within the available corpus, Cob served as notary in 1760 and again in 1765, but never thereafter. However, as Poot was not the incoming notary for the upcoming year of 1766—that job fell to Pablo Tec—he signed as *mahan kab* instead of "notary," perhaps indicating the impromptu nature of his hired services.

As noted, the Ixil corpus is illustrative of the *cah*'s limited literacy and the restriction of the position of notary to select, noble families—the Cetz, Coba, Poot, Cob,

TABLE 1.2. The Dzul lineage as notaries in Ebtun, 1787–1829

	1787	1789	1790	1791	1792	1795	1796
Joseph	X	X	X			X	
Lorenzo				X		X	X
Bernardino					X		
Ignacio							
Manuel							
Lino							

	1808	1809	1811	1812	1813	1815	1816	1817	1822	1823	1825	1829
Joseph												
Lorenzo			X	X	X							
Bernardino	X	X										
Ignacio			X		X							
Manuel						X		X	X	X	X	X
Lino						X	X					

Source: Ebtun notarial documents in Roys (1939).

Tec Chim, Itza, and Yam lineages. Most prolific was Marcos Poot, who appeared serving as notary in 1755, 1766, 1767, and 1777. However, the Cob and Chim lineages also appear repeatedly, with the former having three individuals as notary and the latter having two.[25]

The eastern Yucatecan town of Ebtun also offers an excellent example of the restriction of literacy and the position of notary to select families (table 1.2). Available documents suggest that the Dzul family dominated the position of notary for nearly half a century, if not longer. In Ebtun father likely trained son or nephew in the trade, allowing various members of the Dzul *chibal* to pen the town's written record. In some years, two separate members of the Dzul *chibal* appear as notary for different documents; yet no distinction between notaries such as "notary," "notary public," or "*mahan kab*" is given like that seen in Ixil.

Overall, Ixil's testaments join with documentation from other Maya towns to provide further testimony to the individualized nature of communal politics within the *cahob* while shoring up the assertion that privileged positions such as notary were highly guarded by the traditional precontact Maya elite of the town.

IXIL'S PREAMBLE

Emerging from a Roman tradition, the last will and testament abounded throughout Europe as an effective tool in settling both the temporal and spiritual affairs of the dying. That death came quickly and as a surprise was especially true in the medieval and early modern periods, and the Catholic Church placed an expectation upon all its believers to complete a will. For Gabriel Tec (B15) of Ixil, the composition of a will held such importance that he dictated his when taken ill in the neighboring town of Mama. It is probable that his concern and desire for a will included the benefit of his soul, but it certainly reflected Gabriel's anxiety in settling his estate prior to his passing.

As mentioned, the good fortune of having so many substantive wills over a period of more than forty years gives us a rare view of the Maya notaries who wrote these wills and what they decided to include or omit—documents that would prove the most substantive written record of this colonial town. Moreover, understanding the notary and his role in making testaments likewise helps to distinguish and "hear" the occasional voice of the testator in his/her own will.

The testaments of Ixil not only expose the identity and rotation of their notaries, but also their individual stylistic preferences with regard to composing wills, particularly the preamble.[26] As mentioned, Ixil's testaments follow a prescribed European structure that includes a formulaic preamble. Confirming the testament's sacrality, the preamble in the Spanish-Christian testament, after invoking the Holy Trinity and identifying the testator, consisted of a supplication, a meditation on death and the final judgment, and a profession of faith followed by an encommendation of the soul and body.[27]

Various rubrics existed throughout Europe, but formulae and rubrics in Spanish accompanied Christianity as it crossed the Atlantic to become embedded in New Spain.[28] A few composed model rubrics as templates for indigenous scribes to follow, templates that retained a close familiarity to their Spanish predecessors.[29] In his 1569 *Confesionario mayor*, a reprint of a 1565 earlier version, fray Alonso de Molina instructed indigenous notaries on how properly to fulfill their testamentary duties and compose the preamble to a will. First, Molina provided the notaries with a series of questions intended to determine that the testator's state of mind was sound and that the proper witnesses were present. Then the manual detailed the questions the notary was to ask the testator about his/her possessions after having written the preamble, an example of which Molina provides in his subsequent model testament.[30] Thus, if notaries followed Molina's instructions, they would be responsible for the preamble, and testators would be responsible for the answers to the notary's questions relating to property and its bequeathing.

The Ixil corpus largely confirms this designated pattern.[31] Although spanning forty-one years, and despite variations, the testaments of Ixil demonstrate remarkable consistency and continuation in their preambles. Indeed, it is not uncommon to find large sections of the preamble repeated word for word in testaments written thirty to forty years apart. To facilitate analysis and comparison, we have used common elements found in every preamble from 1738 to 1779 to create a "core" preamble, consisting largely of four distinct parts. Although never appearing in this exact form, this is the basic template that Ixil notaries and testators either augmented or diminished when composing preambles.[32]

The four parts of this core preamble all appear in Molina's model preamble, confirming their overall formulaic and Spanish nature, although admittedly Molina's model is much more verbose. The first part begins with a short declaration of who died and when, usually consisting of a name and a date, and then invokes the name of the Holy Trinity. In the second, the testator declares that the testament will be seen and then identifies his/her parents as residents of Ixil. The third part includes the testator admitting his/her impending death, declaring a sound state of mind—a necessary component when composing a testament as ordered by Alfonso X's thirteenth-century *Siete Partidas*[33]—and expressing his/her wish to be buried in the church. Moreover, the testator supplicates the priest to say a mass for his/her soul. Finally, in the fourth part the testator specifies his/her payment for the mass and donation to the Jerusalem fund.

To be sure, rigid uniformity of any town's preamble over the years, even among the testaments of one notary, is difficult to achieve. Myriad circumstances could alter the testament. Notarial preferences, mistakes, forgetfulness, dying outside the *cah* or dying intestate, and even the testator's social ranking seemed to have shaped the preamble. Scholars have debated the question of who contributed what to the preamble. Some argue that the primary role of author belongs to the testator, others argue for the notary, while most settle on a balance between the two.[34] The general consensus attributes the primary responsibility for the preamble to the local style of the notary while allowing for the occasional contribution of the testator. Of course, diversity exists among Mesoamerican testaments, allowing, for example, Mixtec testators to play a larger role in the composition of the preamble than, say, those of Ixil.[35] Ixil seems to have followed the norm with notaries playing a larger role in the preamble's composition with the possibility of the occasional contribution of a testator. However, what is uncommon about Ixil's corpus is its ability to clearly illustrate this trend.[36]

Having taught and learned from one another, the notaries of Ixil maintained a preamble that followed the same basic core structure while making additions and omissions they deemed appropriate. Many of the additions take the form of

---

TEXT BOX 1.1. Ixil's core preamble

(1) In the name of God the Father, and God the Son, and God the Holy Spirit, three persons, one almighty God, not many. (2) The document of my final words in my testament will be seen, insomuch as I whom am (name), the son of (name), the child of (name), residents here in the *cah* of Ixil. (3) Although I am dying, my heart and my understanding are sound, as it should be. Likewise, I wish my body to be buried inside the home of our temple. Likewise, I supplicate our blessed lord, the guardian priest, that one mass for my soul be said to help the suffering purgatory soul, and that he say a prayer for me in that mass. (4) Likewise, it will be given in alms three *tostones* and two *tomines* for Jerusalem.

---

religious "catchphrases" similar to today's "God forbid," "heaven help me," or "in God's hands." No doubt Ixil notaries were familiar with the popular Christian sayings of their time and surroundings. These religious catchphrases could also be pieces of previous preambles that, for one reason or another, were being phased out or new pieces that were being phased in. Regardless, when they appeared, such catchphrases were duplicated nearly word for word and inserted to augment certain sections of the preamble's core structure.

The selection and popularity of catchphrases depended on the notary's preferences. For example, the third part of the core preamble dictates that all testators designate a burial location after giving the names of his/her parents. Yet Tec, the notary for the 1766 testaments, occasionally inserted before this third part the phrase "Nobody shall redeem themselves from death." His predecessor, Poot, did not share the same preference and included the statement only once, and then just as he was taking over the writing of wills in December of 1766, perhaps showing a brief influence of Tec on Poot that would thereafter cease. Interestingly, when resuming his duties as notary in 1768, Tec again employs the phrase.

These catchphrases, their locations, and corresponding notary provide a clearer understanding of who was responsible for what in the preamble and subsequent testament. Although all Ixil wills subscribe to the same core preamble, certain notaries preferred certain catchphrases to build onto this skeleton. Moreover, because each catchphrase appears in its designated space to augment the core preamble and because such phrases follow the preferences of the notaries, we can assume that the notaries were primarily responsible for such phrases, not the testators.

But this is not to say that testators failed to contribute to their preambles. As seen below, the sporadic insertion at different locations of personal explanations and declarations within the preamble suggests the contributions of testators who were not as strictly bound to formulaic rules of placement and consistency as the notary. In short, the notaries constructed the core preamble, while the testators contributed the random statements and declarations occasionally found throughout the preamble in no consistent pattern as well as the content of the body of the testament concerning bequeathed property. Thus, although all too frequently the voice of the notary and testator were indistinguishable and thereby lost, the following aspires to unscramble the voices and illustrate the influence of the notary and testator though Ixil's core preamble.

THE NOTARY'S INFLUENCE

The testament of Viviana Pech (C1) provides our earliest example of Ixil's preambles. Providing the only glimpse into a 1738 testament, her will contains all the core elements of later Ixil preambles. Although her increased payment for a sung mass corresponds with those from 1748, the major deviation is the insertion of four religious "catchphrases." Two of the four catchphrases continue to occasionally appear in Ixil's testaments. Indeed, the phrases "nobody shall redeem herself/himself from death," and "as [God] wishes to end my life here on this earth" are found not only in Viviana's testament, but inserted throughout the Ixil corpus with little or no variation in orthography and location, especially the latter statement. This, then, reflects the notaries' preference.

The other two catchphrases take the form of explanations not found in any of the subsequent testaments. Viviana's testament (C1) indicates that the will is to "lighten [her] soul before our lord in God" and that through the requested sung mass she "shall be truly worthy." Such additions could be the result of the testator. However, similar phrases are found in Molina's *Confesionario* and were common religious catchphrases among wills. Although the Maya notaries of Ixil never saw Molina's Nahuatl manual, Molina was a Franciscan, and in many ways his testamentary model derived from a Spanish antecedent—one that was common knowledge among the Franciscan ecclesiastics who originally trained the Maya notaries. This also illustrates why, although locally tailored by culture and language, testaments throughout Mesoamerica share fundamental aspects.[37] Yet other than these deviations, Viviana's preamble is standard and nearly indistinguishable in structure from the remaining corpus. Moreover, because most of Ixil's preambles strongly resemble Viviana's, it is likely that her testament represents a standard 1738 preamble.

Ten years later, the preamble had experienced few, albeit significant, changes that reflect the notary's preferences. For example, Ixil preambles in 1748 do not include the residence of the testator's parents. However, two exceptions exist, both

---

Text Box 1.2. Juan Cetz's 1738 changes to the Ixil core preamble

(1) In the name of God the Father, and God the Son, and God the Holy Spirit, three persons, one almighty God, not many. (2) The document of my final words in my testament will be seen, insomuch as I who am (name), the son of (name) the child of (name) residents here in the *cah* of Ixil. (3) Although I am dying, my heart and my understanding are sound, as it should be. Likewise, *as God wishes to end my life here on this earth*, I wish my body to be buried inside the home of our temple. *Nobody shall redeem themselves from death. This is the reason that I now arrange my statement in my will—to lighten my soul before our lord God.* Likewise, I supplicate our blessed lord, the guardian priest, that one mass for my soul be said to help the suffering purgatory soul, and that he say a prayer for me in that mass. *Thus shall I be truly worthy.* (4) Likewise, it will be given in alms three *tostones* and two *tomines* for Jerusalem.

---

occurring when the testator's parents were residents of a *cah* other than Ixil.[38] Perhaps because the wills would be kept in Ixil's book of testaments, the notary of 1748, Salvador Coba, deemed the declaration of the testator's parents as residents of Ixil unnecessary, only noting the exception rather than the rule.

Perhaps most remarkable about the 1748 preambles is their consistent, streamlined nature. The testaments of 1748 begin in January, end in December, and are all written by Coba. It appears that Coba, or a previous notary, removed the religious catchphrases from the preambles of 1738 to create one that was more succinct and that closely resembled the basic core preamble of the surviving Ixil wills. Even still, one would expect some variation in his writing. Yet Coba offers very little, as the 1748 preambles clearly reflect the ability of a notary's personal preferences to shape these religious formulae. Indeed, only twice does a religious catchphrase enter these testaments, and when they do, they are located after the preamble in reference to death (docs. A16, A28).

Interestingly, the catchphrase is the same both times, stating that when God "calls back the life he loaned" to the testator's father, all the goods the testator was to inherit should be passed on to a named individual. Thus, Coba's influence extended beyond the formulaic preamble to include specific religious statements in the body of the text. Regardless, all thirty-four of the 1748 preambles lack any variation in their requests for a church burial, a mass for their soul in purgatory, and the fees for the mass and Jerusalem fund. If Coba did experience the everyday variables that could alter a testament, he triumphed over them to maintain uniformity.

An additional change requires brief attention. In 1738 and 1748 the fee for the mass, without exception, was three *tostones*. One *toston* was equal to four *reales*, thus making the payment equivalent to twelve *reales* or the sum of a sung mass. Thus,

---

TEXT BOX 1.3. Salvador Coba's 1748 changes to the Ixil core preamble

(1) In the name of God the Father, and God the Son, and God the Holy Spirit, three persons, one almighty God, not many. (2) The document of my final words in my testament will be seen, insomuch as I who am (name), the son of (name), the child of (name), ~~residents here in the cah of Ixil~~. (3) Although I am dying, my heart and my understanding are sound, as it should be. Likewise, I wish my body to be buried inside the home of our temple. Likewise, I supplicate our blessed lord, the guardian priest, that one mass for my soul be said to help the suffering purgatory soul, and that he say a prayer for me in that mass. (4) Likewise, it will be given in alms three *tostones* and two *tomines* for Jerusalem.

---

although no 1748 testament included a request for a sung mass, the friar granted all testators a sung mass, which was standard. However, this changed in 1765 as testators began requesting recited masses for a diminished fee of six *reales*. Only 16 percent of testators from 1765 and beyond paid the once-traditional three *tostons* for a sung mass. There is no clear reason for such a change. Although it is tempting to explain the shift as a change in economic factors, even the poorest of Ixil's testators in 1748 requested and received a sung mass. Similarly, we cannot rashly assume a decline in the testator's piety.

More likely, the 1748 testators were simply not presented with the option for a recited mass. The lack of option could stem from the notary's preferences or the friars themselves. Whatever the reason, custom changed, offering 1765 testators and their decedents a more affordable option of a recited mass. Interestingly, the archives are replete with complaints aimed at making required tributes and fees more reasonable. Even though all 1748 testators requested and received sung masses, it is doubtful all were able to pay the full amount owed without the assistance of *cofradías* or other sources. A six-*real* mass would present testators and friars with a more reasonable situation for paying and receiving payment. Although the change fails to firmly represent a notary's preference, it persists throughout the remaining preambles and reflects the reality of colonial life in Ixil.

Over the next seventeen years, Coba's pedantic preferences for a streamlined preamble gave way to tradition as the few extant testaments from 1765 reverted back to declaring the testator's parents as residents of Ixil and even included the occasional religious catchphrase. Indeed, the preambles of 1765 became augmented with two main additions. The first, "although my life is ending on this earth," is a slightly modified version of the 1738 "as [God] wishes to end my life here on this earth" and was placed in the same location as its predecessor, appearing directly before the testator's

---

TEXT BOX 1.4. Marcos Poot's 1765 changes to the Ixil core preamble*

(1) In the name of God the Father, and God the Son, and God the Holy Spirit, three persons, one almighty God, not many. (2) The document of my final words in my testament will be seen, insomuch as I who am (name), the son of (name), the child of (name), residents here in the *cah* of Ixil. (3) ~~Although I am dying, my heart and my understanding are sound, as it should be.~~ Likewise, *although my life is ending*, I wish my body to be buried inside the home of our temple. Likewise, I supplicate our blessed lord, the guardian priest, that one mass for my soul be said to help the suffering purgatory soul, and that he say a prayer for me in that mass. (4) Likewise, it will be given in alms *as we are believing Christians ~~three tostons~~ six tomines and two tomines* for Jerusalem.

---

*Although Joseph Cob was the elected notary for 1765, the few testaments from this year were composed by the *mahan kab*, Marcos Poot.

---

wish to be buried in the church. The other was a new addition to the core preamble and one that Poot seemingly preferred, inserting it into nearly half of the wills he penned later in 1767. It is the inclusion of "as we are believing Christians" before the declaration of fees. Despite these inclusions, Poot failed to include a vital part of the preamble up until this point. The phrase in part three that stated "although I am dying, my heart and my understanding are sound, as it should be" was absent from the 1765 wills. It appears as though the presence of "although my life is ending" largely replaced the previous admittance of death. Indeed, throughout the corpus only once do both phrases coexist within the same testament.[39] As demonstrated below, Poot's avoidance of this phrase remained consistent throughout his wills and further demonstrates the impact of the notary's preferences on the preamble.

The larger quantity of thirty-three testaments for 1766 allows for a better view of the preamble's continuities and changes under Tec. Tec did not seem to mind perpetuating many of the previous year's catchphrases. He continued with some regularity the 1765 addition of "although my life is ending on this earth" but occasionally contributed one main variant: "as it is the wish of our Lord to end my life." Moreover, he continued to include the statement concerning "believing Christians." When they appeared, both catchphrases were consistently placed in the same location as those from the previous wills. In addition, Tec began varying the effect of the requested posthumous mass on the testator's soul in purgatory, sometimes speeding the soul through or offering it protection. Interestingly, under the watch of Tec came the occasional insertion of the *cah*'s patron saint, San Bernabé, within the preamble following the declared residence of the testator's parents. Although lacking real consistency (13 percent of testaments written by Tec include the saint), no

---

TEXT BOX 1.5. Pablo Tec's 1766 changes to the Ixil core preamble

(1) In the name of God the Father, and God the Son, and God the Holy Spirit, three persons, one almighty God, not many. (2) The document of my final words in my testament will be seen, insomuch as I who am (name), the son of (name), the child of (name), residents here in the *cah* of Ixil *governed by our lord San Bernabé of Ixil*. (3) Although I am dying, my heart and my understanding are sound, as it should be.* Likewise, *as it is the wish of our Lord to end my life*, I wish my body to be buried inside the home of our temple. Likewise, I supplicate our blessed lord, the guardian priest, that one mass for my soul be said to help the suffering purgatory soul, and that he say a prayer for me in that mass. (4) Likewise, it will be given in alms *as we are believing Christians three tostons six tomines ~~and two tomines for Jerusalem~~*.

---

*This part typically would be omitted if Tec included "as it is the wish of our Lord to end my life."

---

other notary duplicated this preference, and it thus strongly suggests the impact of Tec's style.

Another change evident with Tec is the decline in frequency of the donations to the Jerusalem fund. The Jerusalem fund was originally intended to support the Christian crusades but eventually became a sinecure and then a part of the local priest's income.[40] Many native testaments throughout New Spain contained donations to this outdated fund, including one as late as 1816 from Ocotitlan, central Mexico.[41] All 1748 testators donated to the fund, and almost all did in 1765. Yet 57 percent of Tec's 1766 testaments failed to include the donation. Although Poot's 1767 testaments excluded the fund only 27 percent of the time, the donations commonly were reduced by half to one *real*. In the end, Jerusalem never received the importance and funding it enjoyed in 1748.

Similar to the change in mass fees, then, it would seem that testators now had the option to reduce or omit the superfluous fund. Again, such an omission should not be considered a decline in personal piety. If the testator was poor, the fund was almost always neglected. However, although the Jerusalem fund declined, the payment for a posthumous mass remained at a near 100 percent for all testators throughout the forty-one-year span of the corpus. Simply put, when poverty or rationality demanded a choice between a requiem and Jerusalem, the testator chose the welfare of his/her soul over those in Jerusalem or chose to donate an amount below that of the standard two *tomines*. No testator paid less than the minimum six *tomines* for a mass or more than the standard two *tomines* to Jerusalem. As discussed later, this insistence on the mass strongly argues for the testators' belief in the benefits of the posthumous mass.

Tec also elected to continue the traditional line "Although I am dying, my heart and my understanding are sound, as it should be." This phrase was firmly established in the early wills of 1738 and 1748 and appeared in every will. Subsequent notaries, however, exhibited personal preferences in the phrase's inclusion (table 1.3). Whereas Poot included the phrase among only three of his wills, Tec included it in nearly 40 percent of his testaments. Domingo Itza, notary of a 1779 will, also included the phrase, suggesting that Poot's stylistic preferences were the primary reason for the phrase's occasional absence from the Ixil corpus. Thus, the inclusion and exclusion of this section in the formulaic preamble reflected the notary's preferences and not necessarily those of the testator.

When Marcos Poot replaced Tec as the year's notary of twenty-four testaments, expected stylistic changes occurred. As mentioned, Poot generally neglected the phrase "Although I am dying, my heart and my understanding are sound, as it should be." He also allowed Tec's mention of Ixil's patron saint San Bernabé to fall by the wayside. Yet Poot compensated for this omission with his increased attention to the religious catchphrase "as God wishes to end my life on this earth," inserted before the testator's wish to be buried in the church. Although this phrase was not uncommon under Tec (appearing in approximately 26 percent of his testaments), after a slight modification it experienced an increase in popularity with Poot. Indeed, Poot uses "as God ends my life on this earth" in 61 percent of his testaments with little variation.[42] Poot also gave increasing preference to the phrase "for we are believing Christians" before the declaration of the given fees; it appears in nearly half of his testaments. It is clear that these two phrases were a result of Poot's preferences. Both phrases appeared in those wills he helped construct in 1765. In addition, the phrases' popularity drastically declined among other notaries.

In 1768 Pablo Tec returned to serve as Ixil's notary, and although the corpus contains only two of his testaments from this time period, they betrayed his notarial tendencies to include the catchphrase "Although I am dying, my heart and my understanding are sound, as it should be"—a phrase that became nearly extinct under Poot. Two additional testaments, one from 1769 and the other from 1779, are insufficient to continue a pattern analysis of the preamble. Yet they do contain glimpses of insight. Both maintain the core preamble while also including San Bernabé as the patron of Ixil, suggesting the saint's slow increase in popularity. The phrase concerning "believing Christians" also appears in both testaments. This suggests a change in the core preamble to include San Bernabé and the catchphrase of "believing Christians." Finally, the 1779 testament includes the dying body/sound mind phrase that all notaries but Poot seem to prefer. Overall, and despite the influence of the notaries' individual preferences, the preamble appears to have changed only slightly by 1779.

TABLE 1.3. Occurrence of "Although I am dying, my heart and my understanding are sound, as it should be"

	1738	1748	1765	1766	1767	1768	1779	Overall
Juan Cetz	1/1							100%
Salvador Coba		34/34						100%
Joseph Cob / Marcos Poot			0/3					0%
Pablo Tec				11/32		2/2		38%
Pablo Tec / Marcos Poot				0/1				0%
Marcos Poot			0/2	1/1	2/24			11%
Domingo Itza							1/1	100%

TEXT BOX 1.6. Marcos Poot's 1767 changes to the Ixil core preamble

(1) In the name of God the Father, and God the Son, and God the Holy Spirit, three persons, one almighty God, not many. (2) The document of my final words in my testament will be seen, insomuch as I who am (name), the son of (name), the child of (name), residents here in the *cah* of Ixil. (3) ~~Although I am dying, my heart and my understanding are sound, as it should be.~~ Likewise, *as God wishes to end my life on this earth* I wish my body to be buried inside the home of our temple. Likewise, I supplicate our blessed lord, the guardian priest, that one mass for my soul be said to help the suffering purgatory soul, and that he say a prayer for me in that mass. (4) Likewise, it will be given in alms *for we are believing Christians* ~~three tostons~~ *six tomines* and two *tomines* for Jerusalem.

THE TESTATOR'S INFLUENCE

Available documentation suggests that roughly 57 of testators in Ixil in the 1760s composed their wills prior to death. The remainder either informed the notary of their wishes prior to death or had relatives or trusted associates speak posthumously for them—a topic discussed later in more detail. The primary role of testators who composed wills prior to death was to inform the notary of the details concerning the inheritance of their property and the settling of debts. However, it appears that they also could contribute random phrases to the preamble. One might imagine the notary writing the preamble at the bedside of the testator when the testator spoke up to contribute a religious catchphrase or blurb to ease his or her mind as he or she prepared to meet God. Unlike those provided by notaries, such phrases and additions followed no pattern, consistent placement, or orthography, and although a certain phrase might be repeated by another testator, its location in the preamble always varied.

Luisa Tec (B56) adds a unique line to the third section of her preamble stating that her payment of one trussed cockerel was to "empower our blessed lord Padre in [his] mediation" for her soul in purgatory. Other contributions took the form of elaborations on preexisting phrases in the preamble. Following the standard phrase "I supplicate our blessed lord, the guardian priest that one mass for my soul be said to help the suffering purgatory soul, and that he say a prayer for me in that mass," Viviana Canche (B23) likely added, "which shall reach my soul there." Although the notary could also be responsible for these random additions, such insertions are neither standard nor formulaic and thus are more likely to represent the individual, spontaneous orations of testators who, unlike the notary, were not strictly bound to formulaic rules of placement and consistency.

Yet the most poignant example of a testator contributing to the preamble comes from a *maestro*. Comparable to the Nahua *fiscales* of central Mexico, the *maestro* was responsible for all matters of religious education and largely fulfilled the mundane tasks of the priest who was often not present. When the opportunity arose, it appears that *maestros* could serve as their own notaries—an act not supported by Spanish law—and composed their own documents. Documents from Ebtun include a *maestro* composing his own will in 1699 and another penning an acknowledgment of sale in 1714.[43] Regarding Ixil, the *maestro* Diego Chan (B14) completely brushed aside the typical formula to compose his own preamble and will. Confidant in his spiritual knowledge and status, he proceeded to include religious statements in no predictable order, inserting, for example, "while my spirit still lives in this world, I present myself to our holy father, the Padre." Indeed, nothing in his preamble resembles or follows the pattern of Ixil's core preamble; he even omits the invocation of the Trinity—the only such omission of the entire corpus![44]

Chan's position in the community gave him a familiarity with Christianity that allowed him the confidence and knowledge to fully participate in—or, better, take over—the construction of his preamble. What of other Ixil residents? Did their position in the community and affluence affect their participation? Generally speaking, yes. Those that spoke up and participated in their preambles were typically members of the noble *chibalob* in the *cah*; being higher ranked, more privileged, better off, meant a closer acquaintance with Christian dogma and its ritual expression. Those testators who had little or nothing to bequeath rarely interfered with the preamble and stuck to the basic core formula. Still, those on the lowest end of the social spectrum were at risk of receiving the barest bones of a preamble. Yet this should come as no surprise. Educational benefits and the right and desire to be heard are attributes traditionally connected with wealth and status. The notary no doubt paid more heed to the wills of such testators, as these were both the wills of his peers and the wills most likely to befall scrupulous examination should contestations arise. As for the poor, the notary presumably knew that the testator lacked the knowledge to contend a poorly scribed will, nor would the scant contents of such a will likely ever be contested. In such cases, the notary's only motives were his habit of penning a formulaic preamble and his Christian concern for the dying.

In general, the corpus of wills confirms that with regard to making testaments in Ixil, notaries were largely responsible for the preamble. Notaries could modify the core preamble with preferred religious catchphrases and insertions that appeared in predictable, stylistic patterns. Testators were primarily responsible for the body of the will and left the preamble to the notary. However, testators, particularly those of means, occasionally contributed random statements and declarations that followed no consistent pattern or repetition.

Three blocks north of Mexico City's famous Zócalo is the Plaza Santo Domingo. On the west side of the plaza beneath the arcades, or Portales de los Evangelistas, street printers, producing anything from business cards to invitations for *quinceañeras* to counterfeit diplomas, share a space with scribes and notaries who arm themselves with pens and typewriters ready to answer the requests of those with myriad documentary needs. Business letters, love letters, letters to government officials, typed copies of expensive textbooks for students, or even completed tax forms can all be acquired from such notaries for as little as twenty *pesos* a page. Ironically, the notaries and printers are stationed across the courtyard from where the Inquisition was headquartered until its closure in 1812. Although some may not be aware of it, such notaries carry on a tradition dating back to the colonial period where, in the very same plaza, their predecessors offered their services to anyone in need of documentation—both legal and illegal.

Indigenous notaries played an important role in the colonial Spanish regime. In Ixil only the nobility could aspire to the prestige of the notary. Elected annually while rotating among a select few, Ixil's notaries played an essential role in the social and religious well-being of the *cah*. The large number of substantive testaments from Ixil within a relatively restricted time frame and the strict annual rotation of the notaries provide an uncommon opportunity to compare the preambles of each notary. Such a comparison offers a rare glimpse into the distinct individual preferences of each notary, and even some testators, thus allowing us to better hear the voice of the notary. Overall, on an individual level, the notary's pen impacted the material life of each testator, and the notaries helped prepare testators' souls for the next life through the preambles they helped compose and tailor. On a corporate level, they also played an important role in the administration of the *cah*—a topic to which we now turn.

NOTES

1. AHAY, Visitas Pastorales, 1788, Sacalum.

2. AHAY, Visitas Pastorales, 1769, Hocobá.

3. GGMM (C0744), no. 66, "Discourses on the Passion of Christ and Other Texts."

4. There are, of course, exceptions where notaries come to play prominent roles in historical studies. See, for example, González Echevarría (1998) and Burns (2010).

5. Burns (2010).

6. Quezada (2014: ch. 3); Gosner (1992: 76–85); Restall (1997: ch. 6).

7. Quezada (2014: 80).

8. Chuchiak (2009: 16n9).

9. Farriss (1984: 184–85); Thompson (1999: 51).

10. For more on *maestros* see Collins (1977); Christensen (2013: 74–80; 2016: 4–5); Chuchiak (2002).

11. Chuchiak (2009: 162). One *peso* had the value of eight *reales*.

12. FS-MY, "registros parroquiales y diocesanos, 1543–1977," Ixil, San Bernabé, Bautismos 1782–1808, image 13 of 551.

13. Ibid., image 352 of 551.

14. Although it is possible that a priest familiar with Yucatec Maya could have composed the entry, the phonetic spelling of the Spanish makes this highly unlikely.

15. The phrase Hoyos commonly uses is "tome esta razon, y yo firme," one commonly used by contemporary notaries when noting and recording something. FS-MY, "registros parroquiales y diocesanos, 1543–1977," Conkal, San Francisco de Asís, Defunciones 1682–1802, images 143 and 220 of 452.

16. The Church of Jesus Christ of Latter-Day Saints has made significant efforts to convert its extensive microfilm collection of worldwide genealogical data into an online database available at *familysearch.org*. This website made possible our search of many parish archives throughout Yucatan to retrieve the data presented here. Digital images of such ledgers for many towns are available on FS-MY. Although curates were instructed to keep individual books for each town, various examples exist of ledgers containing rites from multiple towns. The inaccuracies of the ledgers proved a consistent line of criticism levied against the local curate by ecclesiastical officials performing *visita* inspections.

17. Christensen (2016: 7).

18. GGMM (C0744), no. 66, "Discourses on the Passion of Christ and Other Texts."

19. For the imposition of commoners as governors, see Quezada (2014: 114–22); Gosner (1992: 78–83).

20. León Pinelo (1992: libro VII, titulo X, ley 25, 1833).

21. See Restall (1997: appendix C); Thompson (1999: 51, 279).

22. Restall (1995: 43). See also Restall (1997: 78–83, appendix C).

23. Although some notaries occasionally used *escribano publico* when composing testaments alone, the phrase is especially evident when composing with an assistant as if to distinguish between the appointed notary and the assistant notary, similar to the "*escribano nombrado*" of the Nahuatl testaments of Culhuacan. See Cline and León-Portilla (1984).

24. Restall (1997: 67). Originally, Restall asserted that the *mahan kab* was the pupil of the notary, but Poot's office-holding record and experience long before serving as *mahan kab* to Cob now gives us reason to challenge that initial assumption.

25. Similarly, Tekanto notaries derived from a limited pool of candidates; see DT; Bricker (2015).

26. For an example examining similarities and differences among and between Nahuatl and Maya preambles, see Christensen (2013: ch. 7).

27. Terraciano (1998: 125).

28. For a general overview of the last will and testament and some of its European and American manifestations, see Christensen and Truitt (2015) in general but 2–6 in particular. Restall includes a comparison among wills from various Maya communities and a few from Europe in his *Maya World* (1997: 155–58). For more on the background of wills, see Ramos (2010: 115–29); Cline (1998: 14–17).

29. The Franciscan Alonso de Molina provided one in his 1569 *Confesionario mayor*, as did the Dominican Martín de León in his 1611 *Camino de cielo*. For more on the matter, see Burkhart (2004: 43–47).

30. Molina (1984: 61r–63v). See also Cline (1998).

31. That said, not everyone followed the rubrics, and a great deal of diversity in formulae existed between native communities, illustrating local preferences.

32. In general, Ixil notaries composed the will prior to the death of the testator. This, however, was not the case in all Maya towns, and Tekanto notaries produced a number of strictly formulaic testaments weeks after the testator's death; see Bricker (2015: 434). The following discussion on Ixil's core preamble and notary contributions is a large expansion on the earlier work of Christensen (2013: 234–38).

33. Burns (2001: xi–xii, 1181).

34. Terraciano (1998: 126); Lockhart (1992: 252–56); Restall (1997: 152–55); Cline (1986: 19).

35. Terraciano (1998: 125–27).

36. Any supposition on the topic can never be proven with certainty. Yet the Ixil corpus provides some possible explanations.

37. Restall (1997: 242).

38. Docs. A15, A27. Restall was right in assuming that marriages took place within the *cah* when both sets of parents were from the same *cah*.

39. Restall (1995: 103–5).

40. Ibid., 52.

41. Melton-Villanueva (2016: 181).

42. Poot uses a replacement phrase only twice: once using "now that I face death . . ." and once using "now that my life is summoned. . . ."

43. Roys (1939: 127, 147).

44. Differences in orthography and handwriting further confirm a hand other than that of the notary, Pablo Tec.

2

Defending and Governing Ixil

To the westward of Telchac, 9 miles, is a lookout tower, and a rancho of a few huts, named Yxil, in a grove of cocoanut [*sic*] trees.

—W. W. Gillpatrick, 1885[1]

The road from the town of Ixil is to the south and is a distance of five leagues, from whence comes the aid of the *indios hidalgos* in numbers from 80 to 100 from the two companies present [in Ixil]. [The watchtower] has eight wattle-palm houses (*casas de guano*) and eight *indios de servicio*.

—Juan de Dios González, 1766[2]

It is fitting that in the main ports there be watchtowers (*atalayas*) that monitor the sea at certain hours of the day and night to give warning with smoke and fire.

—Philip IV, 1631[3]

In the spring of 1779, Captain don Pedro Pech was dying. On April 11, with a notary and his relatives in the room, he arranged a last will that included all the usual religious formulae and declarations. Despite being a Pech—the only *hidalgo*-status family in Ixil—and despite having inherited six plots of land from his deceased mother forty-one years earlier, as well as a plot of land from his uncle, Captain don Pedro recorded a short will with few bequeathed items. Yet his title, previous position as *batab*, and the titles and rank of his relatives recorded in the will would

DOI: 10.5876/9781607329220.c002

remove any doubt as to his status that might have been suggested by his seeming lack of fortune. Don Pedro had served as Ixil's *batab* in 1755, and among the consanguineal relatives witnessing his will were the current *batab*, Captain don José Cob, lieutenant don Pasqual Pech, as well as don Antonio Pech and don Manuel Pech. Regarding the latter two, both were listed in the will by their titles, "alferes" (*alférez*). Like "captain," *alférez* indicated a position in Ixil's local militia similar to that of a lieutenant. Thus, feeling death approaching, Captain don Pedro dictated his last wishes in the presence of his peers: the men who defended and governed Ixil.

This chapter employs the testaments of Ixil and various other documents to illustrate how the Maya of Ixil, particularly the elite, deftly negotiated their position within the burgeoning colony.[4] Modern scholarship remains relatively silent on the role that Ixil and its people played in the defense of Yucatan, and studies on native militias are generally few in number.[5] Yet the testaments from Ixil contain individuals bearing the military titles of "captain" and "*alférez*," thus indicating that the town had some experience with a militia or military defense. To be sure, the testaments provide new and exciting insights into the modes and means employed by the Maya to preserve old social hierarchies within the new Spanish colony as they sculpted a system of government in Ixil that would last for hundreds of years. Moreover, the wills shed some much-needed light on the involvement of Maya towns in local militias and their ability to use the colony's need for defense to their social and economic advantage. After a brief overview of the Yucatan's coastal defenses during the colonial period, the following represents the results, however incomplete, of archival and historical sleuthing to uncover Ixil's role in defending Yucatan—results that future discoveries, no doubt, will continue to expand—and the role of Ixil's defenders and nobility in governing the affairs of the town.

DEFENDING IXIL

The Spanish empire's ability to conquer and defend its colony in Yucatan always hinged upon the use of native auxiliaries serving as military allies. Francisco de Montejo failed in his first two attempts at conquering Yucatan because he lacked such allies. Finally, in his third attempt, he and his son dragooned a host of native auxiliaries from a variety of Mesoamerican towns to assist in their efforts and, as a result, established a foothold in the province in 1542 (figure 2.1).[6] Such native auxiliaries—both Nahuas and other Mesoamericans brought into the province in the 1540s, and Mayas of the peninsula's northwest incorporated into the new colony—served as the primary defense of the colony in its first century. As they were officially prohibited from owning firearms of any kind, Mayas formed bow-and-arrow units in order to fight as *indios flecheros*. Local *batabob* led these

FIGURE 2.1. Yucatan's conquest, as imagined by De Bry, 1595. A highly stylized illustration of the Montejo-led conquest of Yucatan engraved by Theodor De Bry. (Girolamo Benzoni, *Historia del Mondo Nuovo* [Frankfurt, 1595], plate XIX, from the copy in the Kislak Collection, Library of Congress)

units and thereby earned for themselves the honorary title of captain, with various other members of Maya *cabildos* also holding militia titles, such as *alférez*, or lieutenant of sorts.[7] Both Merida and Campeche had companies of *indios flecheros y piqueros* (native archers and pikemen) to defend their borders, as did various other burgeoning towns.[8]

As Jorge Victoria Ojeda and Restall explain, the Maya militias initially employed against other Maya during the wars of conquest eventually shifted their role to defending the coastlines by the mid-seventeenth century.[9] A minor nuisance at first, French, English, and Dutch pirates became increasingly concerning beginning in the seventeenth century as attacks and raids continued along the peninsula's shores.[10] Although not rich in precious metals, Yucatan's possession of wood used in dyes (logwood or dyewood) along with honey, wax, hides, and salt made the coast attractive to pirates and privateers. Indeed, pirates threatened or raided the important port town of Campeche thirteen times between 1556 and 1685,[11] and in 1664 pirates likewise "cruelly sacked" the towns of Chicxulub and Ixil.[12]

Spaniards and Mayas alike were tasked with the defense of the colony as the crown began constructing a defensive infrastructure that included *vigías* (coastal watchtowers), forts, *trincheras* (low walls serving as bulwarks), batteries, trenches, and military companies. On April 8, 1600, the *alférez mayor* of Valladolid, Alonso Sánchez de Aguilar—grandson of the Hernando de Aguilar who helped Francisco de Montejo during the conquest of Yucatan and elder brother to Pedro Sánchez de Aguilar, the secular priest known for his report on Yucatan's idolatries—led a small force of Spaniards and *indios flecheros* to defend the port of Rio Lagartos from English pirates. Alonso and his company successfully defended and secured the region, making particular use of *trincheras* to do so.[13] By the second half of the eighteenth century, the British and French threat continued to strengthen. British loggers had established a settlement in the Laguna de Términos, south of Campeche, in 1662, and it prospered—despite regular Spanish attacks—until it was finally overrun and destroyed in 1716. But the loggers immediately started working the banks of the Belize River, on the other side of the peninsula from the Laguna de Términos, and their settlement there survived repeated Spanish attacks throughout the century (figure 2.2). Meanwhile, in 1762, the British seized Havana—an important trading partner with the peninsula's city of Campeche and port of Sisal—heightening colonial concerns of security. When Havana was returned to Spain in the subsequent treaty, British logging activity on the Belize River was made legal (albeit only until war broke out again). Improvements to Yucatan's security continued throughout the colonial period, as did its reliance upon militias. In truth, although free-colored and *pardo* militias came to play an increasingly important role in Yucatan's defense, the region continued to call upon on its native militias for protection, particularly along the coastline.[14]

As mentioned, the continued fortification of Yucatan included coastal watchtowers, *vigías* or *atalayas*, as early as the middle of the sixteenth century and until the middle of the nineteenth. In 1561 Philip II ordered inhabitants close to coastal ports to arm themselves, form squads and companies, and stand in readiness to defend against pirates and to use sentinels if necessary. The governors of Yucatan, don Luis de Céspedes and don Francisco Velázquez Gijón, ordered the appointment of *vigías* in 1564 and 1573 respectively. And later, in 1631, Philip IV ordered the establishment of *vigías* to give warning of pirates or foreign attacks in all the principal ports.[15] The use of such watchtowers to defend waterways was common in medieval and early modern Spain, so their appearance in the New World is not surprising.[16] Each *vigía* was connected to a nearby coastal town by a roadway protected by various *trincheras*. Typically constructed of wood and accompanied by a few huts for those stationed

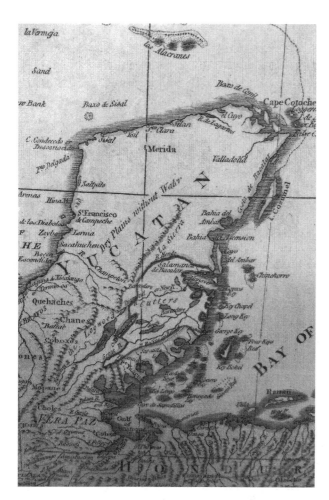

FIGURE 2.2. Map of Yucatan from an eighteenth-century British perspective. The undated (ca. 1790) map shows the extent of British logging activity in southeast Yucatan as well as the coastal location of defensive watchtowers, long of interest to the British—including that of Ixil ("Ysil") (Original map uncatalogued, Library of Congress, Geography and Maps Division)

there, the *vigías* served a more preventative than defensive role along the northern coast of Yucatan. In other words, their purpose was to ward off potential attacks with their presence or, at the very least, provide warning when such danger was spotted.[17] For example, in the 1580s, fray Alonso Ponce visited the port of the coastal town of Sisal where he stated, "Here in this port is a watchtower, and a Spaniard as watchman and native assistants (*atalayeros*), to give warning to Merida as soon as an invasion is discovered."[18] The warnings from the *vigías* came by way of fire, smoke, and/or letter carried by runners from the *vigía* to the proximate town and, eventually, Merida.[19]

The *vigías*, however, served another purpose: the introduction of contraband. Although the official appointment of coastal lookout included primitive living conditions and only a few Mayas to exploit, well-connected Spanish applicants were plentiful.[20] Although the Crown repeatedly condemned the action, contraband seemed an unspoken reality in Yucatan and in other parts of the Spanish realm, particularly for those stationed at the *vigías* with easy access to such traders.[21]

The Mayas stationed at the lookout posts, called *indios atalayeros*, lived more or less in isolation, due to the remote location of the watchtowers and the marshland surrounding the shoreline of the north that was frequently inundated with the seasonal rains. The Maya workers received their assignment, which typically lasted one to two weeks, as a result of forced labor or the *repartimiento*, and their tasks included the physical maintenance of the tower and surrounding *trincheras*, the transportation of messages to and from the *vigía* and Merida, the provision of food for the watchman, and even fishing and salt-making duties. The Mayas originated from the nearby towns and villages, with the rotation being organized by the local *batabob*. At least some received an average salary of two to four *reales* a week.[22] The presence of Maya men at the *vigías* was common, and the sixteenth-century Franciscan Antonio de Ciudad Real noted that in Rio Lagartos "there was constructed a tower of wood, and together with the tower some houses of straw and some other Indians to service it."[23]

In 1722 the governor of Yucatan, don Antonio de Cortaire, conducted a survey of coastal Yucatan's defenses. Inspired by recent events—including the shipwreck of two Dutch frigates on February 6, 1722, close to Sisal containing contraband goods and previous landings of English pirates—the 1722 survey resulted in the earliest known map detailing the defenses and channels of communication for the northern coast of Yucatan (figure 2.3). The map shows *trincheras* along the paths connecting the various towns and their watchtowers as well as houses for those tasked with carrying the warnings. The *trincheras*, oftentimes composed of loose stone and mortar, protected the roads or paths that ran from the *vigías* to the coastal towns and, eventually, to Merida. These low walls provided cover for the militia as they fired upon the enemy while also serving as physical obstacles for anyone attempting to invade from the coast. Of the utmost concern was the security of Merida and its potential invasion from the coast. The map, then, pays particular attention to Merida, placing it in the middle, and illustrates its connection with other towns and their defenses while providing details on the *trincheras* and *vigías*.

As one might expect, the *vigía* of Ixil and the town itself are included in the map, as are details on the *trincheras* accompanying the road connecting the two (figures 2.4 and 2.5). Today Ixil and its surrounding region contain the remains of such *trincheras* along a northern road leading to the coast where a *vigía* once stood.

In 1766, the engineer don Juan de Dios González composed a similar survey and report resulting in a map detailing the defenses, and lack thereof, of the peninsula.

The report mentioned the watchtower of Ixil and described it as being protected by a weak low wall and staffed by *indios de servicio* housed in eight wattle-thatch houses. If the need should arise, the report continued, the road south from the watchtower led to the town of Ixil itself, some five leagues (seventeen miles) away, where *indios hidalgos* commanded two companies of militia totaling 80 to 100 men who could be called upon for assistance.[24]

Beyond general understanding, little is known of the details surrounding Ixil's *vigía*. That said, archival bits and pieces do provide some framework. The exact date of the watchtower's construction is unknown, but it appears to have already been established by the seventeenth century.[25] Although commonly forgotten and overlooked today, the *vigía* appears to have been well known among colonial navigators and cartographers, as it is featured frequently in coastal maps (figures 2.2–2.5).

Regarding the operations of the *vigía*, Jorge Victoria Ojeda recently brought to light Íñigo Escalante, a creole poet who penned various works while serving as the watchman at the *vigía* of Ixil in the late eighteenth century, and archival documents point to him earning a salary of 144 *pesos* a year.[26] Escalante served for three decades until his removal from the post in the late 1790s, meaning he was the sentinel posted at the tower when Ixil composed much of its extant corpus of wills. Escalante and his poems unintentionally reveal the extensive network of colonial officials complicit in the introduction of contraband at *vigías* such as Ixil.[27] Thus, like many others, the *vigía* at Ixil served paradoxical roles of warning off foreign enemies and pirates while facilitating the introduction of contraband to the peninsula, some of it acquired from those same so-called pirates.

More is known concerning the *trincheras* that guarded the road from the *vigía* to the town of Ixil from their archeological remains. A staple in the colonial defense of Yucatan, *trincheras* played an important role in Alonso Sánchez de Aguilar's defense of Rio Lagartos, where he lined them with tanned leather hides for additional protection against the invading English pirates.[28] According to Cortaire's 1722 map, *trincheras* of loose stone once existed at various intervals along the road to Ixil. Today a complex exists of three *trincheras* arranged in L-shaped patterns around a well and the remains of what could have been a residence. Interestingly, the layout of the existing *trincheras* fails to align with Cortaire's 1722 map. Yet among the *trincheras* is a stone with the inscribed date of 1744 that has proved useful in dating the site.[29]

Ixil's *vigía* and *trincheras* provide additional evidence of the continual role that Mayas played in the defense of the peninsula. Because of the inherent distrust of arming the Maya, Spanish officials left the majority of Yucatan's defense to units of free-colored soldiers, oftentimes referred to as *pardo* militias. However, as Mayas remained the majority of the population, Spaniards continued to rely on native

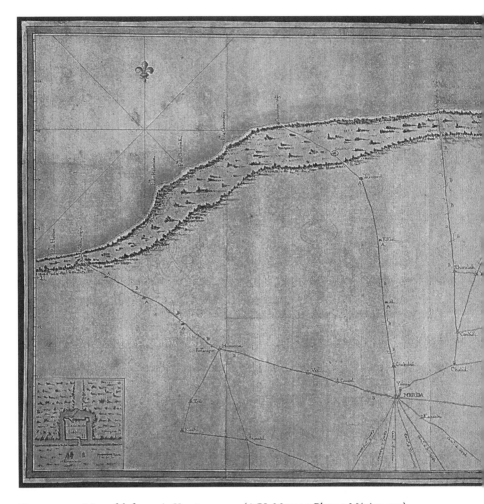

FIGURE 2.3. Map of defenses in Yucatan, 1722. (AGI, Mapas y Planos-México, 119)

auxiliaries in varying degrees, allowing colonial officials in 1704 to lament the lack of Spaniards in the defense of the province.[30] Although admittedly more popular in the northern frontier and coastal areas, militia units of *indios flecheros* continued to appear in the historical record for their role in defending the peninsula. In 1667 don Juan Xiu Cime of Maxcanu was awarded the position of captain in charge of forty *indios flecheros*.[31] And for its colonial defense, Campeche relied on eight companies of *"indios flecheros ó piqueros"* in addition to its other companies of Spanish and *pardo* militias.[32] Moreover, in certain parts of Yucatan, *indios flecheros* continued

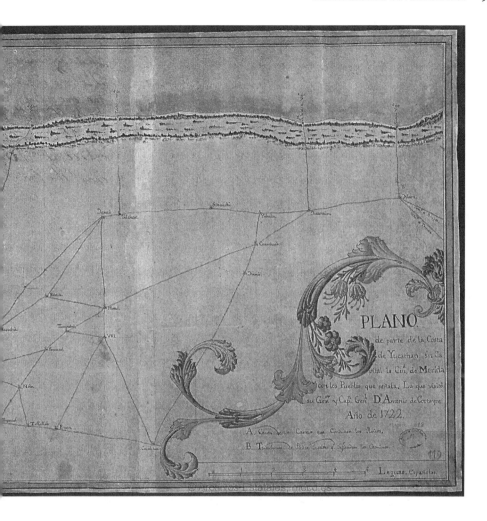

to help Spaniards pacify the region and to serve on conquest expeditions, such as those in the seventeenth century focused on the Itza Maya in what is today northern Guatemala.[33]

The role of the Maya in defending the coastline of Yucatan, particularly in the seventeenth century, is seen clearly in an event recorded by the *bachiller* Gregorio Martín de Guijo of Mexico City. He stated that on March 2, 1663, word reached the governor of Yucatan that an English ship had arrived on the coast. The governor sent Captain Maldonado with 200 Spaniards and 600 *indios flecheros*, who

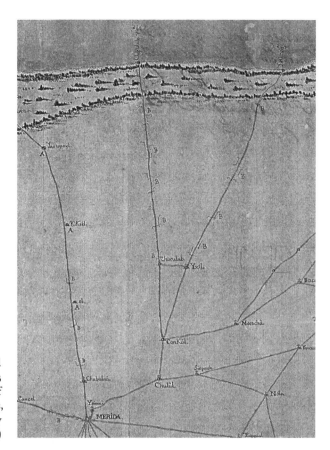

FIGURE 2.4. Detail of map seen in fig. 2.3 showing the *vigía* of Ixil and its defenses, 1722. (AGI, Mapas y Planos-México, 119)

subsequently successfully routed the pirates, causing them to "flee in a hurry" after having burned only one hacienda.[34] Furthermore, the diary of Antonio de Robles recalled a 1686 event in which English pirates disembarked on Yucatan's eastern shore, attacked the town of Tihosuco, and were making their way to Valladolid when, having heard of how many Maya militiamen had now closed the road and stood ready to fight, retreated to their ships.[35]

The organization of indigenous militias throughout New Spain varied from region to region, town to town. Typically, the *cabildo* nominated the officers of a native militia unit, who then subsequently appeared before the Spanish commanding officer, who could call upon the unit for military action when the need arose. However, militiamen could also be assigned to fulfill tasks other than those of battle. For example, Ixil's militia likely held the responsibility of providing the support staff for its *vigía*.

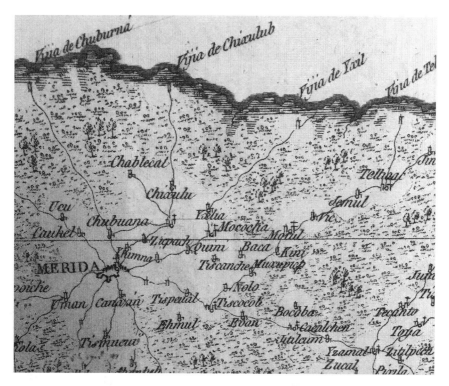

FIGURE 2.5. Detail of a map of Yucatan showing Ixil and its watchtower, 1801. "Vijia de Yxil" is shown on the coast as well as the road down to the town of Ixil ("Yxlia"). (Original map uncatalogued, Library of Congress, Geography and Maps Division)

As mentioned, Spaniards were wary of arming native peoples. Indeed, Spanish law—such as the *Ordenanzas reales* of 1529 and 1531—prohibited "Indians" from possessing firearms, and only nobles could receive permission to carry weapons. In light of this, some towns had an armory of sorts to keep the militia's weapons. Yet the ability of colonial officials to restrict the possession of such weapons among native militias was extremely limited, and conditions varied; for example, some militiamen were allowed to keep their weapons in their homes at all times. The status associated with possessing and carrying weapons held more significance than the weapons themselves. Finally, some native militiamen received exemptions from tribute and the permission to ride a horse with a saddle and reins—something normally limited to Spaniards and native nobles.[36] Indeed, foreign markers of status and prestige were particularly appealing to the native nobility, and the militia provided a legal avenue to achieve such for those privileged individuals.

By the 1790s, indigenous militias throughout New Spain fell victim to a variety of reforms. Upon his appointment in 1789 as viceroy of New Spain, count Juan Vicente de Güemes Pacheco de Padilla y Horcasitas was surprised to discover that native militias even existed. The lack of uniforms, training, organization, and sufficient weapons along with an increasingly pessimistic view of "Indians" in general led Spanish authorities to conclude that although having served Spain in the past out of necessity, the native militias were composed of an "undisciplined people and so poorly maintained that they do not merit the title of troop."[37] In 1792 the viceroy discontinued the official organization of many native militias.[38]

It is here in this context of Ixil's participation in the coastal defense of Yucatan and the region's Maya militias that we find clues to the military titles given to select individuals in Ixil. It remains unclear whether each Yucatecan town with a captain—of which there are more than a few—truly had a militia force or whether the title of captain held more honorary significance than practical.[39] Certainly the title in such towns once held a military responsibility, although it is possible that over the years the title came to serve a more honorary than practical role. In the absence of specific documents from a town, the topic must remain in the realm of speculation. For Ixil, however, we are afforded some clues.

The aforementioned reports and maps all indicate that Ixil, its *vigía*, and *trincheras* held an important defensive role. Moreover, the 1766 report of don Juan de Dios González indicated that Ixil did indeed have a militia force of 80 to 100 men commanded by "*indios hidalgos*." Most importantly, the testaments of Ixil provide evidence of militia offices being held by members of the nobility of the *cah*. Don Francisco Pech, the *batab* of Ixil in 1738, did not hold the title of captain; the first *batab* on record holding the title of captain was don Gaspar Canul in 1748. If Ixil's *trinchera* stone with the date 1744 is an accurate indicator of the wall's initial construction, this would seem to correlate with the appearance of captains in Ixil. Interestingly, the notary, Salvador Coba, only includes Canul's title of captain twice in the wills, perhaps suggesting the novelty of the title in the *cah*.

All *batabob* of record from 1748 to 1779 included the title of captain in their signatures (table 2.1). The last recorded appearance of a captain in Ixil was in 1779; the *batab* from a testament in 1807 does not include the title in his signature, also perhaps reflecting the 1792 crackdown on native militias in general. Such a close connection between the office of *batab* and the military title suggests a general trend of having the leader of a *cah* likewise serve as the leader of its militia.

Moreover, the testaments provide evidence of multiple individuals holding the title of captain in the same year. For example, a 1755 codicil (A2) confirming the receipt of bequeathed goods was done before "our lord, Captain don Juan Pech," although don Pedro Pech, who later refers to himself as "captain," was the sitting

TABLE 2.1. *Batabob* in Ixil holding the title of captain, 1748–79

	1748	1755	1760	1766	1767	1769	1773	1777	1779
Don Gaspar Canul	X								
Don Pedro Pech		X							
Don Ignacio Tec			X	X	X	X			
Don Joseph Cob							X	X	X

Sources: Data from AHAY, "Oficios 1748–1749, 1801–1884," vol. I, "Peten Itza"; Restall (1995; 1997: appendix C).

batab.[40] When don Pedro draws up his will in 1779, he is cited as Captain don Pedro Pech, although Captain don Joseph Cob was the acting *batab*. In Spain, as elsewhere, oftentimes the title of captain remained affixed to the individual long after services rendered. In addition, and perhaps most likely, the multiple captains originate from Ixil's two separate companies. Indeed, the 1766 report of don Juan de Dios González indicated that Ixil had two companies of militia. With a tribute population of 715 in 1721, Ixil could have staffed two companies of militia and, thus, had two captains serving simultaneously.

The other military title that appears in the testaments of Ixil is that of "*alférez*." In the 1779 will of Captain don Pedro Pech (C3), he mentions that it was drafted before his consanguineal relatives, "our lords don Antonio Pech and don Manuel Pech, *alféreces*." As mentioned, the *alférez* stood as second in command to the captain and was a respected position. Indeed, in 1598 Alonso Sánchez de Aguilar became appointed *alférez mayor* of Valladolid in Yucatan and earned 700 *pesos* a year for his service.[41] Although it is possible the position paralleled that of captain in its existence in Ixil, this is the only instance in the wills in which the position is mentioned. Moreover, although both Antonio and Manuel possess the titles, they likely did not serve together in the same company, as a typical militia has only one acting *alférez*.[42] Not surprisingly, the Pech *chibal*—the only one of *indio hidalgo* status in Ixil—held the office.

In the end, the wills provide important corroborating evidence of the importance of Ixil in the defense of Yucatan's coastline and the use of native militias. As expected, those holding the military titles of *capitán* and *alférez* represent noble lineages in the town and no doubt benefited from the various privileges associated with militia service. Indeed, as will be seen in the next chapter, a select few in Ixil bequeathed firearms—the possession of which could only be granted to officers in the militia. Moreover, those holding military titles all held important positions on the *cabildo*, a subject to which we now turn.

GOVERNING IXIL

In general terms, colonial Maya society divided itself between the *almehenob*, or nobles, and the commoners, typically referred to as *macehuales* during the colonial period. Yet within this class of nobles there existed divisions as well. Specifics regarding the preexisting sociopolitical structure and hierarchy of the Maya are oftentimes contested, given the paucity of precontact indigenous sources and the reliance upon Spanish accounts unfamiliar with native governance.[43] Regardless of their specific responsibilities, precontact positions or titles among the Maya nobility persisted through the colonial period, including *batab*, *ah cuch cab*, *ah dzib hun*, *ah kin*, *ah kulel*, *halach uinic*, and *hol pop*. The Maya elite holding these various positions served on councils that oversaw local matters, preserving their status within the new colonial regime and employing a variety of adopted Spanish institutions to do so, including the *cabildo*.

The *cabildo* was a system of local governance that operated in Spain long before its introduction into Yucatan.[44] In 1583 don Diego García de Palacio institutionalized the *cabildo* system in Yucatan, and it continued to spread steadily, soon coming to serve as the official institution of local government in each *cah*.[45] It was here that Maya officials adjudicated legal matters and disputes; handled all official documentation and notarization; collected and delivered civil and ecclesiastical tribute; brokered agreements between Spanish and native interests; and defended the rights of the *cah* and its people. Put simply, the *cabildo* and its officers "formed the crucial interface between the Maya and the major economic and political institutions of the colony."[46] All interactions between the Maya *cah* and the Spanish colonial system fell under its purview.[47]

The *cabildo* not only allowed the Maya *cah* to maintain a degree of cultural autonomy but also provided the elite with the means to establish their position within a new colonial regime. To be sure, colonial rule robbed the traditional elite of many of their previous avenues of attaining social distinction—such as slavery, religious prestige, political power based on traditional networks, and wealth based on a precontact economy.[48] Thus, Maya elite had to employ new ways to establish their social position, including the *cabildo*. Colonial documentation illustrates the wide diversity that existed between each *cah* with regards to the traditional *cabildo* model and its officers. Some, like Cacalchen in 1647, included a *gobernador* (governor), three *alcaldes* (judges and councilmen), six *regidores* (councilmen), and an *escribano* (notary). Others, like Ixil in 1766, included a *batab* (governor), *teniente* (lieutenant and assistant to the governor), two *alcaldes*, four *regidores*, and an *escribano*.[49]

Fortunately, every will and codicil from Ixil contained the names of the cabildo members and the necessary signatures of the *batab* and *escribano*. Thus, the testaments provide an abundant, rich source of data—uncommon for Yucatecan sources—on *cabildo* offices and the Maya who held them. This, then, allows for a localized glimpse both of how the *cabildo* functioned in Ixil from 1738 to 1807 and of those individuals that aspired to governing the *cah*. Certainly, the findings here confirm many of Restall's initial arguments derived from his original corpus of testaments and published in his *Maya World* (1997). However, the expanded corpus of wills now allows for new insights into the 1740s and 1750s, helping to illustrate with more detail those who held office and governed among the elite of Ixil.

In Ixil, as with other *cahob*, the *cabildo* as an institution allowed various preconquest positions to merge with those Spanish. Preexisting rulers among the Maya included the *halach uinic*, or True Man, the highest-ranking, regional ruler who came close to being what we might call "king"; and *batab*, both drawn from the hereditary nobility that dominated the various provinces (or, arguably, kingdoms) of Yucatan. The relationship between the positions of governor and *halach uinic* and *batab* in the late sixteenth and early seventeenth century in Yucatan remains a contested topic. Some scholars argue for a blending of the *batab* into the *cabildo* office of governor as early as the 1580s; others suggest a more gradual incorporation.[50] The extensive documentation available from the Maya town of Tekanto allowed Thompson (1999) to provide a rare view of this relationship. Thompson showed that a dual system of government existed until the beginning of the seventeenth century, with the positions of *batab* and governor being held by separate individuals. The former drew from the traditional hereditary elite; the latter achieved their position by Spanish appointment, which could or could not recognize nobility.[51] Soon, however, the single position of governor dominated the *cabildo* with its office holder being identified as both *batab* and governor.

This is not unlike the situation in central Mexico, where many native rulers (singular, *tlatoani*) of Nahua towns (singular, *altepetl*) identified as both *tlatoani* and governor.[52] Yet in both central Mexico and Yucatan, disagreeable rulers from the traditional ruling class could be replaced with Spanish-appointed governors more compliant with colonial rule. In reality, by the late sixteenth century hereditary rulers played the difficult role of mediator between their town and the Spanish system. Some employed preexisting traditional rites to maintain their legitimacy among their constituents. Others collaborated with Spaniards and friars—even participating in extirpation campaigns—to maintain their power. Still others attempted to appease both sides by engaging in the Spanish system of governance and power, such as the *cabildo*, while also employing (or at least permitting) the continuation of rites seen by the Spanish as pagan.

No doubt many towns followed a similar pattern of integrating preexisting positions into the colonial *cabildo*. Oftentimes the position of *batab* merged into that of governor; Mayas knowledgeable in record keeping, the *ah dzib hun*, and other trained elite could become notaries; and preexisting offices such as the *ah cuch cab*—literally "one who carries honey on his back" but generally used to denote someone of higher status[53]—could become those of the *alcalde* and *regidor*.[54] Yet the individual and autonomous nature inherent in each town allowed for much variety throughout the peninsula, thus preventing a fixed rubric. With regards to the position of governor, at times the hereditary nobility maintained their status as rulers of the *cah* through this office. On other occasions nontraditional lineages dominated the governorship of a town. To the example of Tekanto, Ixil adds another glimpse at local government.

In eighteenth-century Ixil, the head of the *cabildo* identified himself as *batab*. In no instances does the name of a separate individual serving as governor appear in the wills or any other documentation from Ixil, thus suggesting that the *batab* fulfilled the roles of both governor and *batab*—as was the case in many towns. The preconquest title of *halach uinic* appears in an 1807 statement concerning a 1769 will but, interestingly, does so in reference to the Spanish official presiding over a border-dispute litigation. In addition, the title of *ah cuch cab* appears in a 1767 statement (B45) regarding a member of the Ixil community who died intestate. The statement contains the names of the typical *cabildo* members—the *batab*, notary, lieutenant, two *alcaldes*, and four *regidores*—and the necessary signatures. Yet included below the names of the *regidores* is that of Joseph Mis and the title of *ah cuch cab*. This singular inclusion is somewhat of an anomaly and could have been used to dignify Joseph's inclusion in *cabildo* business, perhaps as an executor of the will.[55]

Nonetheless, although none of these preconquest titles appeared in relation to the *batab*, all the individuals holding the office were nobles, and indeed some descended from preconquest hereditary lineages of nobility. Concerning the latter, members of the Pech lineage exerted their influence over the region known as Ceh Pech, which encompassed the town of Ixil long before the arrival of the Spaniards. During the colonial period, the Pech gained official *hidalgo*, or noble, status due to their assistance in helping the Spaniards establish their colony, and they continued to hold influential sway over communal government in Ixil. Indeed, across the wills available from 1738 to 1807 the Pech held seventeen *cabildo* seats. No other *chibal* held as many positions. That said, the Pech held the office of *batab* only twice. The other lineages from Ixil's nobility that occupied the office were the Canul, Cob, and Tec (table 2.2).

In colonial society the Spanish "don" prefix served as an honorific title for those Maya considered *hidalgos* and those serving or having served as *batab*. The Pech represented Ixil's *hidalgos*, to be sure, but that did not award every Pech the title of don, as many appear in the wills without the honorary prefix. That said, eleven Pech appear throughout the wills with the title—some earned through the position of *batab*, for others it is unclear. The only other *chibalob* awarded the title of

TABLE 2.2. *Chibalob* in Ixil with members in the position of *batab*, 1738–1807

	1738	1748	1755	1760	1765	1766	1767	1768	1769	1773	1777	1779	1786	1807
Tec				X	X	X	X	X	X				X	X
Pech	X		X											
Canul		X												
Cob										X	X	X		

Sources: Data from AHAY, "Oficios 1748–1749, 1801–1884," vol. 1, "Peten Itza"; Restall (1995; 1997: appendix C).

TABLE 2.3. The dons of Ixil, by lineage, 1738–1807

Joseph Pech	Ignacio Tec	Joseph Cob	Gaspar Canul	Juan Balam
Lorenso Pech	Clemente Tec			
Juan Pech	Esteban Tec			
Pedro Pech				
Sebastián Pech				
Andrés Pech				
Bartolomé Pech				
Francisco Pech				
Antonio Pech				
Manuel Pech				
Pasqual Pech				

Sources: Data from AHAY, "Oficios 1748–1749, 1801–1884," vol. 1, "Peten Itza"; Restall (1995; 1997: appendix C).

don—most certainly through service as *batab*—were the Cob, Canul, Tec, and Balam (table 2.3).

Seldom does the Ixil corpus of testaments offer sequential, year-after-year examples. However, those from 1765 through 1769 provide useful data in analyzing the rotation of the position of *batab*. In its entirety, it is evident that the position rotated among Ixil's nobility. That said, it also appears that, at least occasionally if not routinely, a *chibal* could occupy the seat of *batab* for years at a time. Such is the case for Captain don Ignacio Tec, who served as *batab* in 1760 and then from 1765 to 1769. If the documentation existed, it would likely indicate that Ignacio held the position for a decade and perhaps longer. Similarly, Captain don Joseph Cob served in 1773, 1777, and 1779. Again, if the documentation were available, it would likely show Cob as *batab* consecutively throughout those years. In truth, the position of *batab* serving as governor in Ixil's *cabildo* more closely aligned with preconquest practices, defying the Spanish tradition of an annually rotating governor.

Interestingly, this lengthened tenure of office applies only to the position of *batab*, as all other *cabildo* positions followed an annual rotation. Certainly this reflects the elevated status of *batab* over that of other *cabildo* members. Although Restall illustrated how the *cabildo*—particularly in Tekanto—could serve to advance careers by ascension through the ranks, he also demonstrated how the elevated status of the positions of *batab*, lieutenant, and notary made them exceptions to this trend.[56] Indeed, no *batab* in Ixil appears to have ever held the office of *alcalde* or *regidor* prior to his appointment. The office of notary, however, does prove the exception to this rule, no doubt due to the elevated position of the scribe in precontact Maya society. For example, Joseph Cob appeared as notary in 1760 and 1765, but then as Captain don Joseph Cob in 1773, 1777, and 1779. Notable are the addition of "captain" and "don" to his name. The latter became awarded to those holding the office of *batab*—the only office with sufficient clout to do so. The former derived, as mentioned, from service in Ixil's militia.

The remaining positions on the *cabildo* included two *alcaldes*, four *regidores*, and a lieutenant. The names of such individuals appear listed in the wills in a fixed order indicating positions and rank (i.e., *regidores* 1°, 2°, 3°, and 4°). The documentation suggests a strict annual rotation among *alcaldes* and *regidores*, although individuals frequently served in their position more than once. For example, Pasgual Coba served as *regidor* in 1755, 1765, and 1798. Pasgual likewise illustrates the general lack of mobility between ranks, as he served in the position of *regidor* throughout his life without ever making the higher ranks of *alcalde* or lieutenant. However, occasionally examples of mobility occur. Sebastián Yam served as *regidor* in 1748 but appeared as lieutenant in 1760. Moreover, Ignacio Coba served as lieutenant in 1748 and then as *alcalde* in 1760.[57] In light of the available data, however, it appears that the nobility of Ixil failed to employ the *cabildo* as a ladder to ascend to the higher rank of *batab*.

As seen in table 2.4., the *hidalgo* lineage of the Pech dominated the *cabildo*, holding more positions than any other *chibal*. Yet other noble *chibalob* such as the Coba and Tec were not far behind and occupied the important positions of *batab* and *escribano* more than once. As will be seen in vivid detail in the next chapter, although the Pech represented Ixil's only *hidalgo chibal*, other noble lineages possessed the political positions and wealth significant enough to rival the Pech and allow for the shared governance of Ixil.[58] In truth, the death tolls of both commoners and elites from multiple epidemics, particularly in the sixteenth and seventeenth

TABLE 2.4. *Chibal* officeholding in Ixil according to annual rotations, 1738–1807

	Batab	Teniente	Escribano	Alcalde	Regidor	Total
Pech	2	1	0	6	8	17
Coba	0	3	1	4	7	15
Tec	5	1	2	2	2	12
Yam	0	1	1	3	5	10
Cob	2	0	4	0	2	8
Canche	0	2	0	0	4	6
Canul	1	0	0	1	3	5
Chim	0	0	2	1	2	5
Couoh	0	0	0	2	2	4

Note: Because a yearly rotation existed in Ixil, and because the same person could occupy the seat more than once, the numbers do not necessarily indicate separate individuals, only the number of rotations for which a *chibal* held a seat. For example, don Ignacio Tec was the only Tec to serve as *batab* but held the seat for five rotations.

Sources: Data from AHAY, "Oficios 1748–1749, 1801–1884," vol. 1, "Peten Itza"; Restall (1995).

centuries, created vacancies for other lesser or aspiring nobles to ascend to governance. The definition of "noble" remained fluid throughout the colonial period and allowed those with or without the necessary socioeconomic status to either enter or leave its purview.[59] Fortunately, the formulaic structure of Ixil's testaments often included the executors of the wills—those who would ensure the desires of the testator would be fulfilled. The testaments described the individuals chosen for this task overwhelmingly as *almehenob*, or nobles. This, then, allows for a more precise view into those *chibalob* considered noble by the Ixil community (table 2.5).

Notably, the only position in Ixil's *cabildo* that demonstrates any significant variance or change over the years is that of the *teniente*, or lieutenant—in some years the position is filled, in others it remains vacant. In many Spanish towns the *alcalde mayor* represented Spanish authority along with his selected lieutenant. Typically, with regard to Maya towns, the position ranked between that of *alcalde* and *batab*, and just below that of notary. In truth, the role, function, and appointment of the *teniente* varied significantly from *cah* to *cah*.[60] Regarding Ixil, bits and pieces of evidence exist to suggest that individuals could hold the position of *teniente* for more than one year (table 2.6) and also that the title remained affixed to the individual after services rendered. In the aforementioned 1779 will of Captain don Pedro Pech, he puts his affairs in order in front of his consanguineal relatives, including Captain don Joseph Cob, the *batab*, and the *alféreces* don Antonio Pech and don Manuel Pech. Included in this list of militia officials is "our lord lieutenant, don Pasqual

TABLE 2.5. *Chibalob* in Ixil described as *almehenob*

	1738	1748	1765–69	1799
Canche		X		
Cante		X	X	
Canul			X	
Chan		X		
Cob			X	
Coba		X	X	
Ek		X	X	
Itza		X		
Ku			X	
Mis			X	
Mitz		X		
Pech		X	X	X
Poot			X	X
Pot			X	
Tec	X	X	X	
Uh		X		
Yam		X	X	

Pech." Interestingly, Pasqual was not the acting lieutenant in 1779—Felipe Canche held that position—and yet he was still referred to as "lieutenant."

The position of *teniente* remained vacant during the years 1738, 1765, 1768, 1769, and 1773 and thus are not represented in table 2.6. Ignacio Coba held the position twice, as did Felipe Canche and Juan de la Cruz Chan. With regard to Canche, he held the position in 1777 and 1779. It is likely that if a will existed for 1778, Canche likewise would appear as *teniente*, thus offering the possibility for a consecutive-year term, like a *batab*. The same possibility exists for Ignacio Coba. This is not overly surprising given that the position of *teniente* was not elected and often resulted from political jockeying within the *cabildo* itself or through personal connections with the *batab*. For Ixil, Restall earlier posited that "it was often a post of indirect political importance, being filled by a man whose social stature in the community derived from his wealth or *chibal* connections, or from both."[61]

TABLE 2.6. Individuals occupying the position of *teniente*, 1738–1807

	1748	1755	1760	1766	1767	1777	1779	1786	1798	1807
Ignacio Coba	X	X								
Sebastián Yam			X							
Gaspar Coba				X						
Andrés Tec					X					
Felipe Canche						X	X			
Juan de la Cruz Chan								X		X
Francisco Coba									X	

Sources: Data from AHAY, "Oficios 1748–1749, 1801–1884," vol. 1, "Peten Itza"; Restall (1995; 1997: appendix C).

Regardless of such uncertainties, the inclusion of the *cabildo* on every will from Ixil certainly opens a wide window of insight into local governance. The wills illustrate not only the corporate workings of town government but also the social standing of various lineages within the town itself. Undoubtedly, the *cabildo* proved useful to noble and elite *chibalob* in shoring up and sustaining preexisting positions of status and power. The Pech were at the apex of social hierarchies before the Spanish arrival, and they continued to be afterward. Yet the signatures found on every last will and testament likewise demonstrate the ability of other elite lineages to employ the *cabildo* in ways that allowed them positions of power within the government of Ixil.

Ixil is still proud of its *trincheras*; they are even portrayed on the town's modern sign (figures 0.5 and 2.6). In recent years, José Encarnación Tejero Poot and José Carlos Cen Rubio, along with others, have labored to increase the ecotourism possibilities of Ixil to include a project titled "Servitur las Trincheras de Ixil." The project petitioned the involvement of INAH and other agencies to restore and preserve the colonial low walls, and envisioned access to and tours of the *trincheras* and the beach beyond for interested tourists. Ironically, perhaps poetically, the low walls once employed by the Maya of Ixil to defend their town have found renewed use in their potential to provide a bit of much-needed revenue for the community.[62]

Indeed, in many ways the local Maya families who still govern Ixil continue in their efforts to maintain the social and economic well-being of the town. In 2015 Anastasio Córdova Chan, as mayor of Ixil, and José Fernando Pech Flota, the

FIGURE 2.6. Ixil's *trincheras*, as portrayed on the *L* of the town sign, 2018. (Photograph by Matthew Restall)

municipal secretary, presided over the nineteenth celebration of "Pa'que te llegue," an event designed to encourage gender equality in Ixil and surrounding towns and to help bring the services of various agencies to those not wanting to go into Merida, particularly women experiencing violence. Representatives from various organizations were present to answer questions, provide instruction, and illustrate potential avenues for future education on matters ranging from daily stress to domestic violence. Although the event and its purposes are something of a novelty for the town, those presiding over it certainly are not. Don Anastasio and don José Fernando were hardly the only men of the Chan and Pech *chibalob* to represent in the twenty-first century the age-old traditions of lineage-based local class and politics (figure 2.7). The patronyms of Chan and Pech are at home in the small town and descend from a long line of Maya who for centuries have borne the burden of defending and governing Ixil.[63]

FIGURE 2.7. A house in Ixil showing Pech influence in modern-day municipal government, 2009. The sign promotes a member of the Pech family's run for the office of municipal president (loosely speaking, the modern equivalent of *batab*). (Photograph by Matthew Restall)

NOTES

1. Gillpatrick (1885: 328).

2. AGI, México, 3157, "Reconocimiento y estado de la Provincia de Yucatán, por el ingeniero Juan de Dios González, en Campeche a 18 de febrero de 1766." A useful transcription of this source appears in Calderon Quijano (1984: 275–84, 395). *Indios de servicio* were typically Mayas who temporarily performed forced labor, at times on a rotational basis.

3. RLRI, lib. VIIII, título XXXXIII, ley 4.

4. A different version of the material in this chapter, including mention of additional sources, is being published as Christensen and Restall (2019).

5. Jorge Victoria Ojeda mentions the role of Maya militias in various publications (1995, 2000, 2007); see also Jones (1998) and Chuchiak (2012).

6. On the conquest of Yucatan, see Restall (1998a; 2014a); Chuchiak (2007).

7. For more on the duties of the *alférez* in the militia see Restall (2009: ch. 5); Vinson (2002: 49).

8. Molina Solís (1904: vol. 1, 309).

9. They were also deployed to the south of the colony into the unconquered zones stretching across the southern Yucatan Peninsula into what is today's northern Guatemala (Jones 1998; Caso Barrera 2002), but we found no evidence that men from Ixil, living as far as they did from those frontiers, were sent south to war in the seventeenth century.

10. For an excellent overview of piracy in the Americas, see Lane (1998).

11. A wall would eventually be constructed around the entire town, becoming the only fully walled town in the Americas.

12. Molina Solís (1910: vol. 2, 255).

13. AGI, Patronato, 80, "Méritos, servicios: Hernando Aguilar: cabo Vela, Cartagena, etc.," fol. 29v. For a more complete account see Cogolludo (1688: bk. 8, ch. 2, 421); Molina Solís (1904: vol. 1, 251–54). Cogolludo, Molina Solís (drawing, no doubt, from Cogolludo), and all subsequent authors who use their works cite the date as having been April 8, 1599. Yet the AGI document places the date as April 8, 1600. It is possible that Cogolludo and/or Molina Solís used a different source with the 1599 date.

14. For an extensive discussion of the Yucatan's defenses and the important role of Afro-Yucatecan militias see Restall (2009: ch. 5). More generally, see Calderon Quijano (1984); Victoria Ojeda (1995); Michel Antochiw (2006). On Spanish-British relations in the Yucatan-Laguna-Belize orbit, see Cromwell (2009); Restall (2014b).

15. RLRI, lib. VIIII, título XXXXIII, ley 3, 4; Peraza Guzmán (2000: 96).

16. Indeed, the word *atalaya* is derived from Islam and *al-talia*. See O'Callaghan (1975: 149). For a general overview and description of the presence of Afro-Yucatecans in staffing the *vigías*, see Restall (2009: 170–73).

17. Scholarly work on *vigías* is scanty, but see Victoria Ojeda (2000; 2007).

18. Ramos (1873: 440); Peraza Guzmán (2000: 97). See also AGI, México, 3157, "Reconocimiento y estado de la provincial de Yucatán, por el ingeniero Juan de Dios González, en Campeche a 18 de febrero de 1766." This report provides useful details on the nine *vigías* of the northeast coast of Yucatan responsible for alerting Merida of impending pirate attacks.

19. Victoria Ojeda (2007: 92–96).

20. Farriss (1984: 37); Victoria Ojeda (1995: 79–82; 2007); Restall (2009: 170–73).

21. Victoria Ojeda provides a few examples in his *Las torres* (2007: 69–73). For more on the trade in contraband in general, see Lane (1998).

22. Victoria Ojeda (2010: 61–82); García Bernal (1972: 135–36).

23. Ciudad Real (1976: 313); Peraza Guzmán (2000: 97). For a survey of native labor and its exploitation at the *vigías* see Victoria Ojeda (2000).

24. AGI, México, 3157.

25. Molina Solís (1910: vol. 2, 428).

26. AGN, Instituciones Coloniales, Indiferente Virreinal, Cárceles y presidios, caja 2499, expediente 020; Victoria Ojeda (2005: 5).

27. Victoria Ojeda (2005: 1–22).

28. Cogolludo (1688: bk. 8, ch. 2, 421). See also Peraza Guzmán (2000: 97).

29. Victoria Ojeda (1995: 111–22).

30. Restall (2009: 160).

31. Quezada and Okoshi Harada (2001: 93).

32. Molina Solis (1904: vol. 2, 427).

33. Jones (1998: 50–51, 133–34); Caso Barrera (2002: 203, 266, 271).

34. Martín de Guijo (1952: 191).

35. Robles (1946: 120); Güereca Durán (2013: 145).

36. Ibid., 148–88. Early in the colonial period indigenous men were recorded as riding on horseback. Indeed, the 1570s and 1580s reports of the journeys of fray Alonso Ponce commented at various times how the Mayas would hurry to meet them upon their arrival at a town, the nobles, at times, on horseback. See, for example, Ciudad Real (1976: 363, 369, 371).

37. Güereca Durán (2013: 261).

38. For more on the topic see ibid., 245–63.

39. For Thompson's thoughts on the matter see his *Tekanto* (1999: 258).

40. It is possible that don Pedro was not serving as captain while acting as *batab* in 1755, although his later reference to this title provides a plausible situation suggesting otherwise.

41. AGI, Patronato, 293.

42. Vinson (2002: 48–49).

43. For the various views of scholars addressing the topic see Roys (1957); Farriss (1984: 231–37); Restall (1997: ch. 7); Thompson (1999: 34–38); Hanks (2010: 26–32); Quezada (2014: ch. 1).

44. O'Callaghan (1975: 578–95).

45. Quezada argues for a slower establishment of the *cabildo* system. See his *Maya Lords* (2014: ch. 3).

46. Thompson (1999: 18).

47. For more on the Maya adaptation of the *cabildo* see Restall (1997: ch. 6). For similarities and differences between Maya *cabildos* in urban and rural areas, see Lentz (2013: 172–98).

48. Patch (1993: 24–25).

49. For more on *cah* variation, see Restall (1997: 66–72).

50. See Farriss (1984: 231–37); Restall (1997: ch. 6); Hanks (2010: 81); Quezada (2014: ch. 3).

51. Thompson (1999: 40–43).

52. For more on the matter see Lockhart (1992: 31–44); Haskett (1991: 99–104).

53. This definition derives from the oldest extant Maya dictionary, the manuscript from Motul (DM), which also includes a definition of "indio principal que tiene cuydado de alguna parcialidad para recoger el tributo y para otras cosas de comunidad."

54. Restall (1997: 61–83); Thompson (1999: 221–304).

55. See Restall (1995: 130–31).

56. Restall (1997: 72–78).

57. For more on *cabildo* career patterns, see Restall (1997: 66–68).

58. For a more intimate view of the Pech in Ixil, see Christensen (2015).

59. Olko, Sullivan, and Szemiński (2018).

60. Restall (1997: 65–66). In some places, such as eighteenth-century Papantla in central Mexico, the lieutenant came from the officer corps of the local militia; Frederick (2016).

61. Restall (1997: 66).

62. *Diario de Yucatán*, October 11, 2011.

63. "Realizan feria 'Pa'que te llegue' en Ixil," *Reporteroshoy.mx*, October 15, 2015, http://reporteroshoy.mx/wp/realizan-feria-paque-te-llegue-en-ixil.html.

3

Ixil's Economic Life

Attached to this convent [Campeche] is the town of the Indians, the *campechanos*, about three hundred tributaries; it is very cool and has many trees, especially that of oranges, bananas, guavas, coconuts, palms, plums and bananas [*sic*] and some that carry a small and very tasty fruit called *huayas*.

    —Fray Antonio de Ciudad Real, 1588[1]

I who am Mateo Coba, I receive three *pesos* plus one *toston*, and one red sapote [orchard], for its sustenance; this well is being cut for me. This closes things with my mothers, Lorensa Pech and Pasquala Yam. I have nothing more to say to them about this.

    —Mateo Coba, 1760 (A5)

Booze had come to Yucatan. Not all at once, but gradually. In the centuries following the arrival of the Spaniards, Mayas had continued with traditional agricultural practices even as the colonial bureaucracy attempted to siphon all surplus away from Maya towns to benefit and feed the colony. Much of this extraction took the form of tribute, religious taxes known as *limosnas* and *obvenciones*, other minor taxes, and mandatory labor service.[2] Because much of the tribute was paid in *mantas*, beeswax, and even maize, the Maya continued to produce those items familiar to their precontact economy. As time progressed, Spanish *estancia* and hacienda owners appeared, oftentimes on the borders of Maya towns. Initial interests revolved

DOI: 10.5876/9781607329220.c003

around stock-raising, but eventually agricultural production became the staple for many landed estates. Indeed, as the eighteenth century progressed and growing Spanish populations demanded more food than the native population could produce, a market for Spanish-produced foodstuffs appeared. And although maize dominated the market of landed estates, sugarcane and its alcoholic byproduct was the runner-up.

Aguardiente, or cane alcohol, emerged as a lucrative and popular by-product of sugar production in Yucatan, particularly in the eighteenth century. Increasing demand encouraged landowners to grow sugarcane on their estates and distill aguardiente. In 1781 the government estimated that local growers and distillers in Yucatan produced 8,000 barrels annually of the intoxicant.[3] Aguardiente was an important part of Yucatan's late colonial economy, and a document from 1814 gives evidence that this rapidly advancing product had reached Ixil. Pedro José Escobedo, a local distiller in Ixil, wrote to the officials of the Real Hacienda inquiring to whom he should deliver the owed taxes on his distillery.[4] The topic seemed to be one of debate between himself and Ixil's *cabildo* and no doubt resulted from the general confusion caused by the Napoleonic wars and the tenuous governance of Spain at the time. Yet aguardiente wrought contention in the region as early as 1785, when the curate responsible for the *doctrina* of Conkal, which included Ixil, complained that the sale of the beverage was the root of all the sins in his parish.[5]

Aguardiente, however, was not the only economic product of Ixil. Indeed, years before the drink's raging popularity, Ixil and its inhabitants made money from beekeeping, *sapote* and banana orchards, and henequen. Many residents owned animals, plots of land, and various personal items. Ixil's corpus of wills provides a glimpse into what the Mayas in this town owned and saw as important enough to pass on to the next generation. No other form of documentation offers such an intimate view. This chapter surveys these wills and the material content left by their testators. In the process, the daily economy of Ixil comes to life in a way that illustrates the economic standing of its *chibalob*, both noble and commoner, as well as general patterns of the ownership and bequeathment of goods according to gender. This chapter also examines the items found in Ixil's local economy and the influence of Spanish goods.

Ixil was always village-like, of modest size and wealth, never a bustling town or a central hub of economic activity. But its inhabitants were illustrative of most Yucatec Maya men and women of the colonial period, preferring to continue traditional ways of economic life while incorporating those Spanish practices and material items seen as potentially beneficial or profitable.

THE DISTRIBUTION OF WEALTH IN IXIL

Wealth is a relative term and subject to the capricious definitions of individuals and society in general. Many of the items listed as wealth in Ixil would fail to meet modern criteria. Yet this does not mean the inhabitants of colonial Ixil had all been reduced to paupers or that the town itself was bereft of economic diversity. Metal spoons, colored yarn, shotguns, animals, saint images, and even house beams do not necessarily scream prestige in today's society, but they were markers of status in eighteenth-century Ixil. Whereas the will of a poor Maya could include a tool or some articles of clothing, a will from an average commoner might contain one or two *kax* (plot of forested land, plural *kaxob*) or even an animal such as a mule or horse. Wealthier Mayas likewise bequeathed such items, but in greater quantity. Moreover, affluent Mayas possessed rarer and more valuable goods, such as metal or silver spoons, chests, saints, or even a gold chain—goods that oftentimes indicated their heightened exposure to Spanish society and economy. A survey of the items bequeathed in the wills further illustrates Ixil's economic diversity.[6]

As mentioned in the previous chapter, the category of "nobility" is best seen as fluid during the colonial period, with economic success or failure playing a large role in determining who wears the title. Admittedly, the wills are limited in their ability to paint a complete picture of Ixil's economy, as they illustrate the wealth of the dying, not the living, for whom no lists of assets were written. Regardless, Restall has shown how wealth could be combined with the social and political status of *cabildo* officeholding to reveal a hierarchy of class and nobility in Ixil. Although this newly expanded corpus does not contradict Restall's earlier findings, it does expand and augment them, adding further depth to our picture of Ixil's wealth.[7]

Table 3.1 analyzes the wealth of the lineages composing the wills in the corpus and is ordered according to the number of *kaxob* held by each. As seen in the previous chapter, the nobility here are those described as such (*almehenob*) or those with the title of don. Out of 105 documents, noble lineages were responsible for 76—a little more than 72 percent. Moreover, it is likely that certain *chibalob* categorized in the table as commoners, due to the absence of any description indicating noble status, were indeed considered noble. For example, although no Chim men are "dons" and nowhere appear as *almehen* executors in the wills, they served in the positions of *alcalde*, *regidor*, and notary, and they married into noble families. As such, they were likely nobles, although they are not listed as such in table 3.1. Given such exceptions, the proportion of 72 percent seems conservative indeed.

This important finding challenges two initial impressions. The first is the impression that most, even all, residents of an indigenous community composed wills, regardless of their socioeconomic status. To be sure, the poor left wills and the testamentary genre remains remarkable for its ability to represent segments of the

TABLE 3.1. Wealth in Ixil, 1738–79

Chibal	Number of Documents	Kax	Animals	Trees, Orchards, Beehives	Tools	Clothing, Cloth	Household Items
Pech	6	45	20	1 orchard	0	23	16
Tec	13	25	18	40 trees	3	5	18
Coba	16	15	0	1 orchard; 7 beehives; 51 trees	3	7	9
Yam	5	13	4	85 beehives	0	5	3
Canche	5	10	2	1 tree; 60 plants	4	7	5
Couoh	6	8	1	0	1	6	6
Chan	6	6	22	1 tree; 2 gardens	3	2	18
Mis	2	6	3	1 orchard	1	3	14
Huchim	4	6	0	0	2	0	6
Tun	2	6	15	0	0	14	3
Itza	4	5	0	0	0	5	3
Poot	5	4	15	0	2	5	15
Canul	4	4	5	1 orchard	3	14	3
Matu	4	4	2	0	1	40	5
Cob	2	4	1	0	0	0	0
Euan	1	3	0	55 banana trees	0	1	6
Cante	3	3	0	6 beehives	0	3	3
Uh	1	2	0	0	0	0	0
Ku	1	1	0	50 banana trees	2	2	6
Cab	2	1	0	4 plots of bananas	2	11	4
Cetz	1	1	0	0	0	0	1
Chim	1	1	0	0	0	0	1
Na	2	0	2	0	0	1	1
Coot	1	0	0	0	2	7	10
Chale	1	0	0	0	1	0	2
Mitz	1	0	0	0	0	0	1
Balam	1	0	0	0	0	0	0
Ek	1	0	0	0	0	0	0
Uitz	1	0	0	0	0	0	0
Can	1	0	0	0	0	0	0
Mo	1	0	0	0	0	0	0
Tacu	1	0	0	0	0	0	0

Note: *Chibalob* are ordered according to the number of *kaxob* held by each. Shaded rows indicate *chibalob* described in the documents as noble.

population—such as the poor and women—who otherwise seldom appear in the historical record. Yet in Ixil there appears to be a stark distinction in the economic status between those who left wills and those who did not. The wills from the neighboring town of Tekanto likewise illustrate this pattern. Thus from the perspective of testamentary evidence, there existed in Maya towns and villages an impoverished, landless underclass, more or less invisible to us.[8]

The second challenged impression is based on the assumption that the nobility by definition are a minority of any given population. But in the Maya world of the eighteenth century, the concept of nobility was broader, more complex, and more multifaceted than that. In Ixil, and likely in other *cahob*, a majority of families making wills considered themselves nobles. A comparison of the death records maintained in Conkal for Ixil in 1766 and 1767 and testaments from Ixil in those years illustrates that the majority of the recorded deceased left wills. A minority of the population constituted the deceased poor, going unnoticed in both the death records and the testamentary record. We cannot access specific numbers, but the approximate gist suggested by the two types of evidence is that some three-quarters of the population are dying with wills, and two-thirds to three-quarters of them are claiming to be descended from at least one noble *chibal*. In other words, roughly half the families in a *cah* like Ixil considered themselves by the mid-eighteenth century to be *almehen*, or Maya nobility.

In the sharper image provided by table 3.1 we find the Pech continuing in their rarefied position, and a brief survey of their wills illustrates larger economic patterns in the town. The Ixil corpus of wills contains only five wills from the Pech—two male and three female—and a codicil from Lorensa Pech detailing her bequeathment of property to a son. Existing death records from Ixil confirm that of the fifty-four recorded deaths in Ixil in 1765, twenty-eight were Pech, although we lack their wills.[9] Perhaps the discrepancy represents lost corpora of wills; perhaps not every Pech left a will; we suspect the former, but perhaps both scenarios are relevant. Yet even with this limited number, the wealth of the Pech is evident: consider that the Pech owned nearly twice the amount of land of their closest rival, the Tec!

Ignacio Pech (A1) died in 1748 and his will and accompanying codicils introduce the 1748 corpus. Ignacio left his three sons and single daughter goods of a variety not matched by any other testator. The bequeathed wealth included three *kaxob*, two house plots with wells, seven horses, two mules, three house beams, two fur blankets, two silver spoons, a multitude of clothing, and household items including two shotguns (table 3.2). The only other male Pech to leave a will, the don Pedro Pech who died in 1779, failed to bequeath much wealth. Indeed, he only mentions two *kaxob*. However, as we have seen, don Pedro held the important positions of *batab* and captain, thus confirming his privileged position in the *cah*.

TABLE 3.2. The wealth of Ignacio Pech, 1748

Land	Clothing	Tools	Cloth	Valuables	Religious Items	Animals	Household Items
2 house plots with wells; 3 forests	3 shirts; 3 pairs of trousers; 3 sashes		3 lengths of cloth	2 metal spoons; 2 shotguns; 2 silver spoons		1 male mule; 4 mares; 1 female mule; 3 geldings	3 house beams; 2 chests; 3 wooden chairs; 1 chair; 2 fur blankets

In his will Ignacio gives a female mule, three geldings, two mares, two house beams, two silver spoons, two wooden chairs, two shirts, two pairs of trousers, two sashes, two lengths of cloth, and two fur blankets to his wife, Bernardina Cante, to distribute to his sons Pasgual and Pedro. Why he charged his wife with distributing the goods instead of directly bequeathing them to his sons is unclear, but perhaps it was simply a matter of convenience. Regardless, following Ignacio's will are four codicils that further elucidate the distribution of goods. The first is a statement from Bernardina Cante and her sons Pasgual and Pedro confirming the receipt of goods according to Ignacio's will. Most interesting, however, is the date of the statement: 1755, seven years after Ignacio composed his will.

This is not the only instance in the corpus of a delayed receipt of goods. The heirs of Francisco Couoh (B35), a wife and daughter, do not gain possession of the horse and furniture bequeathed to them for almost six and a half years. Francisco had stated in his will that the property would be handed over by his father, Ventura, who appeared reluctant to part with the goods; the existence of a notarized record of receipt (B35a) indicates that Francisco's wife, María Huchim, had to resort to legal action and take the matter to the *cabildo* of the *cah*. A hint of the animosity that must have existed between María and her father-in-law is given in the tone of her remarks to the *cabildo*: "*bia bicili*," she says (almost "hey, you, take note of this!"), "*lay tun cin kami chelel*" (now then, at last, I receive); and in closing, "I have nothing to say to Ventura Couoh and he understands this," perhaps meaning "he understands why (I have nothing to say to him)" or "he understands this (and thus agrees with what I have said)."

Technically, executors and those charged with tasks in wills should not delay in carrying out the wishes of the dead. In his large confessional manual of 1569, fray Alonso de Molina asks the penitent, "*Auh yn iquac omomiquilique, açaçomo yciuhca tictequipano yntestamento, yc mocauhtiaque*" (And when [your parents] died, did you perhaps not promptly put into effect the testament which they left behind?).[10] An exemplum, or illustrative story—found in both a colonial collection of Maya-authored religious texts known as the Morley Manuscript and fray Juan Coronel's

1620 *Discursos predicables*—relates the horrible and painful death of a negligent executor who failed to carry out the wishes of the testator.[11] And the theme was also the subject of a play written in Nahuatl.[12] Nevertheless, Bernardina and Ventura, no doubt, had their own reasons to delay the transfer of goods left under their charge.

Ignacio Pech had four children—Salvador, Pasgual, Pedro, and Lorensa. The daughter was given a forest, a house plot and well, one mare, a chest, and a metal spoon. Twelve years later, in 1760, Lorensa and her son, Mateo Coba, make several statements comprising the remaining codicils regarding the funding for the digging of a well. Lorensa states that she gives one red sapote orchard to her son to finance the digging of a well, and Mateo confirms the receipt of such funding. Following the codicils, the corpus returns to the last will and testaments of Ixil's members. Yet the codicils illustrate the law and order maintained in this remote Maya town by the *cabildo*. For in order to settle this business about the well, Mateo needed to "appear before my lord *batab*, and magistrates, and *regidors*, and the notary in order to give my true statement" (A3).

Similar to Spanish women, Maya women could inherit and hold property independent of their husbands.[13] But this should not suggest that the Maya practiced gender equality. More accurate would be to use the term "gender parallelism" where both genders engaged in different, yet important roles. The situation, however, should not be romanticized, as Maya men held principal positions of dominance and power both in the private and public spheres.[14] In general, Maya women labored within the *solar*, or house plot, while the men worked in the *kax* some distance away. Thus, the distribution of wealth between both genders reflects such tasks.[15]

As is demonstrated below in the wills themselves, Maya women typically owned lengths of cloth, looms, and clothing pertaining to both genders; men owned those tools necessary for laboring in the *kax* (machetes, digging sticks, axes, and so on), and men's clothing. Men largely monopolized the ownership of guns, although Bernardina Cante does mention her inheriting a gun, albeit in the context of giving it to her son. As mentioned, men were more likely to own animals, although exceptions for women do exist. Regarding flora, although men likewise owned those orchards, trees, and vegetable gardens found in the *solar*, every bequest in the Ixil corpus was to a female recipient. Land tended to be more mercurial and moved into the hands of those who worked it. Although both genders owned *solares* and *kaxob*, women were much more likely to bequeath a *solar* than a *kax*, and men were slightly more likely to leave a *kax*.

Three of the five Pech testators are female and illustrate these trends and exceptions among property ownership among the genders. The 1738 will of Viviana Pech is the earliest in the corpus and is devoid of many possessions typically associated with women. Instead, she makes a sizeable bequest of six *kaxob* to her sons Pedro (seen above as don Pedro Pech) and Felipe. The bequest of six *kaxob* exceeds that of

TABLE 3.3. Hierarchy of *chibalob* in Ixil according to wealth, 1738–79

Tier	Status	Lineage (chibal)
1	*Indios hidalgos*	Pech
2	Upper nobles	Tec
3	Middle nobles	Coba, Yam, Canche, Chan, Mis
4	Lower nobles	Itza, Poot, Canul, Cob, Cante, Uh, Ku, Mitz, Balam, Ek
5	Upper commoners	Couoh, Huchim, Tun, Coot
6	Middle commoners	Matu, Euan
7	Lower commoners	Cab, Cetz, Chim, Na, Chale, Uitz, Can, Mo, Tacu
8	Underclass	

Note: The "underclass" comprised *chibalob* without a single member making a surviving will.

Source: Modified and updated after Restall (1997: 96).

any other—male or female—and thus confirms her elevated status within the *cah*. More illustrative of common gender patterns, the 1748 wills of Phelipa and Martha Pech (A20 and A21, respectively) include petticoats, chests, *huipiles* (the traditional Maya dress), lengths of yarn, and *solares*. And, as we saw in her 1760 statement to the *cabildo*, Lorensa Pech declares that she gave her son a red sapote orchard along with some money to dig a well.

The holdings of these Pech women confirm their noble and privileged status in the *cah*. Yet despite their status as Ixil's only lineage to be granted the noble status of *hidalgo*, the Pech did not monopolize their elevated socioeconomic position. Indeed, other *chibalob*, including the Tec, Tun, Matu, Chan, and Yam, likewise displayed impressive wealth, and table 3.3 helps to distinguish between and economically rank the many nobles in Ixil. The following examples consider wills from the Tec and Canul lineages to demonstrate both the success of other lineages other than the Pech and the economic life of Ixil.

The Tec came in second to the Pech with regard to local esteem, and their wills indicate a wealth of possessions (table 3.1). Luisa Tec's considerable wealth appears most notably to have been concentrated in her orchard of palm trees—thirty-eight in all—as the leaves of the palm tree were used by the Maya for making roofs. Interestingly, when Luisa (B56) bequeaths the palms to her two sons, each receives nineteen palm trees and one sapote tree, thus creating units of twenty for each son. The Maya used a vigesimal number system (based on a base of twenty with multiples of twenty being used in their calendar to create large numbers). Thus, the number twenty here in the will is a suspiciously significant number even to the colonial Maya. It is possible that this was an age-old method of dividing into two an orchard of many palm trees peppered with the odd sapote. This kind of concern for a numerical symmetry in presentation, often but not always accurately representing reality, can be seen among the colonial Nahuas as well.[16]

In addition to her palm trees, Luisa Tec owned a number of other items rare to the Ixil corpus. While various testators owned horses, Luisa is the only one to mention a saddle, and she is only one of two women to mention any tools: a small iron and bronze tool.[17] Luisa also owns two looms—the only mention in the Ixil corpus of weaving equipment, and a curious one considering that Luisa is rare among the women in not mentioning any cloth or female clothing. A last item found only in the will below is the trussed cockerel, *pota otzin*, that Luisa is giving as payment for her mass rather than selling it to raise the fee in cash. This is consistent with the tribute-product nature of most Maya taxation, but unusual with respect to clerical fees this late in the colonial period. In any case, the will of Luisa demonstrates both the gendered division of labor and ownership in Ixil as well as the noble status of the Tec *chibal* in general.

The Canul *chibal* likewise occupied a privileged position in Ixil's government, and their wealth confirms their status as nobles, although, as lesser nobles, the lineage possessed less esteem than the Pech and Tec (table 3.1). Ignacio Canul (B7), the father of the *batab* don Gaspar who served in 1748, died in 1766 owning two house plots, one with a well, two *kaxob*, four horses and a mule, one house beam, two chests, various items of clothing, and a henequen orchard. Diego Canul (B43), who passed the next year, had more modest holdings of a house plot and well, a single *kax*, and one machete, axe, and iron tool. Yet Martha Canul (A25), who died earlier in 1748 owned two house plots, one with a well, and numerous items of clothing including a length of yarn and a tribute *manta*. With regard to the *manta*, considering that in the eighteenth century a married couple had the annual tribute responsibility of one-half *manta*, a fanega of maize, a turkey, and a chicken—an eighteenth-century value of twenty-five *reales*—the *manta* was a valuable bequest.[18]

Lineages not quite reaching the socioeconomic tier of *almehenob* illustrate their status (or lack thereof) not solely through their limited presence on the *cabildo* and the rare appearance as executors in wills—again, a role typically granted to nobles—but also by their material possessions, which were generally in limited quantity and diversity vis-à-vis nobles. Such qualifiers help us to place the various *chibalob* into two categories: upper and lower commoners. The Canche, for example, are representative of upper commoners. In his 1766 will Gregorio Canche (B6) leaves to his relations one house plot and well, one axe and machete, a blanket, some cloth, and a single red sapote tree. María Canche (B12), who died in the same year, left a similarly modest sum of goods, including a house plot and well, a chest, a house beam, and a few items of clothing. The wills of lower commoners such as Joseph Uitz and Pasquala

Balam (B8 and B44 respectively) would typically end after the religious preamble, sometimes with the terse but accurate statement of *"manbal yan ten"* (I have nothing).

Thus, the wills illustrate a wide distribution of wealth among the Maya of Ixil. The noble *chibalob*, who likewise defended and governed Ixil, composed the most wills, owned the most wealth, and represented a large portion of the families in Ixil. Despite ubiquitous claims of nobility, economic factors distinguished the lineages. Indeed, the top three noble families—the Pech, Tec, and Coba—owned nearly half of the recorded land in Ixil's testaments. The remaining lesser noble and common population ranged in their economic standing, with some possessing wealth in impressive quantities and others lacking any possessions at all. Moreover, the distribution of wealth in Ixil reveals gendered differences: men possessed those goods commonly associated with the *kax* and labor, and women items revolving around the *solar* and domestic roles.

ITEMS IN THE LOCAL ECONOMY

The goods bequeathed in the wills reveal not only the distribution of wealth but also the type of wealth acquired in Ixil. A survey of the items listed in the wills provides an intimate view into the various means and modes of production in Ixil's economy—both traditional and Spanish. Again, the will of Ignacio Pech (A1) proves illustrative, as his wealth illustrates both the local and regional, Spanish economy. Ignacio's possession of house plots and their accompanying wells, the *kaxob*, cloth, and house beams are all products of a traditional Maya economy. An average Maya family would possess a *solar* and a *kax*, with which to cultivate corn, henequen, or other mainstays. As Ignacio's will attests, wells accompanied most house plots. Indeed, testators were particular in their mention of wells, as its inclusion in the house plot certainly added value. As little more than a limestone shelf, Yucatan collected its rainwater not in the soil but below in underground rivers and in sinkholes or cenotes. Thus, wells were a necessary feature, so much so that Mateo Coba went before Ixil's *cabildo* to acknowledge the receipt of money from his two mothers, Lorensa Pech and Pasquala Yam, for the digging of a well (docs. A3–A5).

The thin topsoil and limestone shelf of Yucatan made fallow periods characteristic and, thus, expansion of territory a necessity. As such, *kax* oftentimes were located some distance from the *solar*, thus necessitating specific locational markers when referenced in the wills. Ignacio identifies the location of his first bequeathed *kax* in reference to those surrounding it, stating that "to the east is don Joseph Pech, to the north Manuel Juchim, to the west Joseph Yam, to the south Miguel Tun." Most testators employed a similar technique, although sometimes specific locations appear. Diego Chan (B14) mentions a *kax* that is "on the road to Baca" and another "on the road to Kaknab." And Diego Tec (A24) gives a specific location for a *kax* located "at Silil," a now unknown location within the *cah* boundaries.[19]

Finally, Ignacio's mention of three house beams might seem pedantic. However, it is an indirect reference to the house itself or, in this case, three distinct homes as the Maya seldom mentioned the home itself. Given that the Maya house was ephemeral, in the sense that its walls and roof were composed of wattle and thatch, the central wooden beam—like the less frequently mentioned wooden frame of the house and the smaller wooden beam or lintel for a door or entrance—was one of the more enduring components and thus worthy of mentioning in a will when bequeathing the dwelling as a whole. We may well assume that other testators not mentioning house beams included the unmentioned home in their bequest of the *solar*. Or perhaps the beams of such homes lacked the roof-bearing heft of those specifically mentioned and did not find a place in the will.

Other items in Ignacio's will—his seven horses, two mules, two chests, metal and silver spoons—bespeak his connections to a Spanish, colonial economy, and his ownership of two shotguns certainly indicates Ignacio's involvement in the local militia. In truth, Ignacio's wealth falls into a general pattern seen throughout the testaments of wealthier Maya engaging in a wider, regional economy replete with Spanish goods. With regard to livestock, for example, Diego Chan (B14) bequeathed a donkey, five mules, six cows, and ten horses—an impressive amount of livestock, to be sure. Upon the inclusion of the Spaniards into Yucatan's regional economy, the need for meat and transport of goods to urban centers such as Merida, Campeche, and Valladolid became apparent. The Maya readily adapted to this new demand and began to raise chickens, pigs, and cattle. The meat and lard derived from such livestock could either be sold and consumed or be transported by mule or horse to other centers of consumption. Indeed, as Robert Patch notes, so many Maya came to possess horses and mules that they very nearly monopolized the transport trade.[20] Prior to the Spaniards and their beasts of burden, the Maya met transportation demands with human labor. Now, in the colonial economy, horses and mules filled this role.

This use of transportation can be seen in the will of Joseph Yam (B33). Joseph owned an incredible number of beehives—eighty-five in all. Certainly the Maya had been involved in apiculture long before the arrival of the Spaniards. Honey served as an important ingredient in the fermented drink *balche*, a type of mead associated with pre-Columbian religious rituals. Interestingly, select *batab* seeking to affirm their position in the local social order employed *balche* in clandestine religious and communal rituals throughout the colonial period.[21] Honey also served as an important ingredient in medicinal remedies used in both pre-Columbian and colonial times.[22] The colonial economy, however, brought with it a large demand for beeswax for candles, particularly for the church. As a result, the export of bees-wax became an important commodity for Yucatan, second only to cotton textiles. It even appears in a sixteenth-century confessional manual's question for a Nahua vendor in central Mexico: "*Auh yn campech vitz xicocuitlatl, aço castillan xicocuitlatl ypan oticquixti?*" (And the beeswax that comes from Campeche, did you pass it off as Castilian beeswax?).[23] Joseph's product needed transport to the appropriate mar-kets. Thus, he owned several horses that, no doubt, transported his valuable honey and wax to necessary buyers.

Twenty-four percent of Ixil's testators in the corpus bequeathed animals, thus indicating that stock-raising had found a firm foundation in Ixil by the mid-eighteenth century. Some testators had meager holdings, such as Matias Cob (A36), who owned one mare, or Juan Bautista Matu (A38), who owned one mule. Others, such as Diego Chan, boasted a larger variety and quantity. Consider that Miguel Tun (A9) bequeathed eight cows, two mules, four horses, and a bull; Gaspar Poot (B19) owned four cows and two horses; and Martha Pech (A21) left her relations nine horses and two cows. Because the possession of wealth typically broke along gendered lines, Martha's possession of so much livestock is unusual—particularly because her husband was still living, meaning that she owned the animals independ-ently and was likely involved in the transportation trade.

Ignacio also owned two chests, two metal spoons, and two silver spoons. Spanish-style chests came with a metal lock and functioned to store valuables, such as the silver spoons mentioned, which the Maya likely did not use but preserved for their value as bullion. Various Maya communities today continue to own such chests and preserve documents and items of historical importance.[24] The metal spoons lacked the value of their silver counterparts but were prized nonetheless for their rarity and expense as a Spanish item. Indeed, only seven testators owned metal spoons, and five owned silver ones.

The items in Ignacio's will, of course, do not provide an exhaustive list of goods found in Ixil. One of the most commonly bequeathed items was clothing. The men of Ixil typically wore a shirt, trousers (sometimes accompanied by a belt or sash), and occasionally a cloak and blanket over one shoulder. The shirt was a Spanish introduction (consistently referred to as *camisas* in the wills), as were trousers, although the Maya referred to the latter by its pre-Columbian predecessor—the *ex* or loincloth. Cloaks were rare, and only five Maya men owned one.

Women dressed in the indigenous *huipil* (*ypil*), still popular throughout Yucatan, under which they wore a petticoat (*pic*) and over which could be draped a shawl (*boch*). In addition to these staples, select women owned various accoutrements such as earrings and coral necklaces.[25] The will of Pasquala Matu (B29) provides an illustrative, albeit excessive, example of women's clothing and accessories. Pasquala listed forty items of cloth and clothing in her will, including eleven complete men's outfits (shirts and trousers) and eleven complete women's outfits (*huipiles* and petticoats). She also owned two pairs of necklaces strung with coral beads—a somewhat uncommon luxury for Maya women, as only seven claimed necklaces in their wills. This small fortune was left to five male and six female relatives and is indicative of the kind of economic independence that Maya women sometimes enjoyed. Moreover, it vividly illustrates the role of gender in the community economy. Women testators of Ixil left to their heirs proportionately four times as many items of cloth and clothing as did men. Women also tended to monopolize items such as lengths of cloth and yarn as well as the only ribbons, earrings, bracelets, washing bowl, and looms in the Ixil collection.

Spaniards likewise saw the value in local textiles, particularly given the exorbitant prices of imported cloth. Throughout the colonial period the *repartimiento* system of forced purchase extracted cotton and cotton textiles from the Maya, along with wax, for export and profit. Money could either be advanced to the Maya for a determined quantity of goods or used to purchase items forthwith. Yet in either scenario the Maya received only a fraction of the going market price for their materials and goods. Those colonial officials lauding the *repartimiento* justified the system as a benefit to the Maya, claiming it provided them with money to pay their tribute. Although Spaniards began to demand tribute payments in cash, the appearance of coin use in Ixil—either as bequeathed items such as Gaspar Poot's (B19) six gold coins or as payment for mass and burial fees—reflected its use in the everyday economy as the primary means of purchase, credit advancement and acquisition, and even in the liquidation of assets. Yet the truth was known to both officials and Maya alike that this exploitative system worked primarily in favor of Spaniards.[26]

The practice was so ubiquitous that the bishop of Yucatan, don fray Luis de Piña y Mazo, inquired about it among the thirty questions used in his late eighteenth-century *visitas* throughout the province. Question six specifically asks Maya parishioners if their priest "makes the Indians to spin or weave, or buys from them maize, wax, honey and other fruits of the land to turn around and sell them"; and question twenty-eight asks if when the price of maize is high, the curate obliges his parishioners to pay him in maize.[27] Accusations are not uncommon in the *visita* reports from the various towns, including one made by Joseph Canul of Uman, who accused his curate, among other things, of buying wax from his parishioners for one *real* and then afterward selling it back for four *reales* and of making women spin cotton in his house without pay.[28] In truth, the role of women in providing exportable cotton and cotton textiles was evident, even in Ixil, and Pasquala's clothing empire likely involved the *repartimiento*.

Other testators bequeathed items that testified to the important role of textiles in Ixil. In his terse will Pasqual Huchim (B42) leaves his "cloth-debt" to his father. Pasqual mentions that he has already paid two *pesos* of the debt but that a payment of three *pesos* remains for his father to cover. No other details follow—what was common knowledge to those in Ixil often remains arcane to us today—but again it is possible that this debt is related to the *repartimiento* that could create debts for the Maya if they did not provide the contracted goods. In addition, nearly 10 percent of testators bequeathed lengths of cloth and yarn that could be further developed into clothing or sold outright.

Despite the presence of animal husbandry and a small, but relevant, textile industry, Ixil's primary economic mainstay remained that of agriculture associated with the *kax* and the *solar*.[29] In bequeathing a *kax*, testators relied on tradition and the collective knowledge of the town by locating *kaxob* in relation to surrounding plots. For example, Miguel Tun (A9) gave his wife a forest he located by stating, "Adjacent to the forest to the east is Lucas Cetz; to the south, Juan Bautista Matu; to the west, Lorenso Chan; to the north, Bernardino Chan." Typically, the *kax* provided the maize crop and, as mentioned, resided away from the *solar*. However, some testators make mention of other crops and goods harvested on the *kax*. Diego Euan (A10) left a *kax* to his four children and claimed the *kax* had a "honey crop"; and Francisco Itza (A7) owned *kax* upon which was a "small hill of sapotes." The native sapote tree has a long history with the cultures of Mesoamerica. An important deity of the Nahua (Aztec), Xipe, or "flayed one," wore a sapote leaf skirt. Moreover, the Nahuatl-derived name Zapotec, or *tzapote-catl*, literally means "people of the sapote."[30] The Maya likewise prized the tree for its fruit and hardwood. Indeed, the uncommon durability of the wood inspired its use in roof beams, carved lintels, and decorative boxes—it even appears on King Pakal's renowned stone sarcophagus. Some scholars suggest that the pre-contact Maya elite attempted to control sapote cultivation.[31] Interestingly, the five families in Ixil that record owning sapote trees—Pech, Itza, Canche, Mis, and Coba—are indeed noble *chibalob*.

Other than the occasional mention of nonmaize horticulture on the *kax*, the majority of such seemed to occur in the *solar*. Gregorio Canche (B6) left his share of a house plot to his daughters that included "one red sapote tree," and along with his house plot, Pedro Mis (B30) leaves his wife and adopted child "all that is in my orchard of sapote trees." And Luisa Tec (B56) declared that the thirty-eight palm trees and two sapote trees she left for her sons were on a house plot. To be fair, occasionally a testator failed to mention that a particular orchard or tree was located on the *solar*. Yet the lack of a specific spatial location, similar to that used when bequeathing a *kax*, suggests its inclusion on the house plot.

In addition to palm and sapote trees, other specialty items mentioned on the house plot were beehives, henequen orchards, banana trees, and even a garlic and onion garden. Indeed, a 1665 letter from the governor of Yucatan, Francisco de Esquivel, to Juan Xiu, governor of Oxkutzcab, instructed the latter to ensure that "in the patios and gardens of their [the Mayas'] houses they shall plant chayas, bananas, and other fruit trees."[32] The importance of honey in Yucatan has already been recognized. Yet henequen likewise played an important role in the lives of the precontact Maya. Henequen is native to Yucatan; before the conquest its fibers had been used to make sandals and rope, while rope and sacking were the principal henequen products of the colonial period. The turn of the nineteenth century saw an increase in the demand for such products outside Yucatan, stimulating the development of ports such as Dzilam, Río Lagartos, and Sisal (by which name the English came to refer to the fiber) and the expansion of henequen haciendas.[33] Although Ixil is located close to the henequen ports and within the area of intensive cultivation of the plant, henequen mentioned in the wills—such as Felipe Coba's fifty plants (B10) or Francisco and Tomás Canche's sixty plants (B40a)—reflects earlier patterns of small-scale production by Maya farmers largely for local markets. The explosion of non-Maya-owned henequen haciendas would not take place for a century.[34]

Despite the continuation of traditional Maya agriculture, Ixil also employed various Spanish-introduced plants, including the banana tree. Despite its foreign origin, it seems that bananas quickly found a home among some of the Yucatec Maya as early as the late sixteenth century. Fray Diego de Landa noted the benefit of the banana to the Maya and stated, "There are many bananas, these having been brought by the Spaniards, since previously they did not have them."[35] Throughout the 1570s and 1580s, the commissary general of the Franciscans, fray Alonso Ponce, toured the order's convents in New Spain. In Yucatan bananas make frequent appearances in his reports. Ponce's secretary, fray Antonio de Ciudad Real, recorded that, in Mani, for instance, the Mayas would bring gifts upon their arrival, including "honey, bananas, and other fruits," and that the gardens of the convents themselves often contained banana trees.[36] By the eighteenth century, Ixil's horticulture likewise included bananas and three Maya included them in their wills. Micaela Cab (A8) gave both of her daughters two banana plots each; Pasqual Ku (B54) gave fifty banana trees to his wife; and Diego Euan (A10) left twenty banana trees to his wife, Lorensa, twenty to his son, Nicolás, and fifteen to his son, Francisco.

Along with bananas, there is evidence of onions and garlic being grown as well. Simón Chan (B21) left his wife a garlic garden and an onion garden—two items quickly adopted by the colonial Maya. The Spanish met with frustration the poor soils of Yucatan and thus encouraged those plants grown successfully in irrigated garden plots, such as melons, garlic, cucumbers, radishes, turnips, lettuce, parsley, coriander, mint, borage, onions, and spinach.[37] Other than their inclusion in wills, Spanish-introduced plants betray their appropriation by the Maya in their inclusion in medicinal remedies recorded in various colonial Maya-authored manuscripts. Garlic and onions both appear in medicinal remedies written in the Teabo Manuscript and the Books of Chilam Balam of Kaua and Na.[38]

One wonders whether Simón's vegetable gardens were rare or whether others assumed that such items were included in bequeathed house plots. One clue may be Simón's gender: the overwhelming evidence of sources indicates a division of labor by sex that kept women working on the house plot and men away from it. Thus women may have taken vegetable gardens for granted in their wills but not men, who rarely spent enough time with such gardens to feel proprietorial over them. Simón's vegetable gardens, then, may indeed have been rare—for a man. He left them not to his son but to his wife.

Overall, the wills provide a clearer image of Ixil's agricultural economy with the *kax* generally being associated with maize and the house plot containing a larger diversity, even a specialized form of agriculture. Very few commoners mentioned specialized crops other than maize in the *kax*; instead, the cultivation of honey, sapotes, bananas, henequen, and palm trees largely resided in the hands of the town's nobility. Interestingly, and as noted earlier, Ixil today is known for its small onions—referred to as *cebollitas de Ixil*—and the family names associated with their production descend from colonial nobility: the Yam, Ek, and Coba.

SPATIAL AND TEMPORAL DIVERSITY

A comparison of Ixil's economy with those of other Maya towns and an examination of change in production, if any, from the 1740s to the late 1760s provide a better appreciation of Ixil's local characteristics.[39] Other than those testaments from Ixil, three other towns produced corpora of Maya wills that survive today: Cacalchen, Tekanto, and Ebtun. Like Ixil, all were produced during times of famine and epidemic. Located about twenty miles (as the crow flies) southeast of Ixil, Cacalchen produced some thirty-four testaments from 1646 to 1679.[40] Although written nearly a century before those from Ixil, the wills from Cacalchen contain flora, fauna, and household and clothing items that generally parallel those found in Ixil. This illustrates common patterns of valuation of traditional Maya goods and those Spanish. However, although derived from only thirty-four testaments, Cacalchen bequeathed similar goods in higher quantities. For example, testators bequeathed 187 beehives compared to Ixil's 98. On the other hand, Cacalchen's testators owned few horses and no donkeys, mules, or even cows. The earlier date of these testaments, perhaps, explains this paucity in livestock.

Ebtun is a little over 100 miles southeast of Ixil and produced a collection of documents referred to today as the "Titles of Ebtun" and made accessible through Ralph Roys's transcriptions and translations in his work of the same name.[41] Originally assembled to assert the land rights of the town, the corpus refers to a "Libro de Testamentos" that once existed. The testaments included in the corpus no doubt originated from such a collection, although its location remains unknown today. The few wills range from 1699 to 1813 and what they lack in volume they make up in consistency. It appears that apiculture was more prevalent in Ebtun than in Ixil. Testators from Ebtun overwhelming bequeathed beehives and in numbers greater than those generally seen in Ixil. Moreover, items associated with apiculture, such as wire masks and honey extractors, appear, and jars, possibly for the collection and storage of honey, were ubiquitous. Conversely, although animals do appear in Ebtun's wills, they are few in number compared with those found in Ixil.

About thirty-five miles due east of Ixil is the town of Tekanto. Tekanto produced perhaps the largest number of colonial documents—approximately 550 in all. Wills comprise 412 documents in this corpus, the majority from 1724–59, but only 97 are substantive and include bequests.[42] Similar to Ebtun, Tekanto exhibited a robust apiculture economy—a total of 1,254 bequeathed beehives compared with Ixil's 98—and the town's inhabitants, like Ixil's, were very familiar with livestock, although Tekanto admittedly owned more—ninety horses, twenty-six mules, and 160 head of cattle compared with Ixil's seventy-two horses, fourteen mules, and twenty-two cows. Considering that the number of available substantive wills from Ixil and Tekanto are similar, with Ixil having a slightly larger corpus, the difference in quantity in bequeathed goods is dramatic.

In sum, a comparison of Ixil's local economy with those of its neighboring towns of Cacalchen, Ebtun, and Tekanto reveals similarities and differences and better contextualizes Ixil's economy, which was certainly not at an impressive force in the region. Generally speaking, wills from all four towns illustrate similar ownership in household goods, flora, and fauna. Differences, however, exist in the quantity and frequency with which testators bequeathed such goods, illustrating particular economic preferences, specialties, and development. Livestock, it seems, was still burgeoning in Cacalchen by the mid-seventeenth century, although it seems to have found firm purchase a century later in Ebtun, Ixil, and Tekanto. Ixil falls behind in apiculture when compared with the other towns, although it and Cacalchen bequeath cloth at much higher rates than Ebtun and Tekanto. Indeed, the only mention of cloth and clothing from the wills of Ebtun and Tekanto wills primarily concerns female clothing. It may be that the mention of men's clothing was not customary is these towns, but the absence of lengths of cloth, yarn, and so on reflects perhaps a smaller presence of such in the local economy.

With regard to the temporal change within Ixil's own economy between the 1748 testaments and those from the 1760s, both consistency and small change are evident. Livestock and land ownership among testators remained roughly the same throughout both periods, as did the possession of cloth and clothing. However, the 1760s did exhibit growth in certain sectors of the domestic and local economy. Apiculture was completely absent in 1748 and appears in those wills only from the 1760s. That said, we do not believe that apiculture did not exist in Ixil in the 1740s; the tradition is many centuries old, after all. However, the presence of beekeeping appears to grow throughout the eighteenth century, although it remains a modest undertaking compared with the industry in other *cahob*.

Tools also show a dramatic increase in frequency; indeed, only one testator from 1748 mentions a tool—a machete—whereas 25 percent of the 1760s testators do so, with a variety of tools, particularly those made from metal. Furthermore, the testators from the 1760s bequeathed a larger variety of household items aside from the typical house beam and chest seen in 1748. Blankets, tables, beds, jars, benches, chairs, and dishes were much more common in the wills from the 1760s. Thus, Ixil's economy grew and developed over the eighteenth century, but it was modest and rooted in land and livestock. Those areas seeing the most change concern household items and the diversity of personal tools and goods. One important difference was the personal ownership of saints. Testators start mentioning household saints only in the 1760s, a topic discussed further in the next chapter.

The goods themselves represent the economic world of the colonial Maya that is based in both pre-Columbian and European tradition. The arrival of the Spaniards did not halt traditional means and modes of production, including the use of cotton *mantas* and the cultivation of maize, sapote trees, henequen, and beekeeping, nor eliminate traditional items such as house beams, *huipiles*, and wooden seats. Even the presence of the occasional necklace of coral beads demonstrates a continuation of craft production with roots in the precontact period. However, the Maya of Ixil also adopted Spanish practices, such as animal husbandry and the cultivation of plantains, garlic, and onions, not to mention items of worth such as metal and silver spoons, machetes, chests, shotguns, and so on. In the end, similar to every other aspect of colonization, negotiation between the old and the new became a central theme in Ixil's everyday economy.

As Mexico began its journey to industrialization in the late nineteenth and early twentieth centuries, the demand for energy increased exponentially. Such a demand inspired the creation of various firms and companies devoted to the discovery and recovery of oil, among other things. In 1902 the government granted permission to the Compañía Yucateca de Pozos Artesianos to search for potential oil wells in Ixil on a select piece of land. The specific boundaries were marked by the owners of the surrounding plots: "To the north, the *solar* of Narciso Aguilar; to the south, the *solar* of Florentino Pech; to the east the *ejidos* of Ixil; and to the west, *'calle y solar'* of Clemente Cisneros."[43] Note the mention of Florentino Pech as a local landowner; for although land tenure patterns in Ixil had certainly diversified by the turn of the twentieth century to include Spaniards, the Pech still held on to portions of their ancestral lands and other economic resources. Even the way in which the twentieth-century document described the location of the drill site—using the cardinal directions and the names of adjacent plot owners—was precisely how such descriptions were styled in eighteenth-century wills, with the sole difference being that the 1902 document was in Spanish, not Yucatec Maya. In a way, the search for oil in Ixil continued a pattern reflected in the town's testaments of a century and a half prior—with Ixil maintaining its traditions and its image of a small, economically modest community while slowly reaching out to grasp those economic trends and new material goods deemed most beneficial.

NOTES

1. Ciudad Real (1976: 355–56).

2. For an overview of the Maya colonial economy see Patch (1993: 26–38); Thompson (1999: 15–16).

3. Patch (1993: 142–43).

4. AGN, Instituciones Coloniales, Indiferente Virreinal, Aguardiente de Caña, caja 5051, expediente 74. The Real Hacienda was a treasury of sorts, the accounting and revenue collecting branch of the government.

5. AHAY, Visita Pastorales, Conkal.

6. For additional insights into the wealth and status of the Pech in Ixil, see Christensen (2016).

7. See Restall (1997: 95).

8. Thompson (1999: 90).

9. Bricker and Hill (2009: 248). Bricker and Hill postulate that the lack of Pech wills within the known corpus at the time resulted from the Pech, as *indios hidalgos*, preserving their wills separate from those of other Mayas. Indeed, the death records of the 1760s contain the names of various Pech and state that they composed wills or died "con disposición testamentaria." However, the 1748 wills lack such a separation of Pech wills.

10. Molina (1984: 29v).

11. Christensen (2014: 32–35).

12. Sell and Burkhart (2004: 165–89).

13. For a brief overview of Spanish women's rights, see Socolow (2015: 5–16).

14. Restall (1997: 121–24).

15. For the gendered distribution of wealth in Tekanto, see Thompson (1999: 106).

16. Lockhart (1992).

17. From *baleta* (*bareta*), "small iron bar," here given complementary diminutization by the Maya *chichan*, "small," which we have glossed as "small iron tool" in view of the functional value to the Maya of iron objects; a *bronso*, which could be *bronce*, "copper coin," but considering the low value of one such coin and the context in which Luisa lists the object, we think this may be a bronze-tipped tool similar to the *bronso licil u pabal tunich*, "broken bronze-tipped digging-stick," of Luisa's relative, Pasquala Tec.

18. Patch (1993: 28).

19. For additional examples see docs. A7, A15, A19, A30, A36, A55. Variations in land description and marking existed between *cahob*. For a more extensive discussion, see Restall (1997: ch. 15).

20. Patch (1993: 27). Patch notes that oftentimes town *cofradías*, or religious brotherhoods, owned *estancias* where livestock were raised to supply the town's festivals with lard and meat. However, we have not uncovered evidence of any *cofradías* operating in Ixil, although this could be from a lack of documentation rather than the absence of the sodality itself.

21. See Chuchiak (2004: 137–71).

22. For a few examples, see Bricker and Miram (2002: 371, 408); Christensen (2016: 205).

23. Molina (1984: 38v).

24. For example, see Allen Christenson's experience in his *Popol Vuh* (2003: 17).

25. Ixil's proximity to the coast would make possible its inhabitants' acquisition of coral.

26. Farriss (1984: 43–47); Patch (1993: 81–92); Restall (1997: 185–88).

27. AHAY, Visita Pastorales, 1784, Homun.

28. AHAY, Visita Pastorales, 1782–85, Uman. One Maya in the *visita* report accuses the priest of distributing the wax among the *estancias de cofradías*—property and livestock owned jointly by a *cofradía* to fund celebrations and funerary functions. For more, see Thompson (1999: 25). For ecclesiastics' abuse of *cofradía* estates, see Farriss (1984: 325–26).

29. For a comparison with other towns and in relation to Afro-Yucatecan *milperos*, see Restall (2009: 142–44).

30. Sahagún (1997: 102).

31. Matthews (2009: 13–14).

32. Landa (1937: 130–32); Restall et al. (forthcoming).

33. See Farriss (1984: 367–71); Patch (1993: 206).

34. For an overview of the henequen industry see Evans (2013).

35. Landa (1937: 105, 111); Restall et al. (forthcoming).

36. Ciudad Real (1976: 367). For more on Ponce see Morales (1973: 65–67).

37. Bricker and Miram (2002: 257n1153).

38. Christensen (2016: 207); Bricker and Miram (2002); Gubler and Bolles (2000: 205).

39. Much of the data for the spatial comparison derives from Restall (1997: appendix E).

40. These wills are a part of a larger collection of documents titled "Libro de Cacalchen." Photostats are housed in TULAL. The originals are lost. For more, see Tozzer (1921: 204). For more on the notaries and stylistic changes to the religious preamble see Christensen (2013: 228–30).

41. William Gates was the first to locate and photograph the corpus; the photographs are housed today in the Peabody Museum, Harvard.

42. Thompson (1999: appendix 1). Once lost, the originals are now located in AGEY's notarial collection. We thank Mark Lentz for making us aware of their recent reappearance.

43. *Recopilación de leyes* (1906: vol. 78, 604–5).

4

God in Ixil

The town of Conkal is medium-sized, and the inhabitants, as well as those in the towns of the parish, are Maya Indians, and very devout people.

    —Fray Antonio de Ciudad Real, 1588[1]

It would be very useful for the Indians (Mayas) to have altars, images, and crosses in their homes . . . because in this they are remiss and little devoted, and do not imitate the *Mexicanos* (Nahuas) where each one has his oratory; also, all [Mayas] should carry rosaries around their necks, because there are few who have them.

    —Pedro Sánchez de Aguilar, 1639[2]

This [testament] will snatch my soul away from wicked things.

    —Salvador Camal, 1744[3]

In August of 1588, fray Alonso Ponce's tour of Franciscan convents in New Spain brought him to visit Conkal seven miles south of Ixil. As mentioned, Ixil was a *visita* to the larger Conkal, which served as the *cabecera* and the location of the convent and the residence of the local ecclesiastics. Ponce's secretary, fray Antonio de Ciudad Real, described the experience as follows:

He arrived . . . at the town and convent of San Francisco Conkal where they gave him a very solemn reception. There were an infinite amount of people, men and women, dressed all for Easter and in procession. There were three or four native dances and

DOI: 10.5876/9781607329220.c004

two of Castilian origin. There were many crosses, *ramadas*, music from flutes and trumpets, and they did everything with so much contentment and joy that it all provoked devotion.[4]

This experience differed somewhat from one that Ponce had a month later when visiting the convent of Tekax. Numerous Mayas came out to meet Ponce and make his arrival to the town festive and memorable. Included in the throng were Maya boys, who took part in the celebration in various ways:

[There was] a multitude of boys that celebrated the father commissary on his way to the convent, shouting and raising cheers, throwing oranges at each other and blocking the blows with some shields they carried made of small sticks. There were also two dances of Spanish origin, and another with boys costumed as black boys (*en figura de negrillos*) representing demons, who, when some songs were sang to them in polyphony and in hearing in them the name of Jesus, all fell to the ground and trembled, making a thousand faces and shakings in a sign of fear and terror.[5]

In the end, Ciudad Real would describe the inhabitants of both Conkal and its surrounding towns—including Ixil—and those of Tekax as very devout. Yet both towns expressed their religiosity and devotion in different and distinct ways.

The degree to which the Maya became converted and what that conversion meant to both Spaniards and Mayas alike is an important and ongoing question—and one too large to tackle properly here. But in this chapter, we will address one small part of that question by exploring the religious atmosphere of eighteenth-century Ixil through an examination of both official and unofficial native texts. The official wills recorded with the intent of eventual ecclesiastic review provide details into how the Maya of Ixil prepared body and soul for death according to an approved process. The wills and their bequeathed religious items also illustrate the extension of Catholicism past the corporate and communal sphere into the individual lives of testators. Finally, small details in the wills, from the use of loanwords to the individual friars and *maestros* mentioned in the documents, add further pieces of the puzzle that is religion in Ixil.

Ixil also produced unofficial documentation that likewise illuminates the town's religious experience. Likely produced in the mid-eighteenth century, the Chilam Balam of Ixil (figure 2.6) contains various texts, including those of a religious nature. Technically, the Maya were prohibited from composing handwritten religious texts, thus the Books of Chilam Balam and other manuscripts fall into an unofficial category produced and preserved by the Maya presumably outside the auspices of ecclesiastics (we have called these quasi-notarial manuscripts). Significantly, such unofficial texts provide evidence of those aspects of Catholicism that the Maya chose to preserve of their own accord—in other words, aspects of the religion they valued enough to record in their own books. This, then, like the wills, provides a valuable and intimate view of God in Ixil.

PREPARING FOR AND MANAGING DEATH

An important element in evangelization is the Christianization of death. Upon its arrival in a new culture, Christianity must alter existing traditions surrounding death to align with those sanctioned by the church. This, of course, requires negotiation and often results in a death ritual deriving from both Christian and non- or pre-Christian origins.[6] At times, even ecclesiastics themselves had to alter their burial rituals to align with those preexisting. While in China and after the death of his missionary companion, Antonio d'Almeida, in 1591, Matteo Ricci desired to follow Christian custom and have the body interred next to the church. However, Chinese customs prohibited intramural burials. As a result, Ricci kept his deceased companion in a coffin within the Jesuit residence for two years until it could be shipped back to Macao for burial. As R. Po-chia Hsia states, "In this, at least, the Jesuits kept their death rituals in conformity with Chinese practice."[7]

Regarding Yucatan, fray Diego de Landa provides some of the first reports on the burial practices of the colonial Maya. He mentions the common burial practice of shrouding the body and burying it in the home or somewhere nearby, at times including items significant to the deceased.[8] Today burial practices in Yucatan have both a Christian and non-Christian essence about them. In towns such as Timucuy and Komchen—the latter some fourteen miles west of Ixil—two burials occur. Family members place the deceased in a simple wooden coffin put on display in the home for half a day or so before the burial, which typically takes place within twenty-four hours of death due to the lack of mortuaries and embalming procedures. Mourners enjoy food and alcoholic drink during the wake, which can include stories and even riddles. Loved ones then accompany the coffin to the local cemetery for burial.

If the town lacks a resident priest, the burial proceeds regardless. However, subsequent masses are typically offered for the deceased and his/her family. After two or so years, the body is exhumed to make room for future burials, and the bones are placed in a plastic bag to await their new home in the family *osario*, or bone box. Often in Komchen the family never constructs the *osario*, and the cemetery caretaker eventually discards the bones over the back wall of the cemetery.[9]

Christianity's approaches to death evolved from its roots in Jewish and pagan ritual to include those harboring meaning that is more biblical. Rites and rituals continued to develop throughout the early years of the church and the Middle Ages to include the *Viaticum*—the Eucharist administered on one's deathbed—deathbed reconciliation, prayers, chants, and songs.[10] Growing out of Roman law, wills became ingrained in the ritual of death by the Middle Ages. Indeed, in an effort to unite Castile's legal system, Alonso X ordered the *Siete Partidas* compiled in the thirteenth century, the sixth of which focuses on wills and their proper composition and execution.[11]

By the time Spanish friars began their evangelization of New Spain, a good, Christian death included the writing of a last will and testament. Regarding the Christian death, early friars such as Pedro de Gante and Martín de León employed the fifteenth-century *Ars moriendi* as a model for their own Nahuatl books on how to die well, *Arte de bien morir*. As the Nahua penitent lay dying, a series of questions were asked to ensure his or her proper preparation to meet God, including whether he or she had prepared a will "*inic amo ixpopoyotiliztica miquiz, in yuhqui ce manenenqui*" (so that he will not die with blindness as a beast).[12] Such guidebooks on how to die well also appeared in Yucatec Maya, including one from the town of Teabo. The unknown native author produced a Maya translation of the very popular *Ramillete de divinas flores*, by don Bernardo Sierra, which included various instructions and prayers to help the dying achieve a good death.[13] Indeed, the 1722 Yucatecan synod instructed curates to help the dying "die in a Christian way [*morir cristianamente*], at least those who die in the *cabeceras*." For those living at a distance, the curates should ensure that trained Maya could recite some "brief and clear statements to help the dying believe."[14] Guidebooks such as these no doubt assisted Maya *maestros* charged with helping the sick die well in the *visita* towns that saw their priest only on occasion.[15]

To be sure, last wills and testaments served a legal, secular purpose for the distribution of property. Yet the Christianization of death for the Yucatec Maya included the composition of wills as part of the dying-well process, thus lending the documents a religious character as well. The proper Christian death supported by the wills included the formulaic religious preamble discussed in chapter 1. Here the Maya testators would invoke the name of the Holy Trinity, state their clarity of mind, request a church burial and posthumous mass, and make an offering to Jerusalem. All such insertions added a type of spiritual benefit that contributed to the speedy journey of the soul through the unpleasantness of purgatory, or, as Salvador Camal of Tekanto states in his 1744 will, the formulaic preamble "will snatch my soul away from wicked things."[16]

In Ixil the notary composed this preamble, although, as noted earlier, testators of rank and means could contribute religious catchphrases on occasion. The testator's main contribution to the preamble concerned the insertion of personal preferences regarding the posthumous arrangements for his or her body and soul. Yet the depth of contribution varied widely from town to town, culture to culture, century to century. For example, Nahuas from sixteenth-century Culhuacan left simple requests similar to those found in the preambles of eighteenth-century Ixil. However, eighteenth-century Nahua testators from Toluca included burial instructions that involved masses, requests to wrap their body in a shroud and girt with the rope of a particular saint, specific burial locations, and even requests to ring the church bells.[17] And seventeenth-century Mixtec testators from Teposcolula, Oaxaca, left lengthy offerings to benefit their souls.[18] Consider the following example from the 1731 preamble of Isabel María, a testator from the Toluca Valley:

> My earthly body is to be wrapped in a habit of Carmen of serge, and I will be girt with the rope of my precious father San Francisco. And my grave is to be in the great church behind the holy cross . . . And I say that the help of my spirit and soul is a high mass of requiem . . . and I say that the bells are to be rung for me in my *tlaxilacalli*, and I say that half a *real* is to be given for Holy Jerusalem. And I say that the bells are to be rung for me in Santa María de los Angeles Huitzillan, San Juan Bautista, San Diego, and San Sebastián; half a *real* is to be given for each . . . And I say that I give to the *cofradía* Animas one little maguey.[19]

Generally speaking, Maya testaments from Yucatan and even Guatemala are much simpler in their posthumous arrangements than those from central Mexico and even Peru, negating such things as burial clothing or the ringing of bells—they would never reach the elaboration of Isabel María's preamble.[20] Indeed, it is likely that the Ixil testator played little to no role in making such arrangements, as all were fixed firmly within a formulaic preamble preserved by the notaries (again, see chapter 1). At its most elaborate, posthumous arrangements in Ixil would include a request for a church burial, a mass (either recited or sung), and a donation to Jerusalem. One Ixil testator, Gabriel Tec (B15), mentions a payment to choristers, but the singers were in the *cah* of Mama, where Gabriel was dying. Tekanto wills are simpler, still with no specific burial or mass requests; the *escribano* simply wrote *misa rezada* or *cantada* at the top of the will.[21] Ebtun maintains a very simple preamble that omits specific burial locations, although requests for masses and Jerusalem donations appear by the nineteenth century. Indeed, the religious preambles of seventeenth-century Cacalchen and their requests for masses and occasional donations to Jerusalem come closest to those from eighteenth-century Ixil. Cacalchen wills, however, omit burial requests. Moreover, fees are given in a mixture of coin and kind, with chickens, candles, and maize frequently being used to pay for the requested mass.[22] This perhaps reflects an earlier, seventeenth-century norm that had faded by the eighteenth century.

The vocabulary employed in the wills further illustrates the simple spirituality of Ixil. The formulaic phrases and vocabulary of the preamble reflect the evolution of

Catholicism within the *cah*. It is possible that religious phrases and vocabulary fail to represent the daily dialogue of the town due to the formulaic nature of the preamble. Yet, as seen in chapter 1, the preamble's formula changes slightly from notary to notary, year to year, adapting to the environment of the *cah*. The extended corpus of Ixil testaments, then, provides a unique view into the evolution of the town's ecclesiastical vocabulary and thus its religious maturation.

Attempting to map the degree of Nahua-Spanish interactions through Nahuatl texts, James Lockhart identifies three stages of change. In stage 1, roughly 1519–50, with little sustained contact between individual Nahuas and individual Spaniards, Nahuatl hardly changed at all. In stage 2, roughly 1550–1650, Nahuatl incorporated Spanish nouns as loanwords. The onset of stage 2 reflects not only the growing Spanish presence but also the generation of Nahuas who spent their formative years in the postcontact period. And in stage 3, roughly 1650 to the present, with a growing number of bilingual Nahuas, Nahuatl borrowed other parts of speech, including verbs, and other Spanish conventions, such as Spanish-derived phraseology.[23]

However, Restall states, "Whereas Nahuatl can clearly be seen evolving during the colonial period as a result of contact with Spanish . . . the impact of Spanish on Maya is not so obvious."[24] Due to their peripheral location and cultural characteristics, the Maya seem to have immediately reached a balance between Lockhart's stages 1 and 2 and then remained there throughout the nineteenth century.[25] Lockhart himself explains such variations of his stages through the role of indigenous people in dictating the process of their postcontact evolution.[26] Among other things, the testaments of Ixil illustrate that truth.

Ixil's translation of "church" throughout the corpus provides an excellent example of religious acclimation in the *cah*. Before the arrival of the Spaniards, Maya employed the term *ku* (deity or place to worship a deity, pyramid) to refer to their ancient pyramids. It also appears that Maya used the term *kuna* (deity house) for a place used to worship the supernatural. After the arrival of the Spaniards, the Maya employed the same term to refer to Christian churches. The testaments of 1738 and 1748 unequivocally demonstrate this trend in Ixil and consistently employ *kuna* for "church." The 1748 testament of Felipe Tec (A23) demonstrates how the colonial *kuna* represented a Christian church and not a precontact pyramid or temple. Whereas in his preamble Tec requests his body to be buried in the "*kuna*," when bequeathing his land he locates a particular forest as being next to a "*ku*," or pyramid.

By the 1760s and 1770s, *kuna* had been replaced by variants of the Spanish phrase *santa iglesia* (holy church). Depending on the notaries' preferences, the post-1748 preambles could include *santa iglesia*, *santa na iglesia* (holy mother church), or *cilich nabil iglesia* (holy mother church).[27] Popular throughout Yucatan, this latter phrase appears in texts from various towns and even appears in an postcolonial

1847 catechism.[28] If compared with Lockhart's stages, the Maya's preference for the combined Maya/Spanish phrase places Ixil between stages 1 and 2.

The Maya's hesitancy to replace indigenous terms with those Spanish is not limited to *cilich nabil iglesia*. Another popular Maya phrase among religious texts found in Ixil is the use of *ah bolon pixan* (he of the nine souls) for "blessed" prior to a saint's name. Ubiquitous throughout all Maya texts, the phrase first appears in Ixil in 1766 detailing the residency of the testator's parents to make them "*cahnalen uay tu mektan cahil ca yumilan ah bolon pixan San Bernaber Yxil*" (residents here in the *cah* governed by our lord, the blessed San Bernabé, Ixil). Prior to Catholicism, the phrase *ah bolon* referenced various deities, including Ah Bolon Tzacab, Ah Bolon Ahau, Ah Bolon Caan Chac, and others. Upon the introduction of saints—beings with specific attributes and powers—the Maya applied the preexisting concept of *ah bolon* to the saints.[29]

The use of Maya terminology for the Christian concept of the soul further demonstrates the Maya's general preference for indigenous terms. When referencing the Christian soul, Nahuas consistently favored the Spanish loanword *ánima*, occasionally coupling the word with a Nahuatl approximation (*teyolia*) as in *in teyolia in anima*.[30] The colonial Maya, however, rarely used the term *ánima* and instead preferred the Maya term *pixan*. Modern Maya believe that *pixan* represents one's essence that grows throughout life and that remains close to family and loved ones after death.[31] General similarities between Maya and Christian beliefs allowed *pixan* to become the overwhelmingly popular choice to translate the Christian "soul." Indeed, all Maya ecclesiastical texts employ *pixan* to refer to the immortal essence of a person that survives death—the very definition of a Christian soul.

Again, the testaments provided a vivid example. The notary Salvador Coba consistently used *ánima* in his 1748 testaments. In the 1738 will of Viviana Pech, after the request for a posthumous mass, she explained that the reason for the mass is "*Antebal yn pixan tu numyail purgatoriol*" (to help my soul in the suffering of purgatory). However, Coba's testaments inserted *ánima* in the phrase to read "*yokol in pixan Ca antabac tu numyail anima purgatorio*" (for my soul, that it will be of help to the suffering soul in purgatory). Interestingly, *ánima* appeared only as a formulaic addition to the Spanish loanword "purgatory" and did not replace the preceding use of *pixan* for "soul." Indeed, although subsequent notaries employed *ánima* on occasion, it is always in conjunction with *purgatorio* and never as a replacement for *pixan*.

Perhaps the best example of the preference for Maya terminology over those Spanish is in the testaments' translation of "Almighty" or "Omnipotent." In attempts to translate this Christian idiom, ecclesiastics created the phrase "*uchuc tumen tu sinil*" (power in everything). Interestingly, this idiomatic Maya phrase occurs within all the Ixil testaments without variation and in religious texts always in reference to God. Once formed, the complex, somewhat awkward phrase solidified itself as the accepted formula and experienced no rivals. Later fray Joaquín Ruz would shorten the phrase to *uchucil zinil* in his 1847 catechism.[32]

When compared with preambles from central Mexico, those from Yucatan illustrate a basic simplicity and a preference for Maya terminology. This is not overly surprising when considering the peripheral nature of Yucatan and its overall reference as a colonial backwater vis-à-vis central Mexico. From the corpora available, Ixil presents the most detailed preamble concerning the preparation of the body and soul for the afterlife. It is possible that if wills existed from Cacalchen in the eighteenth century, they would present a more developed process of managing death, as the town was larger and had a stronger ecclesiastic presence than Ixil. Regardless, the static and extremely consistent nature of Ixil's preamble indicates a similar Christian death for all those composing wills, one likely decided long before by local notarial and ecclesiastical preferences.

RELIGION AND GOD IN IXIL

The simplicity of the religious experience as dictated by the will's preamble continues throughout the body of the document. In many towns throughout central Mexico, native testators included numerous bequests of religious items, with saints representing the most common possession. The Catholic belief in saints as otherworldly beings containing specific characteristics and powers paralleled many pre-existing beliefs in Mesoamerica. Thus, indigenous parishioners readily accepted them into their worldviews. With the encouragement of ecclesiastics, native Mesoamericans adopted saint names for their children, towns, and churches. Yet the extent to which the cult of the saints permeated native life varied from culture to culture, town to town, century to century.[33]

In general, saints first enter wills as the patron saint of a town and in formulaic pleas for intercession. By the seventeenth and eighteenth centuries, testators begin to bequeath their household images of saints and even items to specific saints. For example, the Nahua María Hernández from San Miguel Aticpac recorded the following bequests in her 1737 will: "And I say that the Virgen de los Dolores is to go [to be in the church of] Carmen. All the [other] male and female saints are to stay in the house and be residents; Juan Estacio and his precious mother named Polania Antonia are to serve them there."[34] Not only did María own numerous saints, she considered the saints a part of the household. Moreover, her will contains generous donations to specific saints and, no doubt, the *cofradías* that served them.

Whereas Nahua wills of the seventeenth and eighteenth centuries commonly included bequeathed household saint images, such is quite rare for Yucatan. Indeed, nearly 40 percent of testators from the Toluca Valley owned a saint! In contrast, only 6 percent of testators from Ixil's expanded corpus did. Eight percent of testators in Tekanto bequeathed a saint, but wills from both Ebtun and Cacalchen fail to provide any examples of saint ownership. Elsewhere Christensen discusses the various likely reasons for such disparity.[35] Yet an underlying cause concerns a town's exposure to Spanish society and the lack of markets selling religious items—the majority of Yucatecan saint images derived from Mexico or Guatemala. The greater the exposure, the more immersed in the cult of the saints the town became. Ixil—along with Cacalchen, Ebtun, and Tekanto—had limited exposure to Spanish centers of influence and thus adopted the cult at a much more gradual pace than central Mexico.

The saints that do appear in Ixil are one image of San Diego and five of Mary. The popularity of Mary is not surprising, considering her growing status in Spain as both a physical and spiritual intercessor and Franciscan efforts to promote her veneration in Yucatan.[36] It seems that most testators who owned household saints housed them in tabernacles or displayed them on tables, as both typically accompany the bequest of the saint image itself. For example, Bernardino Coot (B24) gave his son Diego "*hunpel ca cilich colebil y u tabernacula*" (one Our Holy Lady and her tabernacle). Illustrating a gradual increase over the years, five of the six images derive from the 1760s and later; the 1748 wills contain only one image, an image of Mary (table 4.1).

The religious possessions of testators in Ixil also included one rosary.[37] Simón Chan's (B21) 1766 will included the bequest of "*hunpel rosario*" (one rosary) to his wife, Magdalena. The only other mention of a rosary in a testament of which we are aware derives from Ebtun and the 1785 will of Rosa Camal. Similar to household saints, then, rosaries and other religious paraphernalia remained outside the grasp of most Maya households. Ecclesiastics viewed the lack of religious items in the home as an obstacle to the Maya's overall conversion. Indeed, some blamed the continuation of idolatry throughout the colonial period on the absence of saints in the home to take their place.[38] And although Pedro Sánchez de Aguilar lamented the lack of saints and rosaries among the Maya, the situation had not improved by 1722, when the bishop Juan Gómez de Parada held a synod to discuss, among other things, evangelization efforts among the Maya. The proceedings of the synod state:

> We advise all our priests and we warn them that the Indians they administer are the most barbarous we have ever known and in which we have seen fewer signs of being Christians and recognized more and greater impediments to be able to become so.... We charge them [the priests] to try to induce them all [the Maya] to carry with them

TABLE 4.1. Owners of religious items in Ixil

Owner	Year	Gender	Rosary	Image of Mary	Tabernacle	Image of San Diego
Felipe Tec	1748	M		1		
Pedro Mis	1766	M			1	1
Juan de la Cruz Coba	1766	M		1	1	
Bernardino Coot	1766	M		2	1	
Simón Chan	1766	M	1			
Marta Mis	1769	F		1		

and pray the rosary of Our Lady and medals of saints, and in their homes put crosses and have some image of Christ our Lord or his saints so that through their eyes and sight their simple-mindedness is accommodated to believe, to hope, and to love God, as is necessary for their salvation.[39]

Certainly, the Maya knew of the saints and rosaries despite their lack of personal ownership of such objects.[40] Curates were expected to pray the rosary daily, and the numerous *cofradías* dedicated to saints and even the rosary throughout Yucatan illustrate their familiarity.[41] Some testators, such as a few from Tekanto, even bequeathed property to *cofradías* dedicated to the saints, such as Ba[l]tesara Chan, who left a house plot and ten palm plants to the *cofradía* of San Antonio Macha.[42] Yet although documents from Tekanto illustrate the existence of five *cofradías*, the testaments of Ixil fail to betray any. The testaments illustrate that exposure to saint images and rosaries remained at the corporate and communal level for most of Ixil's residents, who possibly lacked even the *cofradías* to honor such icons.

In truth, the wills illustrate how socioeconomic standing affected individuals' interaction and relationship with Catholicism in Ixil. All testators bequeathing religious objects derived from upper-level noble *chibalob*, with the only exception being Bernardino Coot. That said, the single Coot testament in the corpus contains items, including those religious, which betray the *chibal* as upper-commoners. In the end, only 6 percent of wills included religious items in their bequests. Noble, wealthier testators certainly had a different experience with Catholicism than other Ixil residents.

The 1766 will of the *maestro* Diego Chan illustrates how socioeconomic status could affect one's experience with Catholicism and its good death. As a noble, Diego became a *maestro* and received training in Spanish notarial practices and religious beliefs. Indeed, as *maestro* he occupied one of the few salaried positions in the town for his instruction of Maya youth in the Catholic doctrine.[43] Already mentioned in chapter 1, Diego dictates his own will instead of enlisting the notary's typical preamble; Diego's preparation for death was to be of a personal making. Two elements leap out as unusual in Diego's will. First, he omits the typical religious preamble for one of his own making—and one that neglects the majority of spiritual invocations and statements. Ironically, the *maestro*'s will is the most secular of any in the corpus! Perhaps Diego's religiosity was so well defined that it did not need further elaboration in his will; perhaps he had already conveyed his posthumous requests to the *cabildo* and priest. Despite its anomalous secular nature, Diego's wealth and status allow him to pay twice the regular mass fee of six *reales* to purchase the more eloquent, more effective sung mass for twelve *reales*.

Second, Diego's property shows him to be a wealthy man, a fact not altogether surprising considering his noble lineage and his position as *maestro*. Diego owned two house plots and two forest plots, and houses (a potential of four, one for each beam-and-frame), along with a few tables, chests, and a silver spoon. Yet his fortune is in livestock. His ten horses, five mules, one donkey, and six cows make him an exception in Ixil at this time. Interestingly, Diego fails to include any religious objects in his will despite his obvious wealth and Catholic training. Thus, Diego's position as *maestro* allowed him to construct his own Christian death, albeit one lacking the typical linguistic accoutrements and trappings.

Presumably more religious than most, Diego and his will illustrates the limitations of testaments in providing the full picture of God in Ixil. Fortunately, another, less official source provides additional insight into the matter—the Chilam Balam of Ixil. The Maya preserved local written records in their own hieroglyphic writing long before the arrival of the Spaniards. Once trained in the friars' colonial schools, Maya *maestros* and notaries served the religious and notarial needs of their towns. Ecclesiastics feared the unsanctioned use of such skills and prohibited Maya men from composing their own handwritten religious texts. Nevertheless, ecclesiastics confiscated numerous manuscript books that the Maya continued to compose throughout the colonial period.[44] Many such books recorded histories, calendrics, medicinal remedies, and religious texts that the town deemed important. Some works survived the colonial period to reach the hands of modern scholars and to be named the Books of Chilam Balam. One such work originated in Ixil.

The Chilam Balam of Ixil, like many other such works, lacks a date and author. Clues exist to place the manuscript in the eighteenth century, possibly around the same time notaries composed some of the wills in this corpus. Moreover, at the bottom of one of the pages, Hipólito Pech boldly declared that he supplied the paper/book (*hun*), thus indicating his role in the composition of the Chilam Balam text. The manuscript itself contains medicinal remedies, calendrics, and redactions of select biblical stories from the Old Testament. Prohibited translations of the Bible existed early in the colonial period, allowing a commissary of the Inquisition, fray Hernando de Sopuerta, to comment in 1586 how Maya translations of the Gospels existed "in the possession of certain natives who know how to read."[45] The passages in the Chilam Balam of Ixil, however, are not faithful translations of the biblical text but redactions of those stories that the Maya found interesting enough to illicitly record.[46]

Examples of Maya-authored and -preserved religious texts exist from other towns. Many of the texts are hagiographies derived from European works such as the *Flos sanctorum*; others are redactions of the Passion of Christ or expositions on the mass and its meaning. Some are found within the pages of Chilam Balam books; others are manuscripts dedicated to religious texts recently identified as Maya Christian copybooks.[47] Either way, the Maya clearly desired to record and preserve religious texts that held specific meaning to their authors and town, and those found in the Chilam Balam of Ixil hint at what certain Maya in Ixil found significant.

The biblical stories included in the Ixil documents relate a history of sorts—from the tower of Babel, to the Abrahamic Covenant and the sacrifice of Isaac, to the Exodus where Moses and Aaron employed miracles to convince Pharaoh to free the enslaved Israelites, to the birth of Christ, an event mentioned but not described.[48] As the manuscript itself is likely an eighteenth-century copy of an earlier original that employed various European works including the Bible, the religious texts indicate Ixil's particular interest in these aspects.[49] Certain religious texts—for example, those recounting the creation of the world, the meaning of the mass, or apocalyptic signs before the end of the world—appear in similar form among various known Maya manuscripts, illustrating a common interest among the Maya. To date, we have not found the religious texts appearing in the Ixil documents in other manuscripts, perhaps illustrating a distinct local preference of the *cah*.[50]

Why the Maya of Ixil chose these texts in particular is uncertain.[51] The Maya worldview included the importance of lineage, genealogy, sacrifice—both human and animal—and gods producing miraculous works. The biblical stories recorded here present such preexisting beliefs within an acceptable Catholic framework that certainly appealed to the Maya. At times Maya leaders read their secretly preserved books to the community.[52] Whether this occurred with the Chilam Balam of Ixil is uncertain. Yet certainly the notaries and *maestro*—including Diego Chan—had access to the text. Thus, the manuscript joins the wills to illustrate the diversity in the experience with and understanding of Catholicism for Ixil residents. Socioeconomic status and education played a large role in determining whether someone engaged Catholicism upon death by composing a will, acquired personal religious objects, or, in the case of the town's Chilam Balam, created them in forbidden works.

ECCLESIASTICS AND IXIL

In addition to the documents and manuscripts discussed, reports and records from ecclesiastics provide additional insight into people's perceptions of God in Ixil and their role in the spiritual life of the town. Although many early ecclesiastics—particularly the Franciscans—viewed the education and potential of the indigenous population with much optimism, the Maya's continuation of precontact rites and rituals tempered such attitudes as early as the mid-sixteenth century. As the seventeenth and eighteenth centuries progressed, expectations for the Maya decreased. The 1722 Yucatecan synod perhaps best captured the prevailing attitude in saying:

> The diligence and care of the curates of Indians must be all the greater, as great is the simplicity and simple-mindedness of their sheep to whom it is not enough to teach and preach the path of their salvation continually, but it is necessary and essential to lead them by the hand so that they do not depart and fall into [the path] of perdition that is so natural to them.[53]

In his 1785 report of his parish of Conkal, the curate fray Francisco Sánchez y Gálvez lamented the spirituality of all the Mayas under his responsibility (including those from Ixil). He claimed that they refuse to send their children to school or even to learn Spanish; only attend mass and other sacraments for the novelty of it and not out of devotion; spend most of their days intoxicated; and go to confession only to satisfy their priest. Indeed, he states quite clearly that the Maya, and even the *gente de color* that have joined the parish, "have greatly wounded my heart to see in them no spirit of comprehension nor that fire that embraces the heart of true penitents."[54] He then goes on to exclude those "naturales" involved in communal politics, some of whom demonstrate sincere devotion in the sight of their priest. This is indeed a sad fate for a *doctrina* that various prominent Franciscans once called home, including Luís de Villalpando, Diego de Landa, and Diego López de Cogolludo.

The report provides details on those administering the *doctrina* in 1785. Ordained a priest seven years prior to his writing the report, Sánchez y Gálvez was from Campeche and served as curate of the *doctrina* of Conkal for three years and two months. Two other ordained, yet novice priests assisted him, along with three other *padre predicadores* who help "with the administration of the *doctrina*."[55] None of the six friars had extensive tenure in the *doctrina*; the most veteran had been there only four years. Moreover, every indication suggests that the religious resided at Conkal and journeyed to the surrounding *visitas* when needed—Ixil was only a two-and-a-half-hour walk from Conkal seven miles away. Even then, it appears that the trained Maya filled in much of the time. When asked if the curate of

Conkal helps the dying achieve a good death, the local Maya indicated that he did, but only those in the *cabecera* as the trained *fiscales*, or *maestros*, assisted those in the *visitas*.[56] This aligned with the instructions and expectations given to ecclesiastics in the 1722 synod.[57]

Also included in the instructions of the 1722 synod was an order for every curate to maintain four books recording the baptisms, confirmations, marriages, and deaths in his parish.[58] Today the availability of such additional documentation is limited at times and sporadic when available. We have been fortunate to locate a few ledgers specifically designated for Ixil's baptisms and marriages; other records for the town are scattered within larger ledgers kept for the entirety of Conkal's jurisdiction. As a whole, the records provide important insight into the role of ecclesiastics in Ixil and the religious climate of the town in general.

It appears that despite its modest size, the residents of Ixil had access to the necessary religious rituals. Often the rituals were performed en masse. For example, on June 15, 1693, fray Antonio Rossado married the Ixil resident Viviana Pech (C1) to Agustín Pech, along with Lucas Pech and Lorensa Chan, and Agustín Tec and Clara Canul.[59] The location of the marriage is uncertain—ecclesiastics varied greatly in the information they included in their entries. Earlier marriages in the ledger from 1655 cite Mococha as a location, and Ixil was indeed a *visita* of Mococha at this time. Yet it is likely that this marriage took place in the church in Ixil, as would be Catholic custom, and the entry is simply one of the many records of rites celebrated in the *cabecera* of Mococha.

Indeed, existing eighteenth-century records and ledgers on Ixil attest to the small town hosting its own rites, albeit with a visiting ecclesiastic. The earliest existing baptismal ledger for Ixil we have found begins in 1728 and includes the record of the son of Martha Pech (A21), Marcos Cime, receiving his baptism in Ixil on June 25, 1729. Later, at the age of fifteen, he would marry Ysabel Pech in 1744.[60] Likewise, the daughter of Pasquala Tec (B51), María Candelaria Cante, married Bernardino Cob in Ixil on April 23, 1762.[61]

The baptismal and marriage rites themselves provide a glimpse into the religious atmosphere that the friars and their assistants provided to Ixil. The records suggest that the friars appeared in Ixil to perform the religious ceremonies on an average of two to three times a month. Thus, as mentioned, it is common to find multiple people being baptized or married on the same day. For example, on June 28, 1731, fray Larsaro (Lázaro) Cantillo baptized five infants in Ixil. His record indicates that the ceremony included the use of the "*Santos oleos*," or holy oils. After a child received baptism by water, the friar would trace the cross with oil on his/her head—a practice continued today. Moreover, the entry also records the godparents of each child tasked with the responsibility of its spiritual instruction, indicating that the popular colonial practice had likewise reached Ixil.[62] Admittedly, the standard script established by the 1722 synod for all ecclesiastics to use when recording baptisms included the mention of holy oils and godparents.[63] Yet the use of the script for Ixil's baptisms seems to confirm the practice in the town.

Regarding marriage, the Council of Trent outlined a rigid procedure to ensure the worthiness of marriage candidates. Indeed, fray Alonso de Molina's 1569 Nahuatl confessional manual contains lengthy instructions, many for the native fiscal, regarding the questions asked of the potential couple.[64] Whereas some existing ledgers for marriages in colonial Yucatan contain the date of the ceremony and those involved, others record the information and interview process of those intending to get married (*informaciones para matrimonios*).

One such example, dated September 27, 1760, relates how Francisco Canul appeared before fray Juan de Hoyos during the friar's visit to Ixil and announced his intention to marry Catalina Chim. To verify the legitimacy of the match, Francisco presented to Hoyos three witnesses. Each witness testified to Francisco's status as a single, chaste, and faithful Christian who, according to their testimonies, was not a relative of Catalina and who had not promised to marry any other woman. Hoyos then met with Francisco and Catalina individually to present the witnesses' testimonies and to verify their free will and desire to marry. The marriage was then announced publicly three times during mass—*inter missarum solemnia*—to ensure that no impediments existed.[65] Finding none, Hoyos married the couple and recorded it "in the book of marriages" (a book we have yet to uncover). The date is uncertain but typically would have occurred a month or so later.[66] Overall, the documentation on baptism and marriage in Ixil suggests that despite its modest size, ecclesiastics provided the town a liturgical climate coterminous with expectations at the time.

Various colonial ledgers containing death records likewise exist to contribute additional insight into the fulfillment of the religious requests in the wills. After the notary completed a will and after recording the death of the testator, he placed the document among others awaiting an ecclesiastic's attention to fulfill the posthumous requests. At the bottom of each will in the Ixil corpus is the signature of the ecclesiastic who completed such requests. At times only a name appears; at other times a brief sentence precedes the signature, describing the rites performed or the fees collected. For example, below the signatures of Lorensa Coba's 1748 testament (A16) fray Diego Pérez Arrias wrote, "*Cumpliose este testamento y se le canto una missa que pidio y lo firme*" (This testament was fulfilled and a mass was sung for her as requested, and I signed it), followed by his signature (figure 4.1).

Unfortunately, the signatures and brief comments in the 1748 wills lack dates to indicate how long after the testator's stated death the friar performed such services.

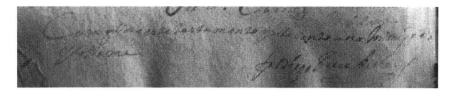

FIGURE 4.1. Signature of fray Diego Pérez Arrias in Lorensa Coba's will, 1748 (A16).

However, two exceptions exist. The will of Pasquala Mitz (A22) states that she died on April 17, 1748 (*"Pasguala mitz cimi en 17 de ablil de 1748 años"*), and fray Joseph Villamil's signature indicated that he had sung a mass for Pasquala Mitz the following day. Moreover, the will of Anna Itza (A35) places her death on November 24, 1748, and fray Joachim Paz sang the mass five days later, on the 29th (we have been unable to find any death records for Ixil in the 1740s). Differences in pen and the incongruent position of the statement and date of death when compared with the rest of the testament suggest its typical insertion after the composition of the will and the death of the testator. The two dated entries of the friars confirm such a hypothesis.

The wills from the 1760s likewise include a statement of death at the top, but it differs from that used in 1748, stating *"Cimi Martha chan en 8 de Nob.e de 1788 anos"* (Martha Chan died on November 8, 1766). Although originally considered an accurate date of death, a comparison with recently discovered death records from Ixil causes uncertainty. For example, the death record entry for Martha Chan, notarized by fray Juan de Hoyos, states that she died on November 5 (three days prior to the date recorded in her will) and was buried the following day. The will of Nicolasa Tec (B20) has a death date of March 28, 1766; yet the death record states March 2. In short, according to the death record, Nicolasa was dead and buried nearly a month prior to her date of death as stated in her testament! At other times the date of death recorded in the will predates that on record, such as Diego Chan (B14), whose will says he died on January 24, 1766, but whose death record states January 25.[67] Out of the fifty death records that correspond to testators in the Ixil corpus, only six, or 12 percent, have matching dates of death. Nor do the death records contain an entry for all the wills composed (see appendix A).

To add to the confusion, most of the death records for the 1760s in Ixil state, as outlined by the 1722 synod, whether the deceased had died with or without a testament (*sin o con disposición testamentaria*). In truth, the designation holds no pattern. At times, testators whose wills report a death weeks after the death record were recorded as having died with wills; other times testators whose wills place their death prior to the date in the death record are sometimes marked as intestate.

What is to be made of such discrepancies between the 1760s testaments and parish records? Firm answers remain elusive. It is possible that errors occurred on both sides. Consider the will of Joseph Cab (B45). Joseph died in Tiho (Merida), not Ixil. Thus, after his death, the *cabildo* gathered to settle his estate on May 30, 1767. The affair was complicated and involved queries into his surviving family and even the finding and researching a relative's will from 1726 to clarify the ownership of a particular *solar* and well. Certainly, such extensive inquiries and research took time. Yet, interestingly, the introductory statement for the will states, "*Josef Cab = Cimi en 30 de Mayo de 1767*" (Joseph Cab died on May 30, 1767). It would have been near impossible for the *cabildo* to learn of the death of Joseph in Tiho, gather on the very same day of his death, perform the inquiries and research, and settle his estate. The introductory statement, then, is referencing the the *cabildo*'s settling of the estate and composition of the will, not the date of death. In other cases, things are not so clear and are even downright bewildering. For example, in a rare example of first-person voice, don Pedro Pech (C3) stated that he was alive and dictating his will on April 11, 1779, and the will's introductory statement dated his death May 25, 1779. Yet his death record claimed the date as June 2, 1779.

In those cases where the notary composed the will posthumously, perhaps the notary simply took notes at the bedside of the testator and later wrote the more formal will, or perhaps close relations provided the details for the deceased. Interestingly, and as with the will of don Pedro, the 1760s corpus contains a few distinct examples of the testator's voice, and all relate to those wills composed prior to the date of the testator's death as stated in the records. Consider Marta Mis (C2), who chastised her daughter for her lack of care, or Luisa Tec (B56), who praised her son for remembering her, or Diego Chan's (B14) role in composing his own will. Such are clear indicators of a living testator's role in the will itself.

Yet some wills were certainly created posthumously. The Yucatecan synod of 1722 commented that "natives" died regularly intestate, and the council provided the outline for death entries that included a statement on whether or not the testator died with a will.[68] Unfortunately, these entries are somewhat unrealiable with regards to Ixil, with some claiming wills that were apparently composed after death, others asserting the absence of wills for those who obviously did in fact have them composed, like Luisa Tec (see appendix A).

Whereas the reasons for such errors and discrepancies between the wills and the death records must remain speculative, they suggest individual priorities. Ecclesiastics seemed to concern themselves more with creating the necessary death record (and one cannot help but wonder at their concern for accuracy), while the notaries in Ixil (at least in the 1760s) focused more on the testament itself. The *cabildo* preserved and, at times, executed the wills of Ixil's residents as part of its responsibility to the town itself. If future disputes arose over the property or inheritance of the deceased, the will was brought forward to settle the matter, as seen already in the codicils and statements accompanying the corpus. Certainly, such issues were local ones; they were family matters that did not concern ecclesiastics busily occupied with the religious administration of the various towns in their purview.

With regard to the burial and accompanying rites, the Yucatecan synod of 1722 instructed ecclesiastics to personally administer to the body of the deceased prior to its burial and not leave it only to the native assistants.[69] Unlike baptismal and marriage records, Hoyos did not state his involvement in the burials when recording deaths. Instead, the statement simply declared that the deceased "received the holy sacraments and was buried in the church the following day." Hoyos then notarized the statement as the curate of Conkal by stating, "*tome esta razon y lo firme*" (I recorded and signed it). As seen with the 1748 will of Anna Itza (A35), ecclesiastics could delay their fulfillment of the requiem mass requested. Indeed, when asked in 1785, the Maya *maestro* of Conkal declared that trained Maya—and not the curate of Conkal—assisted the dying and oversaw their burials in the *visita* towns.[70] Thus, after a locally supervised dying and burial process, it seems that the next time an ecclesiastic came to Ixil, he would recite the requested masses. This, then, allowed Hoyos to sign the death record of Pasqual Coba (B53), and fray Méndez (for example) to collect the mass fees and settle the testament.

In 1785 six ecclesiastics cared for Conkal and its five *visita* towns, which included Ixil. Since friars transferred between towns regularly, it is difficult to know how many were available in the 1740s and 1760s or who was assigned to travel to Ixil, if any at all, and perform necessary rites. The wills and additional ecclesiastical records, again, provide some clues. Tables 4.2 and 4.3 illustrate significant overlap and sharing of ecclesiastical duties in Ixil. Whereas it is possible that the ecclesiastics from Conkal set up a rotation of sorts regarding who traveled to Ixil to perform religious rites, a pattern is difficult to detect. For example, fray Joseph Villamil signed the will of Pasquala Mitz (A22) and attested that he sang a mass for her on April 18, 1748. Two days later, fray Jul Barrera performed a baptism in Ixil for Lorensa Chan, whose sister, Martha (B34), would later die in 1766. Moreover, although fray Manuel de Lara baptized Manuel Pech on November 23, 1748, fray Joachim Paz sang a mass for Anna Itza (A35) six days later, on November 29. Furthermore, for the four wills composed in November and December 1748, four separate friars signed the wills.[71]

A more consistent pattern emerges in the 1760s, with Hoyos signing all wills from 1765 through May of 1767. In fact, as curate of Conkal, the signatures of Hoyos appeared on numerous baptismal, matrimonial, and death records for the *visitas* of Conkal and Conkal itself during the same time frame and until the summer of

TABLE 4.2. Franciscans performing requiem masses in Ixil, 1748–68

Friars	1748 Jan.–Mar.	1748 Apr.	1748 May–Oct.	1748 Nov.	1748 Dec.	1765	1766	1767 Feb.–May	1767 June	1767 July–Oct.	1767 Oct.–Dec.	1768
Diego Pérez Arrias	X											
Joseph Villamil		X										
Francisco Días y Solís			X		X							
Manuel Lara				X								
Joachim Paz				X								
Joseph del Valle y Solís					X							
Juan de Hoyos						X	X	X				
Sebastián Suárez							X					
Ávila									X		X	X
Méndez										X		

Source: FS-MY, "registros parroquiales y diocesanos, 1543–1977," Conkal, San Francisco de Asís, Bautismos 1706–1786, images 499–505.

1773.[72] During the years of 1760s, his signature on the wills and the official death records testify to his traveling between towns. Fray Ávila signs the remaining 1767 wills and those in 1768, with the exception of a four-month hiatus in 1767, when Méndez fills in. Overall, although not permanent and occasionally random, the presence of ecclesiastics in Ixil was certainly regular.

The services the friars performed for the testators likewise varied according to the year. As illustrated in chapter 1, every testator in 1748 left four *tostones* (twelve *reales*) for a sung mass and two *tomines*, or *reales*, for Jerusalem for a total ecclesiastical fee of fourteen *reales*. The consistency of the request for sung masses surely illustrates the standard formulae and routine of the notary and *cah*. The single will from 1738 likewise has similar donations and could represent an earlier example of this pattern.

TABLE 4.3. Franciscans performing baptisms in Ixil, 1748

Friars	Jan.	Feb.	Mar.	Apr.	May	June	July	Aug.	Sept.	Oct.	Nov.	Dec.
Miguel Antonio Sarmiento	X		X									
Pedro Rejón	X	X										
Jul Barrera				X	X	X						
Francisco Días y Solís					X	X	X	X	X		X	
Manuel de Lara					X		X			X	X	X
Joachim Paz										X	X	
Joseph del Valle y Solís								X		X		

Source: FS-MY, "registros parroquiales y diocesanos, 1543–1977," Conkal, San Francisco de Asís, Bautismos 1706–1786, images 499–505.

More affordable yet less powerful, recited masses appear in the wills from 1765 to 1768, with only 16 percent of testators paying for the more expensive sung mass. A recited mass cost six *reales*—half the price of a sung mass—and appeared the more popular choice as the colonial period progressed. When added to the typical donation of two *reales* to Jerusalem, most 1760s testators paid a total ecclesiastical fee of eight *reales*, or one *peso*.

In short, whereas the mass fees and donations to Jerusalem appeared fixed and consistent in every will from 1748, those from the 1760s display more variation and flexibility, with only a few paying the fees of those two decades prior. Regardless, the eighteenth-century priests had received instructions to not allow poverty to prevent a proper burial "because it is not just, nor Christian, for the dead to not have some sort of suffrage."[73] The progressively minded bishop of Yucatan, don Juan Gómez de Parada, labored against the exploitation of the Maya and, thus, established fixed *aranceles*, or fees, for religious and other services, and ordered them to be translated into Maya and posted in every church. Burials were free of charge, and the local curate was not to oblige Mayas to request a mass in their testaments. However, if the Mayas desired to do so voluntarily, the fee was six *reales* for a recited mass and twelve for a sung mass, with an additional *real* for the singers and sacristan each, for a total of fourteen *reales*. There is no mention of the Jerusalem fund, although Gómez de Parada strongly warns priests under severe penalty not to ask for any additional services or charge additional fees.[74] The mass fees in the Ixil wills correspond with those outlined in the 1722 synod;

perhaps the additional two *reales* for Jerusalem paid the singers and sacristan where applicable, or perhaps it was a sinecure too firmly planted in tradition and formula to be removed.

Overall, the official and unofficial documentation from Ixil reveal a religious atmosphere that remained steady, with changes occurring slowly and sometimes not at all. Ixil was Catholic, to be sure, but on terms designated by the *cah* and local traditions. The town's residents arranged their posthumous care through a religious preamble that remained remarkably consistent throughout the eighteenth century. The requested burial, requiem mass, and donation to Jerusalem indicate a simple and unadorned tradition largely unchanged by time if only to include more recited masses. But for a select few, trained Maya—such as those who composed and preserved the Chilam Balam text or those charged with helping the dying achieve a good death—Catholicism remained a consistent yet unobtrusive presence in a daily life removed from Spanish centers; one that is slow-paced and shored up by tradition and one that engages the church primarily for the performance of religious ritual. Indeed, similar to precontact traditions, Ixil residents seem to have found a religious balance in their lives that requires little reduction or augmentation, only maintenance.

In the centuries since they dictated wills to the town notary in the eighteenth century, the residents of Ixil have continued to negotiate the place of God in their lives and town. Sometimes this negotiation allowed for unofficial practices, such as the Maya creating their own Chilam Balam text or even possible membership in forbidden organizations. Regarding the latter—and despite the place of Catholicism as the official religion of New Spain—the aforementioned distiller of aguardiente in Ixil, Pedro José Escobedo, had no trouble signing his name in 1814 with a particular symbol, not once but twice (figures 4.2 and 4.3). Although possibly only a peculiar part of the rubric, that symbol at the end of his name appears to be an interlocking square and compass, which would confirm his identity as a Freemason.

To be fair, Freemasonry is not a religion but a fraternal organization. However, that did not prevent Spain from mounting a significant opposition to Freemasonry beginning with its appearance in the 1720s, particularly in southern Spain and areas adjacent to English-controlled Gibraltar. In 1738 Pope Clement XII issued a papal bull forbidding Catholics from becoming Freemasons—a mandate that remains to this day—and the king outlawed the movement in 1751. The organization spread to New Spain, and, despite the Inquisition's prosecution of a number of Freemasons in Mexico, the first Masonic Lodge formed in Mexico in the early nineteenth century.[75] The circumstances that possibly led Escobedo to sign his

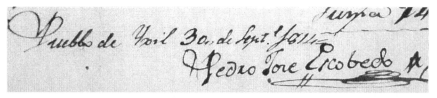

FIGURE 4.2. Possible Masonic signature of Pedro José Escobedo, 1814. (AGN, Instituciones Coloniales, Indiferente Virreinal, Aguardiente de Caña, caja 5051, expediente 74)

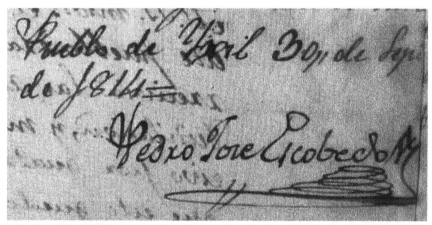

FIGURE 4.3. Additional possible Masonic signature of Pedro José Escobedo, 1814. (AGN, Instituciones Coloniales, Indiferente Virreinal, Aguardiente de Caña, caja 5051, expediente 74)

name with a Masonic mark are uncertain. Yet one could imagine that the liberal ideas of Freemasonry found a tolerable home in an increasingly liberal Mexico, particularly in the early decades of the nineteenth century. Regardless, natives were not the only ones to negotiate their religion to accommodate personal needs and desires.

This is not to say that God lost his role in Ixil. Later, in 1839, a case was brought to the attention of the curate and vicar overseeing Ixil. Don Calixto Antonio Escalante was demanding payment in the sum of twenty *pesos* for the palms and other materials he allegedly invested in the covering of a damaged portion of the church. Escalante had engaged in a verbal agreement with the recently deceased priest of Ixil, don José María Quiñones, and was now demanding payment. Unfortunately, no one could substantiate his claim, and, indeed, others came forward to offer contrary testimony. In the end, the ruling was against Escalante.[76]

FIGURE 4.4.
Church of San
Bernabé, Ixil, 2018.
(Photograph by
Matthew Restall)

Today the church in Ixil remains the centerpiece of the town (figure 4.4). Begun as an open chapel in the sixteenth century and developed into a closed building in the seventeenth, the church serves as a physical conduit between the past and present. Inside the church, polychrome murals dating from the mid- to late eighteenth century (with some more recent "restoration") decorate the sanctuary arch and the apse. Above the archway San Bernabé, the patron saint of Ixil, appears with heavenly angels playing trumpets. God observes the congregation below from the ceiling in the apse, and the rear wall boasts two angels holding ribbons—one saying "*Oración*," the other "*Silencio*"—to remind the Maya parishioners of the reverence expected during services. Floral decorations and friezes accompany the murals and adorn the walls and ceiling (figure 4.5).[77]

FIGURE 4.5. Interior of the Church of San Bernabé, Ixil, 2018. (Photograph by Matthew Restall)

The images testify to a religious atmosphere in Ixil deeply rooted in the past; one that developed slowly and to the dictates of the local Maya population. The murals and religious ornaments, like the church and its eighteenth-century posthumous rites, were simple yet effective, basic and yet sufficient, and reflected an image of God in Ixil that was also delineated by the testaments studied here.

Yet in 2016 other images, more modern and lively, encircled Ixil's church as the town celebrated Carnival—the festive season prior to the liturgical season of Lent. Residents dressed in costumes ranging from those inspired by recent movies, including *Star Wars* and *Despicable Me*, to festive personifications ranging from beer bottles to a Catholic bishop; all danced to a lively band as the *alcalde* of Ixil, Anastacio Córdova Chan crowned the king and queen of Carnival. When Laura Balam, a reporter covering the event, interviewed Alix, Ixil's 2016 king of Carnival, she asked what it all meant to him. Alix responded, "It means a lot to be crowned king of Carnival here in Ixil . . . as everyone knows, Ixil is a town visited more than others because we are very festive and love having fun."[78]

Earlier, in the space directly to the left of the church, a parade of floats and decorated pickup trucks filed in to mark the beginning of a rodeo. The heat of the day caused individuals to crowd in the shade cast by the tall church as they cheered the brave adolescents who entered the arena, taunted the small bull, and then ran frantically from him—as they have been doing for decades, if not centuries. *Dios*, the God of Catholic Christianity, and his church remain central in Ixil today, still perceived with the diversity of perspectives with which they were surely seen in the colonial period. For some, the church represents a key religious component of daily life; for others, it is a grand building of occasional importance during birth, marriage, death, and the occasional festival; for still others, it simply provides shade.

NOTES

1. Ciudad Real (1976: 337).

2. Sánchez de Aguilar (1937: 172).

3. Bricker and Hill (2009: appendix A, 257).

4. Ibid.: 337.

5. Ciudad Real (1976: 363).

6. See Paxton (1990).

7. Hsia (2010: 126).

8. Landa (1937: 57); Restall et al. (forthcoming). For more on the rituals of the precontact Maya, see Fitzsimmons (2009); Scherer (2015).

9. David Bolles, personal communication, June 7, 2017.

10. For more on the development of death's rituals see Paxton (1990: 19–44).

11. Burns (2001: ix–xvii).

12. León (1611: 136v). For more on the evangelization of the Nahuas with regards to death and dying see Burkhart (2004); Hosselkus (2011: 39–43).

13. Christensen (2016: 16–17, 271n66).

14. CS-1722: 110.

15. *Visita* reports indicate that priests were to ensure that such towns had Mayas trained in helping the sick die well. See question nineteen in AHAY, Visita Pastorales, 1784, Homun.

16. Bricker and Hill (2009: appendix A, 257).

17. Pizzigoni (2007).

18. Terraciano (1998).

19. Pizzigoni (2007: 60).

20. Recent works have greatly facilitated the comparisons of native testaments by including transcriptions and translations of such. See Kellogg and Restall (1998); Christensen and Truitt (2015); Restall, Sousa, and Terraciano (2005).

21. For an example of a typical will from Tekanto, see Bricker and Hill (2009: appendix A, 257). For additional insight see Restall (1997: 400n18).

22. The Cacalchen testaments are located in TULAL, Libro de Cacalchen. For examples of three transcribed and translated preambles from Cacalchen, see Christensen (2013: appendix D, 277–78).

23. Lockhart (1992: 263–318).

24. Restall (1995: 13).

25. Restall (1997: 294–319).

26. Lockhart (1992: 434).

27. Catholics believe that the church is the bride of Christ and mother to all its members, thus its common reference as the Holy Mother Church.

28. Ripalda's catechism. For variants in the spelling of *iglesia* in the town of Tekanto, see Bricker (2015: 427–31).

29. For more, see Christensen (2016: 48; 2013: 45–47).

30. *Teyolia*, however, was likely a colonial invention. Christensen (2013: 43–44); Burkhart (2004).

31. Bourdin (2008: 47–68); Gaspar A. Cauich Ramirez, personal communication, August 8, 2007. The precontact meaning of *pixan* as "soul" is difficult to uncover. The Temple of Inscriptions has *pi-xo-ma* in connection with items of clothing, giving a related root of covering—which is another definition of *pixan* in the colonial dictionaries—but not "soul." Stephen Houston, personal communication, June 6, 2017.

32. Ruz (1847: 8–9). See also Hanks's discussion of the phrase in his *Converting Words* (2010: 12–15).

33. For more on the topic, see Christensen (2013: ch. 8).

34. Pizzigoni (2007: 75).

35. Again, see Christensen (2013: ch. 8).

36. See Christensen (2016: 174–78).

37. A few other examples exist where a testator bequeaths "*hunpay u*" (one beaded necklace). Although *u* can also translate as "rosary," it most often appears joined with the Spanish loanword *corales*, or corals, to mean "a necklace of coral beads."

38. Sánchez de Aguilar (1937: 172).

39. CS-1722: 115–16.

40. Of all aspects of Catholicism, saints particularly appealed to indigenous parishioners; Lockhart (1992: 235).

41. Although exceptions exist. In the 1760s it was claimed that the town of Uman had never used or seen a rosary. Chuchiak (2000: 456). *Visita* reports included the question concerning the curate's praying of the rosary. See, for example, question twenty in AHAY, Visita Pastorales, 1784, Homun. For a few examples of *cofradías* see Christensen (2013: 250n26).

42. Thompson (1999: 128).

43. For examples of the salary rates, see Restall (1997: 68–69).

44. Christensen (2016: 3–8); Chuchiak (2004).

45. Fernández del Castillo (1914: 319).

46. Elsewhere, Christensen and others have offered the possibility that not all such forbidden texts went unseen by ecclesiastics. It is possible that the Maya kept such manuscripts away from those who would confiscate them but allowed more lenient priests to know of their existence. Christensen (2016: 17–18); Hanks (2010: 346).

47. For more on religious texts in Chilam Balams and copybooks, see Christensen (2016: 12–22).

48. For a detailed analysis of the individual biblical stories, see Caso Barrera (2011: 19–23).

49. Similar to various European commentaries and *reportorios*, the Maya text seems fascinated with dates and ages. A detailed study of the religious texts in the Ixil would be a worthwhile project, although such lies beyond the scope of this book.

50. The sacrifice of Isaac, however, does appear in certain Nahuatl texts. See Sell and Burkhart (2004: 146–63).

51. For the opinions of Caso Barrera, see her *Ixil* (2011: 19–23).

52. Sánchez de Aguilar (1937: 181).

53. CS-1722: 109.

54. AHAY, Visita Pastorales, 1782–1785, Conkal.

55. *Padre predicadores* were friars with a license from the provincial and chapter of the order as a preacher. They could serve as a professor in a convent school, administer the sacraments, and confess within the *doctrina*.

56. AHAY, Visita Pastorales, 1782–1785, Conkal.

57. CS-1722: 110.

58. CS-1722: 106–7.

59. FS-MY, "registros parroquiales y diocesanos, 1543–1977," Conkal, San Francisco de Asís, Matrimonios 1611–1784, image 198 of 585.

60. FS-MY, "registros parroquiales y diocesanos, 1543–1977," Conkal, San Francisco de Asís, Bautismos 1706–1786, image 417 of 572; FS-MY, "México matrimonios, 1570–1950," Marcos Cime and Ysabel Pech, 02 Feb 1744.

61. FS-MY, "registros parroquiales y diocesanos, 1543–1977," Conkal, San Francisco de Asís, Matrimonios 1757–1786, image 428 of 624.

62. FS-MY, "registros parroquiales y diocesanos, 1543–1977," Conkal, San Francisco de Asís, Bautismos 1706–1786, image 426 of 572.

63. CS-1722: 106.

64. Molina (1984: 45r–58r).

65. A provision laid out by the Council of Trent.

66. FS-MY, "registros parroquiales y diocesanos, 1543–1977," Conkal, San Francisco de Asís, Matrimonios 1757–1786, images 374–75 of 624.

67. For the death records corresponding with the 1760s wills, see FS-MY, "registros parroquiales y diocesanos, 1543–1977," Conkal, San Francisco de Asís, Defunciones 1682–1802, images 167–280 of 452.

68. CS-1722: 110.

69. Ibid.

70. AHAY, Visitas Pastorales, 1782–1785, Conkal, microfilm page 416.

71. Another will from December exists (A38), but it is incomplete and lacks the final signatures.

72. See, for example, his signatures in FS-MY, "registros parroquiales y diocesanos, 1543–1977," Conkal, San Francisco de Asís, Defunciones 1682–1802, image 143 of 452; parroquias Católicas, Yucatan.

73. CS-1722: 242; the instructions came from the 1722 Yucatecan synod to priests serving in Merida, Valladolid, and Campeche.

74. Ibid.: 251.

75. As Freemasonry spread throughout Europe in the seventeenth and early eighteenth centuries and as its members became more political, the church became increasingly wary, thus providing the context for Pope Clement's papal bull. In truth, the topic of Freemasonry in Spain and New Spain is deserving of its own study. A seminal study on the matter remains Greenleaf (1969).

76. AGN, Bienes Nacionales, vol. 9, expediente 20. See also José Ramón Narváez Hernández, *Historia social del derecho y de la justicia* (Mexico City: Editorial Porrúa, 2007), 147.

77. We thank Richard Perry and Niccolo Brooker for sharing their photographs and analysis of the images.

78. Estilo Yucatán, "Noche de Coronación de Reyes de Carnaval de Ixil 2016," www.youtube.com/watch?v=aKdryDGU4bE. As mentioned in our introduction, Restall observed this festival in 1990 and 1996.

5

Family in Ixil

[A]s for my daughter, Agustina Yam, I have left her nothing, because she and her husband do nothing on my behalf, as my lord the *batab* and magistrates know; she has no shame, that one.

—Marta Mis, 1769

[H]ere is my father's house plot; my share of it I leave in the hands of my child, Pablo Tec; he remembered me on this earth.

—Luisa Tec, 1767

On Sunday, April 29, 1714, Joseph Poot (B32) married Dominga Yam and began their life together. As far as we know from existing records, Joseph and Dominga had one son, Salvador (B49), a daughter, and three or four grandchildren. The son, Salvador, eventually married Juana Uh and together, in 1750, they had a child, María, whom Salvador clearly doted upon, referring to her with the affectionate diminutive *chichan* (rarely used in wills) and describing his wife as the woman "who gave life to my daughter, María Poot."[1] Salvador and his wife, Juana, had the opportunity to see their daughter married in Ixil to Lucas Coot on November 10, 1765; Lucas was nineteen years old and María was fifteen. One year later, Salvador's father, Joseph, died, followed by Salvador himself nine months later, on June 24, 1767. The epidemic that swept through Ixil in those years also likely claimed the life of María's husband, Lucas, for in 1769 María married Juan Chan—a second marriage missed by her loving father.[2]

DOI: 10.5876/9781607329220.c005

Such are the intimate details on colonial-era Maya lives that the family wills can provide. Admittedly, some of the data from the story above derived from Conkal's parish matrimonial records. Yet the wills supply not only additional dates and genealogical details but also the emotion and color absent in standard records. This chapter employs Ixil's corpus of testaments to provide a little of that emotion and color needed to make social history effective and engaging. Specifically, the wills illuminate the patterns of inheritance that influenced testators when selecting their heirs, family genealogies and their ties over multiple generations. The wills likewise illustrate marriage patterns evident among the noble lineages of Ixil. Previous works by Restall and by Thompson reveal important insights into many of the matters discussed in this chapter.[3] But unique to our study is an up-close view of how such issues played out in Ixil, a view that both supports and challenges previous analyses while illustrating local variations and preferences expected among the many *cahob*. After all, in a way Ixil was just like any other community in human history: a town where family matters were paradoxically generic and unique all at the same time.

HEIRS IN IXIL

As mentioned, the *Siete Partidas* was a medieval statutory code commissioned by Alfonso X, but still in effect in the Spanish colonial centuries. It includes discussion of testators and their designated heirs, and regarding inheritance it states:

> The lawful share to which the children are entitled is as follows, namely; if there are four of them, or less, they shall have one-third of all the estate of him from whom they inherit. If there are five, or more of them, they are entitled to half of the said estate; and this is called the *legitima*, or legitimate share, for the reason that the law grants it to the children.[4]

Centuries later, the 1722 ecclesiastical synod in Yucatan likewise addressed inheritance, declaring that testators should divide four-fifths of their wealth evenly among their children; the remaining fifth could be disposed of at the pleasure of the testator to benefit his soul, a specific child, or whomever.[5]

Fray Diego de Landa, the sixteenth-century Franciscan friar who spearheaded the "spiritual conquest" in Yucatan with methods that drew lasting controversy, made the following observations regarding existing Maya customs of inheritance:

> Daughters did not inherit equally with their brothers, except as a manner of favor or goodwill, in which case a part of the whole was given them. The rest was divided equally, except where one had helped more in the accumulation of the property, in which case he received an equivalent before the division. . . . Where the heir was not

of sufficient age to receive the property, they entrusted it to the nearest relative as guardian or tutor, who supplied the mother with what she needed for his bringing up; for it was not their custom to place the property in the mother's control. . . . When the heirs reached their majority, the guardians rendered them the property. . . . The transfer was made in the presence of the chiefs and leading men.[6]

As will be seen, Landa's report holds both truth and fiction in eighteenth-century Ixil, where, like all other *cahob*, tradition and individual circumstances ruled the day.

The testaments of Ixil allow us to look in some detail at the heirs of testators, what items they received, and whether the designated inheritance was indeed equal and fair. Recall that property ownership in Ixil typically reflected gender lines: men generally owned those items necessary for laboring in the *kax*, men's clothing, animals, and the *kax* plots of land themselves; women owned items associated with their labor in the *solar*—such as gardens, cloth, looms, and clothing of any kind.[7] As seen below, the vast majority of bequests in the wills consolidated this pattern of gendered ownership, in turn perpetuating the gendered pattern of inheritance. Regarding equality, no real pattern developed within the wills, as the preference of each testator seemingly influenced the will more than official decrees.

If one commonality exists, it is that most testators left at least one item to each child, even if that item was to be shared with other siblings, reflecting the practice of *cetil* and *multial*, or "even distribution" and "joint ownership." For example, when Gaspar Poot (B19) died, he left his share of the house plot that he had inherited from his mother to his children Joseph, María, and Basilia, "the three of them together." A survey of Maya wills from Ixil, Ebtun, Cacalchen, and Tekanto all reveal a general tendency to distribute goods equally among the remaining immediate family.[8] However, as we shall see, exceptions do exist, and testators often favored one heir slightly more than the rest.

The testament of Miguel Tun (A9) provides an illustrative example of Ixil's inheritance patterns. Miguel died a wealthy man on January 20, 1748, and left behind a wife, three sons, and four daughters. After his religious preamble and requests, his first bequest was to his son Juan Tun, who received one well and its *solar*, a house beam, two mules, and two cows. Since this is the only *solar* and house beam bequeathed, we can assume that Miguel bequeathed his family's primary residence to his son Juan. The bequest of *solares* and house beams from father to son was common, perhaps reflecting a desire to leave the family home to the eldest son. Indeed, nearly every occasion of a house beam bequest involved a father and son; with rare exception, men, not women, bequeathed house beams. The vast majority of exceptions to this rule involve multiple house beams, with the son already having received his beam from his father, and others, such as another son or a wife, receiving an additional beam.

The will of Pasquala Tec (B51) provides a notable example and exception to the male gifting of house beams. Pasquala bequeaths her house beam and frame to her son Ambrosio, who buys out other unspecified heirs to the tune of six *reales*. First Clemente Cante and then Agustín Cante renounce all future claims to the beam in first-person declarations, further emphasizing the communal and collective nature of such documents. In this case, Clemente is one of Pasquala's eight living children, while Agustín would appear to be her husband—he is not listed among her children, yet he has their patronym and obviously has claim to the house beam. Indeed, it appears to be through marriage to Agustín that Pasquala originally obtained the house beam. Throughout the wills, the son receiving the house beam often appears favored in the will above his siblings and mother, and such is the case with Ambrosio. The recipient of the house beam and largest inheritance, however, need not be the eldest son, as one would expect in Europe, as Clemente renounces his claim to the beam given to his "younger brother," Ambrosio.

This is not to say that women did not own or bequeath *solares*. For example, Miguel Tun gives a forest plot, its well, and *solar* to his four daughters—Pasquala, Lorensa, Martha, and Phelipa—to share jointly. Such daughters could then pass on the *solar* in their wills, similar to Martha Itza (A17), who left a *solar* and its well to her seven children to share. Women also inherited animals, as Miguel next gives each of his four daughters and a son, Pasqual, a cow. Previously we saw the example of Martha Pech (A21), who owned nine horses and two cows. Yet even in her will she favored her son and husband, giving them nearly three times as many animals as her daughters. Thus, although women did own animals, men both bequeathed and received higher numbers of livestock.

Only some 20 percent of male testators left items to their wives; Miguel was one of them. His wife received two cows, four horses, one chest, one metal spoon, and one forest plot. Considering that spouses were rarely heirs in the wills—only 9 percent of women left goods to their husbands—Ixil's testators certainly favored their children. Consider Ignacio Pech (A1), who devoted considerable space in his will to dividing his goods among his four children. To be fair, he gave his wife a mule, five horses, two house beams, two silver spoons, two wooden chairs, two shirts, two pairs of trousers, two sashes, two lengths of cloth, and two fur blankets. Yet that bequest was followed by a request that she distribute the goods to his sons Pasgual and Pedro.

This and other examples contradict Landa's earlier claim that Maya mothers were not trusted to be guardians of goods for intended heirs. In another instance, Martha Pech (A21) hints at an expected inheritance from her husband by leaving her son "all that my husband gives me when he dies." That said, most testators focused on their children, and Miguel concluded his bequest giving one forest plot to his sons

Juan and Gaspar, to share together, and another forest plot and its well to Juan, Pasquala, Lorensa, Martha, Phelipa, and Pasqual Tun as well as a nephew, Diego Mitz, to share.

In the division of his wealth, Miguel favored his son, Juan, and his wife; both received the most land, animals, and valuables. His remaining children received a fairly even amount of land and animals among them, and even a nephew benefited from the will. One individual, however, received markedly less than all others—Gaspar Tun. He is mentioned only once and is given a forest plot to share with Juan Tun. Admittedly, the will does not refer to Gaspar as a son—perhaps he was simply a relative—but the context suggests an immediate relation. Aside from Juan, gender does not seem to have played a large role in the distribution of goods. Indeed, his daughters received more than Pasqual and Gaspar.

Certainly, myriad examples exist in the corpus of testaments of testators bequeathing property in generally fair and equal proportions to their heirs. Ignacio Tec (A33), for example, distributed equally his wealth among all his sons, as did Martha Itza (A17) with her wealth and seven children. Yet most common is an attempt at an equal distribution while still favoring one heir in particular. The will of Joseph Yam (B33) provides an illustrative example. Joseph owned more beehives than any other testator—eighty-five in all. He also owned three house plots and three parcels of forest land as well as several horses. Joseph's settling of his bee fortune was indicative of his efforts to conform to the custom of *cetil* and *multial*, mentioned earlier, while still favoring his eldest son, Pasqual. Joseph's four other children inherited seven beehives each, but Pasqual was given twenty plus a forest plot, his mother thirty. Likewise, rather than give to Pasqual the house plot, where he presumably lived, Joseph had his son buy the plot for ten *pesos* so that Joseph could then distribute two *pesos* to each of his children (Pasqual himself included). Thus, Joseph obliged his eldest son to buy his siblings out of their shares to a plot that would normally have been jointly inherited.

On the other hand, Ixil also boasted plenty of examples of favoritism and even neglect. As seen in the quotes at the beginning of the chapter, children could lose or gain favor with their parents depending on their actions (or lack thereof). Marta Mis (C2) deliberately left her daughter, Agustina Yam, out of her will because "she and her husband do nothing on my behalf." Conversely, Luisa Tec (B56) favored her son, Pablo Tec, stating that "he remembered me on this earth." Most often the reason for preferential treatment or neglect was unknown. When dividing his wealth among his heirs, Francisco Itza (A7) repeatedly left out his two daughters, Dominga and Viviana, who received only one *solar* and well that they were obliged to share with their four other sisters; no particular reason was given for this. Moreover, Anna Itza (A35) failed to explain her favoritism toward her son, Joseph Mitz, who was included in every bequest with the exception of a *huipil* and petticoat given to her daughter, Pasquala.

Often favoritism is best understood in terms of gendered preferences; or, rather, gendered patterns of labor mean we cannot be sure in some cases whether the bequest really reflected personal favoritism. For example, Micaela Cab (A8) owned numerous items common among women, including clothing, accoutrements, and banana plots. Not surprisingly, the recipients of such were all female, including her two daughters, daughter-in-law, and even her younger sister. Micaela remembered her two sons, Mateo and Martín, using her will to give them a necklace, but they were told to share it with their sister Lorensa. In the absence of daughters, some female testators bequeathed their gendered belongings to extended family. The daughterless Martha Canul (A25) gave a dress and petticoats to her daughters-in-law, Luissa Cul and María Cutz; other items, such as lengths of yarn and a tribute *manta*, went to a son and husband.

As discussed, male testators typically left their sons house beams, *solares*, forest plots, animals, and tools. In the absence of male heirs, land and animals more commonly went to female heirs. For example, Felipe Chim (A30) died without sons and bequeathed to his two daughters his *solar* and well and his wooden chest. To be sure, if Felipe had had a son, he would have been the heir of such property. However, extended family could also benefit from a testator's lack of male heirs. Lacking sons, Salvador Poot (B49) left his forested land to his nephews, described—most unusually for the Ixil wills—with the Spanish term *sobrino*.[9]

Religious items further illustrate gendered preferences. As we have seen, and in contrast to their Nahua counterparts, very few religious items appeared in the wills of Ixil, and those that did appear were mostly in the 1760s, with only one testator from 1748 mentioning an image of Mary (table 5.1). Of the six individuals listing religious items, five are male. Moreover, the only female included in the group, Marta Mis, left her image of Mary to her son. Indeed, all testators left their items to male heirs with the exception of two, who bequeathed such items to their wives, who perhaps could pass them on to male heirs. Thus, we see a strong pattern in Ixil of male ownership and inheritance of religious items.

FAMILY TIES IN IXIL

The wills from Ixil provide not only insight on testamentary heirs and their inheritance but also the opportunity to view select families over multiple generations and the family ties that bound it all together. When Christensen discovered the second corpus of Ixil testaments from 1748, we had hoped to expand our understanding of *chibal* lineages in Ixil prior to the bulk of Restall's wills from the 1760s. We had also

TABLE 5.1. Religious items in Ixil

Owner	Year	Image of Mary	Image of San Diego	Rosary	Heir
Felipe Tec	1748	1			F
Bernardino Coot	1766	2			M × 2
Juan de la Cruz Coba	1766	1			M
Pedro Mis	1766		1		M
Simón Chan	1766			1	F
Marta Mis	1799	1			M

hoped to find genealogical connections between the 1748 and 1760s corpora. And, indeed, we found a few of each.

The first will in the 1748 corpus is that of Ignacio Pech, and the four codicils that follow relate to matters mentioned in Ignacio's testament. In 1748, Ignacio left a wealth of animals and items to his wife, Bernardina Cante, to distribute to his sons, Pasgual and Pedro (again we see the mother serving as guardian). Seven years later, Bernardina distributed some of the goods, as recorded in a codicil appended to the will and recorded in 1755 (A2). Bernardina declares that she is distributing the goods "according to the legal terms of this my husband's testament," while Pasgual and Pedro affirm that they are receiving a variety of goods and even pass some on to their children. Despite the codicil, questions remain. Why did not all the goods left to Bernardina reach the hands of Pasgual and Pedro? Why the delay of seven years? Although one might assume such a distribution of entrusted goods could be handled privately, perhaps the status of the Pech—or some familial discord—required the attention and ratification of the *cabildo*.

Five years later, in 1760, the daughter of Ignacio Pech, Lorensa, found herself having to appear before the *cabildo* and settle an issue with her son, Mateo—an account described in the subsequent three codicils (A3–A5) appended to Ignacio's testament. As Landa attests, the practice of including the town's "leading men" in such a transfer of property predates the colonial period. Here in Ixil the *cabildo* supervised the distribution of Ignacio's wealth from his wife to his sons.

The issue apparently revolved around a well that Mateo desired dug on a house plot. The codicils drop the reader amid a conversation certainly well known to all those present. Mateo declares he has nothing more to say about the house plots and wells except that he was given some money to dig a well by his mothers, Lorensa Pech and Pasquala Yam. Although the digging of wells is commonplace enough given the rocky and shallow state of the limestone bed upon which Yucatan rested, the choice of the kinship word *naob*, "mothers," is more puzzling.

Lorensa confirms her giving the money to her *al*, or child, Mateo thus identifying herself as his direct relation. It is likely, then, that Pasquala, who is only mentioned in the documents, is Mateo's mother-in-law. The whole issue ends with Mateo confirming his receipt of three *pesos*, one *toston*, and one red sapote orchard from his mothers to help fund the well. Mateo states, "I have nothing more to say to them about this"; thus concluded an incident put in motion twelve years prior with the 1748 will of Ignacio Pech.

Another collection of codicils and their accompanying will relates a tale equally dramatic. Sebastián Uh, who appears as an *alcalde* in the 1748 *cabildo*, died nineteen years later, in 1767. In his will (B40) Sebastián left a two-well house plot to his four children, dividing it into two halves, with one-half going to Martín and Juana, the other to Marta and Pasquala. He then mentions an identical property, to go to the same four children together, and it is unclear whether this is a second plot or the same one. Most likely, it was the same one, and a decade of multiple claims by Sebastián Uh's children and grandchildren recorded in the accompanying codicils (docs. B40a and B40b) resulted in the sons of one daughter buying out their aunt and her husband. Two brothers, Francisco and Tomás Canche, appear to purchase one-half of the plot, which is then divided between them (they are described as Marta's children in the first document, but in the second Francisco seems to be referred to as Pasquala's child). The vendors are Juana Uh (an heir in her father's will), her husband Juan Mis, and a previously unmentioned Uh, Andrea. Interestingly, no money is mentioned; instead, the Canche brothers barter their shares of a henequen orchard. This is the only example in the Maya notarial records we have seen of a nonpecuniary land swap. This, combined with the fact that these documents are not conventional sale records (which usually emphasize Spanish legal terms such as *carta de venta* and *conocimiento*), suggests that this exchange may have been the resolution of an inheritance dispute—a resolution brokered by the *cabildo*, as shown in the term *chicanpah*, which often means simply "appear" but also contains the element *pah*, "to judge."

Not all connections within the corpus are so theatrical. Most are quite mundane and provide mere glimpses of the lives of individuals across the decades. The notary for the 1748 wills, Salvador Coba, apparently married Luisa Mo and had a son, Bernardino (B25), who died in 1766; Antonio Huchim (B37), who died in 1766, likewise served on the 1748 *cabildo* as a *regidor*; and don Pedro Pech (C3) served as *batab* in 1755 before he died in 1779. Some connections occur within a much smaller timeframe. María Canche (B12) died in 1766 and bequeathed her son, Gaspar Poot (B19), a share of a house plot and well, along with a house beam and frame shared with his brother, Silvestre. About two months later, Gaspar died and passed to his own children his share of the house plot and well that his mother had left him, along with a variety of other goods including a house beam. Although small, such glimpses still help to focus the image that is eighteenth-century Ixil.

At other times the combined corpus provides clarifying and corroborating details. For example, the 1766 will of Gabriel Tec (B15) refers to his share of a house plot and well established in the testament of his grandfather, Bartolome Tec. The 1748 collection contains the will of his father, Felipe Tec (A26), who states that whatever his father, Bartolome Tec, gives him should be passed on to his son and daughter, Gabriel and María Tec. The epidemic that rocked Ixil in 1748 caused many children to die before their parents. Thus, the intended inheritance of Phelipe from his father passed directly to his son, Gabriel, who suggested as much in his later testament.

One of the more extensive examples comes from the Matu *chibal*. Three testaments within the corpus directly relate to each other and allow for a reconstructed genealogy of five generations (figure 5.1). When Juan Bautista Matu (A38) died in 1748, he favored his grandchildren and single daughter with his property, ignoring his other known sons, Joseph and Marcos, the latter dying without leaving anything in his will, according to his nephew, Mateo (B1). Juan Bautista does not mention the parents of his grandchildren, so it is possible that the grandchildren came from Marcos or some other son not mentioned. Indeed, the identity of his known sons, Joseph and Marcos, are known only through their mention in other wills—Juan Bautista ignores them completely. Perhaps Juan Bautista had a difficult relationship with some of his sons; perhaps Pasquala and the grandchildren mentioned experienced more financial need; or perhaps an agreement not mentioned in the wills existed and thus eludes us. Regardless, it illustrates yet again the personal nature of each testator's distribution of wealth among his heirs, at times favoring his children, at times ignoring them and focusing on grandchildren.

Juan Bautista's will is the final document in the 1748 corpus. Serendipitously, seventeen years later, in 1765, his grandson, Mateo Matu, composes a will that becomes the first in the 1760s collection. Mateo's will employs a variety of kinship terminology that obfuscates his family tree when viewed in isolation. Mateo references Juan Bautista Matu three times and employs a different kinship term each occasion. Juan Bautista appears as Mateo's *sucun*, a term that can mean both "older brother" and "grandfather on the father's side"; as *mam*, which can mean "grandfather on the mother's side" or any male relative through a woman; and as *yum*, meaning "father" or as a term of respect such as "lord." Mateo also mentions a joint inheritance he held with his older brother, Agustín.

Mateo's lineage is difficult to assess without the 1748 will of Juan Bautista, which references both Mateo as his grandchild and the joint inheritance given him, Agustín, and his other grandchildren. When viewed in context of Juan Bautista's

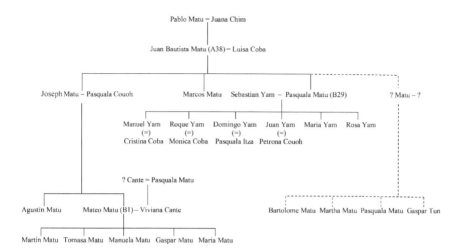

FIGURE 5.1. Genealogy of Pablo Matu and Juana Chim.

will, however, Mateo appears as the grandchild, now all grown up and with a family of his own.[10] The reason for the diversity in kinship terms is unclear but not unheard of. It is possible that the notary, Marcos Poot, was unclear of the particular relationship between Mateo and Juan Bautista, thus employing terms that place the latter as both Mateo's paternal and maternal grandfather. As stated, such errors are not unprecedented, and at times specific kinship definitions elided together. For example, the will of Gabriel Tec (B15) refers to both his paternal and maternal grandfathers as *mam*, and Diego Chan (B14) simply refers to his sons-in-law, Ignacio and Isidro Piste, as sons.

About a year and a half after Mateo's death, Juan Bautista's daughter Pasquala (B29) died, leaving a will that further clarified the blurred genealogical lines. She mentions the joint inheritance given her by her father, Juan Bautista, and even discloses the names of her two older brothers, Joseph and Marcos, and her mother, Luisa Coba. Pasquala's will received mention before for its impressive collection of forty items of cloth and clothing. Moreover, her wealth and noble position allowed her sons to marry into noble and wealthy *chibalob*—the Coba, Itza, and Couoh—a pattern in marriage to which we now turn.

MARRIAGE IN IXIL

A unique feature of the Ixil wills is that each testator named his parents in the preamble (wills from Tekanto, Ebtun, and Cacalchen mentioned the testator's parents only if they were recipients of bequeathed items). This allows for a clear view of marriage patterns in Ixil, which, upon examination, suggest the dominant role of the Pech *chibal*. As is common in most societies, nobility tend to marry nobility to strengthen social, economic, and political alliances. As mentioned, the Tec occupied second place in socioeconomic status. However, other *chibalob*, such as the Cante, Cime, Coba, Uetz, Yam, Tun, and Huchim, also held noble status. When marrying, the Pech chose from this pool of nobles.

Yet the Pech also chose from among their own ranks. Traditionally, scholars claimed that endogamy was a taboo practice among the Maya, largely due to Landa's assertion that "no man or woman marries another of the same name, because this was for them a great infamy."[11] More recently, Philip Thompson's study of Tekanto suggested a more nuanced interpretation. He suggested that "one could not marry members of one's immediate lineage but could marry members of other lineages of the same surname."[12] This is particularly the case when dealing with a large *chibal*, such as the Pech in Ixil. Restall also suggested that nobles were allowed some exception to the rule.[13] Both elements appear to have played a role in Ixil, and although the Pech married other noble *chibalob*—including the Yam, Cime, Coba, Uetz, and Cante—they also married other Pech.

For example, although Alonso Pech married Ursula Cime, their daughter, Viviana Pech (C1), married Agustín Pech.[14] This happened again with the parents of Phelipa Pech (A20), Francisco Pech and María Pech, and again with Martha Pech (A21), whose previous husband was from the Cime *chibal*, but her subsequent husband was Phelipe Pech. Martha's son, Marcos Cime, married Ysabel Pech in 1744; her parents were Francisco and Pasquala Pech.[15] If one were to draw conclusions from the testaments alone, it would seem that the Pech preferred to marry within their own *chibal* 33 percent of the time. The only other occurrence of intra-*chibal* marriage comes from the 1767 will of Lorensa Yam (B50), whose noble parents were Antonio Yam and Petrona Yam. Additional data from Ixil's baptismal records suggest the Pech's overwhelming tendency toward endogamous marriages and indicate that this tendency only increased over time.

Take, for example, Jose[f] Geronimo Pech, who married Ursula Pech on July 8, 1811, in Ixil. His parents were Diego Pech and Simona Poot, but his wife's parents were Mariano Pech and María Paulina Pech.[16] Or Mathias Pech, who married María Pech on January 30, 1714, in the presence of his parents, both of whom had the surname of Pech.[17] Or even María Guadalupe Pech, who was baptized in Ixil on December 26, 1785, and whose recorded parents were Esteban Pech and Francisca Pech, with paternal grandparents Domingo Pech and Ana María Pech.[18] After searching the records of other Yucatecan *cahob*, although endogamous unions between the Pech occasionally occurred, the numbers are nowhere near those seen in Ixil. And although other *chibalob* likewise participated in the practice at times, the frequency pales in comparison with that exhibited by the Pech.[19]

Clearly the Pech increasingly chose to marry other Pech, but why? Two possibilities are likely. Because Mayas seldom married outside their resident *cah*, the dominance of the Pech *chibal* of the Ceh Pech region would make intra-*chibal* marriage an increasing necessity, particularly in the small *cah* of Ixil, where the Pech abounded. The second is not exclusive of the first and would reflect the Pech struggle to maintain lineage landholdings and political dominance within Ixil.[20] As the native population of Yucatan began to rebound and as Spaniards increasingly encroached upon Maya towns, the demand on land increased. Thompson's study of Tekanto again provides an illustrative example. Here, by the mid-eighteenth century, increasing native populations, coupled with an increase in Spanish residents eager to acquire land, all placed pressure on noble landholdings.[21] Whereas Ixil did not have the same Spanish presence as Tekanto, the increasing indigenous population, particularly among other noble *chibalob*, surely pressured the Pech to maintain their dominance of the land and of the local *cabildo* and perhaps led to an increased inclination toward endogamy.[22]

Like that of today, Maya society included extramarital affairs, and the will of Pedro Mis (B30) allows for a small glimpse of one such instance. Pedro mentions his wife, Pasquala Coba, but appears to have no surviving children with her. However, he does bequeath property to a son, Joseph Pech, and to the boy's mother, Felipa Pech, both of whom he refers to as *tzenpal*, which carries the meaning of both "wet nurse" and "adopted child." In fact, it seems clear that Felipa is Pedro's mistress, or extramarital partner, and that Joseph is Felipa's son. Pedro's wife, Pasquala Coba, is still alive; yet Joseph has his mother's patronym. Interestingly, Pedro first describes Felipa as his *mekpal*, "infant," but the word is crossed out and replaced with *tzenpal*, which likewise means "infant" but also "adopted child"—all as though Pedro was searching for the term appropriate to the document (which may be read by the Spanish priest) but a term he would not normally use. This use of "adoption" to thinly veil extramarital relationships also occurred among the Nahuas of colonial central Mexico. After all, the wealthiest *chibal* in Ixil surely had no need of Pedro's supposed charity toward Felipa and her son.

As uncharitable as this may sound toward Pedro, his distribution of property in his will suggests that what he loved most about Felipa Pech was the fact that she had borne him a son (in contrast to his childless marriage). Felipa receives only shares of land in conjunction with her son and Pedro's wife. His wife, Pasquala, does much better, among other things inheriting a house with a house beam and a door (*puerta*) that locked (very rare in a colonial *cah*) and contains the only writing desk (*papirera, papelera*) in the Ixil wills. The son, Joseph, receives not only a house and forest land but also furniture, horses, and valuables such as a statue of San Diego—complete with tabernacle.

At the beginning of the chapter we viewed the strained, eighteenth-century relationship between a mother, Marta Mis, and her daughter, Agustina, to whom she would leave no inheritance. Nearly 250 years later the municipality of Ixil would spend a considerable amount of money and time to provide a startling contrast in maternal relations. Día de las Madres is a celebration akin to Mother's Day in the United States and is celebrated throughout Mexico every May 10; Ixil is no exception. In 2016 the center of town was replete with colorful decorations, lights, and a stage to host the large celebration to honor the town's mothers. Ixil's *alcalde*, Anastacio Córdova Chan, spoke to reporters and invited all mothers to enjoy the large dinner provided, music, performances, and raffle prizes. Chan, along with his wife, passed out free plastic washbowls to those mothers in attendance and then extended, "*de todo corazón*," best wishes to his own mother and wife. Grandmothers sat around tables with daughters who sat with their own children, creating living family trees.[23]

Not that continuities in the foundational nature of family life in Ixil mean that there are no differences between the eighteenth and twenty-first centuries or that change has maintained a steady pace in the town. Although some families remain rooted in Ixil, many children seek educational and employment opportunities elsewhere, particularly in Merida. As is common in many Mexican families, heirs to those owning local stores and businesses in Ixil will inherit the responsibility of their maintenance and continuation. For many others, however, and unlike their eighteenth-century predecessors, future wealth and future spouses await beyond the boundaries of the *cah*, and not from the bequeathed goods of their parents or the town's noble lineages.

NOTES

1. It is possible that Salvador had another daughter, Pasquala, as his father, Joseph, bequeathed items to her as his granddaughter.

2. FS-MY, "México matrimonios, 1570–1950, Lucas Cot and María Poot, 10 Nov 1765; Juan Chan and María Poot, 08 Apr 1769."

3. Restall (1995; 1997); Thompson (1999).

4. Burns (2001: xii, 1183).

5. CS-1722: 110.

6. Landa (1937: 40–41); see also Restall et al. (forthcoming).

7. For a more detailed discussion, see Restall (1997: 124–30).

8. For more on Maya patterns of inheritance, see Restall (1997: ch. 9); Thompson (1999: 94–124).

9. Maya men with sons usually either refer to a nephew with the same Maya term as that for son, *mehen*, or they fail to state the details of what to them (and no doubt to most of the community) was an obvious relationship.

10. Certainly, room for error persists, and the conclusions drawn, although the most likely, retain their malleability.

11. Landa (1937: 40); Restall et al. (forthcoming).

12. Thompson (1999: 210).

13. Restall (1997: 397n29).

14. The parents of Agustín were Antonio Pech and Christian Cutz.

15. FS-MY, "México matrimonios, 1570–1950," Marcos Cime and Ysabel Pech, 02 Feb 1744.

16. Ibid., Joseph Geronimo Pech and Ursula Pech, 08 Jul 1811.

17. Ibid., Mathias Pech and María Pech, 30 Jan 1714.

18. FS-MY, "México bautismos, 1560–1950," María Guadalupe Pech, 26 Dec 1785.

19. The ever-increasing access to marriage and death records will no doubt continually expand our understanding of intra-*chibal* marriage patterns.

20. The work of Paola Peniche Moreno also recognizes the Pech's practice of endogamy in Ixil and views this as a way to maintain material and social benefits. See Peniche Moreno (2007: 175–78).

21. Restall (1997: 220–25) also provides evidence from various *cahob* on the Spanish purchase of land from Maya nobles.

22. Portions of this and the preceding paragraphs in this section derive from Christensen (2015: 125–26).

23. Estilo Yucatán, "Festejo en Ixil Yucatán," May 27, 2016, https://www.youtube.com /watch?v=J94HodAzIvo.

Conclusion

In 2017, a Yucatecan vlogger (video blogger) visited Ixil to ask its residents what Ixil meant to them and what they thought about the idea to have small towns, such as Ixil, portray the town's name in giant letters to encourage tourism. Most agreed that large letters would encourage tourism in their town that, as one woman stated, remained unknown to most. Yet more interesting were the answers indicating what Ixil meant to them. Nearly all professed their pride in originating from Ixil and in living in a place that "continues traditions." Nearly all respondents associated the town with family. One woman said, "To me, Ixil means home, it's where my family is." And Felipe Tec declared that to him Ixil means "love, love for my family, love for my home, love for my homeland, love for being here, it means my family, my home, years of tradition, my culture, my people, my *cebollitas de Ixil*, of course!"[1]

As we have argued in the chapters above, and as is shown in the translated wills that follow, Maya life in eighteenth-century Yucatan was *family* life. The newly expanded corpus of wills from Ixil coupled with new sources from the archives allow us to paint a portrait of the Maya town with more vivid and vibrant shades of detail than ever before. And as we conclude our portrait and step back to observe the image, what stands out as the focal point and what ties everything together is the family unit.

This should not be overly surprising, after all. A town is nothing more than a macrocosm of myriad individual family units. Economic and material life, political machinations, and relations with the outside world were all anchored in family

DOI: 10.5876/9781607329220.c006

in Ixil, where the roots and bonds of *chibal* and *cah* intersected. A shared colonial experience, lineage and economic ties, and religious obligations served to unite the individual family units into Ixil's community.

As in times past, notaries derived from elite families within the town and received their training from such. Their service to both the community and Ixil's individuals made valid the corporate and religious standing of the town and its residents through documentation. Indeed, the notaries played an important and unparalleled role in ensuring that Ixil and its family units—outlined painstakingly in the preamble of each will—survived in historical memory. Those that took up arms in defense of Ixil and Yucatan and who served in the town government did so for the safety and benefit of the town and its families—including their own—and a desire to see their family patronym, their *chibal*, continue in its position of authority as it had for centuries prior. Such concerns likewise included economic prosperity. The Maya certainly had financial responsibilities to the Spanish colonial system, but what seemed to concern them most as they compiled their wills was the proper distribution of their material goods among family members. Even religion, which can be very individualistic in nature, became familial to the Maya of Ixil as they married into specific lineages, even their own; preserved local religious texts; and passed along to family members whatever simple religious objects they possessed. On more than one occasion, family members of the deceased became entrusted with ensuring the payment for requested masses and burials—the family would help to ensure salvation. Finally, in many ways the families in Ixil mirror our own in their personal and gendered preferences for inheritance; their close-knit family relations; and even their family feuds.

Yet the archival sources on Ixil—especially the expanded corpus of wills presented in this book—do more for us than permit the reconstruction of a small town's social history; they also help locate that town within the larger context of colonial Yucatan. As a result, our understanding of how indigenous peoples lived under Spanish rule, while at the same time governing themselves in their various towns, has expanded, allowing for comparative analyses. So too has our view of the larger picture of colonial Maya society sharpened. Actions once determined to be universal among all Maya towns can now been seen as local, and vice versa; details have emerged on how religious, political, and economic norms for the colony played out in individual towns; and the impact that both Maya and Spaniard had on the other's colonial experience has become clearer. Eighteenth-century Ixil allows us to better comprehend how Mayas and Spaniards jointly ran a colonial machine with political, economic, religious, and defensive cogs, each one helping to turn the other and keep the mechanism operating in both local and regional spheres.

Ironically, those cogs and spheres often turned and were operated without much thought given to the other, or to the larger machine of which they were part. Consider our own lives. Local concerns and priorities within the community and family absorb much of our daily thought and priorities, and little attention is paid to the role of our actions in shaping a larger environment. This certainly was the case in Ixil. The wills and records of Ixil's Mayas all betray a concern for the local and the family, without giving much concern for the broader Spanish colonial world in which they lived. Indeed, the penning of wills, marriages, religious funerals and masses, bequests, even the formation of militias, relate to the benefit of the family and the town, not the Spanish colonial system. Yucatec Maya largely continued to be the language in which Ixil kept its records, primarily because its world was simply that—Maya. Of course, Ixil was not ignorant of its colonial status, nor did it resist those aspects of Spanish life seen as beneficial. Yet then, as even now, Ixil's priority was its own citizens, its own families, those that continued to call it home.

NOTE

1. Gilmereb, "En Ixil la gente construy sus Letras Turísticas," September 15, 2017, https://www.youtube.com/watch?v=LOWSiAauNKE.

Appendix A

List of the Ixil Testaments, by Date, 1738–79

Doc.	Testator	Testament Date	Death Record Date	Testament Status
A1	Ignacio Pech	01-08-1748		
A2	Bernardina Cante (statement)	04-22-1755		
A3	Mateo Coba (statement)	10-19-1760		
A4	Lorensa Pech (statement)	10-21-1760		
A5	Mateo Coba (statement)	10-21-1760		
A6	Pasgual Coba	01-15-1748		
A7	Francisco Itza	01-20-1748		
A8	Micaela Cab	01-20-1748		
A9	Miguel Tun	01-20-1748		
A10	Diego Euan	01-27-1748		
A11	Lorensa Ek	02-16-1748		
A12	Bernardo Chan	03-06-1748		
A13	Pasquala Itza	03-20-1748		
A14	Nicolasa Yam	03-20-1748		
A15	Cristina Can	03-20-1748		
A16	Lorensa Coba	03-20-1748		

DOI: 10.5876/9781607329220.c007

Doc.	Testator	Testament Date	Death Record Date	Testament Status
A17	Martha Itza	04-05-1748		
A18	Juan Cante	04-05-1748		
A19	Bernardina Tec	04-05-1748		
A20	Phelipa Pech	04-05-1748		
A21	Martha Pech	04-17-1748		
A22	Pasguala Mitz	04-17-1748		
A23	Felipe Tec	05-18-1748		
A24	Diego Tec	05-18-1748		
A25	Martha Canul	05-18-1748		
A26	Felipe Tec	07-05-1748		
A27	Joseph Chale	08-04-1748		
A28	Marcos Huchim	08-04-1748		
A29	Diego Cetz	08-04-1748		
A30	Felipe Chim	08-14-1748		
A31	María Candelaria Cante	08-19-1748		
A32	Manuel Coba	10-04-1748		
A33	Ignacio Tec	10-23-1748		
A34	María Tec	11-14-1748		
A35	Anna Itza	11-14-1748		
A36	Mathias Cob	12-02-1748		
A37	Pasgual Canche	12-02-1748		
A38	Juan Bautista Matu	12-02-1748		
B1	Mateo Matu	[1765]		
B2	Antonia Cante	[1765]		
B3	Manuel Cob	[1765]	11-19-1765	T
B4	Pedro Couoh	11-28-1765	11-29-1765	T
B5	Andrés Coba	[1765]		
B6	Gregorio Canche	01-12-1766		
B7	Ignacio Canul	01-03-1766		
B8	Joseph Uitz	10-15-1765		
B9	Antonia Coba	01-10-1766	01-04-1766	I
B10	Felipe Coba	01-12-1766	01-10-1766	T

Doc.	Testator	Testament Date	Death Record Date	Testament Status
B11	Pedro Matu	01-26-1766	01-27-1766	I
B12	María Canche	01-28-1766	01-09-1766	T
B13	Petrona Na	02-12-1766	02-08-1766	?
B14	Diego Chan	01-24-1766	01-25-1766	T
B15	Gabriel Tec	01-30-1766		
B16	Joseph Couoh	01-05-1766	01-03-1766	I
B17	Geronimo Tec	02-15-1766	02-07-1766	I
B18	Bernardina Couoh	03-05-1766	03-13-1766	?
B19	Gaspar Poot	03-10-1766	02-21-1766	T
B20	Nicolasa Tec	03-28-1766	03-02-1766	T
B21	Simón Chan	04-04-1766	04-04-1766	T
B22	Ventura Yam	04-04-1766	04-05-1766	I
B23	Viviana Canche	04-28-1766	04–2?-1766	T
B24	Bernardino Coot	04-29-1766	04-27-1766	T
B25	Bernardino Coba	05-02-1766	04-27-1766	T
B26	María Chan	05-07-1766	05-02-1766	T
B27	Juan Tacu	07-20-1766	07-19-1766	T
B28	Juan de la Cruz Poot	06-15-1766	05-11-1766	I
B29	Pasquala Matu	08-25-1766	?-?- 1766	T
B30	Pedro Mis	08-17-1766		
B31	Martha Coba	08-06-1766	08-02-1766	—
B32	Joseph Poot	09-17-1766		
B33	Joseph Yam	11-20-1766		
B34	Martha Chan	11-08-1766	11-05-1766	T
B35	Francisco Couoh	12-23-1766	11-?8–1766	?
B36	Juan de la Cruz Coba	11-12-1766		
B37	Antonio Huchim	12-20-1766	12-21-1766	T
B38	Martha Coba	12-03-1766	12-?-1766	T
B39	Diego Coba	01-14-1767	01-13-1767	I
B40	Sebastián Uh	01-10-1767	01-04-1767	T
B41	Mateo Canche	11-26-1766	11-16-1766	T
B42	Pasqual Huchim	02-11-1767	03-01-1767	T
B43	Diego Canul	02-30-1767	03-07-1767	T
B44	Pasquala Balam	05-05-1767	05-06-1767	I
B45	(settling of Joseph Cab's estate)	05-30-1767		

Doc.	Testator	Testament Date	Death Record Date	Testament Status
B46	Tomasa Tec	06-09-1767	06-09-1767	I
B47	Juana Mo	06-09-1767	06-09-1767	—
B48	Juana Tun	06–1..-1767		
B49	Salvador Poot	06-24-1767	06-24-1767	?
B50	Lorensa Yam	07-18-1767	07-07-1767	I
B51	Pasquala Tec	07-18-1767	07-09-1767	I
B52	Micaela Tec	08-09-1767	08-06-1767	I
B53	Pasqual Coba	09-20-1767	09-20-1767	T
B54	(settling of Pasqual Ku's estate)	10-08-1767	10-07-1767	I
B55	Antonia Coba	10-21-1767	10-27-1767	T
B56	Luisa Tec	11-02-1767	11-03-1767	I
B57	Pedro Huchim	11-20-1767	11-05-1767	I
B58	Antonio Coba	11-11-1767		
B59	Monica Na	12–04-[1767]	12-02-1767	I
B60	Nicolás Chan	n.d.	11-30-1767	
B61	Jacinto Poot	12-14-1767		
B62	Lorensa Canul	12-27-1767	12-19-1767	I
B63	Ignacia Coba	01-08-176[8]	01-?-1768,	I
B64	Mateo Yam	11-15-1767	11-18-1767	—
B65	Luisa Couoh	01-13-1768	01-12-1768	T
C1	Viviana Pech	07-04-1738		
C2	Marta Mis	10-14-1769	10-14-1769	
C3	Don Pedro Pech	05-25-1779	06-02-1779	

Note: Testament dates are from the wills themselves. Death records could not be found for any pre-1765 testator. Testament status is taken from the death records. The letter T (= testate) represents those whose death record states that they died with a testament; the letter I (= intestate) denotes those who died without a testament, according to the death records. As discussed above, those notations were not always correct. At times, the death record remained silent regarding the matter, marked in this table with a dash (—) or was illegible, marked with a question mark (?).

Sources: Death records are taken from FS-MY, "registros parroquiales y diocesanos, 1543–1977," Conkal, San Francisco de Asís, Defunciones 1682–1802, images 219-268. The Christensen (A) corpus originals are in AHAY, "Oficios, 1748–1749, 1801–1884," vol. 1; those in the Restall (B) corpus are in CAIHY (see Restall 1995). The individual wills in the C corpus are in ANEY, 1819iv, fols. 19r, 19v, and 37r (now in AGEY).

Appendix B

The Testaments of Ixil

In our transcriptions of the wills, we have tried to retain the original orthography as much as possible, including such details as capitalization, word breaks (although Maya notaries were inconsistent in that regard), and paragraph breaks. Thus, dashes and equal signs follow the original. Where words or letters are lost—mostly at the end of a line, where the paper frayed—we have added the missing letters in brackets where their identity seemed clear or added ellipses in brackets where it was not clear. Because Maya notaries spelled Christian names inconsistently, we have styled names in our translations with the usage most common among notaries—both Maya and Spanish—in eighteenth-century Yucatan. We have left the inconsistent spellings of Christian names in the transcriptions without the clutter of "*sic*" clarifications.

FOLS. 1R–1V DOCUMENT A1[1]

WILL OF IGNACIO PECH
8 JANUARY 1748

YGNASIO PECH CIMI EN 8 DE ENERO DE 1748 AÑOS

tu Kaba dios yumbil y dios mehenbil y dios espiritu santo oxtul personas huntulili dios uchuc tumen tusinil maix pimobi lai bin ylabac u hunil yn tokyahthan tin testamento hibicil tenil Cen ygnasio pech u mehen pedro pech u yalen lorsensa yam u Bacacix cimil yn Cah toh uol tin pucsikal y tin nat uet sihcie Baixan olah mucul in cucutil ychil y othoch ca Kuna lae = Baixan cin uoktic ynbah ca pixanil yum padre

DOI: 10.5876/9781607329220.c008

guardian ca yalab hunpeɔ missa yokol in pixan ca antabac tu numyail anima purgatorio y̰ ca u masen tu payalchi ychil u missa lae Baixan bin ɔabae u limosnayl oxpel
tostones y̰ Capel tumin helulalem lai

Bayxan hunpok macho y̰ hunpok yeua tzimin y̰ hunpel u hol Na y̰ hunpay caha
y̰ hunɔit cuchara takin y̰ hunpay silla kanche licil cutal y̰ hunpel camisa hunpel ex
hunpay kaxnak hunpel panio y̰ hunpel u silla bim Cin ɔaic tin mehen Sar^{or} pech
Bayxan hunɔit ɔoon cin ɔaic tin mehen Sar^{or} pech y̰ pasgual pech Ca nupobi lae
Baixan hunpok mula y̰ oxtul capon tzimin y̰ catul yeua tzimin y̰ Capel u hol Na y̰
Ca ɔit cuchara taKin u frata y̰ Capel silla kanche licil cutal y̰ capel camisa y̰ capel ex y̰
capel kaxnak y̰ capel panyo y̰ capel tzotz Cin patic tin u atan Ber^{na} cante ca u thoxe tin
mehenob pasgual pech pedro pech lae Bayxan hunɔit ɔoon cin ɔaic tin mehen pedro
pech Bayxan hunpel cħeen y̰ u solalil u pach cin ɔaic tin mehenob y̰ ti yxmehen Sar^{or}
pech pasg^{l} pech pedro pech lorensa pech Can nupobi lae Bayxan hunpet Kax Cin
ɔaic tin mehenob Sarua^{or} pech pasgual pech pedro pech y̰ lorensa pech Can napobi
lae u tzayal lai Kax ti lakin D^{n} Joseph pech ti xaman man^{i} Juchim ti chikin Joseph
yam ti nohol Miguel tun lae—

Bayxan hunpok yeua tzimin y̰ hunpay caha y̰ hunɔit cuchara takin Cin ɔaic ti
yxmehen—lorensa pech lae Baixan hunpel cħeen y̰ u solil u pach y̰ hunpet Kax yan
bolon cħob u tzayal ti lakin clemente cime ti xaman Diego pech ti chikin mechor
canche = ti nohol xp. toba tec—y̰ hunpet u lak kax yan Nac ac u tzayal ti lakin u
Kax Cah ti xaman pedro pech ti chikin D.^{n} Ju.^{o} pech ti nohol pedro pech cin ɔaic tin
mehenob saruador pech pasgual pech pedro pech y̰ tin u ɔinob Damian pech Jasinto
pech lae ca nupobi lae—halil u xul in tohyahthan tin testamento lae lic yn uacuntil
catul al mehenob albaseasob lae mathe.^{o} tec y̰ mathe.^{o} Na—

ygnasio coba the^{e}	D.^{n} gaspar canul	gaspar tun
Bar.^{me} pech ald^{e}	Batab	Diego mitz
Sebastian uh ald^{e}	Sarua^{or} Coba ess^{no}	an.^{tto} Juchim
		Sebastian yam
		Regidoresob

Cumpliose este testamento y se le canto una missa que pidió y lo firme
   fr. Diego Perez Arrias

IGNACIO PECH DIED JANUARY 8, 1748

In the name of God the Father, and God the Son, and God the Holy Spirit, three persons, one almighty God, not many. This document of my final words in my testament
will be seen, insomuch as I who am Ignacio Pech, the son of Pedro Pech, the child of
Lorensa Yam. Although I am dying, my heart and my understanding are sound, as
it should be. Likewise, I wish my body to be buried inside the home of our temple.
Likewise, I supplicate our blessed lord, the guardian priest, that one mass for my soul
be said to help the suffering purgatory soul, and that he say a prayer for me in that
mass. Likewise, it will be given in alms three tostons and two tomins for Jerusalem.

Likewise, a male mule, a mare, a house beam,[2] a chest, a metal spoon, a wooden chair from this time on, a shirt, a pair of trousers, a sash, a length of cloth, and a chair I give to my son Salvador Pech. Likewise, one shotgun I give my son Salvador Pech and Pasgual Pech, both of them together. Likewise, a female mule, three geldings, two mares, two house beams, two silver spoons, two wooden chairs from this time on, two shirts, two pairs of trousers, two sashes, two lengths of cloth, and two fur blankets I leave to my wife Bernardina Cante to distribute to my sons Pasgual Pech, Pedro Pech. Likewise, a shotgun I give to my son Pedro Pech. Likewise, one well together with its house plot I give to my sons and daughter Salvador Pech, Pasgual Pech, Pedro Pech, Lorensa Pech, the four of them together. Likewise, one forest I give to my sons Salvador Pech, Pasgual Pech, Pedro Pech, and Lorensa Pech, the four of them together. Adjacent to the forest to the east is don Joseph Pech, to the north Manuel Juchim, to the west Joseph Yam, to the south Miguel Tun. Likewise, one mare, a chest, and a metal spoon I give to my daughter Lorensa Pech. Likewise, one well together with its house plot, and a forest where there are many holes; adjacent to the east is Clemente Cime, to the north Diego Pech, to the west Mechor Canche, to the south Cristóbal Tec; and one other forest next to the willow tree adjacent to the east is the cah forest, to the north Pedro Pech, to the west don Juan Pech, to the south Pedro Pech I give to my sons Salvador Pech, Pasgual Pech, Pedro Pech, and to my grandchildren Damian Pech, Jacinto Pech, the two of them together. That is all; this is the end of my words in my testament. I appoint two noblemen as executors, Mateo Tec and Mateo Na.

Ignacio Coba, lieutenant	don Gaspar Canul	Gaspar Tun
Bartolomé Pech, alcalde	batab	Diego Mitz
Sebastián Uh, alcalde	Salvador Coba, notary	Antonio Huchim
		Sebastián Yam
		Regidors

This testament was fulfilled and a mass was sung for him as he requested, and I signed it

fray Diego Pérez Arrias

FOL. 2R DOCUMENT A2

STATEMENT

22 APRIL 1755

TESTAMENTO THAN LAE HELE EN = 22 DE ABLIL DE 1755

Ten cen Ber.^{na} cante cin ceemsic yn yum batab y yn yum Jus^{as} y Regidolesob lae y ess^{no} y Ca yum D.ⁿ Juan pech Cappⁿ lae bay biguili tu yarmahthan yn uicham ychirla testameto lae lay tumen cin thoxic u barl u baob lae =

Ten cen pasguar pech tin Kamah Capok mulas tu kab yn Na lae y hunpay Sia Kanche lae licil cutar lae y hunper u hor Na lae y huper Cuchala taKin lae y hunpay

caha lae y canpis yxim lae y hunper olpa lae = Bayxan lae hunper camissa y ex y kaxnaK
y panio lae Cin Kubic tin u ar lae = u matanob lae u kas cen yokor cabob lae =

Ten cen po pech tin Kamah ca poK mulas tutukab yn Na lae y hunpay sia kanche
lae liguil cutar lae y huperl uhor Na lae y hunpay Caha lae y hunper Cuchala taKin lae
y canpis yxim lae Bayxan Cin Kubic hunper Camissa y ex y KaxNa y panio utial yn u
ar pedro pech lae u Kas cen yoKor cabob lae - - -

bayxan hunper macho y hun ɔit ɔoon lae cu cu tar tin kab uchic u ɔocor yn thox-
tiob lae halilibe ten Ber.^{na} cante lae - - -

ygnasio Coba then^e	Juan Pech in	An^{tto} Juchim Bonifa.^{o} Cob
Sebas.^{n} couoh alcar^s	D.^{n} p.^{o} pech Batab	pasg.^{l} Coba pasguar pech
Sarua.^{or} coba alcar^s	marcos poot ess^{no}	
		Regidoresob lae

tutanil ca yum capp^n Dn Juan pech lae

TESTAMENT OF TODAY, THE 22ND OF APRIL, 1755

I who am Bernardina Cante bow down before my lord batab and my lord magistrates
and regidors and notary and our lord captain don Juan Pech. It is according to the
legal terms of this my husband's testament through which I distribute his household
goods.

I who am Pasgual Pech received two female mules from the hands of my mother
and one wooden chair that is here now and one house beam and one metal spoon
and one chest and two measures of corn and one similar to it. Likewise, one shirt and
trousers and sash and length of cloth that I deliver to my child; they are receiving a
little while I am on this earth.

I who am Pedro Pech received two female mules from the hands of my mother and
one wooden chair that is here now and one house beam and one chest and one metal
spoon and two measures of corn. Likewise, I deliver one shirt and trousers and sash
and length of cloth to my child Pedro Pech, a little of it while I am on this earth.

Likewise, one male mule and one shotgun that comes to my hands; they were
already distributed to me before; this is the truth. I, Bernardina Cante.

Ignacio Coba, lieutenant	I am Juan Pech	
Sebastián Couoh, alcalde	don Pedro Pech, batab	Antonio Huchim, Bonifacio Cob
Salvador Coba, alcalde	Marcos Poot, notary	Pasgual Coba, Pasgual Pech
		Regidors

Before our lord, captain don Juan Pech

FOL. 3R DOCUMENT A3

STATEMENT

19 OCTOBER 1760

ten cen mathe° coba chicanpahen tu tanil in yum Batab y̱ Justisiasob y̱ Regidoresob
y̱ ess^{no} utial in ɔab in hahal than Bicil minan in than yoklal lay solalob y̱ u chenillob
lae chenbel halili chen cu bin u ɔab u taKinilob ca holoc ten lae catun cu lac yetellob
lae heix uac in sutup tu pach in thane catun in kam u tzecul lay tumen chican pahen
tutanil in yum Batab y̱ Jus^{as} y̱ Regidoresob y̱ ess.^{no} lae utial in ɔab u hahil in than Bicil
cu ɔaic lay u parte takin in Naob lorensa pech y̱ pasq^{la} yam utial holbal in chen lae lay
u hahil licil in ɔaic in firma yalan Cabal hele en 19 de oc.^{re} de 1760 a^{s}

Sebas^n yam th^e	Cap^n D^n ygo tec	mathias ake
ygo coba agus^n cante	Batab	Gaspar coba
alcardes	Jph Cob ess^{no}	fran^{co} pech Jasinto pech
		Regidoresob

I who am Mateo Coba appear before my lord batab, and magistrates, and regidors
and the notary in order to give my true statement; which is that I have nothing to
say about those house plots and wells. There is simply no more about the well other
than the money was given for it to be dug for me. Then, with the others, there were
six all together that I turned to in my statement. Then I received a reprimand when I
appeared before my lord the batab and magistrates and regidors and notary in order
that I give my true statement; which is that my mothers Lorensa Pech and Pasquala
Yam gave part of the money for the digging of my well there. This is the truth; now I
give my signature below today the 19th of October of the year 1760.

Sebastián Yam, lieutenant	Captain don Ignacio Tec	Mathias Ake
Ignacio Coba, Agustín Cante	batab	Gaspar Coba
Alcaldes	Joseph Cob, notary	Francisco Pech, Jacinto Pech
		Regidors

FOL. 3V DOCUMENT A4

STATEMENT

21 OCTOBER 1760

ten cen lorensa pech cin ɔaic u hahil in than Bicil cin ɔaic huncul in pakal chacar haz
ti in u al mathe° coba yoklal u hanlil lay u chenil cubin potbil lae Bay u chic in u alic
tutanil in yum Batab y̱ Jusasob y̱ Regidoresob y̱ ess^{no} uay ti audenzia lae = lay u hahil
in firma cabal hele en 21 de oc.^{re} de 1760 anōs

Sebas^n yam th^e	d ygo tec	mathias ake
ygo coba agus^n cante	Batab	gaspar Coba

alcardesob   fran^co pech Jasinto
                                                        pech Regidoresob

tin tanil cen Jph Cob ess^no

I who am Lorensa Pech give my true statement; which is that I give one red sapote
orchard of mine to my son Mateo Coba; it will be for its sustenance, when the well is
drilled there. I am explaining this before my lord the batab and magistrates and regidors and notary here in the courthouse. This is the truth; my signature below, today,
the 21st of October of the year 1760.

Sebastián Yam, lieutenant   don Ignacio Tec   Mathias Ake

Ignacio Coba, Augustine Cante   batab   Gaspar Coba

Alcaldes   Francisco Pech, Jasinto Pech
                                                     Regidors

Before me, Joseph Cob, notary

FOL. 3V DOCUMENT A5

STATEMENT

21 OCTOBER 1760

ten cen mathe° coba cin kamic oxpel peso catac hunpel toston y huncul chacar haz
utial u hanlil lai chen cahil chahal ten lae tu kal in Naob lorensa pech y pasquala yam
minan tin than yetelob lae lay tumen cin ɔaic u hahil tutan ca yum Batab y Jus^asob y
Regidoresob y ess^no uay ti audensia lae lay u hahil in firma cabal hele en 21 de oc^re de
1760

sebas^n yam th^e   D^n ygo tec   mathias ake

ygo coba agus^n cante   Batab   gaspar coba fran^co

alcardesob lae   Jph Cob ess^no   pech Jasinto pech
                                                         Regidoresob

I who am Mateo Coba, I receive three pesos plus one toston, and one red sapote
[orchard], for its sustenance, this well is being cut for me. This closes things with my
mothers, Lorensa Pech and Pasquala Yam. I have nothing more to say to them about
this, for I give the truth before our lord batab and magistrates and notary here in the
courthouse. This is the truth; my signature below, today, the 21st of October of 1760

Sebastián Yam, lieutenant   don Ignacio Tec   Mathias Ake

Ignacio Coba, Augustine Cante   batab   Gaspar Coba, Francisco Pech

Alcaldes   Joseph Cob, notary Jacinto Pech
                                                       Regidors

FOL. 4R DOCUMENT A6

WILL OF PASGUAL COBA

15 JANUARY 1748

PASGUAL COBA CIMI EN 15 DE ENERO DE 1748 ANŌS

Tu kaba Dios yumbil y Dios mehenbil y Dios espiritu Santo oxtul personas huntul Dios uchuc tumen tusinil maix pimobi lay bin ylaba u hunil yn takyahthan tin testamento hibicil tenil cen pasqual Coba u mehen Alonso coba u yalen Ber^na tec lae bacacix cimil yn cah lae toh uol tin pucsikal y ti nat uet sihcie = Bayxan u olah mucul in cucutil ychil y otoch ca kuna lae Bayxan cin u oktic ynba ti ca pixanil yum padre guardian ca yalab hunper missa yokol yn pixan ca antabac tu numiayl anima purgatorio y ca u masen tu payal [chi] ychil u missa lae Bayxan bin ɔabae u limosnayl oxpel tostones y capell tumin helusalem lae

Bayxan Capel cheen y u solalil u pach y hunpet kax in mul matuh ma y yn sucunob lae tin yā cin patic ti mehenob matheº coba = phelipe coba = mathia cob = maria coba can nupobi lae Bayxan hunpel solal manan cheenil lae cu yalic yn sucunob Bicil bin u holoba u chenil ca ukubeob tin mehenob ca mananai u thanob yokol lay Capel cheen lai in mehenob y yxmehen lae halil in than tin testamento minan u bal inba lae cin uacuntic huntul almehen matheo tec albaseas

ygnasio Cob[a] the^e	D.^n gaspar canul	gapar tun
Bar.^me pech ald^e	Batab	Diego mitz
Sebastian uh ald^e	Saruador Coba ess^no	antº Juchim
		Sebastian yam
		Regidoresob

Cumpliose este testamento y se le canto una missa que pidió y lo firme
    fr. Diego Perez Arrias

PASGUAL COBA DIED ON THE 15TH OF JANUARY, 1748

In the name of God the Father, and God the Son, and God the Holy Spirit, three persons, one almighty God, not many. This document of my final words in my testament will be seen, insomuch as I who am Pasgual Coba, the son of Alonso Coba, the child of Bernardina Tec. Although I am dying, my heart and my understanding are sound, as it should be. Likewise, I wish my body to be buried inside the home of our, temple. Likewise, I supplicate our blessed lord, the guardian priest, that one mass for my soul be said to help the suffering purgatory soul, and that he say a prayer for me in that mass. Likewise, it will be given in alms three tostons and two tomins for Jerusalem.

Likewise, two wells, together with their house plot, and one forest I received them together with my older brothers; what is mine I deliver to my sons Mateo Coba, Felipe Coba, Matias Coba, María Coba, the four of them together. Likewise, one house plot that has no well; my older brothers say that a well will be drilled and they will deliver it to my sons; they have no more to say about it; those two wells [are] for my sons and daughter. There is no more to my words in my testament about my household goods. I appoint one nobleman Mateo Tec as executor.

Ignacio Coba, lieutenant	don Gaspar Canul	Gaspar Tun
Bartolomé Pech, alcalde	batab	Diego Mitz
Sebastián Uh, alcalde	Salvador Coba, notary	Antonio Huchim
		Sebastián Yam
		Regidors

This testament was fulfilled and a mass was sung for him as requested, and I signed it
　fray Diego Pérez Arrias

FOLS. 4V–5R DOCUMENT A7

WILL OF FRANCISCO ITZA
20 JANUARY 1748

FRANCO YTZA CIMI EN 20 DE ENERO DE 1748 ANŌS

Tu kaba dios yumbil y Dios mehenbil y dios espiritu santo oxtul personas huntulili Dios uchuc tumen tu sinil maix pimobi lay bin ylabac u hunil yn tokyahthan tin testament[to] hibicil tenil cen fran^{co} ytza u mehen mathe^o ytza yalen mag.^{na} pech lae Bacacix cimil yn cah lae toh uol tin pucsikal y tin nat uet sihcie Bayxan u olah mucul yn cucutil ychil y othoch ca kuna lae Baixan cin u oktic ynba ti ca pixanil yum padre guar^a ca yalab hunpe ɔ missa yokol yn pixan ca antabac tu numyail anima purgatorio y ca u masen tu payalchi ychil u missa lae Baixan bin ɔabae u limosnayl oxpel tostones y capel tumin helusalem lae

　Bayxan hunpel cheen y u solalil u pach cin ɔaic ti y yxmehenob Martha ytza Bar.^{na} ytza Ber.^{na} ytza Dominga ytza Bibiana ytza y cic Anna ytza uac nulobi lae Baixan hunpet kax yan tzuc ya cin ɔaic ti yxmehenob Martha ytza Bar.^{na} ytza Ber.^{na} ytza cic anna ytza y clemente canche yxpl Juc^{h}im Juan pech u tzayal lai kax ti lakin fran^{co} cante ti xaman lae ygnasio ba ti chikin merchor pech ti nohol diego pech Baixan hunpet kax cin ɔaic ti yxmehenob Martha ytza Bar.^{na} ytza Ber.^{na} ytza y cic anna ytza y clete canche xpl Juc^{h}im Juan pech u tzayal lai kax ti lakin agustin ake ti xaman Pablo couoh ti chikin clemente cime ti nohol pasgual pech Bayxan hun kax yan tun utial Martha ytza Bar.^{na} ytza Ber.^{na} ytza anna ytza Juan pech clemente canche xpl Juc^{h}im u tzayal lai kax lae ti lakin mathe^o tec ti xamā Ber.^{na} cob ti chikin marcos batz ti nohol micolas [. . .] halil u xul in than tin testamento

ygnasio Coba the^e	D.^{n} gaspar canul	gaspar tun
Bar.^{me} pech ald^e	Batab	Diego Mitz
Sebastian uh ald^e	Saruador Coba ess^{no}	an.^{tto} Juc^{h}im

Sebastian yam

Regidoresob

Cumpliose este testamento y se le canto una missa que pidió y lo firme
  fr Diego Perez Arrias

FRANCISCO ITZA DIED ON THE 20TH OF JANUARY, 1748

In the name of God the Father, and God the Son, and God the Holy Spirit, three
persons, one almighty God, not many. This document of my final words in my testament will be seen, insomuch as I who am Francisco Itza, the son of Mateo Itza, child
of Magdalena Pech. Although I am dying, my heart and my understanding are sound,
as it should be. Likewise, I wish my body to be buried inside the home of our temple.
Likewise, I supplicate our blessed lord, the guardian priest, that one mass for my soul
be said to help the suffering purgatory soul, and that he say a prayer for me in that
mass. Likewise, it will be given in alms three tostons and two tomins for Jerusalem.

Likewise, one well together with its house plot I will give my daughters Martha
Itza, Bartolina Itza, Bernardina Itza, Dominga Itza, Viviana Itza, and the older sister
Anna Itza, the six of them together. Likewise, there is one forest, where there is a
small hill of sapotes, that I give my daughters Martha Itza, Bartolina Itza, Bernardina
Itza, the older sister Anna Itza, and Clemente Canche, and Cristóbal Juchim, Juan
Pech; adjacent to this forest to the east is Francisco Cante, to its north Ignacio Ba, to
the west Melchor Pech, to the south Diego Pech. Likewise, I give one forest to my
daughters Martha Itza, Bartolina Itza, Bernardina Itza, and the older sister Anna Itza
and Clemente Canche Cristóbal Juchim, Juan Pech; adjacent to this forest, to the
east is Agustín Ake, to the north Pablo Couoh, to the west Clemente Cime, to the
south of Pasqual Pech. Likewise, there is one forest to go to Martha Itza, Bartolina
Itza, Bernardina Itza, Anna Itza Juan Pech, Clemente Canche, Cristóbal Juchim;
adjacent to this forest there is to the east Mateo Tec, to the north Bernardina Cob, to
the west Marcos Batz, to the south Nicolás [. . .]. This is no more; this the end of my
words in my testament

Ignacio Coba, lieutenant	don Gaspar Canul	Gaspar Tun
Bartolomé Pech, alcalde	batab	Diego Mitz
Sebastián Uh, alcalde	Salvador Coba, notary	Antonio Huchim
		Sebastián Yam
		Regidors

This testament was fulfilled and a mass was sung for him as requested, and I signed it
fray Diego Pérez Arrias

FOL. 5V DOCUMENT A8

WILL OF MICAELA CAB

20 JANUARY 1748

MICAELA CAB CIMI EN 20 DE ENERO DE 1748 AÑOS

Tu kaba dios yumbil y dios mehenbil y Dios espiritu santo oxtul personas huntulili Dios uchuc tumen tusinil maix pimobi lay bin ylabac u hunil yn takyahthan tin testamento hibicil tenil cen micaela cab u yxmehen gaspar cab u yalen christina coba lae bacacix cimil yn cah lae toh uol tin pucsikal y tin nat uet sihcie Bayxan u olah mucul yn cucutil ychil y otoch ca kuna lae Baixan cin u oktic ynba ti ca pixanil yum padre guardian ca yalab hunper missa yokol in pixan ca antabac tu numyail anima purgatorio y ca u masen tu payalchi ychil u missa lae Baixan bin ɔabae u limosnayl oxpel tostones y capel tumin helusalem lae

Baixan hunpel pic y hunpel ypil y hunpel tup y hunpay u y capel sor ti hatz y hunpel boch cin ɔaic tin u al pasg.ᵗᵃ uh Baixan hunpel pic y hunpel ypil y capel sor ti hatz cin ɔaic tin u al lorensa uh Baixan hunpel pic cin ɔaic tin u ilib lorensa canul Baixan hunpay u colaris cin ɔaic tin u alob matheo uh martin uh lorensa uh ox nupobi lae Baixan hunpay u y hunpay sinta cin ɔaic tin u i ɔin luissa Canul lae halil u xul in than tin testamento lae cin uacuntic huntul almehen agustin yam albaseas

ygnasio coba theᵉ	D.ⁿ gaspar canul	gaspar tun
Bar.ᵐᵉ pech	Batab	diego mitz
Sebastian uh	Saruador Coba essⁿᵒ	Anᵗᵗᵒ Juchim
alcardesob		Sebastian yam
		Regidoresob

Cumpiose este testamento y se le canto una missa que pidió y lo firme
  fr. Diego Perez Arriz

MICAELA CAB DIED ON THE 20TH OF JANUARY, 1748

In the name of God the Father, and God the Son, and God the Holy Spirit, three persons, one almighty God, not many. This document of my final words in my testament will be seen, insomuch as I who am Micaela Cab, the daughter of Gaspar Cab, the child of Cristina Coba.

Although I am dying, my heart and my understanding are sound, as it should be. Likewise, I wish my body to be buried inside the home of our temple. Likewise, I supplicate our blessed lord, the guardian priest, that one mass for my soul be said to help the suffering purgatory soul, and that he say a prayer for me in that mass. Likewise, it will be given in alms three tostons and two tomins for Jerusalem.

Likewise, one petticoat and one huipil and one bracelet and one beaded necklace and two banana plots and one shawl I give to my child Pasquala Uh. Likewise, one petticoat and one huipil and two banana plots I give to my child Lorensa Uh.

Likewise, one petticoat I give to my daughter-in-law Lorensa Canul. Likewise, one beaded necklace I give to my children Mateo Uh, Martín Uh, Lorensa Uh, the three of them together. Likewise, one necklace and one belt I give to my younger sister Luisa Canul. There is no more; this is the end of my words in my testament. I appoint one nobleman, Agustín Yam as executor

Ignacio Coba, lieutenant	don Gaspar Canul	Gaspar Tun
Bartolomé Pech	batab	Diego Mitz
Sebastián Uh		Antonio Huchim
Alcaldes	Salvador Coba, notary	Sebastián Yam
		Regidors

This testament was fulfilled and a mass was sung for her as requested, and I signed it
fray Diego Pérez Arrias

FOLS. 6R–6V DOCUMENT A9

WILL OF MIGUEL TUN

20 JANUARY 1748

MIGUEL TUN CIMI EN 20 DE ENERO DE 1748 AÑOS

Tu kaba dios yumbil y dios mehenb y dios espiritu santo oxtul personas huntulil dios uchuc tumen tu sinil maix pimobi lai bin ylabac u hunil yn tokyahthan tin testamento hibilcil tenil cen Miguel tun u mehen Juanchin tun u yalen Sesilia pech lae Bacacix cimi yn cah lae toh uol tin pucsikal y tin nat uet sihcie Bayxan u olah mucul yn cucutil ychil y otoch ca kuna lae Bayxan cin u oktic ynba ti ca pixanil yum padre guardian ca yalab hunpeɔ missa yokol yn pixan ca antabac tu numyail anima purgatorio y ca u masen tu payalchi ychil u missa lae Bayxan bin ɔabae u limosnayl oxpel tostones y capel tumin helusalem lae

   Bayxan hunpel cħeen y u solalil u pach y hunpetz u hol Na y Capok mula y Capok Baca cin ɔaic tin mehen Juan tun Bayxan hunpel cħeen y u solil u pach y hunpet kax cin ɔaic tin yxmehenob pasgual[a] tun lorensa tun martha tun phelipa tun can nupobi lae u tzayal lay kax ti xaman agustin pech ti chikin diego coba ti nohol andres coba Baixan hunpok Baca cin ɔaic ti pasguala tun Baixan hunpok Baca cin ɔai[c] ti lorensa tun Baixan hunpok Baca cin ɔaic ti Martha tun Baixan hunpok Baca cin ɔaic ti phelipa tun Baixan hunpok toro—cin ɔaic ti pasgual tun Baixan capok Baca y cāpok capon tzimin y hunpay caha y hun ɔit cuchara takin y hunpet kax cin ɔaic tin u atan ma[. . .][. . .] u tzayal lai kax ti lakin lucas cetz ti nohol Juan bausta matu ti chikin lorenso chan xaman Berno chan Baixan hunpet kax yan ca cin ɔaic ti Juan tun y gaspar tun ca nupobi lae Baixan hunpel cħeen y u kaxil u pach cin ɔaic tin mehen y yxmehenob juan tun pasguala tun lorensa tun martha tun phelipa tun y u iɔin pasgual tun y sobrino diego mitz u multialob lai cħeen lae halibe cin uacunti catul almehenob ygnasio coba Silvestre pech albaseasob lae

ygnasio Coba the^e		gaspar tun
Bar.^me pech	D.^n gaspar canul	diego mitz
Sebastian uh	Batab	an.^tto Juchim
alcardesob	Saruador Coba ess^no	Sebastian yam
		Regidoresob

Cumpliose este testamento y se le canto una missa que pidió y lo firme
fr. Diego Perez Arriaz

MIGUEL TUN DIED ON THE 20TH OF JANUARY, 1748

In the name of God the Father, and God the Son, and God the Holy Spirit, three persons, one almighty God, not many. This document of my final words in my testament will be seen, insomuch as I who am Miguel Tun, the son of little Juan Tun, the child of Cecilia Pech. Although I am dying, my heart and my understanding are sound, as it should be. Likewise, I wish my body to be buried inside the home of our temple. Likewise, I supplicate our blessed lord, the guardian priest, that one mass for my soul be said to help the suffering purgatory soul, and that he say a prayer for me in that mass. Likewise, it will be given in alms three tostons and two tomins for Jerusalem.

Likewise, one well together with its house plot and one house beam and two female mules and two cows I give to my son Juan Tun. Likewise, one well together with its house plot and one forest I give to my daughters Pasquala Tun, Lorensa Tun, Martha Tun, Phelipa Tun, the four of them together. Adjacent to the forest to the north is Augustine Pech, to the west Diego Coba, to the south Andrés Coba. Likewise, one cow I give to Pasquala Tun. Likewise, one cow I give to Lorensa Tun. Likewise, one cow I give to Martha Tun. Likewise, one cow I give to Phelipa Tun. Likewise, one bull I give to Pasqual Tun. Likewise, two cows and four geldings and one chest and one metal spoon and one forest I give to my wife María Tep [?]. Adjacent to the forest to the east is Lucas Cetz; to the south, Juan Bautista Matu; to the west, Lorenso Chan; to the north, Bernardino Chan. Likewise, there is one forest that I give to Juan Tun, and Gaspar Tun, the two of them together. Likewise, one well together with its forest I give to my son and daughters Juan Tun, Pasquala Tun, Lorensa Tun, Martha Tun, Phelipa Tun, and her younger brother Pasqual Tun and a nephew Diego Mitz. This well is their joint property. That is all. I appoint two noblemen Ignacio Coba, Silvester Pech as executors.

Ignacio Coba, lieutenant		Gaspar Tun
Bartolomé Pech	don Gaspar Canul	Diego Mitz
Sebastián Uh	batab	Antonio Huchim
Alcaldes	Salvador Coba, notary	Sebastián Yam

Regidors

This testament was fulfilled and a mass was sung for him as requested, and I signed it
fray Diego Pérez Arrias

FOLS. 7R–7V DOCUMENT A10

WILL OF DIEGO EUAN

27 JANUARY 1748

DIEGO [EUAN CI]MI EN 27 DE ENERO DE 1748 AÑŌS

Tu kaba dios yumbil y̱ dios mehenbil y̱ dios espiritu Santo oxtul personas huntulili
dios uchuc tumen tusinil ma ix pimobi lai bin ylabae u hunuil yn takyahthan tin
testamento hibicil tenil cen diego euan u mehen fransisco euan u yalen Anna canche
lae Bacacix cimi yn cah lae toh uol tin pucsikal y̱ tin nat uet sihcie—Bayxan u olah
mucul yn cucutil ychil y̱ otoch ca kuna lae Bayxan cin u ohtic ynba ti ca pixanil ym
padre guardian ca yalab hunpe ɔ missa yokol yn pixan ca antabac tu numyail anima
purgatorio y̱ Ca u masen tu payalchi ichil u missa lae Bayxan bin ɔa lae u limosnayl
oxpel tostones y̱ capet tumin helusalem lae

Bayxan hunpel cħeen y̱ u solil u pach cin ɔaic tin mehenob fran^{/··} euan y̱ Nicolas
euan ca nu pobi lae Bayxan heix in mehen gra^l euan y̱ yxmehen M^a can^d euan lae u
chi[c]tiob lae ca u mulmanteob hunpel cħeen y̱ u solil u pach ychil cantulob utial
cahlah[e]balob lai grab^r euan y̱ lag M^a can^d euan lae Bayxan hunpel u hol na cin
ɔaic tic mehen Nicolas euan Baixan hunpet Kax cin ɔaic tin mehenob fran^{co} euan y̱
Nicolas euan y̱ yxmehen pasguala euan u tzayal lai kax yan yabal cibili lae ti lakin D.^n
Juan pech ti xaman Sebastian Canche ti chikine Bar.^{me} pech ti nohol gaspar pech lae
Bayxan hunpet kax yan tahil cin ɔaic tin mehenob fran^{co} coba y̱ sar^{or} coba y̱ gra^l euan
y̱ yxmehen maria can^d euan can nupobi lae u tzayal kax ti lakin fran^{co} Coba ti xaman
fran^o canche ti chikine lorenso canche ti nohol mathe^o Canche = Bayxan hunpet
kax yan xelyah cin ɔaic tin mehen[ob] fran^{co} euan y̱ Nicolas euan [. . .] euan y̱ in
mam mechor canche y̱ Sebastian canche yn sobrina lae Bayxan hunpay caja cin ɔaic
tin yxmehen pasg^{la} euan—Bayxan hunpay mesa cin ɔaic tin mehen[ob] fran^{co} euan
y̱ nicolas euan y̱ pasguala euan Baixan hun ɔit ɔoon y̱ hun kalcul u chun hatz cin
ɔaic tin u atan lorensa pech Baixan hol huncul u chun hatz cin ɔaic tin mehen fran^{co}
euahn = Baixan hun kalcul u chun hatz cin [ɔaic] tin mehen Nicolas euan lae Bayxan
hunpay sablon y̱ u cayl cin ɔaic tin mehen Nicolas euan lae Bayxan Junpel tzotz cin
ɔaic tin u atan Lorensa pech lae halil u xul in than tin testamento cin uacuntic catul
almehenob mathe.^o tec Andre ytza albaseas

ygnasio Coba the^e	D.^n gaspar canul	gaspar tun
Bar.^{me} pech ald^e	Batab	diego mitz
Sebastian uh ald^e	Saruador Coba ess^{no}	an.^{to} hucħim

Sebastian yam

Regidoresob

Cumpliose este testamento y se le canto una missa que pidió y lo firme
fr. Diego Perez Arriaz

DIEGO EUAN DIED ON THE 27TH OF JANUARY, 1748

In the name of God the Father, and God the Son, and God the Holy Spirit, three persons, one almighty God, not many. This document of my final words in my testament will be seen, insomuch as I who am Diego Euan, the son of Francisco Euan, the child of Anna Canche. Although I am dying, my heart and my understanding are sound, as it should be. Likewise, I wish my body to be buried inside the home of our temple. Likewise, I supplicate our blessed lord, the guardian priest, that one mass for my soul be said to help the suffering purgatory soul, and that he say a prayer for me in that mass. Likewise, it will be given in alms three tostons and two tomins for Jerusalem.

Likewise, one well together with its house plot I give to my sons Francisco Euan and Nicolás Euan, the two of them together. Likewise, for my son Gabriel Euan and daughter María Candelaria Euan together what was jointly purchased for them, one well together with its house plot; among the four of them its contents are to belong to Gabriel Euan and María Candelaria Euan. Likewise, one house beam I give to my son Nicolás Euan. Likewise, one forest I give to my sons Francisco Euan and Nicolás Euan, and daughter Pasguala Euan adjacent to the forest, where there is a lot of wax, to the east is don Juan Pech, to the north Sebastián Canche, to the west Bartolomé Pech, to the south Gaspar Pech. Likewise, there is a forest where there is a honey crop I give to my sons Francisco Coba and Salvador Coba and Gabriel Euan and daughter María Candelaria Euan, the four of them together. Adjacent to the forest to the east is Francisco Coba, to the north Francisco Canche, to the west Lorenso Canche, to the south Mateo Canche. Likewise, one forest that is divided I give to my son[s] Francisco Euan and Nicolás Euan [and Gabriel] Euan and my maternal grandfather Melchor Canche and Sebastián Canche my cousin.

Likewise, one chest I give to my daughter Pasquala Euan. Likewise, one table I give to my sons Francisco Euan and Nicolás Euan, and Pasquala Euan. Likewise, one shotgun and 20 banana trees I give to my wife Lorensa Pech. Likewise, 15 banana trees I give to my son Francisco Euan. Likewise, 20 banana trees I [give] to my son Nicolás Euan. Likewise, one table and its gourd I give to my son Nicolás Euan. Likewise, one cloak I give to my wife Lorensa Pech. There is no more; this is the end of my words in my testament. I appoint two noblemen, Mateo Tec, Andre Itza, as executors.

Ignacio Coba, lieutenant	don Gaspar Canul	Gaspar Tun
Bartolomé Pech, alcalde	batab	Diego Mitz
Sebastián Uh, alcalde	Salvador Coba, notary	Antonio Huchim

Sebastián Yum

Regidors

This testament was fulfilled and a mass was sung for him as requested, and I signed it
fray Diego Pérez Arrias

FOL. 8R DOCUMENT AII

WILL OF LORENSA EK

16 FEBRUARY 1748

LORENSA EK CIMI EN 16 DE FEB[RERO] DE 1748 ANŌS

Tu kaba dios yumbil y dios mehenbil y dios espiritu santo oxtul personals huntulil
dios uchuc tumen tusinil maix pimobi lay bin ylabac u hunil in tokyahthan tin
testameto hibicil tenil cen lorensa ek u yxmehen agustin ek u yalen maria canche
lae Bayxan u olah mucul in cucutil ychil y otoch ca kuna lae Baixan cin uoktic ynba
ti ca pixanil yum padre guardian ca yalob hupeɔ missa yokol in pixan ca antabac tu
numy[ai]l anima purgatorio y Ca u masen tu payalchi ichil u missa lae Baixan bin
ɔabae u limosnayl oxpel tostones y capel tumin helusalem lae Baixan halil in than
tin testamento minan u bal inba lae Cin uacuntic Juntul almehe Bartasar canche
albaseas lae

ygᵒ Coba theᵉ	Cappⁿ D.ⁿ gaspar canul	gaspar tun
Bar.ᵐᵉ pech aldᵉ	Batab	Diego Mitz
Sebastian Uh aldᵉ	Saruador Coba essⁿᵒ	Anᵗᵗᵒ Juchim
		Sebasⁿ yam
		Regidoresob

Cumpliose este funeral y se le canto una missa que pidió y lo firme
   Fr. Diego Perez Arriaz

LORENSA EK DIED ON THE 16TH OF FEBRUARY, 1748

In the name of God the Father, and God the Son, and God the Holy Spirit, three
persons, one almighty God, not many. This document of my final words in my testament will be seen, insomuch as I who am Lorensa Ek, the daughter of Agustín Ek,
the child of María Canche. Likewise, I wish my body to be buried inside the home of
our temple. Likewise, I supplicate our blessed lord, the guardian priest, that one mass
for my soul be said to help the suffering purgatory soul, and that he say a prayer for
me in that mass. Likewise, it will be given in alms three tostons and two tomins for
Jerusalem.

Likewise, I have no more words for my testament; I have no more things. I appoint
one nobleman, Baltasar Canche, as executor.

Ignacio Coba, lieutenant	captain don Gaspar Canul	Gaspar Tun
Bartolomé Pech, alcalde	batab	Diego Mitz
Sebastián Uh, alcalde	Salvador Coba, notary	Antonio Huchim
		Sebastián Yam
		Regidors

This testament was fulfilled and a mass was sung for her as requested, and I signed it
fray Diego Pérez Arrias

FOL. 8V DOCUMENT A12

WILL OF BERNARDO CHAN
6 MARCH 1748

BERNO CHAN CIMI EN 6 DE MARSO DE 1748 ANŌS

Tu kaba dios yumbil y dios mehenbil y dios espiritu santo oxtul personas huntulili
dios uchuc tumen tusinil maix pimobi lay bin ylabal u hunil in tokyahthan tin
testamento hibicil tenil cen—Ber.^{no} Chan u mehen Juan chan u yalen—Fran^{ca} tun
Bacacix cimil in cah lae toh uol tin pucsikal y tin nat uet sihcie Bayxan u olah mucul
in cucutil ychil y otoch ca kuna lae Bayxan Cin u oktic inba ti ca pixanil yum padre
guardian Ca yalob hunpe ɔ missa yokol in pixan ca antabac tu numyail anima purgatorio y ca u masen tu payal chi ychil u missa lae Bayxan bin ɔabac u limosnail oxpel
tostones y Capel tumin helusalem lae Baixan hunpel Cħeen y u solalil u pach Cin
ɔaic tin yxmehen dominga chan y mehen lorenso chan y Martha chan ox nupobi lae
Bayxan hunpet kax cin kubic ti lorenso chan lae bic u nal u yum lae Bayxan hunpet
kax y hun ɔit machete cin ɔaic ti lorenso chan lae yoklal u mucicen lae halil u xul in
than tin testamento lae lic in uacunic catul almehenob albaseasob lae grabiel Chan y
Andres ytza

ygnacio Coba the^{e}	D.^{n} gaspar Canul	gaspar tun
Bar.^{me} pech ald^{e}	Batab	Diego Mitz
Sebastian Uh ald^{e}	Sar.^{or} Coba ess^{no}	an^{tto} juchim
		Sebastian yam
		Regidoresob

Cumpliose este testamento y se le canto una missa que pidió y lo firme
Fr. Diego Perez Arrias

BERNARDO CHAN DIED ON THE 6TH OF MARCH, 1748

In the name of God the Father, and God the Son, and God the Holy Spirit, three
persons, one almighty God, not many. This document of my final words in my

testament will be seen, insomuch as I who am Bernardo Chan, the son of Juan Chan, the child of Francisca Tun. Although I am dying, my heart and my understanding are sound, as it should be. Likewise, I wish my body to be buried inside the home of our temple. Likewise, I supplicate our blessed lord, the guardian priest, that one mass for my soul be said to help the suffering purgatory soul, and that he say a prayer for me in that mass. Likewise, it will be given in alms three tostons and two tomins for Jerusalem.

Likewise, one well together with its house plot I will give to my daughter Dominga Chan, and son Lorenso Chan and Martha Chan, the three of them together. Likewise, one forest I deliver to Lorenso Chan from his mother and father. Likewise, one forest and one machete I give to Lorenso Chan. Concerning how I am to be buried, there is no more; this is the end of my words in my testament. I appoint two noblemen as executors, Gabriel Chan and Andrés Itza.

Ignacio Coba, lieutenant	don Gaspar Canul	Gaspar Tun
Bartolomé Pech, alcalde	batab	Diego Mitz
Sebastián Uh, alcalde	Salvador Coba, notary	Antonio Huchim
		Sebastián Yam
		Regidors

This testament was fulfilled and a mass was sung for him as requested, and I signed it
fray Diego Pérez Arrias

FOL. 9R DOCUMENT A13

WILL OF PASQUALA ITZA

20 MARCH 1748

PASGUALA ITZA CIMI EN 20 DE MARZO DE 1748 ANŌS

Tu kaba dios yumbil y dios mehenbil y dios espiritu santo oxtul personas huntulili dios uchuc tumen tusinil maix pimobi lai bin ylabac u hunil yn tohyahthan tin testamento hibicil tenil cen pasguala itza u yxmehen Adres ytza u yalen fran^ca yam Bacacix cimil ȳ cah lae toh uol tin pucsikal y tin nat uet sincie Bayxan u olah muculin cucutil ychil y othoch ca kuna lae Baixan cin uoktic ynba ti ca pixanil yum padre guardian ca yalob hunpe ɔ missa yokol yn pixan ca antabac tu numyail anima purgatorio y ca u [ma]sen tu payalchi ichil u missa lae Baixan bin ɔabae u limosnayl oxpel tostones y capel tumin helusalem lae

Bayxan hunpel boch y hunpel pic y hunpay U y hun ɔaam tup cin ɔaic tin u al pasguala Chan Baixan heix Cabin cimic yn yume heix bal cubin u ɔa tene Ca u ɔae tin u al pasguala chan lae halil u xul in than tin testamento lae cin uacuntic huntul almehen grabier chan albaseaslae Baixan catzil u hebal nok cin ɔaic tin u icham lorenso chan

ygnasio Coba the^e	D.^n gaspar canul	gaspar tun
Bar.^me pech ald^e	Batab	Diego Mitz
Sebastian Uh ald^e	Saruaor Coba ess^no	an^tto juchim
		Sebastian yam
		Regidoresob

Cumplio este testamento y se le canto una missa que pidió y lo firme
    Fr. Diego Perez Arrias

PASQUALA ITZA DIED ON THE 20TH OF MARCH, 1748

In the name of God the Father, and God the Son, and God the Holy Spirit, three persons, one almighty God, not many. The document of my final words in my testament will be seen, insomuch as I who am Pasguala Itza, the daughter of Andrés Itza, the child of Francisca Yam. Although I am dying, my heart and my understanding are sound, as it should be. Likewise, I wish my body to be buried inside the home of our temple. Likewise, I supplicate our blessed lord, the guardian priest, that one mass for my soul be said to help the suffering purgatory soul, and that he say a prayer for me in that mass. Likewise, it will be given in alms three tostons and two tomins for Jerusalem.

Likewise, one shawl and one petticoat, and one necklace, and one pair of earrings I give to my child Pasquala Chan. Likewise, when my father dies, anything he would give to me he should give my child Pasquala Chan. This is no more; this is the end of my words in my testament. I appoint one nobleman, Gabriel Chan, as executor. Likewise, two lengths of cloth I give to my husband Lorenso Chan

Ignacio Coba, lieutenant	don Gaspar Canul	Gaspar Tun
Bartolomé Pech, alcalde	batab	Diego Mitz
Sebastián Uh, alcalde	Salvador Coba, notary	Antonio Huchim
		Sebastián Yam
		Regidors

This testament was fulfilled and a mass was sung for her as requested, and I signed it
    fray Diego Pérez Arrias

FOL. 9V DOCUMENT A14

WILL OF NICOLASA YAM
20 MARCH 1748

NICOLASA YAM CIMI EN 20 DE MARSO DE 1748 AÑOS

Tu kaba dios yumbil y dios mehenbil y dios espiritu san[to] oxtul personas huntulili dios uchuc tumen tusinil maix pimobi lai bin ylabae u hunil in tokyahthan tin

testamento hibicil tenil cē Nicolosa yam u yxmehen agustin yam u yalen Clara chim
Bacacix cimil yn cah lae toh uol tin pucsikal y tin nat uet sihcie Baixan uolah mucul
in cucutil ychil yotoch ca kuna lae Baixan Cin uoktic ynba ti ca pixanil yum padre
guardian ca yalab hunpe ɔ missa yokol yn pixan ca antabac tu numyail anima purgatorio y ca u masen tu payalchi ychil u missa lae Baixan bin ɔabae u limosnail oxpel
tostones y capel tumin helusalem lae

 Baixan heix bal cubin u ɔa ten in yum cabin Cimice ca u ɔae tin ualob halil u xul
in than tin testamen lae cin uacuntic huntul almehen Sebastian Uh albaseas lae—

ygnasio Coba the^ᶜ	D.ⁿ gaspar Canul	gaspar tun
Bar.^{me} pech ald^ᶜ	Bata[b]	diego Mitz
Sebastian Uh ald^ᶜ	Sarua.^{or} Coba ess^{no}	an.^{tto} huchim
		Sebastian yam
		Regidoresob

Cumpliose este testamento y se le canto una missa que pidió y lo firme
 Fr. Diego Perez Arrias

Nicolasa Yam died on the 20th of March, 1748

In the name of God the Father, and God the Son, and God the Holy Spirit, three
persons, one almighty God, not many. This document of my final words in my testament will be seen, insomuch as I who am Nicolasa Yam, the daughter of Agustín Yam,
the child of Clara Chim. Although I am dying, my heart and my understanding are
sound, as it should be. Likewise, I wish my body to be buried inside the home of our
temple. Likewise, I supplicate our blessed lord, the guardian priest, that one mass
for my soul be said to help the suffering purgatory soul, and that he say a prayer for
me in that mass. Likewise, it will be given in alms three tostons and two tomins for
Jerusalem.

 Likewise, what my father gives me when he dies, he should give my children. There
is no more; this is the end of my words in my testament. I appoint one nobleman,
Sebastián Uh, as executor.

Ignacio Coba, lieutenant	don Gaspar Canul	Gaspar Tun
Bartolomé Pech, alcalde	batab	Diego Mitz
Sebastián Uh, alcalde	Salvador Coba, notary	Antonio Huchim
		Sebastián Yam
		Regidors

This testament was fulfilled and a mass was sung for her as requested, and I signed it
 fray Diego Pérez Arrias

FOL. 10R DOCUMENT A15

WILL OF CHRISTINA CAN

20 MARCH 1748

XP.ⁿᵃ CAN CIMI EN 20 DE MARZO DE 1748 AÑŌS

Tu kab[a] Dios yumbil y dios mehenbil y Dios espiritu santo oxtul personas huntulilil
Dios uchuc tumen tusinil maix pimobi lai bin ylabac u hunil yn takyahthan tin
testamento hibicil tenil cen xp.ⁿᵃ Can u yxmehen gaspar can u yalen Maria Ui Cab
ah otochnalen ti Cah tis lae Bacacix cimil yn Cah lae toh ual tin pucsikal y tin nat
uct sihcie Bayxan uolah mucul in cucutil ychil yotoch Ca kuna lae Baixan Cin uoktic
ynba ti ca pixanil yum padre guardian Ca yalob hunpe ɔ missa yokol in pixan ca anta-
bae tu numyail anima purgatorio y Ca u masen tu payalchi ychil u missa lae Baixan
Bin ɔabae u limosnayl oxpel tostenes y Capel tumin helusalem lae
    halil u xul in than tin testamento lae Cin uacuntic huntul almehen Barsar Canche
albaseas lae

ygnacio Coba theᵉ	D.ⁿ gaspar canul	gaspar tun
Bar.ᵐᵉ pech aldᵉ	Batab	Diego mitz
Sebastian uh aldᵉ	Sarua.ᵒʳ Coba essⁿᵒ	an.ᵗᵗᵒ Juchim
		Sebastian yam
		Regidoresob

Cumpliose este testamento y se le canto una missa que pidió y lo firme
    fr Diego Perez Arrias

CHRISTINA CAN DIED ON THE 20TH OF MARCH, 1748

In the name of God the Father, and God the Son, and God the Holy Spirit, three persons, one almighty God, not many. This document of my final words in my testament
will be seen, insomuch as I who am Christiana Can, the daughter of Gaspar Can, the
child of María Ui Cab resident of the cah Tiz.[3] Although I am dying, my heart and
my understanding are sound, as it should be. Likewise, I wish my body to be buried
inside the home of our temple. Likewise, I supplicate our blessed lord, the guardian
priest, that one mass for my soul be said to help the suffering purgatory soul, and that
he say a prayer for me in that mass. Likewise, it will be given in alms three tostons and
two tomins for Jerusalem.

    There is no more; this is the end of my words in my testament. I appoint one
nobleman, Baltasar Canche, as executor.

Ignacio Coba, lieutenant	don Gaspar Canul	Gaspar Tun
Bartolomé Pech, alcalde	batab	Diego Mitz
Sebastián Uh, alcalde	Salvador Coba, notary	Antonio Huchim

Sebastián Yam

Regidors

This testament was fulfilled and a mass was sung for her as requested, and I signed it
fray Diego Pérez Arrias

FOL. 10V DOCUMENT A16

LORENSA COBA
20 MARCH 1748

LORENSA COBA CIMI EN 20 DE MARSO DE 1748 AÑŌS

tu kaba Dios yumbil y Dios mehenbil y Dios espiritu santo oxtul personas huntulili
Dios uchuc tumen tusinil maix pimobi lai bin ylabac u hunil yn takyathan tin testamento hibicil tenil Cen lorensa Coba u yxmehen Jacinto Coba u yalen margalita euan
lae BacaCix Cimil yn Cah lae toh uol tin pucsikal y tin nat uet sihcie Baixan u olah
mucul in cucutil ychil yotoch Ca Kuna lae Baixan Cin uoktic ynbah ca pixan yum
padre guardian ca yalab hunpe ɔ missa yokol in pixan Ca antabac tu numyail anima
purgatorio y ca u masen tu payalchi ychil u missa lae Baixan bin ɔabae u limosnail
oxpel tostones y Capel tumin helusalem

Baixan he u chenil yn yum lae cin ɔaic tin ualob lae andres Juchim y maria Juchim
Maria Juchin ox nupobi lae Baixan he Cabin payac u cuxtal in mahan yum tumenel
Ca yumil ti dios lae heix bal cubin u ɔa ten Cachie Ca u ɔae tin U alob oxtulob
andres Juchim maria Juchim maria Juchim u bolil u chic in meyah tic lai in yum
damian pech lae halil u xul in than tin testamento lae Cin uacuntic hunul almehen
Bartatzar canche alceasias

ygnasio Coba the^e	D.^n gaspar Canul	gaspar tun
Bar.^me pech ald^e	Batab	Diego mitz
Sebastian uh ald^e	Sarua.^or Coba ess^no	an.^tto Juchim
		Sebastian yam
		Regidores

Cumpliose este testamento y se le canto una missa que pidió y lo firme
fr. Diego Perez Arrias

LORENSA COBA DIED ON THE 20TH OF MARCH, 1748

In the name of God the Father, and God the Son, and God the Holy Spirit, three persons, one almighty God, not many. This document of my final words in my testament
will be seen, insomuch as I who am Lorensa Coba, the daughter of Jacinto Coba, the
child of Margarita Euan. Although I am dying, my heart and my understanding are

sound, as it should be. Likewise, I wish my body to be buried inside the home of our temple. Likewise, I supplicate our blessed lord, the guardian priest, that one mass for my soul be said to help the suffering purgatory soul, and that he say a prayer for me in that mass. Likewise, it will be given in alms three tostons and two tomins for Jerusalem.

Likewise, the well of my father I give to my children Andrés Huchim and María Huchim, María Huchim, the three of them together. Likewise, when our lord God calls the life loaned to my father, what is given to me will then be given to my three children Andrés Huchim, María Huchim, María Huchim; these things I arrange are made clear to my lord Damian Pech. There is no more; this is the end of my words in my testament. I appoint one nobleman, Baltasar Canche, as executor.

Ignacio Coba, lieutenant	don Gaspar Canul	Gaspar Tun
Bartolomé Pech, alcalde	batab	Diego Mitz
Sebastián Uh, alcalde	Salvador Coba, notary	Antonio Huchim
		Sebastián Yam
		Regidors

This testament was fulfilled and a mass was sung for her as requested, and I signed it
    fray Diego Pérez Arrias

FOL. 11R DOCUMENT A17

WILL OF MARTHA ITZA

5 APRIL 1748

MARTHA YTZA CIMI EN 5 DE ABLIL DE 1748 AÑŌS

Tu kaba dios yumbil y dios mehenbil y dios espiritu santo ox[tul] personas huntulil dios uchuc tumen tusinil maix pimobi lai bin [ylabac] u hunil yn thakyahthan tin testamento hibicil tenil cen Martha ytza u yxmehen fran⁽ᶜᵒ⁾ ytza u yalen luissa couoh BaCaCix Cimil in Cah lae toh uol tin pucsikal y tin nat—uet sihcie Baixan u olah mucul in cucutil ychil yotoch Ca kuna lae Baixan Cin uokti ynba ti Ca pixanil yum padre guardian ca yalab hunpe ɔ missa yokol in pixan cantabac tu numyail anima purgatorio y ca u masen tu payalchi ychil u missa lae Baixan bin ɔabac u limoxnayl oxpel toston y Capel tumin helusalem lae

Baixan hunpel cħeen y u solalil u pach Cin patic tin u alob lae Miguel tun gaspar tun Juan tun—Barᵐᵉ Tun Franco tun maria tun thomasa tun halib minan u bal inba Cin uacuntic huntul al[mehen] Bar.ʳ canche arbaseas lae

ygnasio Coba	D.ⁿ gaspar canul	gaspar tun
Bar.ᵐᵉ pech aldᵉ	Batab	diego Mitz
Sebastian Uh aldᵉ	Saruador Coba essⁿᵒ	anᵗᵗᵒ Juchim
		Sebastian yam

Regidoresob

Perez   Cumpliose este testamento y se le canto su missa con su vigilia y responso qe pidió y lo firme

    fr Joseph Villamil

MARTHA ITZA DIED ON THE 5TH OF APRIL, 1748

In the name of God the Father, and God the Son, and God the Holy Spirit, three persons, one almighty God, not many. This document of my final words in my testament will [be seen], insomuch as I who am Martha Itza, the daughter of Francisco Itza, the child of Luissa Couoh. Although I am dying, my heart and my understanding are sound, as it should be. Likewise, I wish my body to be buried inside the home of our temple. Likewise, I supplicate our blessed lord, the guardian priest, that one mass for my soul be said to help the suffering purgatory soul, and that he say a prayer for me in that mass. Likewise, it will be given in alms three tostons and two tomins for Jerusalem.

    Likewise, one well together with its house plot I leave to my children Miguel Tun, Gaspar Tun, Juan Tun, Bartolome Tun, Francisco Tun, María Tun, Thomas Tun. That is all; I have no more things. I appoint one nobleman, Baltasar Canche.

Ignacio Coba	don Gaspar Canul	Gaspar Tun
Bartolomé Pech, alcalde	batab	Diego Mitz
Sebastián Uh, alcalde	Salvador Coba, notary	Antonio Huchim
		Sebastián Yam
		Regidors

[fray Diego] Pérez [Arrias]. This testament was fulfilled and a mass was sung for her with its vigil and responsory prayer that she requested, and I signed it

    fray Joseph Villamil

FOL. 11V DOCUMENT A18

WILL OF JUAN CANTE

5 APRIL 1748

JUAN CANTE CIMI EN 5 DE ABLIL DE 1748 AÑŌS

Tu kaba dios yumbil yetel dios mehen yetel dios espiritu santo oxtul personas huntu-lili dios uchuc tumen tusinil maix pimobi lai bin in ylabac u hunil in thakyahthan tin testamento hibicil tenil Juan Cante u mehen Fran.ᶜᵒ cante u yalen Nicolasa Coba lae Bacacix cimili cah lae toh uol tin pusikal y̨ tin nat uet sihcie Baixan u olah mucul in cucutil ychil yotochil [*sic*] yotoch Ca kuna lae Baixan cin uoktic inbah Ca pixanil yum padre guardian Ca yalab hunpe ɔ missa yokol in pixan Ca antabac numyail

anima purgatorio yetel ca u masen tu payalchi ychil u missa lae Baixan bin ɔabae u
limosnayl oxpel tostones y̧ capel tumin helusalem lae =

Baixan hūpai caJa Cin ɔaic tin Miguel cante y̧ hunpel tzotz utial xan Baixan
hē cabin cimil in yum lae hecexbal bin u ɔa tene ca u ɔae tin mehenob lae halibe
min[an] u bal inba lae Bar.ʳ canche albasias lae

ygnasio Coba theᵉ	D.ⁿ gaspar cunul	gaspar tun
Bar.ᵐᵉ pech aldᵉ	Batab	Diego mitz
Sebastian Uh aldᵉ	Sarᵒʳ Coba essⁿᵒ	an.ᵗᵗᵒ Juchim
		Sebastian Yam
		Regidoresob

Perez   Cumpliose este funeral y se le canto una missa con su responso y vigilia como
lo pidió el difᵗᵒ y yo firme

fr. Joseph Villamil

JUAN CANTE DIED ON THE 5TH OF APRIL, 1748

In the name of God the Father, and God the Son, and God the Holy Spirit, three
persons, one almighty God, not many. This document of my final words in my testament will be seen, insomuch as I who am Juan Cante, the son of Francisco Cante
the child of Nicolasa Coba. Although I am dying, my heart and my understanding
are sound, as it should be. Likewise, I wish my body to be buried inside the home
of our temple. Likewise, I supplicate our blessed lord, the guardian priest, that
one mass for my soul be said to help the suffering purgatory soul, and that he say a
prayer for me in that mass. Likewise, it will be given in alms three tostons and two
tomins for Jerusalem.

Likewise, one chest I give to my [son] Miguel Cante and also the cloak in it.
Likewise, when my father dies and he leaves, what will be given to me will be given to
my sons. That is all; I have no more things. Bartolomé Canche, executor.

Ignacio Coba, lieutenant	don Gaspar Canul	Gaspar Tun
Bartolomé Pech, alcalde	batab	Diego Mitz
Sebastián Uh, alcalde	Salvador Coba, notary	Antonio Huchim
		Sebastián Yam
		Regidors

[fray Diego] Pérez [Arrias]. This funeral was completed, and a mass with its vigil and
responsory prayer was sung as the deceased requested, and I signed

fray Joseph Villamil

FOL. 12R DOCUMENT A19

WILL OF BERNARDINA TEC

5 APRIL 1748

BERNA TEC CIMI EN 5 DE ABLIL DE 1748 ANŌS

Tu kaba dios yumbil y dios mehenbil y dios espiritu santo oxtul personas huntilil dios uchuc tumen tusinil maix pimobi lai bin ylabac u hunil yn thakyahthan tin testamento hibicil tenil Cen Ber^na tec u yxmehen Ben^na tec u yalen pasguala Chan lae baCaCix Cimil yn Cah lae toh uol tin pucsakal yetel tin nat uet sihcie Baixan u olah mucul yn cucutil ychil yotoch Ca kuna lae Baixan Cin uokti ynbah ca pixanil yum padre guardian Ca yalab hunpe ꜫ missa yokol yn pixan Ca antabac nunumiayl anima purgatorio y Ca u masen tupayalchi ychil u missa lae Baixan bin ꜫabae u limoxnayl oxpel toston yetel Capel tumin helusalem lae

   Baixan hunpel cħeen yetel u solalil u pach Cin patic tin u alob lae yetel hunper kax u tzayal lai kax ti lakin matheo Na ti xama phelipe pech ti nohol afalisio Coba y u lak hunpet kax yan cen ox u tzaial ti nohol Joseph Uh ti lakin Joseph Yam ti xaman diego Yam ti chikin agus^n canche y u lak hunpet yan Ber Bena u tzayal ti nohol Ber.^na tec ti lakin Bena ti xaman Clete Yam y Joseph yam ti chikin diego pech lae yetel Capay CaJa U multial lai in u alob lae Miguel Coba Agustin Coba andre ian Coba Ber.^na Coba ychil Cantulob lae halili u xul i[n] than tin testamento lae li ci[n] uacuntic hutul al mehen gaspar pech alseas lae

ygnasio Coba the^e	D.^n gaspar cunul	gaspar tun
Bar.^me pech ald^e	Batab	Diego mitz
Sebastian Uh ald^e	Saruador Coba ess^no	An.^tto Juchim
		Sebastian yum
		Regidoresob

Perez   Cumpliose este funeral y se le canto una missa con su vigilia y responso como lo pidió el dif.^to antes de morir y firme

   fr. Jospeh Villamil

BERNARDINA TEC DIED ON THE 5TH OF APRIL, 1748

In the name of God the Father, and God the Son, and God the Holy Spirit, three persons, one almighty God, not many. This document of my final words in my testament will be seen, insomuch as I who am Bernardina Tec, the daughter of Bernardo Tec, the child of Pasquala Chan. Although I am dying, my heart and my understanding are sound, as it should be. Likewise, I wish my body to be buried inside the home of our temple. Likewise, I supplicate our blessed lord, the guardian priest, that one mass for my soul be said to help the suffering purgatory soul, and that he say a prayer for me in that mass. Likewise, it will be given in alms three tostons and two tomins for Jerusalem.

Likewise, one well together with its house plot I leave for my children and one forest; adjacent to the forest to the east is Mateo Na, to the north Phelipe Pech, to the south Aparicio Coba; and there is another forest of mine whose three neighbors are, to the south is Joseph Uh, to the east Joseph Yam, to the north Diego Yam, to the west Agustín Canche and another one at the road to Bena adjacent to the south is Bernardo Tec, to the east Bena, to the north Clemente Yam and Joseph Yam, to the west Diego Pech; and two chests to belong jointly to my children Miguel Coba, Agustín Coba . . . Coba, Bernardo Coba. That is all. There are no more of my words in my testament. I appoint one nobleman, Gaspar Pech, as executor.

Ignacio Coba, lieutenant	don Gaspar Canul	Gaspar Tun
Bartolomé Pech, alcalde	batab	Diego Mitz
Sebastián Uh, alcalde	Salvador Coba, notary	Antonio Huchim
		Sebastián Yam
		Regidors

[fray Diego] Pérez [Arrias]. This funeral was completed, and a mass with its vigil and responsory prayer was sung as the deceased requested before dying, and I signed
fray Joseph Villamil

FOL. 12V DOCUMENT A20

WILL OF PHELIPA PECH
5 APRIL 1748

PHELIPA PECH CIMI EN 5 DE ABLIL DE 1748 AÑŌS

Tu kaba dios yumbil y dios mehenbil y dios espiritu santo ox tul personas huntu-lilil dios uchuc tumen tusinil maix pimobi lai bin ylabac u hunil yn takyahthan tin testamento hibilcil tenil Cen phelipa pech u yxmehen fran.co pech u yalen maria pech lae bacacix cimil yn Cah lae toh uol tin pucsikal y tin nat uet sihcie Baixan u olah mucul in cucutil ychil yotoch Ca kuna lae Baixan Cin uoktic ynba ca pixanil yum padre guardian ca yalab hunpeɔ missa yokol in pixan ca antabac tu numyail anima purgatorio y ca u masen tu payalchi ychil u missa lae Baixan bin ɔabae u limosnail oxpel tostones y Capel tumin helusalem lae

Baixan hunpel pic y hunpel ypil bin ɔai ti maria pech Baixan hunpel pic cin ɔaic Juana pech Baixan hunpel pic cin ɔaic ti Rossa pech—Baixan hunpel ypil cin ɔaic ti manuela pech Baixan hunpai caJa Cin ɔaic ti diego pech Baixan huntzil u chel kuch Cin ɔaic ti Ber.no pech Baixan huntzil u chel kuch cin ɔaic ti Martha pech Baixan he cheen y u solalil u pach utial in yume tic u than in u alob tu uuctulilob lae Baixan he lai kax capet utial in yume ti cu than in u alob xani halibe—minan u bal inba cin cucuntic Catul almehenob abaseasob franco Cante Bartasar Canche lae

ygansio Coba the^e	D.^n gaspar canul	gaspar tun
Bar.^me pech ad^e	Saruador Coba ess^no	Diego mitz
Sebastian Uh ad^e		an^tto Juchim
		Sebastian yam
		Regidoresob

Perez   Cumpliose con este funeral y se le canto su missa con su vigilia y responso como desponeo como lo pidió el difto y yo firme

    Joseph Villamill

PHELIPA PECH DIED ON THE 5TH OF APRIL, 1748

In the name of God the Father, and God the Son, and God the Holy Spirit, three persons, one almighty God, not many. This document of my final words in my testament will be seen, insomuch as I who am Phelipa Pech, the daughter of Francisco Pech, the child of María Pech. Although I am dying, my heart and my understanding are sound, as it should be. Likewise, I wish my body to be buried inside the home of our temple. Likewise, I supplicate our blessed lord, the guardian priest, that one mass for my soul be said to help the suffering purgatory soul, and that he say a prayer for me in that mass. Likewise, it will be given in alms three tostons and two tomins for Jerusalem.

Likewise, one petticoat and one huipil will be given to María Pech. Likewise, one petticoat I give to Juana Pech. Likewise, one petticoat I give to Rosa Pech. Likewise, one huipil I give to Manuela Pech. Likewise, one chest I give to Diego Pech. Likewise, one length of blond yarn I give to Bernardo Pech. Likewise, one length of blond yarn I give to Martha Pech. Likewise, the well along with its house plot, the property of my father, that he declared (gave) to my seven children. Likewise, there is a forest, two of them, the property of my father that he also declared to my children . . . That is all; I have no more things. I appoint two noblemen as executors: Francisco Cante, Baltasar Canche.

Ignacio Coba, lieutenant	don Gaspar Canul	Gaspar Tun
Bartolomé Pech, alcalde	batab	Diego Mitz
Sebastián Uh, alcalde	Salvador Coba, notary	Antonio Huchim
		Sebastián Yam
		Regidors

[fray Diego] Pérez [Arrias]. This funeral was completed, and a mass with its vigil and responsory prayer was sung as the deceased stipulated and requested, and I signed

    fray Joseph Villamil

FOL. 13R DOCUMENT A21

WILL OF MARTHA PECH

17 APRIL 1748

MARTHA PECH CIMI EN 17 DE ABLIL DE 1748 ANŌS

Tu kaba dios yumbil y̱ dios mehen y̱ dios espiritu santo oxtul personas huntulili dios uchuc tumen tusinil maix pimobi lai bin in ylabae u hunil yn thokyahthan tin testamento hibicil tenil Martha pech u yxmehen marcos pech u yalen Juana uetz Bacacix cimil yn cah lae toh uol tin pucsikal y̱ tin nat uet sihcie Baixan u olah mucul yn cucutil ychil yotoch ca kuna lae Baixan Cin uoktic ynba ti ca pixanil yum padre guardian ca yalab hunpeɔ missa yokol in pixan ca antabac tu numyail anima purgatorio y̱ ca u masen tu payalchi ychil u missa lae Bayxan bin ɔabae u limosnyl oxpel tostones y̱ Capel tumin helusalen lae

　Baixan Capok yeua tzimin y̱ hunpok capon tzimin y̱ hunpok uacax cin ɔaic tin u al marcos cime = Baixan hunpok yeua tzimin y̱ hunpok podro tzimin y̱ hunpel pic cin ɔaic tin u al manla cime = Baixan hunpok yeua tzimin y̱ hunpel pic cin ɔaic tin u al aguitina pech = Baixan hunpel ipil cin ɔai tin u al pasguala pech = Baixan hunpok yeua tzimin y̱ hunpok podro y̱ hunpok capon tzimin y̱ hunpok uacax cin ɔaic tin u icham phelipe pech = Baixan he cen bal cubin u ɔa ten in u icham Cabin cime lae ɔae tin u al marcos cime lae halibe mathe.° tec abaseas

ygnasio coba the^e	Dⁿ gaspar canul	gasp.ʳ tun
Batolme pech ad^e	Batab	Diego mitz
Sebastian uh ad^e	Saruador Coba es^no	an^tto Juchim
		Sebastian yam
		Regidoresob

Cumpliose este funeral y se le canto una missa como la pidió el difto y lo firme
　fr. Joseph Villamil

MARTHA PECH DIED ON THE 17TH OF APRIL, 1748

In the name of God the Father, and God the Son, and God the Holy Spirit, three persons, one almighty God, not many. This document of my final words in my testament will be seen, insomuch as I who am Martha Pech, the daughter of Marcos Pech, the child of Juana Uetz. Although I am dying, my heart and my understanding are sound, as it should be. Likewise, I wish my body to be buried inside the home of our temple. Likewise, I supplicate our blessed lord, the guardian priest, that one mass for my soul be said to help the suffering purgatory soul, and that he say a prayer for me in that mass. Likewise, it will be given in alms three tostons and two tomins for Jerusalem.

　Likewise, two mares and one gelding and one cow I give to my child Marcos Cime. Likewise, one mare and one colt and one petticoat I have to my child Manuela Cime. Likewise, one mare and one petticoat I give to my child Agustina Pech. Likewise, one huipil I give to my child Pasquala Pech. Likewise, one mare and one colt and one gelding and one cow I give to my husband Phelipe Pech. Likewise, all that my husband gives me when he dies will be given to my child Marcos Cime. There is no more. Mateo Tec, executor.

Ignacio Coba, lieutenant	don Gaspar Canul	Gaspar Tun
Bartolomé Pech, alcalde	Batob	Diego Mitz
Sebastián Uh, alcalde	Salvador Coba, notary	Antonio Huchim
		Sebastián Yam
		Regidors

This funeral was completed and a mass was sung for her as the deceased requested, and I signed it

fray Joseph Villamil

FOL. 13V DOCUMENT A22

WILL OF PASGUALA MITZ

17 APRIL 1748

PASGUALA MITZ CIMI EN 17 DE ABLIL DE 1748 AÑŌS

Tu kaba dios yumbil y dios mehenbil y dios espiritu santo oxtul pēsonas[4] huntulil Dios uchuc tumen tusinil maix pimobi lai bin ylabac u hunil in takayahthan tin testamento hibicil tenil Cen pasguala mitz u yxmehen mathe.° mitz uyalen lorensa Cetz Bacacix cimil yn cah lae toh uol tin pucsikal y tin nat uet sihcie Baixan u olah mucul in cucutil ychil yotoch ca kuna lae

Bayxan Cin uoktic ynba ti ca pixanil yum padre guardian ca yalab hunpe ɔ missa yokol in pixan ca antabac tunamyuil anima purgatorio y ca u masen tu payalchi ychil u missa lae Baixan bin ɔabae u limosnail oxpel tostones y Capel tumin helusalem lae Baixan hunpai u cin ɔaic tin u al thomasa tun halilibe Cin uacuntic huntul almehen gra[l] chan albaseas lae

ygnasio Coba the[e]	D.[n] gaspar canul	gaspar tun
Bar.[me] pech ald[e]	Batab	Diego Mitz
Sebastian Uh ald[e]	Sar.[or] Coba ess[no]	an[tto] Juchim
		Sebastian yam
		Regidoresob

Cumpliose este funeral y se le canto la missa, como lo pidió el df[to] y lo firme en 18 de Abril de 48

fr. Joseph Villamil

PASQUALA MITZ DIED ON THE 17TH OF APRIL, 1748

In the name of God the Father, and God the Son, and God the Holy Spirit, three persons, one almighty God, not many. This document of my final words in my testament will be seen, insomuch as I who am Pasquala Mitz, the daughter of Mateo Mitz, the child of Lorensa Cetz. Although I am dying, my heart and my understanding are sound, as it should be. Likewise, I wish my body to be buried inside the home of our temple. Likewise, I supplicate our blessed lord, the guardian priest, that one mass for my soul be said to help the suffering purgatory soul, and that he say a prayer for me in that mass. Likewise, it will be given in alms three tostons and two tomins for Jerusalem.

Likewise, one necklace I give to my child Thomasa Tun. That is all. I appoint one nobleman, Gabriel Chan, as executor

Ignacio Coba, lieutenant	don Gaspar Canul	Gaspar Tun
Bartolomé Pech, alcalde	Batob	Diego Mitz
Sebastián Uh, alcalde	Salvador Coba, notary	Antonio Huchim
		Sebastián Yam
		Regidors

This funeral was completed and the mass was sung for her as the deceased requested, and I signed it on the 18th of April, 1748

fray Joseph Villamil

FOLS. 14R–14V DOCUMENT A23

WILL OF PHELIPE TEC

18 MAY 1748

PHELIPE TEC CIMI EN 18 DE MAYO DE 1748 ANŌS

Tu Kaba dios yumbil y dios mehenbil y dios espiritu santo oxtul personas huntulili dios uchuc tumen tusinil maix pimobi lai bin ylabac u huntil yn tokyahthan tin testamento hibicil tenil cen—phelipe tec u mehen dⁿ Clemente tec u yalen maria xuchimi ca = Bacacix cimil yn cah lae touol tin pucsikal y tin nat uet sihcie Bayxan u olah mucul yn cucutil ychil yotoch ca Kuna lae Bayxan Cin Uoktic ynba ti ca pixanil yum padre guardian ca ya lab hunpe ɔ missa yokol yn pixan ca antabac tu numyl anima purgatorio lae y Ca u masen tu payalchi ychil u missa lae Bayxan bin ɔabae u limosnayl oxpel tostones y Capel tumen helusalem lae

Bayxan hunper solal y u chenil Cin patic tin i ɔin helonimo tec y fran.ᶜᵒ tec y in u atan lorensa yam he Cabin Cimice ca mucuc tumen helonimo tec y fran.ᶜᵒ tec lai yn u atan lorensa yam Cutun u y ate hei solal y chen tu kab helonimo tec y fransisco tec lae Bayxan hun ɔit tzimin[?] y hunpok yeua tzimin y hunpay caha y hunpel u hol na—y hun ɔit cuchara takin Cin ɔaic ti fran.ᶜᵒ tec lae Bayxan he lai ye u alae ye Cabin alnace [u] ca u ɔaic yal hun pek ti lai yn tzenpal marcos coba lae Baixan hunpet kax yan ku

u tzayal ti chikin fran.^{co} tec [ti no]hol fran.^{co} pech ti lakin gaspr tob[?] Bayxan hunpet
kax cin ɔaic ti Berna tec y̱ fran.^{co} tec u tzayal lai kax ti noh Ber.^{na} tec ti lakin Bena
ti xan clemente yam y̱ Joseph yam ti chikin Diego pech = Baixan hunpel mesa y̱ ca
cilich colelbil cin ɔaic tin u atan lorensa yam halil u xul in than tin testamento lic yn
[ua] cunti catul almehenob mathe.° tec mathe.° ek albaleaseob lae

Bar.^{me} pech ald^e	D.ⁿ gaspar canul	gaspar tun
Sebastian uh ald^e	Batab	Diego mitz
	Sar^{or} Coba ess^{no}	an.^{tto} Juchim
		Regidoresob

Fr Franco Dias y Solis

FELIPE TEC DIED ON THE 18TH OF MAY, 1748

In the name of God the Father, and God the Son, and God the Holy Spirit, three persons, one almighty God, not many. This document of my final words in my testament
will be seen, insomuch as I who am Felipe Tec, the son of don Clemente Tec, the child
of María Huchim. Although I am dying, my heart and my understanding are sound,
as it should be. Likewise, I wish my body to be buried inside the home of our temple.
Likewise, I supplicate our blessed lord, the guardian priest, that one mass for my soul
be said to help the suffering purgatory soul, and that he say a prayer for me in that mass.
Likewise, it will be given in alms three tostons and two tomins for Jerusalem.

Likewise, one house plot and its well I leave to my younger brother Geronimo
Tec and Francisco Tec, and my wife Lorensa Yam; when I am dead and buried, from
Geronimo Tec and Francisco Tec, immediately it will be left to my wife, Lorensa
Yam, this house plot and well that is in the hands of Geronimo Tec and Francisco
Tec. Likewise, one horse and one mare and one chest and one house beam and one
metal spoon I give to Francisco Tec. Likewise, there is a mare; when it gives birth its
foal will be given to my adopted child Marcos Coba. Likewise, one forest where there
is a pyramid adjacent to the west is Francisco Tec, [to the] south Francisco Pech, to
the east Gaspar Cob[?] Likewise, one forest I give to Bernardina Tec and Francisco
Tec. Adjacent to the forest to the south is Bernardina Tec, to the east Bena, to the
north Clemente Yam and Joseph Yam, to the west Diego Pech. Likewise, one table
and Our Holy Lady I give to my wife Lorensa Yam. There is no more; this is the end
of my words in my testament in which I appoint two noblemen, Mateo Tec, Mateo
Ek, as executors.

Bartolomé Pech, alcalde	don Gaspar Canul	Gaspar Tun
Sebastián Uh, alcalde	batab	Diego Mitz
	Salvador Coba, notary	Antonio Huchim
		Regidors

fray Francisco Días y Solís

FOL. 15R DOCUMENT A24

WILL OF DIEGO TEC

18 MAYA 1748

DIEGO TEC CIMI EN 18 DE MAYO DE 1748

Tu Kaba dios yumbil y dios mehen y dios espiritu santo oxtul personas huntulili dios uchuc tumen tusinil maix pimobi lay bin ylabac u hunil yn thakyahthan tin testamento hibicil tenil cen Diego tec u mehen Ber.[no] tec u yalen Juana huchin = Bayxan bacacix cimil yn Cah lae touol tin pucsikal y tin ti na uet sihcie Bayxan u olah mucul yn Cacuhil ychil yotoch ca kuna lae Bayxan Cin uoktic ynba ti Ca pixanil yum padre guardian ca yalab hunpe ɔ missa yokol yn pixan Ca antabac tu numyuil anima purgatorio y ca u masen tu payalchi ychil u missa lae Bayxan bin ɔabae u limosnayl oxpel tostones y Capel capel tumin helusalem lae

   Bayxan hunpel cħeen y u solalil u pach y hunpak tzimin yeua hunpay caJa Cin ɔaic tin u atan Martha chim lae—Bayxan hunpel solal manan u cħenil y oxtul tzimin cin ɔaic tin na Juana Jucħim lae y hunpet kax yan silil utial xan halibe—tic yn uacuntic ca tul albaieasob marcos Coba—Silvestre pech

Bar.[me] pech ald[e]	D[n] gaspar canul	gaspar tun
Sebastian uh	Batab	Diego Mitz
	Sar[or] Coba ess[no]	an[tto] Jucħim
		Sebastian yan
		Regidoresob

   Fr Franco Dias y Solis

DIEGO TEC DIED ON THE 18TH OF MAY, 1748

In the name of God the Father, and God the Son, and God the Holy Spirit, three persons, one almighty God, not many. This document of my final words in my testament will be seen, insomuch as I who am Diego Tec, the son of Bernardo Tec, the child of Juana Huchim. Although I am dying, my heart and my understanding are sound, as it should be. Likewise, I wish my body to be buried inside the home of our temple. Likewise, I supplicate our blessed lord, the guardian priest, that one mass for my soul be said to help the suffering purgatory soul, and that he say a prayer for me in that mass. Likewise, it will be given in alms three tostons and two tomins for Jerusalem.

   Likewise, one well together with its house plot and one mare, one chest I give to my wife Martha Chim. Likewise, one house plot without a well and three horses I give to my mother Juana Huchim; and one forest that is at Silil belonging to her also. That is all. I appoint two executors, Marcos Coba, Silvestre Pech.

| Bartolomé Pech, alcalde | don Gaspar Canul | Gaspar Tun |
| Sebastián Uh | batab | Diego Mitz |

Salvador Coba, notary   Antonio Huchim

Sebastián Yam

Regidors

fray Francisco Días y Solís

FOLS. 15V–16R DOCUMENT A25

WILL OF MARTHA CANUL

18 MAY 1748

MARTHA CUNUL CIMI EN 18 DE MAYO DE 1748 AÑŌS

Tu kaba dios yumbil y Dios mehenbil y Dios espiritu santo oxtul personas huntulili
Dios uchuc tumen tusinil maix pimobi lay bin ylabae U hunil yn tokyahthan tin
testamento hibicil tenil Cen Martha cunul u yxmehen Bar.ᵐᵉ canul u yahen clara coba
lae Bacacix cimil yn Cah lae toh uol tin pucsikal y tin nat uet sihcie Baixan u olah
mucul yn Cucutil ychil yotoch Ca kuna lae Bayxan in uok ti ynba ti ca pixanil yum
padre guardian ca yalab hunpeɔ missa yokol yn pixan ca antabac tu numyail anima
purgatorio y ca u masen tu payalchi ychil u missa lae Bayxan tin ɔabae u limosnayl
oxpel tostones y Capel tumin helusalem lae

   Baixan hunpel ypil yetel hunpay sinta Cin ɔaic tin u ilib luissa cul Bayxan huntil
u cħeel kuche in ɔaic tin u al mathe.° tun lae—Baixan huntzil yubte y oxpel Kuch
Cim ɔaic tin u icham gaspar tun—Bayxan hunpel pic cin ɔaic tin u alob fran.ᶜᵒ tun =
mathe.° tun—Nicolas tun = ox nupobi lae Bayxan uacumentic oxpel mehen camisa
lai yn u ilib maria Cutz U ɔa tin u alob lae ca cec la[u]c lai pic ti yn u ilib lae Bayxan
hunpel cħeen y u solal u pach utial yn yum u mul matah y yn tillo catulob hehele lae
ca cu lae tanbuhteni y u iɔin luissa canul Baixan tan beh tin yum phelipe canul lae
Bayxan helay tanbuh solal yntial y luissa canul ti cabin than yn u alob xani lay tumen
cin ɔaic te[s]tamento lae halib lic yn uacuntic catul albaseasob Diego Mitz Juan bauᵗᵃ
matu =

Bar.ᵐᵉ pech aldᵉ	D.ⁿ gaspar Canul	gaspar tun
Sebastian uh aldᵉ	Batab	Diego Mitz
	Saruador Coba essⁿᵒ	an.ᵗᵗᵒ Juchim
		Sebastian yam
		Regidoresob

Fr. Franco Dias y Solis

MARTHA CANUL DIED ON THE 18TH OF MAY, 1748

In the name of God the Father, and God the Son, and God the Holy Spirit, three persons, one almighty God, not many. This document of my final words in my testament will be seen, insomuch as I who am Martha Canul, the daughter of Bartolome Canul, the child of Clara Coba. Although I am dying, my heart and my understanding are sound, as it should be. Likewise, I wish my body to be buried inside the home of our temple. Likewise, I supplicate our blessed lord, the guardian priest, that one mass for my soul be said to help the suffering purgatory soul, and that he say a prayer for me in that mass. Likewise, it will be given in alms three tostons and two tomins for Jerusalem.

Likewise, one huipil and one belt I give to my daughter-in-law Luissa Cul. Likewise, one length of blond yarn I give to my child Mateo Tun. Likewise, one tribute manta and three lengths of yarn I give to my husband Gaspar Tun. Likewise, one petticoat I give to my children Francisco Tun, Mateo Tun, Nicolás Tun, the three of them together. Likewise, ... three sons, shirt of my daughter-in-law María Cutz is given to my children. ... petticoat to my daughter-in-law. Likewise, one well together with its house plot belonging to my father and my uncle that they both received jointly today I divide it between the younger sibling Luissa Canul. Likewise, today I divide my house plot between Luissa Canul with my words to my children also, thus I give testament. There is no more. At this time I appoint two executors: Diego Mitz, Juan Bautista Matu

Bartolomé Pech, alcalde	don Gaspar Canul	Gaspar Tun
Sebastián Uh, alcalde	batab	Diego Mitz
	Salvador Coba, notary	Antonio Huchim
		Sebastián Yam
		Regidors

fray Francisco Días y Solís

FOL. 16V DOCUMENT A26

WILL OF PHELIPE TEC

5 JULY 1748

PHELIPE TEC CIMI EN 5 DE JULIO DE 1748 AÑŌS

Tu kaba dios yumbil y̨ dios mehenbil y̨ dios espiritu santo oxtul pelsonas huntuli dios uchuc tumen tusinil maix pimobi lay bin ylabac u hunil yn tokyahthantin testamento hibicil tenil cen phelipe tec U mehen = Bar.^me tec u yalen Maria Uh lae Bacacix cimil yn Cah lae toh uol tin pucsikal y̨ tin nat uet sihcie = Bayxan u olah mucul yn cutil ychil yotoch ca kuna lae Bayxan cin uoktic ynba ti ca pixanil yum padre guardian ca yalab hunpe ꜧ missa yokol yn pixan caantabae tu numyail anima purgatorio y̨ ca u masen tu payalchi ychil u missa lae = Bayxan bin ꜧabae u limosna oxpel toston y̨ capel tumin helusalen—

Bayxan heix bal bin u ɔa ten yn yum cabin cimice ca u ɔac tin mehen y̱ ti yxmehen lae—gra.ˡ tec = maria tec = halile minan ubal ynba lae cin uacunti huntul al mehen matheo tec albaseas

Bar.ᵐᵉ pech ald.ᵉ	D.ⁿ gaspar canul	gaspar tun
Sebastian Uh ald.ᵉ	Batab	diego mitz
ygnasio Coba the.ᵉ	Saruador Coba ess.ⁿᵒ	Sebastian yam
		an.ᵗᵗᵒ Juchim
		Regidoresob

Fr. Franco Dias y Solis

PHELIPE TEC DIED ON THE 5TH OF JULY, 1748

In the name of God the Father, and God the Son, and God the Holy Spirit, three persons, one God almighty, not many. The document of my final words in my testament will be seen, insomuch as I who am Phelipe Tec, the son of Bartolome Tec, the child of María Uh. Although I am dying, my heart and my understanding are sound, as it should be. Likewise, I wish my body to be buried inside the home of our temple. Likewise, I supplicate our blessed lord, the guardian priest, that one mass for my soul be said to help the suffering purgatory soul, and that he say a prayer for me in that mass. Likewise, it will be given in alms three tostons and two tomins for Jerusalem.

Likewise, what my father will give to me when he dies will be given to my son and my daughter, Gabriel Tec, María Tec. That is all, I have no more things. I appoint one nobleman, Mateo Tec, as executor.

Bartolomé Pech, alcalde	don Gaspar Canul	Gaspar Tun
Sebastián Uh, alcalde	batab	Diego Mitz
Ignacio Coba, lieutenant	Salvador Coba, notary	Sebastián Yam
		Antonio Huchim
		Regidors

fray Francisco Días y Solís

FOL. 17R DOCUMENT A27

WILL OF JOSEPH CHALE

4 AUGUST 1748

TESTINMONIO

JOSEPH CHALE CIMI EN 4 DE AGOSTO DE 1748 AÑŌS

Tu kaba dios yumbil y̱ dios mehenbil y̱ dios espiritu santo oxtul pelsonas huntulili dios uchuc tumen tusinil maix pimobi lay bin ylaba u hunil yn tokyahthan tin

testamento hibicil tenil cen Joseph Chale u mehen Fran.ᶜᵒ chale U yalen—mag.ⁿᵃ
cauich ah cah nalen ti cah mococha lae Bacacix cimil yn cah lae toh uol tin pucsikal y̱
tin nat uet sihcie Bayxan u olah mucul yn cucutil ychil yotoch ca Kuna lae Bayxan cin
uoktic ynba ti ca pixanil yum padre guardian ca yalab hunpeɔ missa yokol yn pixan
ca antabac tu num yail anima purgatorio y̱ ca u masen tu payalchi ychil u missa lae—
Bayxan bin ɔabae u limosnayl oxpel toston y̱ capel tumin helusalem

Bayxan hunpel cħeen y̱ u solalil u pach lic ca Kubic ti Manuela cante y̱ u yalob
agustin chale Juan Joseph chale y̱ luissa chale Bayxan hunpay caJa y̱ hunpay tabron
y̱ hunpay u bateyail po lae halil u xul yn than tin testamento lae—agustin yam pasg̱ʲ
pech albaseasob lae—

ygnasio coba theᵉ	D.ⁿ gaspar canul	gaspar tun
Bar.ᵐᵉ pech aldᵉ	Batab	Diego Mitz
Sebas.ᵃⁿ Uh aldᵉ	Saruador Coba essⁿᵒ	an.ʳᵗᵒ Jucħim
		Sebastian yam
		Regidoresob

    Fr. Franco Dias y Solis

TESTIMONY

JOSEPH CHALE DIED ON THE 4TH OF AUGUST, 1748

In the name of God the Father, and God the Son, and God the Holy Spirit, three persons, one God almighty, not many. The document of my final words in my testament
will be seen, insomuch as I who am Joseph Chale, the son of Francisco Chale, the
child of Magdalena Cauich, residents of the cah Mococha. Although I am dying, my
heart and my understanding are sound, as it should be. Likewise, I wish my body to
be buried inside the home of our temple. Likewise, I supplicate our blessed lord, the
guardian priest, that one mass for my soul be said to help the suffering purgatory soul,
and that he say a prayer for me in that mass. Likewise, it will be given in alms three
tostons and two tomins for Jerusalem.

Likewise, one well together with its house plot will be delivered to Manuela Cante
and her children Augustin Chale, Juan Joseph Chale, and Luisa Chale. Likewise, one
chest, and one table, and one axe head. That is all; this is the end of my words in my
testament. Augustin Yam, Pasgual Pech, executors

Ignacio Coba, lieutenant	don Gaspar Canul	Gaspar Tun
Bartolomé Pech, alcalde	Batob	Diego Mitz
Sebastián Uh, alcalde	Salvador Coba, notary	Antonio Huchim
		Sebastián Yam
		Regidors

    fray Francisco Dias y Solís

FOL. 17V DOCUMENT A28

WILL OF MARCOS HUCHIM

4 AUGUST 1748

MARCOS JUCHIM CIMI EN 4 DE AGOSTO DE 1748 ANŌS

Tu kaba dios yumbil y dios mehenbil y dios espirtu santo oxtul pelsonas huntulili dios uchuc tumen tu sinil maix pimobi lay ben ylabac u hunil yn tokyahthan tin testamento lae—hibilcil tenil cen marcos Juchim u mehen Joseph Juchim u yalen An.^tta chim lae Baca cix cimil yn Cah lae toh uol tin pucsikal y tin nat uet sihcic Bayxan u oloah mucul yn cucutil ychil yotoch ca Kuna lae Bayxan cin uoktic ynba ti ca pixanil yum padre ca yalab hunpeↄ missa yokol yn pixan ca antabac tu numyalyl anima purgatorio lae y ca u masen tu payalchi ychil u missa lae Bayxan bin ↄabae u limosnayl oxpel tostones y capel tumin helusalem lae

Bayxan hebal cubin u ↄaab ten yn yum Cabin payac u cuxtal tumen ca yumil ti d.^s lae ca u ↄab tin mehen gra^l Juchim y lix lay yoman lae halil u xul in than tin testamento lae—gra^l chan albaseas lae

ygnasio Coba the^e	D.^n gaspar canul	gasp.^r tun
Bar.^me pech ald^e	Batab	diego mitz
Sebastian Uh ald^e	Saruador coba ess^no	an.^tto Juchim
		Sebas.^an yam
		Regidoresob

Fr. Franco Dias y Solis

MARCOS HUCHIM DIED ON THE 4TH OF AUGUST, 1748

In the name of God the Father, and God the Son, and God the Holy Spirit, three persons, one God almighty, not many. The document of my final words in my testament will be seen, insomuch as I who am Marcos Huchim, the son of Joseph Huchim, the child of Anneta Chim. Although I am dying, my heart and my understanding are sound, as it should be. Likewise, I wish my body to be buried inside the home of our temple. Likewise, I supplicate our blessed lord, the guardian priest, that one mass for my soul be said to help the suffering purgatory soul, and that he say a prayer for me in that mass. Likewise, it will be given in alms three tostons and two tomins for Jerusalem.

Likewise, what is given to me by my father when our lord God calls his life is given to my son Gabriel Huchim and . . . That is all; this is the end of my words in my testament. Gabriel Chan, executor.

Ignacio Coba, lieutenant	don Gaspar Canul	Gaspar Tun
Bartolomé Pech, alcalde	Batob	Diego Mitz
Sebastián Uh, alcalde	Salvador Coba, notary	Antonio Huchim

Sebastián Yam

Regidors

fray Francisco Días y Solís

FOL. 18R DOCUMENT A29

WILL OF DIEGO CETZ

4 AUGUST 1748

DIEGO CETZ CIMI EN 4 DE AGOSTO DE 1748 AÑŌS

Tu kaba dios yumbil y dios mehenbil y dios espiritu santo oxtul personas huntulili dios uchuc tumen tusinil maix pimobi lay bin ylabae u hunil yn tokyathan tin
testamento hibicil tenil cen diego cetz u mehen pedro cetz u yalen—Bar.ⁿᵃ pech lae
bacacix cimil yn Cah lae toh uol tin pucsikal y tin nat uet sihcie Bayxan u olah mucul
yn cucutil ychil yotoch cu Kuna lae Bayxan cin uoktic ynba ti ca pixanil yum padre
guardian ca yalab hunpeɔ missa yoklal yn pixan—ca antabac tu numyail anima purgatorio y ca u masen tu payalchi ychil u missa lae Bayxan bin ɔabae u limosnayl oxpel
tostones y capel tumin helusalem lae

Bayxan hunpel cħeen y u solalil u pach y hunpel kax yan tan u tzayal lay kax ti
lakine Juachin pech—ti xaman dn Joseph Cob chikine marcos cante ti nohol lucas
couoh lae cin ɔaic ti mehen diego cetz—Bayxan hunpay caJa cin ɔaic tin mehen
marcos cob halil u xul in than tin testamento lae—cin uacuntic huntul al mehen graˡ
chan albaseas

ygnasio Coba theᵉ	D.ⁿ gaspar canul	gaspar tun
Bar.ᵐᵉ pech aldᵉ	Batab	Diego mitz
Sebastian Uh aldᵉ	Saruador Coba ess.º	An.ᵗᵗº Juchim
		Sebastian yam
		Regidoresob

Fr. Frano Dias y Solis

DIEGO CETZ DIED ON THE 4TH OF AUGUST, 1748

In the name of God the Father, and God the Son, and God the Holy Spirit, three persons, one God almighty, not many. The document of my final words in my testament
will be seen, insomuch as I who am Diego Cetz, the son of Pedro Cetz, the child of
Bernardina Pech. Although I am dying, my heart and my understanding are sound,
as it should be. Likewise, I wish my body to be buried inside the home of our temple.
Likewise, I supplicate our blessed lord, the guardian priest, that one mass for my soul
be said to help the suffering purgatory soul, and that he say a prayer for me in that
mass. Likewise, it will be given in alms three tostons and two tomins for Jerusalem.

Likewise, one well together with its house plot and one forest—adjacent to the forest to the east is Juaquin Pech, to the north don Joseph Cob, west Marcos Cante, to the south Lucas Couoh—I give to my son Diego Cetz. Likewise, one chest I give to my son Marcos Cob. That is all; this is the end of my words in my testament. I appoint one nobleman, Gabriel Chan, as executor.

Ignacio Coba, lieutenant	don Gaspar Canul	Gaspar Tun
Bartolomé Pech, alcalde	batab	Diego Mitz
Sebastián Uh, alcalde	Salvador Coba, notary	Antonio Huchim
		Sebastián Yam
		Regidors

fray Francisco Días y Solís

FOL. 18V DOCUMENT A30

WILL OF FELIPE CHIM
14 AUGUST 1748

FELIPE CHIM CIMI EN 14 DE AGOSTO DE 1748 ANŌS

Tu kaba dios yumbil y dios mehenbil y dios espiritu santo oxtul personas huntulili Dios uchuc tumen tusinil maix pimobi lay bin ylabac u hunil yn tokyakthan tin testamento hibilcil tenil cen phelipe chim U mehen Agustin chim u yalen—Martha Coba = Bacacix cimil yn cah lae toh uoltin pucsikal y tin nat uet sihcie = Bayxan u olah mucul yn cucutil ychil yotoch ca kuna lae Bayxan cin uoktic ynba ti ca pixanil yum padre guardian ca yalab hunpeɔ missa yoklal yn pixan ca antabac tu numyail anima purgatorio y ca u masen tu payalchi ychil u missa lae Bayxan bin ɔabae u limosnail oxpel tostones y capel tumin helusalem lae—

Bayxan hunpel cheen y u solalil u pach yn mul ma tah y yn cicob lae cin patic tin yxme martha chim y maria chim y lay yaman lae Bayxan hunpay caJa utial utial Martha chim y maria chim lae—halil u xul yn than tin testamento lae = graꞁ chan albasias

Bar^me pech ald^e	D.^n gaspar canul	gaspar tun
Sebastian Uh ald^e	Batab	diego mitz
yg.° Coba the^e	Saruador Coba ess^no	an^tto Juchim
		Sebastian yam
		Regidoresob

Fr. Franco dias y Solis

FELIPE CHIM DIED ON THE 14TH OF AUGUST, 1748

In the name of God the Father, and God the Son, and God the Holy Spirit, three persons, one God almighty, not many. The document of my final words in my testament will be seen, insomuch as I who am Phelipe Chim, the son of Augustin Chim, the child of Martha Coba. Although I am dying, my heart and my understanding are sound, as it should be. Likewise, I wish my body to be buried inside the home of our temple. Likewise, I supplicate our blessed lord, the guardian priest, that one mass for my soul be said to help the suffering purgatory soul, and that he say a prayer for me in that mass. Likewise, it will be given in alms three tostons and two tomins for Jerusalem.

Likewise, one well together with its house plot I received jointly with my older sisters I leave to my daughter[s] Martha Chim and María Chim, jointly. Likewise, one chest belonging to Martha Chim and María Chim. That is all; this is the end to my words in my testament. Gabriel Chan, executor

Bartolomé Pech, alcalde	don Gaspar Canul	Gaspar Tun
Sebastián Uh, alcalde	batab	Diego Mitz
Ignacio Coba, lieutenant	Salvador Coba, notary	Antonio Huchim
		Sebastián Yam
		Regidors

fray Francisco Días y Solís

FOL. 19R DOCUMENT A31

WILL OF MARÍA CANDELARIA CANTE
19 OF AUGUST 1748

M.ᵃ CAN.ᵃ CANTE CIMI EN 19 DE AGOSTO DE 1748 AÑŌS

Tu kaba dios yumbil y dios mehenbil y dios espiritu Santo oxtul personals huntulili Dios uchuc tumen tusinil maix pimobi lay bin ylabac u hunil—yn tokyahthan tin testamento hibilcil tenil cen maria can.ᵃ cante u yxmehen agustin cante u yalen lorensa canul = Bacacix cimi tin cah lae toh uol tin pucsikal y tin nat uet sihcie—Bayxan u olah mucul yn cucutil ychil yotoch ca Kuna lae Bayxan cin uoktic ynba tic pixanil yum padre guardian ca yalab hunpeɔ missa yoklal yn pixan ca antabac tu numyail anima—purgatorio y ca u masen tu payalchi ychil u missa lae Bayxan bin ɔaba u limosnayl oxpel tostones y Capel tu tumin helusalem lae—

Bayxan he cħeen y u solalil u pach cah lic yn yum lae ti cu than yn u alobi = graˡ Juchim = lorensa Juchim halil u xul in than tin testamento lae—Andres ytza = ygnasio Coba albaseasob lae—

ygnasio coba theᵉ	D.ⁿ gaspar canul	gaspar tun

Bartolme pech ald^e	Batab	diego mitz
Sebas.^n Uh ald^e	Sar.^or Coba ess^no	an.^tto Juchim
		Sebastian yam
		Regidoresob

Fr. Franco Dias y Solis

MARÍA CANDELARIA CANTE DIED ON THE 19TH OF AUGUST, 1748

In the name of God the Father, and God the Son, and God the Holy Spirit, three persons, one God almighty, not many. The document of my final words in my testament will be seen, insomuch as I who am María Candelaria Cante, the daughter of Augustin Cante, the child of Lorensa Canul. Although I am dying, my heart and my understanding are sound, as it should be. Likewise, I wish my body to be buried inside the home of our temple. Likewise, I supplicate our blessed lord, the guardian priest, that one mass for my soul be said to help the suffering purgatory soul, and that he say a prayer for me in that mass. Likewise, it will be given in alms three tostons and two tomins for Jerusalem.

Likewise, here is a well together with its house plot where my father resides, is spoken for by my children Gabriel Huchim, Lorensa Huchim. That is all; this is the end of my words in my testament. Andrés Itza, Ignacio Coba, executors.

Ignacio Coba, lieutenant	don Gaspar Canul	Gaspar Tun
Bartolomé Pech, alcalde	batab	Diego Mitz
Sebastián Uh, alcalde	Salvador Coba, notary	Antonio Huchim
		Sebastián Yam
		Regidors

fray Francisco Días y Solís

FOL. 19V DOCUMENT A32

WILL OF MANUEL COBA

4 OCTOBER 1748

MANUEL COBA CIMI EN [4] DE OCTUBRE DE 1748

Tu kaba dios yumbil y dios mehenbil y dios espiritu santo oxtul personas huntu-lili dios uchuc tumen tusinil maix pimobi lai bin ylaba u hunil in tokyahthan tin testamento hibicil tenil cen manuel Coba U mehen Sebastian Coba U yalen pasguala canche lae bacacix cimil in cah lae toh uol tin pucsikal y tin nat uet sihcie—Baixan u olah mucul in cucutil ychil ca kuna lae Baixan cin uoktic inbah ti ca pixanil yum pe guardian ca yalab hunpeɔ missa yoklal in pixan ca antabac tu numiayl anima purgatorio y ca u masen tu payalchi ichil u missa lae—Baixan bin ɔabae u limosnayl oxpel tostones y capel tumin helusalem lae—

Baixan hunpai caha Cin ɔaic tin u atun—pasguala Juchim lae = graˡ chane Ber.ⁿᵒ coba albaseasob lae =

Bar.ᵐᵉ pech aldᵉ	D.n gaspar canul	Gaspar tun
Sebastian Uh aldᵉ	Batab	Diego Mitz
	Sar.ᵒʳ Coba essⁿᵒ	An.ᵗᵗᵒ Juchim
		Sebastain yam
		Regidoresob

Fr. franco Dias y Solis

MANUEL COBA DIED ON THE 4TH OF OCTOBER, 1748

In the name of God the Father, and God the Son, and God the Holy Spirit, three persons, one God almighty, not many. The document of my final words in my testament will be seen, insomuch as I who am Manuel Coba, the son of Sebastián Coba, the child of Pasguala Canche. Although I am dying, my heart and my understanding are sound, as it should be. Likewise, I wish my body to be buried inside the home of our temple. Likewise, I supplicate our blessed lord, the guardian priest, that one mass for my soul be said to help the suffering purgatory soul, and that he say a prayer for me in that mass. Likewise, it will be given in alms three tostons and two tomins for Jerusalem.

Likewise, one chest I give to my wife, Pasguala Juchim. Gabriel Chan, Bernardo Coba, executors.

Bartolomé Pech, alcalde	don Gaspar Canul	Gaspar Tun
Sebastián Uh, alcalde	Batob	Diego Mitz
	Salvador Coba, notary	Antonio Huchim
		Sebastián Yam
		Regidors

fray Francisco Días y Solís

FOLS. 20R–20V DOCUMENT A33

WILL OF IGNACIO TEC

23 OCTOBER 1748

YGNASIO TEC CIMI EN 23 DE OCTUBRE DE 1748 AÑŌS

Tu kaba dios yumbil y dios mehenbil y dios espirtu santo oxul personas huntulili dios uchuc tumen tusinil maix pimobi lay bin y labac u hunil yn tokayahthan tin

testamento lae hibicil tenil cen ygnasio tec u mehen xpⁱ tec U yalen Juana Uh =
Bacacix cimil in cah lae toh uol tin pucsikal y̠ tin nat uet sihcie = Bayxan u olah
mucul in cucutil ychil yotoch ca kuna lae = Bayxan Cin uoktic ynba ti ca pixanil yum
padre guardian ca yalab Junpe ꜫ missa yoklal in pixan ca antabac tu numiayl anima
purgatorio y̠ ca u masen tu payalchi ychil u missa Bayxan Sin ꜫabae u limosnayl oxpel
toston y̠ Capel tumin Jelusalem lae—

Bayxan hunpel cɧeen y̠ U solalil u pach in mul matahma y̠ in sucunob cin patic in
mehenobi yn he lint = Bayxan heix u cɧenil in mam lae ti Cu than in mehenob xani
= tu nohol Miguel tun yan lay cɧeen lae—Bayxan hunpok capon tzimin y̠ hunpok
yeua tzimin y̠ hunpet kax yan cacal U tzayal lai kax ti xami clemente tec ti lakin
mathias ake ti chikin Diego Couoh ti nohol agustin Coba Cin patic ti lai i mehenob
lae Saruador tec pasgⁱ tec Bar.ᵐᵉ tec ant.ᵒ tec can nupobi lae Bayxan hunpay CaJa u
multial in mehenob xan Bayxan hunpok yeua tzin in u yal lai tzimin lae cin ꜫaic tin
Na Juana Uh = Baixan hunpel u hol in mul matahma y̠ in sucuni andres tec Cin patic
in mehenob xani can nupobi lae halil u xul in than tin testamento lae Cin uaCuntic
Juntul al mehen mathe.ᵒ tec albaseas lae—

Batalome pech aldᵉ	D.ⁿ Gaspar canul	Gasp.ʳ tun
Sebastian Uh aldᵉ	Batab	Diego mitz
	Saruador Coba essⁿᵒ	an.ᵗᵗᵒ Jucɧim
		Sebastian yam
		Regidoresob

Fr. Franco Dias y Solis

IGNACIO TEC DIED ON THE 23RD OF OCTOBER, 1748

In the name of God the Father, and God the Son, and God the Holy Spirit, three
persons, one almighty God, not many. The document of my final words in my testament will be seen, insomuch as I who am Ignacio Tec, the son of Cristóbal Tec, the
child of Juana Uh. Although I am dying, my heart and my understanding are sound,
as it should be. Likewise, I wish my body to be buried inside the home of our temple.
Likewise, I supplicate our blessed lord, the guardian priest, that one mass for my soul
be said to help the suffering purgatory soul, and that he say a prayer for me in that
mass. Likewise, it will be given in alms three tostons and two tomins for Jerusalem.

Likewise, one well together with its house plot I received jointly with my older
brothers I leave to my sons . . . Likewise, here is a well of my grandfather, this is
spoken for by my sons also; to the north is Miguel Tun and there is the well. Likewise,
one gelding and one mare, and one forest—adjacent to the forest to the north is
Clemente Tec, to the east Matias Ake, to the west Diego Couoh, to the south Agustín
Coba—I leave it to my sons Salvador Tec, Pasgual Tec, Bartolomé Tec, Antonio Tec,
the four of them together. Likewise, one chest to belong jointly among my sons also.
Likewise, one mare and its colt[?] I give to my mother, Juana Uh. Likewise, one beam

I received jointly with my older brother Andrés Tec I leave to my sons also, the four of them together. That is all; this is the end of my words in my testament. I appoint one nobleman, Mateo Tec, as executor.

Bartolomé Pech, alcalde	don Gaspar Canul	Gaspar Tun
Sebastián Uh, alcalde	batob	Diego Mitz
	Salvador Coba, notary	Antonio Huchim
		Sebastián Yam
		Regidors

fray Francisco Días y Solís

FOL. 21R DOCUMENT A34

WILL OF MARÍA TEC

14 NOVEMBER 1748

MARIA TEC CIMI EN 14 DE NOB.ʳᵉ 1748 ANŌS

Tu kaba dios yumbil y dios mehenbil y Dios espiritu santo oxtul personas Juntulili dios uchuc tu men tusinil maix pimobi lay bin ylabac u hunil in tokyahthan tin testamento hibicil tenil cen ma tec u yxmehen Miguel tec u yalen Agustina Canul— BacaCix Cimil in Cah lae toh uol tin pucSikal y tin nat uet sihcie = Bayxan u olah mucul in cucutil ychil yotoch ca kuna lae = Bayxan Cin uoktic ynba ti ca pixanil yum padre guardian ca yalab Junpeɔ missa yoklol pixan caan tabai tu numyail anima purgatorio y ca u masen tu payalchi ychil u missa lae = Bayxan bin ɔabae u limosnayl oxpel toston y Capel tumin helusalem lae

halil u xul in than tin testamento lae pasgual pech albaseas—

ygnasio Coba theᵉ	D.ⁿ Gaspar canul	Gasp.ʳ tun
Barme pech aldᵉ	Batab	Diego Mitz
Sebastian Uh aldᵉ	Saruador Coba essⁿᵒ	anᵗᵗᵒ juchim
		Sebas.ⁿ yam
		Regidoresob

Cumpliose este funeral y se le canto una missa, Viga y response: y lo firme
    fr. Manˡ de Lara

MARÍA TEC DIED ON THE 14TH OF NOVEMBER, 1748

In the name of God the Father, and God the Son, and God the Holy Spirit, three persons, one God almighty, not many. The document of my final words in my testament will be seen, insomuch as I who am María Tec, the daughter of Miguel Tec, the child of Augustina Canul. Although I am dying, my heart and my understanding are sound, as it should be. Likewise, I wish my body to be buried inside the home of our temple. Likewise, I supplicate our blessed lord, the guardian priest, that one mass for my soul be said to help the suffering purgatory soul, and that he say a prayer for me in that mass. Likewise, it will be given in alms three tostons and two tomins for Jerusalem.

That is all; this is the end of my words in my testament. Pasgual Pech, executor.

Ignacio Coba, lieutenant	don Gaspar canul	Gaspar Tun
Bartolomé Pech, alcalde	batab	Diego Mitz
Sebastián Uh, alcalde	Saruador Coba, notary	Antonio Huchim
		Sebastián Yam
		regidors

This funeral was completed and a mass was sung for her, vigil, and responsory prayer, and I signed it

fray Manuel de Lara

FOLS. 21V–22R DOCUMENT A35

WILL OF ANNA ITZA

14 NOVEMBER 1748

ANNA YTZA CIMI EN [1]4 DE NOB.ʳᵉ DE 1748 ANŌS

Tu kaba dios yumbil y dios mehenbil y dios espiritu santo oxtul personas huntulili dios uchuc tumē tusinil maix pimobi lay bin ylabac u hunil yn testamento hibicil tenil Cen Anna ytza u yxmehen phelipe ytza U yalen xpⁿᵃ ba BacaCix Cimil yn Cab lae toh uol tin pucsikal y tin nat uet sihcie—Bayxan u olah mucul yn cucutil ychil yotoch ca kuna lae Bayxan cin uoktic ynba ti ca pixanil yum padre guardian ca yalab hunpeɔ missa yoklal pixan ca antabac tu numyail anima purgatorio y cu u masen tu payalchi ychil u missa lae—Bayxan bin ɔabae U limosnayl oxpel tostones y Capel tumin helulalem lae—

Bayxan hunpel cħeen y u solalil u pach cin—ɔaic tin u al Joseph mitz y catⁿᵃ Mitz y Rogue Mitz = Bayxan hunpet kax yan ber ConKal tu katbe mo ca chaobi u tzayal ti lakin D.ⁿ Jospeh pech ti nohol pedro tun ti chikin D.ⁿ Sebastian pech ti xaman pasgual pech Cin ɔaic tin u al Josseph Mitz y agustin chan ca nupobi lae—Bayxan hunpel u holna Cin ɔaic tin uol Joseph Mitz y Martin Canul ca nupobi lae—Bayxan hun ɔit cuchara takin Cin ɔaic tin u al Jospeh Mitz y Cata.ⁿᵃ Mitz ca nupobi—Bayxan hunpay caha cin ɔaic tin u al Joseph Mitz Bayxan hunpel ypil y hunpel pic cin ɔaic ti Pasguala canul lae halil u xul in than tin testamento lae minan u bal inba lae Bayxan Cin uacuntic Capel al mehenob Joseph Mitz y Andres Itza Albaseasob lae utial u tanolte u katicob [m]issa yoklal in pixan tutan Batab y Justisias—

ygnasio Coba theᵉ   Cnppⁿ D.ⁿ Gaspar canul   Gaspʳ tun

Bar.^me pech ald^e	Batab	D.° Mitz
Sebastian Uh ald^e	Saruador Coba essno	an^tto Juchim
		Sebastian yam
		Regisdoresob

Cumpliose con este testameto y se le canto una missa vigilia y responio como lo pidió y lo firme en 19 de Nobe de 1748 ano

    fr. Joachim Paz[5]

ANNA ITZA DIED ON THE 24TH OF NOVEMBER, 1748

In the name of God the Father, and God the Son, and God the Holy Spirit, three persons, one God almighty, not many. The document of my testament will be seen, insomuch as I who am Anna Itza, the daughter of Phelipe Itza, the child of Christina Ba. Although I am dying, my heart and my understanding are sound, as it should be. Likewise, I wish my body to be buried inside the home of our temple. Likewise, I supplicate our blessed lord, the guardian priest, that one mass for my soul be said to help the suffering purgatory soul, and that he say a prayer for me in that mass. Likewise, it will be given in alms three tostons and two tomins for Jerusalem.

    Likewise, one well together with its house plot I give to my child Joseph Mitz and Catarina Mitz, and Roque Mitz. Likewise, one forest there on the road to Conkal . . . adjacent to the east is don Joseph Pech, to the south is Pedro Tun, to the west don Sebastián Pech, to the north Pasgual Pech, I give to my child Joseph Mitz and Agustín Chan, the both of them together. Likewise, one metal spoon I give to my child Joseph Mitz and Catarina Mitz, the both of them together. Likewise, one chest I give to my child Joseph Mitz. Likewise, one hupil and one petticoat I give to Pasguala Canul. That is all; this is the end of my words in my testament. I have no more things. Likewise, I appoint two noblemen, Joseph Mitz and Andrés Itza, as executors; they will take care to ask for the mass for my soul; before the Batab and Justices

Ignacio Coba, lieutenant	captain don Gaspar Canul	Gaspar Tun
Bartolomé Pech, alcalde	batab	Diego Mitz
Sebastián Uh, alcalde	Salvador Coba, notary	Antonio Huchim
		Sebastián Yam
		Regidors

This testament was fulfilled and a responsory mass was sung for her and a vigil as she requested, and I signed it on the 29th of November, 1748

    fray Joachim Paz

FOL. 22V DOCUMENT A36

WILL OF MATHIAS COB

2 DECEMBER 1748

MATHIAS COB CIMI EN 2 DE DIZ.ᶜ 1748 ANŌS

Tu kaba dios yumbil yetel Dios mehenbil y̆ Dios espiritu santo oxtul personas huntulili dios Uchuc tumen tusinil maix pimobi lay bin ylabac u hunil yn tokyahthan tin testamento hibicil tenil cen mathias Cob u mehen Andres Cob u yalen lusia tec—BacaCix cimil yn Cah lae toh uol tin pucsikal y̆ tin nat uet sihcie Bayxan uolah muculin cucutil ychil yotoch ca kuna lae Bayxan cin uoktic ynba ti ca pixanil yum padre guardian ca yalab hunpe ɔ missa yoklal yn pixan ca antabac tu numiayl anima purgatorio y̆ ca u masen tu payalchi ychil u missa lae—Bayxan bin ɔabae u limosnayl oxpel toston y̆ capel tumin helusalem lae—

Bayxan hunpok yeua tzimin cin ɔaic tin mehen Berⁿᵒ Cob he cabin alnace ca u ɔae yal ti yin ursura Cob lae—Baybic tu ɔaah ten in yum lae mama bin luksic ti in mehenob lae halil u xul in than tin testam.ᵗᵒ Joseph Mitz aluasias

yg.° Coba theᶜ	D.ⁿ gaspar canul	gaspar tun
Bar.ᵐᵉ pech aldᶜ	Batab	Diego Mitz
Sebastian Uh aldᶜ	Saruador Coba ess.ⁿᵒ	an.ᵗᵗᵒ huchim
		Sebastian yam
		Regidoresob

Joseph del Valle y Solis

MATIAS COB DIED ON THE 2ND OF DECEMBER, 1748

In the name of God the Father, and God the Son, and God the Holy Spirit, three persons, one God almighty, not many. The document of my final words in my testament will be seen, insomuch as I who am Matias Cob, the son of Andrés Cob, the child of Lusia Tec. Although I am dying, my heart and my understanding are sound, as it should be. Likewise, I wish my body to be buried inside the home of our temple. Likewise, I supplicate our blessed lord, the guardian priest, that one mass for my soul be said to help the suffering purgatory soul, and that he say a prayer for me in that mass. Likewise, it will be given in alms three tostons and two tomins for Jerusalem.

Likewise, one mare I give to my son Bernardo Cob. When . . . he will give . . . to Ursula Cob. Likewise, that which my father gave to me, no one will take away from my sons. That is all; this is the end of my words in my testament. Joseph Mitz, executor.

Ignacio Coba, lieutenant	don Gaspar Canul	Gaspar Tun
Bartolomé Pech, alcalde	batab	Diego Mitz
Sebastián Uh, alcalde	Salvador Coba, notary	Antonio Huchim

Sebastián Yam

regidors

Joseph del Valle y Solís

FOL. 23R DOCUMENT A37

WILL OF PASGUAL CANCHE

2 DECEMBER 1748

PASGUAL CANCHE CIMI EN 2 DE DIZ.ᵉ DE 1748 AÑŌS

Tu kaba dios yumbil y dios mehenbil y dios espiritu santo oxtu personas huntulili
dios uchuc tumen tusinil maix pimobi lay bin ylabac u hunil yn tok yahthan tin testamento hibiCil tenil cen pasgual canche u mehen Gaspar canche u yalen Rossa Coyi
lae—Bacacix cimil yn cah lae toh uol tin pucSikal y tin nat uet sihcie = Bayxan u olah
mucul in cucutil ychil yotoch ca kuna lae Bayxan Cin uoktic ynba ti ca pixanil yum
padre guardian ca yalab hunpe ɔ missa yoklal in pixan ca antabac tu numiayl anima
purgatorio y ca u masen tu payalchi ychil u missa Bayxan bin ɔabae u limosnayl oxpel
tostones y capel tumin helusalem lae—

fran.ᶜᵒ Na aluaseas

yg.ᵒ Coba theᵉ	D.ⁿ Gaspar canul	gaspar tun
Bar.ᵐᵉ pech aldᵉ	Batab	Diego Mitz
Sebastian Uh aldᵉ	Saruador Coba essⁿᵒ	an.ᵗᵗᵒ Juchim
		Sebastian yam
		Regidoresob

Fr. Francisco Dias y Solis

PASGUAL CANCHE DIED ON THE 2ND OF DECEMBER, 1748

In the name of God the Father, and God the Son, and God the Holy Spirit, three persons, one God almighty, not many. The document of my final words in my testament
will be seen, insomuch as I who am Pasgual Canche, the son of Gaspar Canche, the
child of Rossa Coyi. Although I am dying, my heart and my understanding are sound,
as it should be. Likewise, I wish my body to be buried inside the home of our temple.
Likewise, I supplicate our blessed lord, the guardian priest, that one mass for my soul
be said to help the suffering purgatory soul, and that he say a prayer for me in that
mass. Likewise, it will be given in alms three tostons and two tomins for Jerusalem.
Francisco Na, executor.

Ignacio Coba, lieutenant	don Gaspar Canul	Gaspar Tun
Bartolomé Pech, alcalde	Batob	Diego Mitz

Sebastián Uh, alcalde   Salvador Coba, notary   Antonio Huchim

Sebastián Yam

Regidors

fray Francisco Días y Solís

FOL. 23V DOCUMENT A38

WILL OF JUAN BAUTISTA MATU

2 DECEMBER 1748

JUAN BAUTA MATU CIMI EN 2 DE DIZ.ᶜ DE 1748 ANŌS

Tu kaba dios yumbil y̱ dios mehenbil y̱ dios espiritu santo oxtul personas huntulili
dios uchuc tumen tusinil maix pimobi lay bin ylabac U hunil yn tokyahthan tin
testamento hibicil tenil cen Juan bau.ᵗᵃ matu U mehen Pablo matu = u yalen juana
chim lae—Bacacix cimil yn cah lae toh uol tin pucsikal y̱ tin nat uet sihcie = Bayxan u
olah mucul in cucutil ychil yotoch ca kuna lae—Bayxan cin uoktic ynba ti ca pixanil
yum padre guardian ca yalab hunpe ɔ missa yoklal in pixan caantabac tu numyail
anima purgatorio lae y̱ ce u masen tu payalchi ychil u missa lae—Bayxan bin ɔabae u
limosnayl oxpel tostones y̱ capel tumin helusalem lae—

Bayxan hunpel cħeen y̱ u solalil u pach Cin ɔaic tin u i ɔinob y̱ yxmehen pasguala
matu = Mathe.° matu Bar.ᵐᵉ matu = Martha matu = agustin matu = pasg.ˡᵃ matu =
Bayxan hunpel cħeen y̱ u kaxil u pach cin ɔaic tin u i ɔinob y̱ tin yxmehen = pasguala matu = mathe.° matu Bar.ᵐᵉ matu = Martha matu = agaustin matu = pasg.ˡᵃ
matu Bayxan hunpel Cħen y̱ u solal u pach cin ɔaic tin u i ɔin Gaspar tun y̱ tin mam
Manuela Chim = lae Bayxan hunpel cuchara takin y̱ hunpok macho y̱ hunpay tabron
utial agustin matu lae—Bayxan hunpet kax cin ɔaic tin ui ɔinob lae agustin matu = y̱
Bar.ᵐᵉ matu ca nupobi[. . .] u tzayal lay kax ti nohol ygnasio chim ti lakin Simon pis
[?] [. . .] = ti xaman u kax ca ti yol [. . .]kin xam =⁶

JUAN BAUTISTA MATU DIED ON THE 2ND OF DECEMBER, 1748

In the name of God the Father, and God the Son, and God the Holy Spirit, three persons, one God almighty, not many. The document of my final words in my testament
will be seen, insomuch as I who am Juan Bautista Matu, the son of Pablo Matu, the
child of Juana Chim. Although I am dying, my heart and my understanding are sound,
as it should be. Likewise, I wish my body to be buried inside the home of our temple.
Likewise, I supplicate our blessed lord, the guardian priest, that one mass for my soul
be said to help the suffering purgatory soul, and that he say a prayer for me in that mass.
Likewise, it will be given in alms three tostons and two tomins for Jerusalem.

Likewise, one well together with its house plot I give to my grandchildren
and my daughter Pasguala Matu: Mateo Matu, Bartolome Matu, Martha Matu,

Augustín Matu, Pasguala Matu. Likewise, one well together with its forest I give to my grandchildren and to my daughter Pasguala Matu: Mateo Matu, Bartolome Matu, Martha Matu, Augustin Matu, Pasguala Matu. Likewise, one well together with its house plot I give to my grandchild Gaspar Tun and to my cousin Manuela Chim. Likewise, one metal spoon and one male mule and one large table belonging to (to belong to) Augustin Matu. Likewise, one forest I give to my grandchildren Augustin Matu and Bartolome Matu, both of them together . . . adjacent to the forest to the south is Ignacio Chim, to the east Simon Pis[?] . . . to the north a forest. . . .

FOL. 1R DOCUMENT B1[7]

WILL OF MATEO MATU

[1765]

CIMI MATHEO MATU [. . .] 1765

[tukaba Ds yumbil y Ds mehenbil y Ds espiritu santo oxtul per]sonas huntulil hahal Dios uchuc tumen tusinil maix pimobi lay bin ylabac u hunil yn takyahthan tin testamento hibicil tenil cen Mathe.° Matu u Mehenen Joseph Matu u yalen Pasguala couoh ah caharnarlob yxil lae Bayxan cuxul yn cuxtal yokol cab lae Volah mucul yn Cucutil ychil santa ygressia Bayxan cin uoktic ynba ti ca pixanil yum pe ca u yalab Junpeɔ missa yn pixan bin ɔabac U limosnayl tumen yalab otzil christianob rae uacper tumin y caper tumin Jelusalem—8 rrs—

Bayxan Junac zolal yl u chenil lae yn Mul Matan y yn u ix Jan pasguala matu lae y yn Sucun AGus.ⁿ Matu lae ychill u testamento yn yum cimi lae Bayxan helay yixmehen yn tio Marcos Matu cimi lae cu ɔayi ychil testamento tumen Minan ychil lay solal lae hele tune cin yocsici tin testamento pasg.ʳᵃ Matu V kaba lae bay[. . .] lacabil lae Bayxan yn parteob rae yoklal lay solal lae cin patic tin palillob rae caac solal yn yanil tu testamento yn sucun Jun bautista Matu y Jupet kax yn mul matan yter yn Sucun aGusⁿ matu lae = Cin patic tin mehenob rae Mar.ⁿ Matu thomassa matu Manʳᵃ Matu Gaspar Matu Malia Matu = Bayxan Junpok = Mula cin patic tin uatan bibiana cante y yn palilob rae Bayxan Junper Batela[?] Vtial yn Man Juan bautista Matu lae conbil Bay bin tun tin manah hunpok chichan uacax Vtiall u hat yn yum Juan bau.ʳᵃ Matu lae Bay tun be CuCutar tin kab y yn Su = cun AGusn Matu y ten Matheo Matu Cucutar tu kab yn palillob rae yl u yixmehen yn Sucun Agus.ⁿ Matu = lae halili V xul yn than tin testamento cin Uacuntic Juntur almehenob rae Joseph Mis y Matheo Canul albasseassob rae lay bin tun ortic V katic missa tin pixan obrae tu tan Batab y Jusᵃˢ—

Andres pech	Dⁿ. ygn°. tec	pasguar coba marcos couoh
Nicolas Couoh	Batab	pasguar pech pasguar canche
Joseph cob essⁿᵒ puᶜᵒ	Marcos pot essⁿᵒ	Regidorlessob rae s

Mahan Kab

Dijose esta missa resada y lo firme
fr Juan de Hoyos

MATEO MATU DIED ON [. . .] 1765

In the name of God the Father, God the Son, God the Holy Spirit, three persons, one true almighty God, not many, the paper of my final statement in my testament will be seen, as I who am Mateo Matu, the son of Joseph Matu and child of Pasquala Couoh, residents here in Ixil. Although my life is ending on this earth, I wish my body to be buried in the holy church. Likewise, I supplicate our blessed lord the Padre, that he say one mass for my soul. The fee shall be given, as we are believing Christians; six tomins and two tomins for Jerusalem.

Likewise, one house plot and its well given to me jointly with my mother-in-law, Pasquala Matu, and with my older brother, Agustín Matu, in the will of my late father; also [with] the daughter of my uncle, Marcos Matu, who died leaving nothing in his will. This house plot, that today I place in my will, came down from the hands of Pasquala Matu. Likewise, my share of this house plot I leave for my children; the same house plot mentioned as mine in the will of my grandfather, Juan Bautista Matu; and one forest plot, my joint inheritance with my older brother, Agustín Matu, which I leave to my sons, Martín Matu, Tomasa Matu, Manuela Matu, Gaspar Matu, [and] María Matu. Likewise, one female mule I leave to my wife, Viviana Cante, and these my children. Likewise, one small iron tool belonging to my grandfather, Juan Bautista Matu—to be sold. Thus I shall then have purchased one calf for the measure [of cloth] of my lord Juan Bautista Matu. Therefore, what was in my hands, with my older brother, Agustín Matu, and me, Mateo Matu, from now on shall be in the hands of these my children, with the daughter of my older brother, Agustín Matu.

There is no more; here ends my statement in my will. I designate one [sic] nobles, Joseph Mis and Mateo Canul, as executors; they shall take care to request mass for my soul. Before the batab and magistrates:

Andrés Pech	don Ignacio Tec	Pasqual Coba, Marcos Couoh
Nicolás Couoh	batab	Pasqual Pech, Pasqual Canche
Joseph Cob, public notary	Marcos Poot, notary	regidors
	hired hand	

This recited mass was said and I signed it
fray Juan de Hoyos

FOL. 1V DOCUMENT B2

WILL OF ANTONIA CANTE

[1765]

cimi Antonia Cante [. . .] 1765

tukaba Dios yumbil Dios mehenbil Dios espiritu Santo oxtul personas huntulil
hahal Dios uchuc tumen tusinil maix pimobi lay bin ylabac uhunil yn takyahthan
tin testamento hibicil tenir cen An.ᵗᵗᵃ cante u yix Mehenen Mar.ⁿ cante u yalen Bar.
ⁿᵃ canche ah caharnarob uay ti cah yxil lae Bayxan c u xul yn cuxtar uolah mucur yn
Cucutil ychir Santa ygressia lae Bayxan cin uoktic ynba ti ca pixanil yum paᶜ c u la
ca yalab Junpeꜟ missia Resada yokor yn pixan ca u masen tu payalchi ychirl u missa
ca antacbac yn pixan tu numiayayl purgatolio bin ꜟabac u limosnayl uacper tumin y
caper tumin gielusalem—

Bayxan Junper caha utial yn tzenpar Juan Canul Bayxan Junpay poycheyl u cayl
utial pedro canul Bayxan hunper ca missa yl uhunperl uakal kuch u matan yn uichan
lucas cou[oh] hunpay cab y yikil utial Juana canul hunpay cab y yikil u Juriana canul
hunpay ti bibiana canul hunpay ti malia can[ul] hunpay martha canul hunpay ti
pedro canul halili Yxu[l] yn than tin testamento cin uacuntic huntur alMehen albasseas tan ortic u katic missa tin pixan Joseph Mis =

Andres pech	Dⁿ. ygnᵒ. tec	pasgᴵ. coba marcos couoh
Nicolas Couoh	Batab =	pas pech = pasgᴵ. canche
alcardessobrae	Marcos pot essⁿᵒ	Reg.ᵒlessobrae
Mahan Kab		

Dijose esta missa resada y lo firme
fr Juan de Hoyos

ANTONIA CANTE DIED ON . . . 1765

In the name of God the Father, God the Son, God the Holy Spirit, three persons, one
true God almighty, not many, the paper of my final statement in my testament will be
seen, inasmuch as I who am Antonia Cante, the daughter of Martín Cante and child
of Bernardina Canche, residents here in the cah of Ixil. Although my life is ending on
this earth, I wish my body to be buried in the holy church. Likewise, I supplicate our
blessed lord, the Padre, that he say one said mass for my soul, that he send a prayer in
the mass that will assist my soul in the sufferings of purgatory. The fee shall be given,
six tomins and two tomins for Jerusalem.

Likewise, one chest for my infant Juan Canul. Likewise, one bed that is now the
property of Pedro Canul. Likewise, one shirt and one measure of yarn, the inheritance of my husband, Lucas Couoh. One beehive with bees for Juana Canul, one
beehive with bees is Juliana Canul's, one to Viviana Canul, one to María Canul, one
Marta Canul, one to Pedro Canul. This is the truth, the end of my statement in my

will. I designate one nobleman as executor responsible for requesting mass for my soul: Joseph Mis.

Andrés Pech	don Ignacio Tec	Pasqual Coba, Marcos Couoh
Nicolás Couoh	batab	Pasqual Pech, Pasqual Canche
alcaldes	Marcos Poot, notary	regidors
Joseph Cob, public notary	hired hand	

This recited mass was said and I signed it
  fray Juan de Hoyos

FOL. 2R DOCUMENT B3
WILL OF MANUEL COB
[1765]
CIMI MANUEL COB [. . .] 1765

[tukaba Dios yumbil y̱ Dios mehen]bil Dios espiritu santo huntulil hahal D^s uchuc tumen tusinil maix pimobi lay bin ylabac u Junil yn thakyahthan tin testamento hibiguil tenil cen Manuer cob u mehenen Josef Cob u yalen Dominga ek ah otochnalob uay ti cah Yxil = [. . .] cin Ualic U ant xul yn cuxtar yokol caab rae Volah mucul yn CuCutil ychil Santa ygressia lae Bayxan cin uoktic ynba ti ca pixanil yum p.^{c} c u la ca yalab hunpeɔ missa Ressa da yl ix ca V masen tu payalchi ychill u missa lae antabar yn pixan tu numyayl pulgatolio lae bin ɔabac U limosnayl tumen yalab otzil christianob rae = 6 rr^s y 2 rr^s gilusalem halili U xul yn than tin testamento cin uacuntic almehenJoseph mis albaseas =

Andres pech	Capp^n D.^{n} ygn^o. tec	pasg^l. coba Marcos couoh
Nicolas Couoh	Batab =	pasg^l. pech pasg^l. canche
alcardessob rae	Marcos pot ess^{no} Mahan Kab	Regidolessob rae

Dijose esta missa resada y lo firme
  fr Juan de Hoyos

MANUEL COB DIED ON [. . .] 1765

In the name of God the Father, God the Son, God the Holy Spirit, one true God almighty, not many; it will be seen, the paper of my final statement in my will, as I who am Manuel Cob, the son of Joseph Cob and child of Dominga Ek, householders here in the cah of Ixil. . . . I state that my life on this earth is ending, and I wish the burial of my body to be in the holy church. Likewise, I supplicate our lord the Padre that he say one said mass and also that he send up for me a prayer in the mass to assist my soul through the suffering in purgatory. The fee will be given, for we are believing Christians; six reales, with two reales for Jerusalem. This is the truth, the end of my statement in my will. I designate the nobleman Joseph Mis as executor.

Andrés Pech	don Ignacio Tec	Pasqual Coba, Marcos Couoh
Nicolás Couoh	batab	Pasqual Pech, Pasqual Canche
alcaldes	Marcos Poot, notary	regidors
	hired hand	

This recited mass was said and I signed it
  fray Juan de Hoyos

FOL. 2R DOCUMENT B4

WILL OF PEDRO COUOH

28 NOVEMBER 1765

CIMI PEDRO COUOH EN 28 DE NOBLEM^c DE 1765 Ã

tukaba dios yumbil Dios mehenbil Dios espiritu santo oxtul personas huntulili hahar
Dios Uchuc tumen tusinil mayx pimobi lay bin ylabac U Junil yn takyahthan tin
testamento hibicil ten pedrocouoh U Mehen Juan couoh u yalen ynes cante Bayxan
c u xul yn cuxtal ic yokol cab rae Volah mucul yn Cucutil ychil Santa ygressia lae
Bayxan cin uoktic ynba ti ca pixanil yum p.^{c} uardia ca yalab Junpe ɔ missa Ressa yokol
yn pixan bin ɔabac u limosnayl uacper tumin y caper tumin gielusalem—8 rr^s—

Bayxan Junac chen yl u solalil Vpach yn parte lae cin patic tukab yn palillob gregolio couoh apolonia couoh malia couoh man.^{ra} couoh Bayxan Junpay caha utial aplo-
nia couoh y malia couoh canupobi y hun ɔit bate y Junpec tirma hun ɔit bac y camissa
y es y kaxnak y panio u matanyn mehen gregolio couoh tu hunar hunpay caha Vtial
man.^{ra} couoh = Bayxan hunper yn man kax y yn ui ɔin yan ti xculix cin patic tu kab
yn palil lobrae Bay u lak kax yan tzucya yn parte xan cin patic tu kab yn palilob [. . .]
halilil y xul yn than tin testamento cin uacuntic huntul almehenalbasseas D^n Gaspar
Canul lay bin tan ortic u katic missa tin pixan lae tu tan batab y Justissiassob rae

Andres pech	D^n. ygn^o. tec Batab	pasg^l coba marcos couoh pasg^l pech
Nicolas Couoh	Joseph cob ess^{no} pu^{co}	pasg^l canche Regidorlessob rae
alcardessob rae	Marcos pot ess^{no} Mahan Kab	

Dijose esta missa y lo firme
  fr Juan de Hoyos

PEDRO COUOH DIED ON THE 28TH OF NOVEMBER, 1765

In the name of God the Father, God the Son, God the Holy Spirit, three persons, one
true God almighty, not many. The paper of my final statement in my testament will
be seen, inasmuch as I am Pedro Couoh, the son of Juan Couoh and child of Inés
Cante. Likewise, as my life is ending on this earth, I wish the burial of my body to be
in the holy church. Likewise, I supplicate our blessed lord, the guardian priest, that

he say one said mass for my soul. The fee will be given: six tomins and two tomins for Jerusalem: 8 reales.

Likewise, I leave my share of one well with the house plot to which it belongs in the hands of my children: Gregorio Couoh, Apolonia Couoh, María Couoh, Manuela Couoh. Likewise, one chest for Apolonia Couoh and María Couoh, both together; and one axe and one cloak, one beam, and shirt and trousers and belt and blanket, the inheritance of my son Gregorio Couoh, alone; one chest for Manuela Couoh. Likewise, one forest, purchased with my younger brother, at Xculix, I leave in the name of my children. Likewise, my share of the other forest, at Tzucya, I also leave in the hands of my children . . . this is the truth and end of my statement in the will. I designate one nobleman as executor, don Gaspar Canul; he is responsible for requesting mass for my soul. Before the batab and magistrates:

Andrés Pech	don Ignacio Tec	Pasqual Coba, Marcos Couoh
Nicolás Couoh	batab	Pasqual Pech, Pasqual Canche
alcaldes	Joseph Cob, public notary	regidors
	Marcos Poot, notary, hired hand	

This recited mass was said and I signed it
fray Juan de Hoyos

FOL. 2V DOCUMENT B5

WILL OF ANDRES COBA

[1765]

tukaba Dios yumbil Dios mehenbir Dios espiritu santo oxtul personas Juntulili hahar Dios Uchuc tumen tusinil mayx pimobi lay lae c u xul yn cuxtar lae hibicir ten cen Andres Coba U Mehenen pasguar Coba U yalen Ruissa Cob ah caharNarlob Uay ti cah yxil lae bayxan Volah mucul yn Cucutil ychil Santa ygressia lae bin ɔabac U limosnayl tumen yalab otzil christianob rae hunpeɔ missa Ressada uac per tumin U thohor lae =

Andres pech	D^n. ygn^o. tec	$pasg^l$ coba marcos couoh
Nicolas Couoh	Batab	$pasg^l$ pech $pasg^l$ canche
alcardessob rae	Joseph cob ess^{no}	Regidorlessob rae
	Marcos pot ess^{no}	
	MarJan Kab	

Dijose esta missa resada y lo firme
fr Juan de Hoyos

In the name of God the Father, God the Son, God the Holy Spirit, three persons, one true God almighty. My life is ending, inasmuch as I am Andrés Coba, the son of Pasqual Coba and child of Luisa Cob, residents here in Ixil. Likewise, I wish my body buried in the holy church. The fee shall be given, as we are believing Christians, for one said mass: six tomins. This is the truth.

Andrés Pech	don Ignacio Tec	Pasqual Coba, Marcos Couoh
Nicolás Couoh	batab	Pasqual Pech, Pasqual Canche
alcaldes	Joseph Cob, public notary	regidors
	Marcos Poot, notary, hired hand	

This recited mass was said and I signed it
    fray Juan de Hoyos

FOLS. 2V–3R DOCUMENT B6

WILL OF GREGORIO CANCHE
12 JANUARY 1766

CIMI EN 12 DE ENERO DE 1766 AÑ CIMI GREG⁰ CANCHE

tukaba Dios yumbil y Dios mehenbil y Dios esspiritu santo oxtul personas huntulil Dios uchuc tumen tusinil maix pimobi lay bin ylabac ᵘ hunil yn takyahthan tin testamento hibicil ten cen greg.⁰ canche u mehenen Cleᵗᵉ canche u yalen Agus.ⁿᵃ [huchim?] lae bay bic xulul u cah in cuxtal uay yokol cab lae Bayxan uolah u mucul in cucutil ychil Santa Yglesia lae Bayxan licix uoktic inba ti ca pixanil yum padre gar.dian ca u yalab hunpeɔ missa Resada yokol yn pixan Bayxan bin ɔabac u limossnayl uacpel tumin lae

   Bayxan hunac chen y solar yanil yn yum lae he in parte laye cin patic tu kab in uixmehen Maria Canche y maria nebes canche y hun ɔit bat y hun ɔit machete y hunpel s(d)arga (shield) y hunpel hergeta y hun cul chacal Jaas—utial lay catuliⁿ uixmehenob lae halili u xul in than tin testamento lae—cin uacuntic huntul almehen albasias A[ndres] tec lay bin tan oltic katicab missa yokol in pixan tu tan batab y Jusᵃˢ Regiᵒʳsoblae y essⁿᵒ lae—
[fol. 3r]

Joseph pech	Dn Ygo tec batab	Anᵗᵗᵒ tec
Diego may	gaspar coba thenᵉ	franᶜᵒ canul
alcaldesob lae	pablo tec essⁿᵒ	Anᵗᵗᵒ pech
		pedro canul
		Regiʳsoblae

   Dijose esta missa y lo firme
      Fr Juan de Hoyos

ON THE 12TH OF JANUARY, 1766, HE DIED; GREGORIO CANCHE DIED

In the name of God the Father, God the Son, God the Holy Spirit, three persons, one almighty God, not many. The paper of my final statement in my testament will be seen, inasmuch as I am Gregorio Canche, the son of Clemente Canche and child of Agustina [Huchim?]. As, therefore, my life is ending on this earth, I likewise wish the burial of my body to be in the holy church. Likewise, I also now supplicate our blessed lord, the guardian priest, that he say one said mass for my soul. Likewise, the fee will be given: six tomins.

Likewise, there is one well with the house plot where my father is, my share of which I leave in the name of my daughter, María Canche, with María Neves Canche, with one axe and one machete and one blanket and one piece of crude cloth and one red sapote tree; these are for both my daughters. This is the truth, the end of my statement in my will. I designate one nobleman as executor, Andrés Tec; he shall be responsible for requesting mass for my soul. Before the batab and magistrates, regidors, and notary:

[fol. 3r]

Joseph Pech	don Ignacio Tec	Antonio Tec
Diego May	batab	Francisco Canul
alcaldes	Pablo Tec, notary	Antonio Pech
		Pedro Canul
		regidors

This recited mass was said and I signed it

  fray Juan de Hoyos

FOLS. 3R–3V DOCUMENT B7

WILL OF IGNACIO CANUL

3 JANUARY 1766

CIMI Yg.º CANUL EN 3 DE ENERO DE 1766 AÑ—

tukaba Dios yumbil y Dios mehenbil y Dios esspiritu santo oxtul personas huntulil Dios uchuc tumen tusinil maix pimobi lay bin ylabac u hunil yn takyahthan tin testamento hibil tenil cen Yg.º canul u mehenen Diego canul u yal Monica chim Bayxan uan c u xul in cuxtal uay yokol cab lae Uolah mucul in cucutil Ychil Santa na Yglesia lae licix uoktic inba ti ca pixanil yum paᵉ[guardian] ca u yalab hunpeɔ missa yokol yn pixan caix ɔabac u limosnayl tumen yalab otzil christianob lae uacpel tumin y capel tumin helusalem lae—

  Bayxan heix yn parte ti chen y solal lae cin patic tukab in mam Joseph Coba y Agusⁿ coba—y ygnasia coba oxnupobi [. . .] micolas couoh bay bic in matan ti in han Diego [Co]uoh lae canupobi [. . .] aixnob lae y hunac kax yan tu xaman ti ixualahtun

tzayal kax lae Nicolas couoh ti nohol—ti lakin phelipe canche ti chikin Juan coba—-
Yg.° Juchim ti xaman—utial Jos[e]ph coba tu hunal

Bayxan hunac chen y u solalil u pach tu kubah ten yn mehen—Dn gaspar canul
uhel lay solal cah lic lae cin patic tun tukab yn mam Joseph coba utial xan—Bayxan
hunac kax yan tu nohol cah—utial in mam Agus.ⁿ coba—bay bic in matan ti in
haan franc.° couoh—u tzayal ti lakin Juan pech—ti xaman Juan Ytza—ti chikin
Joseph pech—Bayxan capok capon tzimin y hunpok macho—utial yn mam
Joseph coba tu hunal—Bayxan hunpok yeua y yal potro utial in uatan lorensa ek
y hunpel hol na utial Joseph coba y hunpel caha—y hunpel camisa y hunpel ex
hunpay kaxnak—

[fol. 3v] Bayxan hunpay caha utial in uatan lorensa ek—y hunpel camisa y ex utial
in mekpal Nicolas chan—Bayxan heix in pakal Ciobe utial yn mam Jōph coba y in
uatan lae halili uxul Yn than tin testamento cin uacun tic catul almehen albasiasob
lae—Jōph Mis y Andrez tec lay bin tan olticob u katicob missa ti in pixan tu tan
batan [*sic*] y Jus.ᵃˢ lae—

Joseph pech al^de	Cap.ⁿ Dⁿ Yg° tec	An^tto tec
Diego may al^de	batab	franco canul
	gaspar coba then^e	An^tto pech p° canul
	pablo tec ess^no	Regi^rsob lae

Dijose esta missa y lo firme
  Fr Juan de Hoyos

IGNACIO CANUL DIED ON THE 3RD OF JANUARY, 1766

In the name of God the Father, God the Son, God the Holy Spirit, three persons,
one almighty God, not many. The paper of my final statement in my testament will
be seen, for I am Ignacio Canul, the son of Diego Canul and child of Monica Chim.
Likewise, as my life is ending here on this earth, I wish the burial of my body to be
in the holy house, the church. Also, I now supplicate our blessed lord, the guardian
priest, that he say one mass for my soul. We shall also give the fee, because we are
believing Christians: six tomins and two tomins for that Jerusalem.

Likewise, here is my share of a well with a house plot which I leave in the hands
of my grandson[s], Joseph Coba and Agustín Coba, with Ignacia Coba, the three of
them together.

From Nicolás Couoh, this then was my inheritance, [also] from my father-in-law,
Diego Couoh, both of them together; also with one forest, which is to the north at
Ixualahtun, Nicolás Couoh the neighboring forest to the south, to the east Felipe
Canche, to the west Juan Coba, Ignacio Huchim to the north—for Joseph Coba
alone. Likewise, one well with the house plot to which it belongs, that was delivered
to me by my son, don Gaspar Canul, who is currently resident on this house plot,
which I leave in the name of my grandson, Joseph Coba; it too is his. Likewise, one

forest—to the south is the cah—for my grandson, Agustín Coba. Next, my inheritance from my father-in-law, Francisco Couoh; its neighbor to the east is Juan Pech; to the north, Juan Itza; to the west, Joseph Pech. Likewise, two geldings and one male mule for my grandson, Joseph Coba, for him alone. Likewise, one mare and its foal child for my wife, Lorensa Ek, and one house beam for Joseph Coba with one chest and one shirt and one pair of trousers and one sash.

[fol. 3v] Likewise, one chest for my wife, Lorensa Ek, and one shirt and trousers for my infant, Nicolás Chan. Likewise, here is my henequen orchard, for my grandson, Joseph Coba, and this my wife. This is the truth, the end of my statement in my will. I designate two noblemen as executors—Joseph Mis and Andrés Tec; they shall be responsible for requesting mass for my soul. Before these the batab and the magistrates:

Joseph Pech, alcalde	captain don Ignacio Tec	Antonio Tec
Diego May, alcalde	batab	Francisco Canul
	Gaspar Coba, teniente	Antonio Pech, Pedro Canul
	Pablo Tec, notary	

This recited mass was said and I signed it
fray Juan de Hoyos

FOL. 3V DOCUMENT B8

WILL OF JOSEPH UITZ
15 OCTOBER 1765

CIMI JPH UITZ EN 15 DE OCTUBRE DE 1765 AÑ

tu kaba Dios yumbil y Dios mehenbil y Dios espiritu santo oxtul personas huntulil Dios uchuc tumen tusinil maix pimobi lay bin ylabac u hunil in testamento hibil tenil Cen Joseph uitz u mehenen ming.¹ uitz u yalen Juana chulim ah cahnal ti la [...] kantiho lae Bacacix cimil in cah tin cucutil lae y tin pucsikal uet sihci lae Bayxan lic uoktic inba ti ca pixanil yum padre cura ca yalab hunpel missa re sada utial yn pixan bin ɔabac u limosnayl uacpel tumin tumen yalab otzil christianob lae—lay u xul in than tin testamento cin uacuntic huntul almehen pedropech u met yatzil tin pixan lae—

Joseph pech al^de	D^n Yg° tec batab	An^tto tec
Diego may al^de	pablo tec ess^no	fran^co canul
		An^tto pech

Dijose esta missa y lo firme
Fr Juan de Hoyos

JOSEPH UITZ DIED ON THE 15TH OF OCTOBER, 1765

In the name of God the Father, God the Son, God the Holy Spirit, three persons, one almighty God, not many. It will be seen, the document of my testament, inasmuch as I who am Joseph Uitz, the son of Miguel Uitz and the child of Juana Chulim, resident there in [. . .] Tiho. Although I am dying with respect to my body, my heart is sound, as it should be. Likewise, I supplicate our blessed lord the Padre Curate that he say one said mass for my soul. The fee shall be given: six tomins, for we are believing Christians here. This is the end of my statement in my will. I designate one nobleman, Pedro Pech, to ensure mercy for my soul.

Joseph Pech, alcalde	don Ignacio Tec	Antonio Tec
Diego May, alcalde	batab	Francisco Canul
	Pablo Tec, notary	Antonio Pech

This recited mass was said and I signed it
    fray Juan de Hoyos

FOL. 6R DOCUMENT B9

WILL OF ANTONIA COBA
10 JANUARY 1766

CIMI AN^tta COBA—EN 10 DE ENERO DE 1766 AÑ SORTERA—

tu kaba Dios yumbil y Dios mehenbil y Dios espiritu santo oxtul pelsonas huntulil Dios uchuc tumehen tusinil mix pimobi lay bin ylabac u hunil Yn testamento
hibicil—tenil An^tta coba u Yixmehen Sar.^ol coba u yalen Juana canul heix ua tu yoltah
ca Yumil ti Dios u xules in cuxtaluay yokol cabe uolah mucul in cucutil Ychil yotoch
santa yglesia lae Bayxan lic cix uoktic ynba ti ca pixanil yum pae cura ca yalab hunpeɔ
missa Rezada utial in pixan lae bin ɔabac u limosNayl uacpel tumin lae—6 rr^s

Joseph pech al^de	D^n Yg^o tec batab	An^tto tec—Reg^or
Diego may al^de	pablo tec ess^no	fran^co canul Reg^or
		An^tto pech Reg^or

Dijose esta missa y lo firme
    Fr Juan de Hoyos

ANTONIA COBA DIED ON THE 10TH OF JANUARY, 1766. SINGLE.

In the name of God the Father, God the Son, God the Holy Spirit, three persons, one almighty God, not many. It will be seen, the document of my testament, inasmuch as I who am Antonia Coba, the daughter of Salvador Coba and child of Juana Canul. As—alas!—it is the wish of our lord in God to end my life here on this earth, I wish my body buried in the house of the holy church. Likewise, I supplicate our blessed lord the Padre Curate that he say one said mass for my soul. The fee shall be given: six tomins. 6 reales.

Joseph Pech, alcalde	don Ignacio Tec	Antonio Tec, regidor
Diego May, alcalde	batab	Francisco Canul, regidor
	Pablo Tec, notary	Antonio Pech, regidor

This recited mass was said and I signed it
  fray Juan de Hoyos

FOLS. 6R–6V DOCUMENT B10

WILL OF FELIPE COBA
12 JANUARY 1766

CIMI PHELIPE COBA EN 12 DE ENERO DE 1766 AÑ

tu kaba Dios yumbil y Dios mehenbil y Dios esspiritu santo oxtul personas huntulil ^{ds} uchuc tumen tusinil maix pimobi lay bin ylabac u hunil Yn testamento hibicil tenenil phelipe coba u mehenen pasqual coba u yalen phelipa couoh heix ua tu yoltah ca Yumil ti D.ˢ u xules Yn cuxtal lae uolah mucul yn cucutil Ychil santa Yglesia lae—Bayxan lic ix uoktic ynba ti ca pixanil yum padre cura ca yalab hunpel missa ti in pixan lae bin ɔabac u limosnayl uacpel tumin ~~halili~~ u masen tu payalchil ychil u misa lay tumen cin uaCuntic huntul almehen Joseph cob albasias lay bin tan oltic u katic missa ti in pixan lae halili u xul yn than tin testamento lae—6 rrs

  Bayxan heix in Mul matan ~~chen~~ y solal lae cin patic tukab in uatan pasguala Juchim y yn uixmehen Juana Coba y hunac kax yan ti subinche lae utial xan y hunpel Jergueta y hunpel sarga tzotz y hun ɔit bat y lahuyox [fol. 6v] kal u chun Ci lae—cin patic tin uatan y in uixmehen tumen [l . . .] ~~chen~~ y solal lae in mul matan y in sucun Mathe° coba y in ui[ɔin] Mathias coba xan tumen bay yanil ychil u testamento yn y[um] pasqual coba lae halili u xul yn than tin testamento [l]ae halili cin uacuntic Joseph cob albasias lae lay bin tan oltic[ob] katicob missa tu tan batab y Jusᵃˢ—

Gaspar coba then^e	Dⁿ Yg° tec batab	Anᵗᵗ° tec
Joseph pech aldess	Pablo tec ess^{no}	fran^{co} canul
Diego may aldess		Anᵗᵗ° pech
		pedro canul
		Regiosoblae

FELIPE COBA DIED ON THE 12TH OF JANUARY, 1766

In the name of God the Father, God the Son, God the Holy Spirit, three persons, one almighty God, not many. It will be seen, the document of my testament, inasmuch as I am Felipe Coba, the son of Pasqual Coba and child of Felipa Couoh. As—alas!—it is the wish of our lord in God to end my life here, I wish my body buried in the holy church. Likewise, I now also supplicate our blessed lord the Padre Curate that he say one mass for my soul. The fee shall be given: six tomins. This is the truth [deleted]. [May] he send up a prayer in that mass for me. I appoint one nobleman, Joseph Cob, as executor. He shall take care to request a mass for my soul. This is the truth, the end of my statement in my will. 6 reales.

Likewise, here is my jointly inherited well with house plot, which I leave in the name of my wife, Pasquala Huchim, with my daughter, Juana Coba, with one forest that is at Subinche, also for her; and one crude blanket and one fur blanket and one axe and fifty [fol. 6v] henequen plants. I leave to my wife and my daughter, for [them, a] well and house plot, which was my joint inheritance with my older brother, Mateo Coba, and also my younger brother, Matias Coba, as it is in the will of my father, Pasqual Coba. This is the truth, the end of my statement in my will. This is the truth; I designate Joseph Cob as executor; he shall be responsible for requesting mass. Before the batab and the magistrates:

Gaspar Coba, teniente	don Ignacio Tec	Antonio Tec
Joseph Pech, alcalde	batab	Francisco Canul
Diego May, alcalde	Pablo Tec, notary	Antonio Pech
		Pedro Canul
		regidors

FOL. 6V DOCUMENT B11

WILL OF PEDRO MATU
26 JANUARY 1766

CIMI PEDRO MATU HELE EN 26 DE JENERO DE 1766 Ā

tu kaba Dios yumbil y Dios mehenbil y Dios espiritu santo oxtul personas huntulil Dios uchuc tumen tusinil maix pimobi lay bin ylabac u hunil yn takyahthan tin testamento hibicil tenil cen pe° matu u mehen Ju° matu u yal thomasa couoh ah otochnalob Uay ti cah Yxil Bayxan uolah mucul Yn cucutil Ychil Yotoch Santa Yglesia lae Bayxan lic uoktic ynba ti ca pixanil yum padre guardian ca yalab hunpeɔ missa utial yn pixan Bayxan bin ɔabac u limosnayl uacpel tumin lae—caix u masen tu pay-alchi lae Ychil u misa lay bin xul yn than tin testamento lae Bayxan yan yn yum ɔaic u limosnayl [. . .] misa lae bin u tan olte u katic misa tu tan batab y Jus^as—

Joseph pech al^de	D^n Yg° tec batab	An^tto tec
Diego may al^de	pablo tec ess^no	fran^co canul
		An^tto pech
		pedro canul

Regi^{or}sob lae

Dijose esta missa resada y lo firme
fr Juan de Hoyos

PEDRO MATU DIED ON THE 26TH OF JANUARY, 1766

In the name of God the Father, and God the Son, and God the Holy Spirit, three persons, one almighty God, not many. It will be seen, the document of my final statement in my testament, inasmuch as I who am Pedro Matu, the son of Juan Matu and child of Tomasa Couoh, householders here in the cah of Ixil. Likewise, I wish my body buried in the home of the holy church here. Likewise, I now supplicate our blessed lord, the guardian priest, that he say one mass for my soul. Likewise, the fee shall be given: six tomins. Also that he send up a prayer in the mass. Here shall end my statement in my will. Likewise, there is my lord to give the fee [for] the mass; he shall take care to request the mass. Before the batab and magistrates: Don Ignacio Tec, batab; Pablo Tec, notary;

Joseph Pech, alcalde	don Ignacio Tec	Antonio Tec
Diego May, alcalde	batab	Francisco Canul
	Pablo Tec, notary	Antonio Pech
		Pedro Canul
		regidors

This recited mass was said and I signed it
fray Juan de Hoyos

FOL. 7R DOCUMENT B12

WILL OF MARÍA CANCHE
28 JANUARY 1766

CIMI MARIA CANCHE HELE EN 28 DE JENERO DE 1766 AÑ =

tu kaba Dios yumbil y Dios mehenbil y Dios esspiritu santo oxtul personas huntulili Dios uchuc tumen tusinil maix pimobi lay bin ylabac u hunil yn thakyahthan
tin testamento hibiCil tenil cen maria canche u yixehen gaspar canche u yal fran.^{ca}
Mo—ah otochnalob uay ti cah Yxil lae Bayxan u an tu yoltah ca yumil ti Dios V xules
yn cuxtal uay yokol cab lae uolah Uolah mucul yn cucutil ychil yotoch cilich Nauil
Yglesia lae Bayxan licix uoktic ynba ti ca pixanil yum padre cura—ca u yalab hunpeɔ
missa kabil missa yokol yn pixan y ca u masen tu payalchi ychil u missa. Bayxan bin
bin ɔabac u limosnayl tumen yalab otzil christianob lae oxpel tostones y capel tumin
helusalem lae emebal u cuch yn pixan tu tan ca yumil ti Dios manhebal u xantal tu
numYaYl Animas purgatorio lae—

Bayxan pat can yn cah tu bal yn balae—hunpel chen y u solaril u pach yn matan ti yn mam matheo canche hele tune cin patic tukab yn ualob—u multialoblae—gaspar pot—y Juo pot—y u lak gaspar pot y silbes^te pot—y pasquala pot—y maria pot—y fran^ca pot u matanob lae—hunpel hol na y marco lae utial gaspar pot y silbes^te pot canupobi yokol lae—hunpay caha utial silbeste pot tu hunalae y hunpel pic utial pasquala pot—y hunpel pic utial franca pot y hunpel ypil u tial maria pot y hunpel pic utial pasquala pot—y hunpel ypil utial Madalena coba—y hunpel camisa utial Silbeste pot halili u xul yn than tin testamento—licix yn uacuntic catul almehenob laeJoseph mis y Jasinto pech albasiasob lay bin tan oltic u katic missa tin pixan tu tan batab y Jus^as lae—

gaspar coba then^e	Cap^n d^n Yg^o tec batab	An^tto tec fran^co canul
Joseph pech al^de	pablo tec ess^no	An^tto pech p^oe canul
Diego may al^de		

Cantose esta missa y lo firme
  fr Juan de Hoyos

María Canche died on the 28th of January, 1766

In the name of God the Father, God the Son, God the Holy Spirit, three persons, one almighty God, not many. It will be seen, the document of my final statement in my will, inasmuch as I who am María Canche, the daughter of Gaspar Canche and the child of Francisca Mo, householders here in the cah of Ixil. Likewise, as our lord in God wishes to end my life here on this earth, I wish my body buried in the home, the holy mother church. Likewise, I supplicate our blessed lord the Padre Curate that he say one mass, a sung mass, for my soul and that he send up for me a prayer in the mass. Likewise, the fee shall be given, for we are believing Christians: three tostons and two tomins for Jerusalem; it will lighten the burden of my soul before our lord in God so as not to detain it in the suffering of souls in purgatory.

Likewise, I declare the settlement of my goods and property: one well with its accompanying house plot, given to me by my grandfather, Mateo Canche; now, therefore, I leave it in the name of my children, to be their joint property—Gaspar Pot and Juan Pot and the other Gaspar Pot and Silvestre Pot and Pasquala Pot and María Pot and Francisca Pot—their inheritance; one house beam with its frame for Gaspar Pot and Silvestre Pot, for them both together; one chest for Silvestre Pot, for him alone; and one petticoat for Pasquala Pot; and one petticoat for Francisca Pot; and one huipil for María Pot; and one petticoat for Pasquala Pot; and one huipil for Magdalena Coba; and one shirt for Silvestre Pot. This is the truth, the end of my statement in my will. I now designate two noblemen, Joseph Mis and Jacinto Pech, as executors; they shall take care to request mass for my soul. Before these the batab and the magistrates:

Gaspar Coba, teniente	captain don Ignacio Tec	Antonio Tec, Francisco Canul

Joseph Pech, alcalde	batab	Antonio Pech, Pedro Canul
Diego May, alcalde	Pablo Tec, notary	

This mass was sung and I signed it
    fray Juan de Hoyos

FOL. 7V DOCUMENT B13

WILL OF PETRONA NA
12 FEBRUARY 1766

CIMI PET.^{na} NA HELE EN 12 DE FEB^{ro} DE 1766 Ā

tu kaba Dios yumbil y Dios mehenbil y Dios esspiritu santo oxtul personas huntulil
hahal Diosuchuc tumen tusinil maix pimobi lay bin ylabac u hunil yn testamento
hibicil tenil cen pet.^{na} Na u yixmehen Apa.^{o} Na—u yal Ant.^{a} mas ah otochnalob Uay
ti cah Yxil lae Bayxan ti lic yn uoktic ynBa ti ca pixanil yum padre Cura ca u yalab
hunpeɔ missa ti yn pixan uchebal sebtal u manel yn pixan tu numyayl animas purgatorio Bayxan bin ɔabac u limosnayl tumen u yalab otzil christianob lae u hunpel peso
y helusa

[inserted:] Bayxan hunpok yn keken utial y tilla marta bas lae—lem lae = Bayxan
hunac chen y u solalir u pach cin patic tu kab yn uichan marcos ek—y Sarua^a pech u
yal yn cic lae—y hunpel capon tzimin utial yn uichan y hunpel caha y hunpel pic lae
utial marcos ek lae Bayxan cin uaCuntic huntul almehen Jasinto pech—albasias lay
bin tan oltic u katic misa yokol yn pixan tu tan batab y Justiasias lae halili u xul yn
than tin tes tamento lae—

Jph pech Diego may	D^n Yg^o tec	An^{tto} tec
alcaldesob lae	Batab	fran^{co} canul
Gaspar coba then^e		An^{tto} pech
		p^{o}e canul
		Regidoresob

tin tanil Cen pablo tec ess^{no}

Dijose esta missa resada y lo firme
    fr Juan de Hoyos

PETRONA NA DIED ON THE 12TH OF FEBRUARY, 1766

In the name of God the Father, and God the Son, and God the Holy Spirit, three
persons, one true God almighty, not many. It will be seen, the document of my testament, inasmuch as I who am Petrona Na, the daughter of Aparicio Na and the child
of Antonia Mas, householders here in the cah of Ixil. Likewise, I now supplicate our
blessed lord the Padre Curate that he say one mass for my soul, so that my soul pass

quickly through the suffering of souls in purgatory. Likewise, the fee will be given, for we are believing Christians: one peso, [also for] Jerusalem.

[inserted:] Likewise, one pig of mine, for my aunt Marta Bas. Likewise, one well with its accompanying house plot I leave in the name of my husband, Marcos Ek, with Salvadora Pech, the child of my elder sister; and one gelding for my husband, and one chest and one petticoat for this Marcos Ek. Likewise, I appoint one nobleman, Jacinto Pech, as executor; he shall take care to request a mass for my soul. Before the batab and magistrates. This is the truth, the end of my statement in my will.

Joseph Pech, Diego May	don Ignacio Tec	Antonio Tec
alcaldes	batab	Francisco Canul
Gaspar Coba, teniente		Antonio Pech
		Pedro Canul
		regidors

Before me, Pablo Tec, notary

This recited mass was said and I signed it
    fray Juan de Hoyos

FOL. 8R DOCUMENT B14

WILL OF DIEGO CHAN, MAESTRO

24 JANUARY 1766

EN 24 HENELO DE 1766 Aᵒˢ

testamento Vtial Diego chan Maestro V mehenen Mathias chan V yalen pasquala Cante ah caharnarlob yxil Bayxan Van cuxul yn cuxtar yokol cab rae quin uoktic ynba ti ca Pixanir yum pa.e utial ca yalab Junpeɔ missa kay billae bin ɔabac V tulul Mis 14 rrˢ y gieluSalem lae

Bayxan cin tzolic yn than tin testamento lae Vtial yn thoxic he cen bar yɔama ten ca yumir ti Dios lae tin palillob rae Bayxan Junac chen yl u solalil u pach quin patic tukab yn uatan Josepha canche lay yn cah lic lae y Junpok yeua tzimin y capok yar tu pach y oxtur mula y capok macho y Junpok burro y Junpok baca uacax y Junperl u hor Na yl u marcoyl lae y Junpay caha lae y caper messa = Vtial y uatan Josepha canche tulacar lay tin tzolah lae—Bayxan Junpok yeua tzimin y Junpok baca y Junperl u hor na yl u mar coyl lae y Junper cuchala takin Vtial yn uixmehen pasquala chan Bayxan Junpok yeua tzim y Junpok baca y Junperl u horna yl u marco yl lae utial yn uixmehen Juana chan y Junac chen yl u solal lil u pach yan tu lakin cah ber baca Vtial yn uixmehenob pasqʳᵃ chan y Juana chan canupobi lae = Bayxan Junpok yeua tzimin y hunpok baca = y Junpay caha utial yn mehen ygn.ᵒ piste = Bayxan Junpok yeua tzimin y Junpok baca y Junpay caha utial yn mehen yzidr[o] piste Bayxan junperl u horna y Junac kax yanac V multial y ygnᵒ piste yzidro piste lae V tzayar kax lac ti lakin Sarua.

ᵒʳ coba ti xaman gaspa[r] coba ti chikin Jassinto yam Bayxan Junpok yeua tzimin y̱
Junpok baca y̱ J[un] ac kax yan ber Kaknab Vtial yn Mam grabrier tec u tzayar ti lakin
Andres cob Bayxan Junpok capon tzimin Vtial yn Mam Juana canche Bayxan Junpok
yeua tzimin con bir yn Muc bar lae halili xul yn tin testamento lae cin uacuntic catur
almehenob rae albassiassob rae gaspar canul y̱ Andres tec =

Joseph pech alcardes	cappⁿ Dⁿ ygn° tec Batab	An^{tto} tec fran^{co} can[ul]
Diego may alcardes	Marcos pot ess^{no} pabro tec	An^{tto} pech pedro ca[nul]
	ess^{no} pu.^{co}	Reg.^{or}lessob rae

ON THE 24TH OF JANUARY, 1766

The will of Diego Chan, maestro, the son of Matias Chan, the child of Pasquala
Cante, residents of Ixil. Likewise, while my spirit still lives in this world, I present
myself to our holy father, the Padre, that one mass be said, be sung. The value of the
mass, 14 reales, shall be given, including Jerusalem.

Likewise, I arrange my statement in my will in order to divide among my children
these things that our lord God has given me. Likewise, one well with its accompanying house plot I leave in the name of my wife, Josepha Canche; it is where I am now
living; and one mare with her two foals, and three female mules, and two male mules,
and one donkey, and one cow, and one house beam with its frame, and one chest, and
two tables—I have arranged for all this to go to my wife, Josepha Canche. Likewise,
one mare and one cow and one house beam with its frame and one silver spoon for
my daughter, Pasquala Chan. Likewise, one mare and one cow and one house beam
with its frame and one silver spoon for my daughter, Juana Chan; and one well with
the house plot that goes with it, which is to the east of the cah on the road to Baca,
for my daughters, Pasquala Chan and Juana Chan, both together. Likewise, one
mare and one cow, and one chest, for my son, Ignacio Piste. Likewise, one mare and
one cow and one chest for my son, Isidro Piste. Likewise, one house beam and one
forest go jointly to Ignacio Piste and Isidro Piste; its neighboring forest to the east is
Salvador Coba's, to the north Gaspar Coba, to the west Jacinto Yam. Likewise, one
mare and one cow and one forest, which is on the road to Kaknab, for my grandson,
Gabriel Tec; its neighbor to the east is Andrés Cob. Likewise, one gelding for my
mother-in-law, Juana Canche. Likewise, one mare shall be sold for my burial. This
is the truth, the end of this my testament. I designate these two nobles as executors:
don Gaspar Canul and Andrés Tec.

Joseph Pech, alcalde	captain don Ignacio Tec	Antonio Tec, Francisco Canul
Diego May, alcalde	batab	Antonio Pech, Pedro Canul
	Marcos Poot, notary	regidors
	Pablo Tec, public notary	

FOL. 8V DOCUMENT B15

WILL OF GABRIEL TEC

30 JANUARY 1766

CIMI GRAVIER TEC EN 30 DE HENERO DE 1766 Ā—

tukaba Dios yumbil y̨ Dios mehenbil y̨ Dios esspiritu santo—oxtul personas
huntulili Dios uchuc tumen tusinil maix pimobi lay bin ylabac u hunil yn testamento
hibicil tenil cen gravier tec u Mehen nen phelipe tec u yalen Juana chan ah otoch
nalob uay ti cah Yxil lae—bay bic uay ti cah MaMa tu payah yn cuxtul ca yumil ti Ds
lae lay u chun lic ualic ychil yn testamento uchebal yoheltic hemac bin ylic tu kinil
lae—Bayxan heix u limosnal misa u chic yn mucul lae—ynchich Josepha canche tu
ɔah u takinil y̨ u chic u botabal ah kayob ti cah Mama—

Bayxan heix yn parte solal y̨ chen yan tu testamento yn mam Bar.^{me} tec lae cin patic
tukab yn uixmehen phelipa tec y̨ lay yoman tumen yn uatan pasguala cutz xane—y̨
hunac kax yan chen ychil bel bena tu nohol be yan lae nak cah y̨ ulakax yan tu xaman
cah bel pacchen y̨ hunpay caha—lae—Bayxan heix bal tu hahal thantah yn Man
Diego chan maessto—ychil u testamento caat cimie lae cin patic tu kab yn palil phelipa tec y̨ layli yomano—Bayxan hun pel uacax ba^{ca} y̨ hunpok yeua tzimin y̨ hunac cax
yan bel kaknab tin matah tin mam Diego chan maestro lae u tzayal kax lae—Andrez
cob ti lakin lay yan nak cah utial lay yn uixmehen phelipa tec y̨ yan tu nak in uatan lae
lay u xul u xul yn takyahthan tin testamento cin ɔocsic lae—tu tan batab y̨ Jus^{as} ti cah
Mama lae—

gaspar coba then^e	D^n Yg^o tec	An.^{tto} tec
Jph pech a^{de}	Batab	fran.^{co} canul
Diego may a^{de}	pablo tec ess^{no}	An.^{tto} pech
		pedro canul
		Regi.^{or}sob lae

GABRIEL TEC DIED ON THE 30TH OF JANUARY, 1766

In the name of God the Father, and God the Son, and God the Holy Spirit, three
persons, one God almighty, not many. It will be seen, the document of my will,
inasmuch as I who am Gabriel Tec, the son of Felipe Tec and the child of Juana Chan,
householders here in the cah of Ixil. However, here in the cah of Mama, our lord God
has called my life. For this reason I am dictating my will, so that it can be known by
whomever shall see it on whatever day. Likewise, here is the mass fee for the occasion
of my burial; my grandmother, Josepha Canche, gave the money and at that time the
choristers of the cah of Mama will be paid.

Likewise, here is my share of a house plot and well that is in the testament of my
grandfather, Bartolomé Tec; I leave it in the hands of my daughter, Felipa Tec, also
with her by whom she was born, my wife Pasquala Cutz. And one forest, within

which there is a well; it is next to the cah, on the road south to Bena; with the other forest that is to the north of the cah, on the road to Pacchen. And one chest for her. Likewise, here is the property in the truthful statement made by my grandfather, Diego Chan, maestro, in his testament, when he died—which I leave in the hands of my child, Felipa Tec, with her who bore her. Likewise, one cow and one mare and one forest on the road to Kaknab, given to me by my grandfather, Diego Chan, maestro; its neighboring forest to the east is Andrés Cob's, which is beside the cah. It is for my daughter, Felipa Tec, and is next to my wife's. This is the end of my final statement in my will; I have finished it. Before the batab and magistrates in the cah of Mama.

Gaspar Coba, teniente	don Ignacio Tec	Antonio Tec
Joseph Pech, alcalde	batab	Francisco Canul
Diego May, alcalde	Pablo Tec, notary	Antonio Pech
		Pedro Canul
		regidors

FOL. 9R DOCUMENT B16

WILL OF JOSEPH COUOH

5 JANUARY 1766

CIMI JOSEPH COUOH 5 V MEHEN GASPAR COUOH V YAR BAR.^{na} BAS CIMIN
JOSE COUOH EN 5 DE ENERO DE 1766 Ã

tu kaba D.^{s} yum bil y Dios mehenbir Dios espilitu santo oxtur perzonas Juntulili hahar Dios uchuc tumen tusinir mayx pimobi lay u hahil cin katic ti ca yum p.^{c} uarDian ca u yalab Junpeɔ missa Rezar utial yn pixan y ca u mantzen tu payarchi tu missa lae antabar yn pixan tu numiayl purgatolio lae bin ɔabac u limosnayl uacper tumin y halili be yn than tin testamento lae

Joseph pech	Capp^n D^n ygnassio tec	An.^{tto} tec fran.^{co} canul
Diego may	Batab	An.^{tto} pech pedro canul
alcardessob	Gaspar coba then.^{c}	Reg.dorlessob lae
	pablo tec ess^{no}pu.^{co}	6 rr^s

Dijose esta missa resada y lo firme =
  fr Juan de Hoyos

JOSEPH COUOH DIED; 5; THE SON OF GASPAR COUOH AND CHILD OF
BERNARDINA BAS. JOSEPH COUOH DIED ON THE 5TH OF JANUARY, 1766
In the name of God the Father, and God the Son, God the Holy Spirit, three persons, one true God almighty, not many. This is the truth. I ask our lord, the guardian priest,

to say one recited mass for my soul, and to send up for me a prayer in the mass to aid my soul in the suffering of purgatory. The fee shall be given: six tomins. And this then is my true statement in my will.

Joseph Pech	captain don Ignacio Tec	Antonio Tec, Francisco Canul
Diego May	batab	Antonio Pech, Pedro Canul
alcaldes	Gaspar Coba, teniente	regidors
	Pablo Tec, public notary	6 reales

This recited mass was said and I signed it
  fray Juan de Hoyos

FOL. 9R DOCUMENT B17

WILL OF GERONIMO TEC
15 FEBRUARY 1766

CIMI GELONIMO TEC EN 15 DE FEBRERO DE 1766 Ã ==

V mehen andres tec V yalen pasg.ʳᵃ poot cimi tin cah lae cin uoktic ynba ti ca pixanir yum p.ᵉ uardia ca yalab Junpeɔ missa Ressada lae bin ɔabac u tulul uacper tumin halili be ==

joseph pech	Cappⁿ Dⁿ Ygᵒ tec Batab	An.ᵗᵗᵒ tec fran.ᶜᵒ canul
Diego may	gaspar coba then.ᵉ	An.ᵗᵗᵒ pech pedro canul
	pablo tec essⁿᵒ	Reg.ᵒʳlessob lae
		6 rrs

Dijose esta missa resada y lo firme
  fr Juan de Hoyos

GERONIMO TEC DIED ON THE 15TH OF FEBRUARY, 1766

The son of Andrés Tec and child of Pasquala Poot. He died here in the cah. I supplicate our blessed lord, the guardian priest, to say one recited mass. The payment will be given: six tomins. This is the truth then.

Joseph Pech	captain don Ignacio Tec	Antonio Tec, Francisco Canul
Diego May	batab	Antonio Pech, Pedro Canul
	Gaspar Coba, teniente	regidors
	Pablo Tec, public notary	6 reales

This recited mass was said and I signed it
  fray Juan de Hoyos

FOL. 9V DOCUMENT B18

WILL OF BERNARDINA COUOH
5 MARCH 1766

CIMI BER.NA COUOH EN 5 DE MARZO DE 1766

ā tu kaba Dios yumbir Dios mehenbir Dios espilitu santo Juntulili hahar Dios uchuc
tumen tusinir mayx pimobi lay bin ylabac u hunir yn thakyahthan tin testamento
hibicir tenir cen ber.na couoh u yix mehenen Joseph couoh u yalen thomassa canul
Bayxan cin uoktic ynba ti ca pixanir yum p.e uardian ca yalab Junpeɔ missa Ressar
missa bin ɔabac u thulul uacper tumin ɏ caper tumin gielusaRem =

Bayxan hunper yn mul mathan chen ɏ yn lakob rae yl u solar lil u pach cin patic tu
kab yn uicham Ming.l coba lae tumen yn matan tu testamento yn yum lae ɏ Junper
boch utial yn uicham xan lae Jassinto pech albasseas =

Josph pech	Capp^n D.^{n} Yg.^{o} tec Batab	An^{tto} tec fran^o
Diego may	gaspar coba then.^{c}	canul p^o canul
alcardessob rae	pablo tec ess^{no}pu^{co}	an^{tto} pech Reg^{or}zob rae

Dijose esta missa resada y lo firme
  fr Juan de Hoyos

BERNARDINA COUOH DIED ON THE 5TH OF MARCH, 1766

In the name of God the Father, God the Son, God the Holy Spirit, one true God
almighty, not many. It will be seen, the document of my final statement in my testament, inasmuch as I who am Bernardina Couoh, the daughter of Joseph Couoh and
child of Tomasa Canul. Likewise, I supplicate our blessed lord, the guardian priest,
that he say one mass, a recited mass. The payment will be given: six tomins and two
tomins for Jerusalem. Likewise, my one well—jointly inherited with my relatives—
and the house plot that goes with it, I leave in the hands of my husband, Miguel
Coba; for I inherited it in my father's will. And one shawl for my husband, too.
Jacinto Pech, executor.

Joseph Pech	captain don Ignacio Tec	Antonio Tec, Francisco Canul
Diego May	batab	Pedro Canul
alcaldes	Gaspar Coba, teniente	Antonio Pech, regidors
	Pablo Tec, public notary	

This recited mass was said and I signed it
  fray Juan de Hoyos

FOLS. 9V–10R DOCUMENT B19

WILL OF GASPAR POOT

10 MARCH 1766

CIMI GASPAR POT EN 10 DE MARSO DE 1766

ã tu kava Dios yumbil y Dios mehenbil y Dios esspiritu santo huntulil hahar Dios uchuc tumen tusinil maix pimobi lay bin ylabac u hunil yn takyahthan tin testamento hibicil tenil cen Gaspar pot u mehenen pedro pot u Yalen maria canche Bayxan ua tuc u xul yn cuxtal tumen hahal Dios uay yokol cab lae uolah mucul yn uinicil ychil Yotoch cilich nabil Yglesia lae Bayxan lic uoktic yn ba ti ca pixanil yum padre Cura ca u yalab hunpeɔ missa Resada bin ɔabac u limosnayl hunpel peso—tumen yalab otzil christianob lae uchebal u yantabal yn pixan tu numyayl purgatorio tumen ca yumil ti D.ˢ lae—

Bayxan heix parte ti lay solal lae tu patah ten yn Na lae ca mul matan yanil ychil u testamento yn Na lae cin patic tu kab yn palilob Jph pot—y maria pot = y bassilia pot oxnupobi = Bayxan cantul uacax y catul capon tzimin y hunpel u puertayl u hol Na = y hunpel caha y yn parte ti lay sitillo lae cin patic tu kab tu yoxtulilob y hunpel pic [fol. 10r] Utial Maria pot—y bassia pot y hunpel ex utial Jph pot y hunpel camisa utial xan—y hunpel tzotz sarga lae y hunpel bat y hun ɔit machete y hunpach u colares y uacpel cueta de oro a medio u tohol lae lay u xul yn takyahthan tin testa-mento cin uacuntic hutul almehen Jasinto pech aluasias lae lay bin tan oltic u katic misatin pixan tu tan batab y Jus.ᵃˢ lae—8—

Jph pech aᵈᵉ	Dⁿ Ygᵒ tec batab	An.ᵗᵗᵒ tec
Diego may aᵈᵉ	pablo tec essⁿᵒ pulico	fran.ᶜᵒ canul
		An.ᵗᵗᵒ pech
		pedro canul

Dijose esta missa resada y lo firme
    fr Juan de Hoyos

GASPAR POOT DIED ON THE 10TH OF MARCH, 1766

In the name of God the Father, and God the Son, and God the Holy Spirit, one true God almighty, not many. It will be seen, the document of my final statement in my will, inasmuch as I who am Gaspar Poot, the son of Pedro Poot and child of María Canche. Likewise, when the true God ends my life here on this earth I wish my body buried in the home, the holy mother church. Likewise, I supplicate our blessed lord, the Padre Curate, that he say one recited mass. The fee shall be given—one peso— for we are believing Christians—to provide assistance to my soul in the suffering of purgatory, through our lord in God.

Likewise, here is the share of the house plot that my mother left me, which was a joint inheritance in my mother's will; I leave it in the hands of my children, Joseph

Poot and María Poot and Basilia Poot, the three of them together. Likewise, four cows and two geldings and one beam, a house beam, and one chest, with my share of that plot, which I leave in the hands of the three of them. And one petticoat [fol. 10r] for María Poot and Basilia Poot, and one pair of trousers for Joseph Poot and one shirt for him, too, with that one fur blanket and one axe and one machete and one necklace of coral beads and six gold coins. This is the end of my final statement in my will. I appoint one nobleman, Jacinto Pech, as executor. He shall take care to request mass for my soul. Before the batab and magistrates here.

Joseph Pech, alcalde	don Ignacio Tec	Antonio Tec
Diego May, alcalde	batab	Francisco Canul
	Pablo Tec, public notary	Antonio Pech
		Pedro Canul

This recited mass was said and I signed it
  fray Juan de Hoyos

FOLS. 10R–10V DOCUMENT B20

WILL OF NICOLASA TEC

28 MARCH 1766

CIMI NICOLASSA TEC = EN 28 DE MARSO DE 1766 Ã

tu kaba d.ˢ yumbil y Dios espiritu santo oxtul perso nas huntulil d.ˢ uchuc tumen tusinil maix pimobi lay bin ylabac u hunil yn takyahthan tin testamento hiBicil tenil cen Nicolasa tec = u yixmehenen Marⁿ tec U yalen maria coba ah cahnalen uay tu mekᵗᵃⁿ cahil ah bolon pixan sabernaber Yxil lae Bacacix cimil yn cah lae toh uol tin naat y tin pucsikal uet sihci lae = Bayxanlic ix uoktic ynba ti ca pixanil yum padre cura ca u mansen tu payalchi Ychil u misa Bayxan uolah mucul yn uinicil Ychil santa Ygᶜsia lae—Bayxan bin ɔabac u limosnayl misa uacpel tumin

Bayxan pat caan yn cah tubal yn balae Bayxan hunpel ch̶e̶n y tan buh solal cin ɔaic ti yn ual Juan chan y hunac kax [fol. 10v] yan tu chikin ti xculix u tzayal chikin lae agusn Yam ti nohole Andres Yam y hunpel boch utial utial yn uabil pet.na chan Bayxan heix lay ch̶e̶n y solal yn cah lic lae yan u hahal than Rosa coyi yn uetel u chic yn mul mantic lay solal y ch̶e̶n y lae cin patic tun tu kab yn ual Juan chan u calah y cabin xuluc u cuxtalob hunhuntultiob lae lay u chun licil in uacuntic c̶a̶t̶u̶l̶ a̶l̶m̶ huntul almehen Andrez cob aluasias lay bin tan oltic u katic misa Tu tan batab y Jusᵃˢ—

Joseph pech aᵈᵉ	Capⁿ Dⁿ Ygᵒ tec	An.ᵗᵗᵒ tec =
Diego may aᵈᵉ	Batab	fran.ᶜᵒ canul =
	Pablo tec essⁿᵒ	An.ᵗᵗᵒ pech =
		pedro canul =

Regi^{or}sob lae =

Dijose esta missa resada y lo firme
   fr Juan de Hoyos

NICOLASA TEC DIED ON THE 28TH OF MARCH, 1766

In the name of God the Father, and God the Holy Spirit, three persons, one almighty God, not many. It shall be seen, the document of my final statement in my will, inasmuch as I who am Nicolasa Tec, the daughter of Martín Tec and the child of María Coba, resident here in the cah governed by the blessed San Bernabé Ixil. Although I am dying, my heart and my understanding are sound, as it should be. Likewise, I also supplicate our blessed lord, the Padre Curate, to send up for me a prayer in the mass. Likewise, I wish my body buried in the holy church. Likewise, the mass fee shall be given: six tomins.

Likewise, I am declaring the settlement of my goods and property. Likewise, one well with half a house plot, I give to my child, Juan Chan, with one forest plot [fol. 10v] which is to the west of Ixculix; its western neighbor is Agustín Yam; to the south is Andrés Yam. And one shawl for my granddaughter, Petrona Chan. Likewise, here is the well and house plot where I live—this is a true statement—together with Rosa Coyi. This, my jointly purchased house plot and well, I leave in the hands of my child, Juan Chan. All lives lose their strength one by one; for this reason, I now appoint [deleted: two nob . . .] one nobleman, Andrés Cob, as executor; he shall take care to request a mass. Before the batab and magistrates:

Joseph Pech, alcalde	captain don Ignacio Tec	Antonio Tec
Diego May, alcalde	batab	Francisco Canul
	Pablo Tec, notary	Antonio Pech
		Pedro Canul
		regidors

This recited mass was said and I signed it
   fray Juan de Hoyos

FOLS. 10V–11R DOCUMENT B21

WILL OF SIMON CHAN

4 APRIL 1766

CIMI SIMON CHAN = EN 4 DE ABLIL DE 1766 Ã

tu kaba Dios yumbil y Dios mehenbil y Dios espiritu santo oxtur personas huntulil Dios uchuc tumen tusinil maix pimobi lay bin ylabac u hunil yn takyahthan tin testamento hibicil tenil cen simon chan u mehenen Agus.ⁿ chan u Yalen catalina

coba ah cahnalob uay tu mektan cahil ca yumilan ah bolon pixan sabernaber = yxil
= bacacix cimil yn cah in cucutilae toh uol tin pucsikal y̱ tin nat uet sihci lae mamac
bin u loh ba ti cimil = Bayxan ua cu xulel yn cuxtal uay yokol cab lae uolah mucul
yn uinicil ychil yotoch cilich Nabil Y̱glesia lae = Bayxan lic uoktic ynba ti ca pixanil
yum padre guardian ca u yalab hunpeɔ misa utial yn pixan yetel ca ca u masen
tu payalchi ychil u misa uchebal yantabal tumen ca Yumil ti Dios tu numYayl
[*sic*] purgatario—mahebal u xan tal tu tan ca Yumil ti d.ˢ lae Bayxan bin ɔabac u
limosnayl tumen yalab otzil christianob lae uacpel tumin y̱ capel t[umin] [fol. 11r]
helusalem lae—

Bayxan hunpel u canal cheyl ynah y̱ hunpel tabronil Juch y̱ u cayl y̱ hunpel boch
ma ɔococ yn botici cin patic ca payera anJos y̱ ca payera Sebollas u cone u ɔoc botic
lae y̱ hunpel rosario u lae utial yn uatan madalena couoh Bayxan hunpel caJa—y̱
hunpel botihuela y̱ hun ɔit bat y̱ machete = y̱ tirma tzotz lae utial yn mehen Joseph
chan = Bayxan—hunpel botihuela lae = y̱ hunpach colares utial yn uixmehen Juana
chan Bayxan heix Yn parte ti lay solal y̱ chen yn cah lic y̱ yn Yum lae he cabin cimic
Yn Yum Agusn chan tumen ca Yumil ti D.ˢ uay yokol cab lae ca u ɔab u parte =
Yn mehenob lae = halili u xul Yn than tin testamento cin uacuntic catul almehen
gaspar ek y̱ marcos pot albasiasob lay bin tan oltic u katic missa tin pixan tu tan
batab y̱ Jusᵃˢ—

Jph pech aᵈᵉˢ	Dⁿ Yg° tec	=An.ᵗᵗᵒ tec—
Diego may aᵈᵉˢ	Batab	=fran.ᶜᵒ canul—
	pablo tec essⁿᵒ audenᵃ	—An.ᵗᵗᵒ pech—
		—pedro canul—
		—Regidoreso lae =

Dijose esta missa resada y lo firme
  fr Juan de Hoyos

SIMON CHAN DIED ON THE 4TH OF APRIL, 1766.

In the name of God the Father, and God the Son, and God the Holy Spirit, three
persons, one almighty God, not many. The document of my final statement in my
testament may be seen, inasmuch as I who am Simon Chan, the son of Agustín Chan,
the child of Catalina Coba, residents here in the cah governed by our lord the blessed
San Bernabé Ixil. Although I am dying, my heart and my understanding are sound, as
it should be. Nobody shall free himself from death. Likewise, when my life ends here
on this earth, I wish the burial of my body to be in the home, the holy mother church.
Likewise, I supplicate our blessed lord, the guardian priest, that he say one mass for
my soul and that he send up for me a prayer in the mass to provide the protection of
our lord in God through the suffering of purgatory, and not to be burdened before
our lord in God. Likewise, the fee will be given, as we are believing Christians: six
tomins and two tomins for Jerusalem.

Likewise, one tall-tree seed and one polished table with its gourd and one shawl; I have not finished paying for it; I leave our garlic garden and our onion garden; it was sold and is just paid for; with one rosary; all for my wife, Magdalena Couoh. Likewise, one chest and one jar and one axe and machete, with a fur cloak, for my son, Joseph Chan. Likewise, one jar, with one [necklace] of coral beads, for my daughter, Juana Chan. Likewise, here is my share of this house plot and well where I live with my father—he who, when he died, my father, Agustín Chan, through our lord in God here on this earth, he gave his share to us—[me and] my sons. This is the truth, the end of my statement in my will. I appoint two noblemen, Gaspar Ek and Marcos Poot, as executors. They shall take care to request a mass for my soul. Before the batab and magistrates:

Joseph Pech, alcalde	don Ignacio Tec	Antonio Tec
Diego May, alcalde	batab	Francisco Canul
	Pablo Tec, council notary	Antonio Pech
		Pedro Canul
		regidors

This recited mass was said and I signed it
    fray Juan de Hoyos

FOL. 11R DOCUMENT B22

WILL OF VENTURA YAM

4 APRIL 1766

CIMI BEN^{ra} YAM EN 4 DE ABLIL DE 1766 Ã

tu kaba Dios yumbil y Dios mehenbil y Dios esspiritu sato oxtur personas humtulil Dios uchuc tumen tusinil maix pimobi lay bin ylabac u hunil yn testamento hibicil tenil ben^{ra} Yam u mehen An.^{tto} Yam u Yal Juan canul ah cahnal ua ti cah Yxil lae Bayxan uolah mucul ychil santa Yleia lae lic ix uoktic ynba tin pixanil yum padre ^{cura} ca yalab hunpel misa utial yn pixan bin ɔabac u limosnayl uacpel tumin tumen yalab otzil christianob lae halili u xul yn than lae—

Jph pech a^{des}	Dⁿ Yg^o tec	An.^{tto} tec—
Diego may a^{des}	Batab	fran.^{co} canul—
	pablo tec ess^{no}	An.^{tto} pech—
		pedro canul—
		Regi^{or}sob lae

Dijose esta missa resada y lo firme
    fr Juan de Hoyos

Ventura Yam died on the 4th of April, 1766.

In the name of God the Father, and God the Son, and God the Holy Spirit, three persons, one almighty God, not many. The document of my testament may be seen, inasmuch as I am Ventura Yam, the son of Antonio Yam and child of Juana Canul, resident here in the cah of Ixil. Likewise, I wish to be buried in the holy church. Also I supplicate my blessed lord, the Padre Curate, that he say one mass for my soul. The fee will be given—six tomins—as we are believing Christians. This is the truth, the end of my statement.

Joseph Pech, alcalde	don Ignacio Tec	Antonio Tec
Diego May, alcalde	batab	Francisco Canul
	Pablo Tec, notary	Antonio Pech
		Pedro Canul
		regidors

This recited mass was said and I signed it
fray Juan de Hoyos

FOL. 11V DOCUMENT B23

WILL OF VIVIANA CANCHE
26 APRIL 1766

Cimi bibiyana canche en 26 de Ablil de 1766 ã

tu kaba d.ˢ yumbil y Dios mehenbil y Dios esspiritu santo—oxtur personas huntulili hahal d.ˢ uchuc tumen tusinil maix pimobi lay bin ylabac u hunil yn takyahthan tin testamento hibicil tenil bibiana canche u yixmehen Cleᵗᵉ canche u Yal Marta Uh ah otochnalon uay ti cah yxil = lae bacacix cimil yn cah hele lae toh uol tin pucsikal y tin nat lae Bayxan uolah Mucul yn cucut uinicil ychil yotoch ca nabil ti Santa Yglesia. Bayxan lic uoktic ynba ti ca pixanil yum padre curadian utial u yalab hunpe ɔ missa Resada utial yn pixan mahebal u xantal tu numyayl purge torio Bayxan lic uoktic Ynba ti ca pixanil Yum padre utial ca u masen tu payalchu ychil u missa heix bin nahaltic yn pixan lae bin ɔabac u limosnayl uacpel tumin y capel tumin helusalem lae

Bayxan hunpok yeua tzimin y u yal yeua xan cin patic tu kab yn uichan marcos cante y yn ual Juan cante = Bayxan heix yn parte chen y solal tu patah ten Yn Yum ychil u testamento ca cimi lae cin patic tu yn uicham xan y Juan cante—tebin ylabac tu testamento yn Yum lae bix yanili ca Yumil ti Dˢ bin ɔaic u nucul y ca Yum Jusᵃˢ tu kinil tumen oxac lay chen y solalae heuac multial bil licil yn patic tu kab uicham y yn ual y yn tio y yn sucunob y ui ɔinob lae lay u nucul cin patic almehen peᵒ cob aluasias lay bin tan oltic u kati misa tu tan batab y Jusᵃˢ lae

Jph pech aᵈᵉ=	Dⁿ Ygᵒ tec Batab	An.ᵗᵗᵒ tec
Diego may aᵈᵉ=	pablo tec essⁿᵒ	fran.ᶜᵒ canul

An.ᵗᵗᵒ pech

pedro canul

Regiᵒʳsob lae

Dijose esta missa resada y lo firme
    fr Juan de Hoyos

VIVIANA CANCHE DIED ON THE 26TH OF APRIL, 1766

In the name of God the Father, and God the Son, and God the Holy Spirit, three persons, one true God almighty, not many. It may be seen, the document of my final statement in my testament, inasmuch as I am Viviana Canche, the daughter of Clemente Canche, the child of Marta Uh; we are householders here in the cah of Ixil. Although I am dying, my heart and my understanding are sound. Likewise, I wish the burial of my body to be in the home, our house in holy church. Likewise, I supplicate our blessed lord, the priest, that he say one recited mass for my soul so as not to detain it in the suffering of purgatory. Likewise, I supplicate our blessed lord, the Padre, that he send up for me a prayer in the mass, which shall reach my soul there. The fee shall be given: six tomins and two tomins for Jerusalem.

Likewise, one mare and also its filly I leave in the hands of my husband, Marcos Cante, and my child, Juan Cante. Likewise, here is my share of a well and house plot left to me in the will of my father, now deceased; I leave it to my husband also and to Juan Cante. It may be seen in the testament of my father, who is with our lord in God—it will be given; his instrument (of will) is with our lord magistrates—why today these three wells and this house plot I now leave jointly in the hands of my husband and my child and my uncle and my older brothers and my younger siblings. This instrument I leave with the noble Pedro Cob, as executor; he shall take care to request a mass. Before the batab and magistrates.

Joseph Pech, alcalde	Don Ignacio Tec	Antonio Tec
Diego May, alcalde	batab	Francisco Canul
	Pablo Tec, notary	Antonio Pech
		Pedro Canul
		regidors

This recited mass was said and I signed it
    fray Juan de Hoyos

FOL. 12R DOCUMENT B24

WILL OF BERNARDINO COOT

29 APRIL 1766

CIMI BER^{no} COT EN 29 DE ABLIL DE 1766 Ã =

tu kaba Dios yumbil y̱ Dios mehenbil y̱ Dios esspiritu santo oxtul personas huntulili Dios uchuc tumen tusinil maix pimobi lay bin ylabac u hunil yn takyahthan tin
testamento hibicil tenil cen ber^{no} cot u mehenen Diego cot u yalen YSaber mukul ah
cahnalob uay ti cah Yxil lae—bacacix cimil yn cah tin cucutilae toh uol tin pucsikal y̱
tin nat uet sihci lae Bayxan uolah mucul Yn cucutil Ychil Yotoch cilich nabil Yglesia
lae Bayxan ~~uolah mucul~~ lic uoktic ynba ti ca pixanil Yum pa.^{e} cura ca u yalab hunpeɔ
missa Resada yokol Yn pixan y̱ ca u masen tu payalchi Ychil u missa ca mansabac
tu numyayl purgatorio Bayxan bin ɔabac u limosnayl uacpel tumin y̱ capel tumin
helusalem lae = 8 rr^s

Bayxan hunpel ~~chen~~ y̱ u solalil u pach lae cin patic tu kab yn mehenob—Diego cot y̱
Joseph cot u multialob lae bay yanil ychil u testamento—yn uatan Dominga tec—bay
bic Uɔama ten Ca Yum lucas canche—ychil u testamento caat cimi lae = Bayxan
hunpel ca cilich colebil—y̱ u tabernacula = y̱ hunpel chichan caJa = y̱ hunpay chichi
na ^{ho}[^{l}] puerta = y̱ hunpel camissalob y̱ capel ex = y̱ hun ɔit bat lay tin tzolah canal lae
utial Diego cot = Bayxan heix yn mehen Jph cot lae—cin ɔaic hunpel ca cilich
colebil ti xan y̱ u messayl lae y̱ tanbuh chichan hol na lae—bay bic canup hol na cachilae
lay tumen cin ɔaichun hun xetil tiob lae = y̱ hunpel camissa tun bul ben = y̱ capel ex y̱
hunpel caha y̱ machete y̱ lob che mascab y̱ hunpel cama lae—Bayxan heix yn canan pic
lae y̱ Ypil lae cin patic tu kab luuissa cob ca u kub ti la ypal pasguala cot u kaba lae bax
bic u matan Ychil u testamento Yn uatan Dominga tec lae—lay tumen cin kochbesic
yn uixmehen luuisa cob u kube lae lay tumen cin uacuntic catul almehen = Jph miss y̱
mathe.^{o} canul lay bin tan oltic u katic misa ti in pixan tu tan batab y̱ Justisiass lae—

Jph pech a^{de}	D.^{n} Yg.^{o} tec	An^{tto} tec—
Diego may a^{de}	Batab	fran^{co} canul—
alcaldesob lae	pablo tec ess^{no}	An^{tto} pech—
		pedro canul
		Regi^{or}sob lae

Dijose esta missa Resada y lo firme
  fr Juan de Hoyos

BERNARDINO COOT DIED ON THE 29TH OF APRIL, 1766

In the name of God the Father, and God the Son, and God the Holy Spirit, three
persons, one almighty God, not many. The document of my final statement in my testament will be seen, inasmuch as I who am Bernardino Coot, the son of Diego Coot
and the child of Isabel Mukul, residents here in the cah of Ixil. Although I am dying,

my heart and my understanding are sound, as it should be. Likewise, I wish my body buried in the home, the holy mother church. Likewise, I now supplicate our blessed lord, the Padre Curate, that he say one recited mass for my soul, and that he send up for me a prayer in the mass so as to pass through the suffering of purgatory. Likewise, the fee will be given: six tomins and two tomins for Jerusalem. 8 reales.

Likewise, one well with its accompanying house plot I leave in the hands of my sons, Diego Coot and Joseph Coot, together. This property is in the will of my wife, Dominga Tec, for it was given to me by our father, Lucas Canche, in his will—he has since died. Likewise, one Our Holy Lady and her tabernacle, and one small chest, and one small house beam for a door—and one shirt, and two pairs of trousers, and one axe, which I have arranged to be the property of Diego Coot. Likewise, here is my son Joseph Coot, to whom I also give one Our Holy Lady with its table, and half a small house beam; thus here are both house beams today, for I give one to each one, dividing them thus. And one shirt, which goes undivided [to Joseph], with two pairs of trousers and one chest and machete and digging-stick and one bed. Also I have looked after this slip and dress, which I leave in the hands of Luisa Cob, to deliver to her child, named Pasquala Coot. It was given to her in the testament of my wife, Dominga Tec, which is why I charge my daughter[-in-law], Luisa Cob, to deliver it to her. I designate two noblemen, Joseph Mis and Mateo Canul, to take care of requesting a mass for my soul. Before the batab and magistrates here:

Joseph Pech, alcalde	don Ignacio Tec	Antonio Tec
Diego May, alcalde	batab	Francisco Canul
alcaldes	Pablo Tec, notary	Antonio Pech
		Pedro Canul
		regidors

This recited mass was said and I signed it
    fray Juan de Hoyos

FOL. 12V DOCUMENT B25

WILL OF BERNARDINO COBA

2 MAY 1766

CIMI BER^no^ COBA EN 2 DE MAYO DE 1766 Ã—

tu kaba Dios yumbil y Dios mehenbil y Dios esspiritu santo oxtul personas huntulili hahal Dios uchuc tumen tusinil maix pimobi lay bin ylabac u hunil yn takyahthan tin testamento hibicil tenil cen Ber^no^ coba u mehen sar.^or^ coba—u yalen luuisa mo ah cahnalob uay ti cah Yxil lae Bayxan uolah mucul Yn uinicil Ychil cilich nabil Yglesia lae Bayxan lic uoktic ynba ti ca pixanil Yum padre cura ca u yalab hunpeɔ missa Resa da utial Yn pixan y ca u masen tu payalchi Ychil u missa lae bayxan bin ɔabac u limos-nayl yn missa uacpel tumin lae—6 r^s^

Dijose esta missa y lo firme
    fr Juan de Hoyos

Jph pech a^{de}	D.^{n} Yg.^{o} tec	An^{tto} tec =
Diego may a^{de}	Batab	fra^{no} canul
	pablo tec ess^{no}	An^{tto} pech
		pedro canul
		Regi^{or}sob lae

BERNARDINO COBA DIED ON THE 2ND OF MAY, 1766.

In the name of God the Father, and God the Son, and God the Holy Spirit, three persons, one true God almighty, not many. It will be seen, the document of my final statement in my testament, inasmuch as I who am Bernardino Coba, the son of Salvador Coba and the child of Luisa Mo, residents here in the cah of Ixil. Likewise, I wish my body buried in the holy mother church. Likewise, I now supplicate our blessed lord, the Padre Curate, that he say one recited mass for my soul, and that he send up for me a prayer in the mass. Likewise, the fee for my mass will be given: six tomins. 6 reales. This recited mass was said and I signed it,
    fray Juan de Hoyos

Joseph Pech, alcalde	don Ignacio Tec	Antonio Tec
Diego May, alcalde	batab	Francisco Canul
	Pablo Tec, notary	Antonio Pech
		Pedro Canul
		regidors

FOL. 12V DOCUMENT B26

WILL OF MARÍA CHAN
7 MAY 1766

CIMI MARIA CHAN EN 7 DE MAYO DE 1766 Ã

tu kaba Dios yumbil y Dios mehenbil y Dios esspiritu santo oxtul personas huntulil Dios uchuc tumen tusinil maix pimobi lay bin ylabac u hunil yn thakyahthan tin testamento hibicil Cenil Maria chan u Yixmehen pasgual chan u Yal Andrea balam lae ah cahalnalen tu cahal hoctun Bacacix cimil Yn cah hele lae toh uol tin pucsikal uet sihci lae maix mac bin u loh uba ti cimil lae Bayxan tin uoktah ynba ti ca pixanil Yum padrecura ca u yalab hunpeɔ missa Resada lae y ca u masen tu payalchi ychil u missa lae emebal u cuch Yn pixan tu tan ca yumil ti d^{s} ca sebac u manel tu numYayl purgatorio lae Bayxan bin ɔabac u limosnayl yn misayl uacpel tumin lae—

Jph pech a^{de} D.^{n} Yg.^{o} tec   An^{tto} tec

Diego may a^{de}   Batab   fran° canul

pablo tec ess^{no}   An^{tto} pech

pedro canul

Regi^d—

Dijose esta missa y lo firme

fr Juan de Hoyos

MARÍA CHAN DIED ON THE 7TH OF MAY, 1766

In the name of God the Father, and God the Son, and God the Holy Spirit, three persons, one almighty God, not many. It will be seen, the document of my final statement in my testament, inasmuch as I am María Chan, the daughter of Pasqual Chan and the child of Andrea Balam, residents of the cah of Hoctun. Although I am dying today, my heart is sound, as it should be. It is certain that nobody shall redeem himself from death. Therefore, I supplicate our blessed lord, the Padre Curate, that he say one recited mass, and that he send up for me a prayer in the mass to alleviate the guilt of my soul before our lord in God, so that my soul pass quickly through the suffering of purgatory. Likewise, the fee for my mass will be given: six tomins.

Joseph Pech, alcalde	don Ignacio Tec	Antonio Tec
Diego May, alcalde	batab	Francisco Canul
	Pablo Tec, notary	Antonio Pech
		Pedro Canul
		regidors

This recited mass was said and I signed it

fray Juan de Hoyos

FOL. 13R DOCUMENT B27

WILL OF JUAN TACU

20 JULY 1766

CIMI JUAN TACU HELE EN 20 DE JULIO DE 1766 AÑ = =

tu kaba Dios yumbil y Dios mehenbil y Dios espiritu santo oxtul pesonas huntulil Dios uchuc tumen tusinil maix pimobi lay bin ylabac u hunil yn takyahthan tin testamento hibicil tenil cen Ju° tacu u mehenen Jph tacu u yalen Margarita mex ah cahnalen uay tu mektan cahil ca yumilan ah bolon pixan Sa bernaber Yxil Bacacix cimil Yn cah lae toh uol tin pucsikal y tin naat uet sihci lae lae—uolah mucul yn uinicil Ychil Santa Yglesia lae Bayxan licix yn uoktic ynba ti ca pixanil Yum padre guardian ca u Yalab hunpel chichan Misa Resada utial Yn pixan y ca u masentu payalchi Ychil u

missa Bayxan bin ɔabac u limosnayl tumen yalab otzil christianob la uacpel tumin lay
u xul Yn than tin testamento lae halili be minan U bal Ynba lae—

Jph pech a[de]	D.[n] Yg.[o] tec	An[tto] tec ==
Diego may a[de]	Batab	fran[o] canul =
	pablo tec ess[no]	An[tto] pech =
		pedro canul
		Regi[r]es lae

Dijose esta missa resada y lo firme
    fr Hoyos

JUAN TACU DIED ON THE 20TH OF JULY, 1766

In the name of God the Father, and God the Son, and God the Holy Spirit, three
persons, one almighty God, not many. It will be seen, the document of my final statement in my testament, inasmuch as I who am Juan Tacu, the son of Joseph Tacu and
the child of Margarita Mex, residents here in the cah governed by our lord the blessed
San Bernabé of Ixil. Although I am dying, my heart and my understanding are sound,
as it should be; I wish my body buried in the holy church. Likewise, I also now supplicate our blessed lord, the guardian priest, that he say one small recited mass for my
soul, and that he send up for me a prayer in the mass. Likewise, the fee for my mass
will be given, for we are believing Christians: six tomins. This is the end of my statement in my will. This is the truth. I have no household goods.

Joseph Pech, alcalde	don Ignacio Tec	Antonio Tec
Diego May, alcalde	batab	Francisco Canul
	Pablo Tec, notary	Antonio Pech
		Pedro Canul
		regidors

This recited mass was said and I signed it
    fray Hoyos

FOL. 13R DOCUMENT B28

WILL OF JUAN DE LA CRUZ POOT
15 JUNE 1766

CIMI JU[o] DE ☩ POT EN 15 DE JUNIO DE 1766 AÑ

tu kaba Dios yumbil y Dios mehenbil y Dios esspiritu santo oxtul personas huntulil
Dios uchuc tumen tusinil maix pimobi lay bin ylabac u hunil yn testamento bicil tenil
cen Juo de ☩z pot u mehen Agus[n] pot—u yalen luuisa Juchim lae Bayxan cin uoktic

ynba ti ca pixanil Yum padre cura ca u u yalab hunpel chinchan misa Resada utial Yn
pixan y ca u masen tu payalchi Ychil u misa uchebal u Yantal Yn pixan tu numYayl
animas purgatorio lae binix ɔabac u limosnayl uacꝑel tumin lae halili u xul Yn than
tin testamento—6 rˢ

Jph pech aᵈᵉ	Dⁿ Yg.º tec	Anᵗᵗᵒ tec
Diego may aᵈᵉ	Batab	franᵒ canul
	pablo tec essⁿᵒ	Anᵗᵗᵒ pech
		pedro canul
		Regiᵒʳsob lae

Dijose esta missa y dieron seis rrˢ
  fr Hoyos

Juan de la Cruz Poot died on the 15th of June, 1766

In the name of God the Father, and God the Son, and God the Holy Spirit, three persons, one God almighty, not many. It will be seen, the document of my testament, as I
who am Juan de la Cruz Poot, the son of Agustín Poot and the child of Luisa Huchim.
Likewise, I supplicate our blessed lord, the Padre Curate, that he say one small recited
mass for my soul, and that he send up for me in a prayer in the mass, empowered to
aid my soul through the suffering of souls in purgatory. Also the fee will be given: six
tomins. This is the truth, the end of my statement in my will. 6 reales.

Joseph Pech, alcalde	don Ignacio Tec	Antonio Tec
Diego May, alcalde	batab	Francisco Canul
	Pablo Tec, notary	Antonio Pech
		Pedro Canul
		regidors

I said this mass and they gave six reales
  fray Hoyos

FOLS. 13V–14R DOCUMENT B29
WILL OF PASQUALA MATU
25 AUGUST 1766

PASGUALA MATU—Cimi en 25 de Agosto de 1766 añ—

tu kaba D.ˢ yumbil y D.ˢ mehenbil y D.ˢ esspiritu santo oxtur personasob lae huntulil
D.ˢ uchuc tumen tusinil maix pimobi lay bin ylabac u hunil yn takyahthan tin testamento hibicil tenil cen pasq.ˡᵃ matu u yalen luissa coba ah cahalnalen uay tu mektan
cahil ca yumilan ah bolon pixan Sabernaber Yxil lae Bacacix cimil in cah lac toh uol

tin pucsikal y tin nat lae mamac bin u loh uba ti cimil lae—Bayxan uolah mucul yn
cucutil ych Yotoch Santa Yglesia lae. Bayxan lic ix uoktic ynba ti ca pixanil yum padre
cura. ca u Yalab hunpe ɔ missa utial Yn pixan y ca u masen tu payalchi Ychil u missa
uchebal U yantabal Yn pixan tu tan ca yumil ti d.ˢ tu numYayl animas purgatorio
Bayxan bin ɔabac u limosNayl misa—oxpel tostones y capel tumin Jelusalem lae ==

Bayxan pat can Yn cah ti hebal yan tene—Bayxan hopel camissa y hopel ex y
canpay kaxnak y capel panilloyl lae—utial Yn uicham Sebas.ⁿ Yam mamacbin luksic
ti lae—Bay = xan hunpel camissa y hunpel ex utial yn ual man.ʲ yam—Bayxan hunpel
camissa y hunpel ex utial Rogue Yam—Bayxan Domingo Yam hunpel camissa y
ex utial xan = hunpel camissa y hunpel ex Bayxan oxpel camissa y oxpel ex utial Yn
ual Juᵒ yam = Bayxan capel Ypil y capel pic y hunpel boch—y hunpay u ca lot u
hulul colares utial maria Yam = Bayxan hunpel pic y hunpel ypil y hunpel boch—y
hunpay u ca lot u hulul colares xan utial Rosasa yam Bayxan hunpel pic utial Yn uilib
christina coba = Bayxan hunpel pic utial Yn uilib monica coba—Bayxan hunpel ypil
utial yn uilib pasgʲᵃ ytza—Bayxan hunpel ypil utial yn uilib pet.ⁿᵃ couoh Bayxan heix
Yn mul matan chen y solal lae yan ychil u testamento Yn Yum Juᵒ bauᵗᵃ matu lae capel
chen y u solalil u pachob lae Bay bic Yn mul matan y yn sucunob lae—Jph matu—y
marcos = matu—cin patic tun tu kab Yn ualob xiblalob lae Man.ˡ Yam y Rogue
Yam—y Domingo Yam—y Juo Yam—y Juo Yam—y Yn chupul al maria Yam—u multialob lae—halilibe cin uacuntic catul almehen albasiasob lae—Jph mis—y Dⁿ An.ᶻ
pech thenᶜ lay bin tan oltic u katicob missa yokol Yn pixan tu tan batab y Ju.ᵃˢ lae
[fol. 14r]

Jph pech aᵈᵉ	Cap.ⁿ D.ⁿ Yg.ᵒ tec	Anᵗᵗᵒ tec—
Diego may aᵈᵉ	Batab	francᵒ canul—
	tin tan pablo tec essⁿᵒ	Anᵗᵗᵒ pech—
		pedro canul Regiᵒsob lae

Cantose esta missa y lo firme
   fr Hoyos

PASQUALA MATU DIED ON THE 25TH OF AUGUST, 1766

In the name of God the Father, and God the Son, and God the Holy Spirit, three
persons, one God almighty, not many. It will be seen, the document of my final
statement in my testament, inasmuch as I who am Pasquala Matu, the daughter of
Luisa Coba, resident here in the cah governed by our lord the blessed San Bernabé of
Ixil. Although I am dying, content is my heart and my understanding; nobody shall
redeem themselves from death. Likewise, I wish my body buried in the home of the
holy church. Likewise, I also now supplicate our blessed lord, the Padre Curate, that
he say one mass for my soul, and that he send up for me a prayer in the mass empowered to protect my soul before our lord in God in the suffering of souls in purgatory.
Likewise, the mass fee will be given: three tostons and two tomins for Jerusalem.

Likewise, I am declaring the items of cloth that are mine. Likewise, five shirts and five pairs of trousers and four belts and two lengths of cloth for my husband, Sebastián Yam; nobody is to take it from him. Likewise, one shirt and one pair of trousers for my child, Manuel Yam. Likewise, one shirt and one pair of trousers for Roque Yam. Likewise, one shirt and one pair of trousers also for Domingo Yam. [deleted: one shirt and trousers] Likewise, three shirts and three pairs of trousers for my child, Juan Yam. Likewise, two huipiles and two petticoats and one shawl, and one pair of strung necklaces for María Yam. Likewise, one petticoat and one huipil and one shawl, and also one pair of strung coral necklaces, for Rosa Yam. Likewise, one petticoat for my daughter-in-law Cristina Coba. Likewise, one petticoat for my daughter-in-law Monica Coba. Likewise, one huipil for my daughter-in-law Pasquala Itza. Likewise, one huipil for my daughter-in-law Petrona Couoh. Likewise, here is my jointly inherited well and house plot, which is in the will of my father, Juan Bautista Matu; two wells go with the house plot there. Now then my joint inheritance—with my elder brothers Joseph Matu and Marcos Matu—I leave in your hands, my boys, Manuel Yam and Roque Yam and Domingo Yam and Juan Yam and Juan Yam and my girl, María Yam, all of them together. This is the truth. I appoint two noblemen as executors, Joseph Mis and don Andrés Pech, lieutenant; they shall take care to request a mass for my soul. Before the batab and magistrates here: [fol. 14r]

Joseph Pech, alcalde	captain don Ignacio Tec	Antonio Tec
Diego May, alcalde	batab	Francisco Canul
	Before me, Pablo Tec, notary	Antonio Pech
		Pedro Canul, regidors

This mass was sung and I signed it
   fray Hoyos

FOLS. 14R–14V DOCUMENT B30

WILL OF PEDRO MIS

17 AUGUST 1766

CIMI PEDRO MIS—EN 17 DE AG^to DE 1766 AÑ—

tu kaba Dios yumbil y Dios mehenbil y Dios essp^to. s.—oxtur personas huntulil Dios uchuc tumen tusinil maix pimobi lay bin ylabac u hunil yn takyahthan tin testamento hibicil tenil cen pedro miss u mehenen Diego miss U Yalen lusia tun lae Bayxane tamuk u pay cen ca yumil ti d^s. hele lae cin ɔaic yn than ti yn hahal d^s. uchebal Yn kubic Yn pixan ti ca yumil ti d^s. heix in Cucutial lumil lae Uolah mucul Ychil Yotoch Santa nabil Yglesia lae—licix uoktic ynba ti ca pixanil yum padre guardian ca u yal hunpe ɔ missa kaybil missa utial yn pixan yl ix bin u masen tu payalchi Ychil u misa lae emebal u cuch yn pixan tu tan ca yumil ti d^s. y ca sebac u manel tu NumYayl

animas purgatorio lae Bayxan bin ɔabac u limosnayl missa lae oxpel tostones y̆ capel
tumin Jelusalem lae

Bayxan hunpel Na—y̆ hunpel u puertayl V hol na—y̆ u yabeyl y̆ hunpel yeua—y̆
yal potro—y̆ u lak yal chichan yeua—y̆ hunpel messa y̆ hunpel silla kanche—y̆ hun ɔit
ɔopatan coch bol—y̆ hunpel tabernacula—y̆ c ium San Diego—y̆ hunpay caha—y̆
hun ɔit cuchara takin—y̆ hunpel botihuela—y̆ hunpel u bancoyl ħuch—y̆ hunpel
kax yan tu chikin multun lae—u matan Joseph lae—yn tzenpal lae—utzayalob—Ju°
miss ti nohol—ti chikin marcos cime ti xaman D.ⁿ bar.ᵐᵉ pech—ti lakin Yg.° bas—tili
yan bay tuhole—u lak kaxcapel lob lae = Bayxan hunpel kax yan tu chikin u hol cah
tu takal u parte gaspar pot cin ɔaic tin m̶e̶k̶p̶a̶l̶a̶l̶o̶b̶ tzenpal phelipa pech y̆ yalob u
matanob lae—Bayxan hunpel kax yan ti ixtohil—u matan kax yn uatan cin ɔaic ti
mathais Juchim y̆ clara Juchim canupobi = Bayxane hunpel cħen y̆ u solaril u pach lae
cin patic tukab yn uatan pasgla coba y̆ lay yn tzenpal Jph pech lae u yal ix lay phelipa
pech xane canupob xani y̆ hecen tulacal yn pakal cheob ya ychile u multialob—
Bayxan hunpel Na y̆ mac lae y̆ u Yabeylae y̆ hunpel nuc lae y̆ yn papirera y̆ hunpel sia
kanche y̆ hunac kax yan ti ixtohil utial Yn uatan pasgla coba lae he u tzayale Diego
[fol. 14v] pech halili be lic yn uacuntic aluasiassob Dⁿ gaspal canul lae lay bin tan oltic
u katicob missa yoklal yn pixan tu tan batab y̆ Jus.ᵃˢ Regi°ʳsob lae—

Jph pech aᵈᵉ	D.ⁿ Yg.° tec	Anᵗᵗᵒ tec—
Diego may aᵈᵉ	Batab	fran° canul
	pablo tec essⁿᵒ	Anᵗᵗᵒ pech =
		pedro canul =
		Regi°ʳsob lae

Cantose esta missa y lo firme
    fr Hoyos

PEDRO MIS DIED ON THE 17TH OF AUGUST, 1766

In the name of God the Father, and God the Son, and God the Holy Spirit, three
persons, one God almighty, not many. It will be made public, the document of my
final statement in my testament, inasmuch as I who am Pedro Mis, the son of Diego
Mis and the child of Lucia Tun. Likewise, while our lord in God calls me today, I give
my statement to my true God so that I may deliver my soul to our lord in God. Here
is my earthly body; I wish it buried in the home, the holy house, the church. Also I
now supplicate our blessed father, the guardian priest, that he say one mass, a sung
mass, for my soul, and also send up for me a prayer in the mass to alleviate the guilt
of my soul before our lord in God and so it will pass quickly through the suffering of
souls in purgatory. Likewise, the fee for that mass will be given: three tostons and two
tomins for Jerusalem.

Likewise, one house, with one house beam for a door, with its lock, and one
mare with one colt, and the other offspring—the little mare, and one table, and one

wooden chair, and one blunt digging-stick, and one tabernacle with our lord San Diego, and one chest, and one silver spoon, and one jar, and one polished bench, and one forest plot, which is to the west of the stone mound; it is the inheritance of this Joseph, my adopted child. Its neighbors are Juan Mis to the south, Marcos Cim over to the west, don Bartolome Pech to the north, Ignacio Bas to the east. In the same place is the entrance to these other two forests. Likewise, one forest is to the west of the cah entrance, next to Gaspar Poot's share; I give it to my [deleted: infants] wet nurse, Felipa Pech, with her children together. Likewise, one forest at Ixtohil—my wife's inherited forest—I give to Matias Huchim and Clara Huchim, both together. Likewise, one well with the house plot that goes with it I leave in the hands of my wife, Pasquala Coba, with my adopted child, Joseph Pech—he is also the child of Felipa Pech here, also to both of them together; and all that is in my orchard of sapote trees is for them together. Likewise, one house and door with its key, and one seat with my writing desk, and one wooden chair, and one forest, which is at Ixtohil, for my wife Pasquala Coba—its neighbor is Diego [fol. 14v] Pech. This is the truth. I now appoint as executor don Gaspar Canul. He shall take care to request a mass for my soul. Before the batab, magistrates, and regidors:

Joseph Pech, alcalde	dcdon Ignacio Tec	Antonio Tec
Diego May, alcalde	batab	Francisco Canul
	Pablo Tec, notary	Antonio Pech
		Pedro Canul
		regidors

This mass was sung and I signed it
    fray Hoyos

FOL. 14V DOCUMENT B31

WILL OF MARTHA COBA

6 AUGUST 1766

en 6 de Agosto de 1766 ã cimi Martha coba u yixmehen manuel coba U yal An.ᵗᵗᵃ yzta = tu kaba Dios yumbil y Dios mehenbil y Dios esspiritu santo oxtul personas huntulil Dios uchuc tumen tusinil maix pimobi lay bin ylabac u hunil—cin katic ti ca pixanil Yum padre cura ca yalab hunpel misa Resada utial antabal Yn pixan tu NumiaYayl animas purgatorio lae bin ɔabac u limosnayl uac pel tumin lae halili u xul Yn than tin testamento lae

Jph pech aᵈᵉ	D.ⁿ Yg.° tec	Anᵗᵗᵒ tec =
Diego may aᵈᵉ	Batab	fran° canul =
	pablo tec essⁿᵒ	Anᵗᵗᵒ pech ==

pedro canul

Regi^{or}sob lae

Dijose esta missa resada y lo firme
 fr Juan de Hoyos

On the 6th of August of 1766 died Martha Coba, the daughter of Manuel Coba and
child of Antonia Itza. In the name of God the Father, and God the Son, and God the
Holy Spirit, three persons, one almighty God, not many. This document will be seen.
I request from our blessed father, the Padre Curate, that he say one said mass to assist
my soul through the sufferings of purgatory. The fee shall be given: six tomins. This is
the truth, the end of my statement in my will.

Joseph Pech, alcalde	don Ignacio Tec	Antonio Tec
Diego May, alcalde	batab	Francisco Canul
	Pablo Tec, notary	Antonio Pech
		Pedro Canul
		regidors

This recited mass was said and I signed it
 fray Juan de Hoyos

FOL. 15R DOCUMENT B32

WILL OF JOSEPH POOT
17 SEPTEMBER 1766

CIMI JPH POT EN 17 DE SEP^{e} DE 1766 AÑO

tu kaba Dios yumbil y Dios mehenbil y Dios espiritu santo oxtul personas huntulil
hahal Dios uchuc tumen tusinil maix pimobi lay bin Ylabac u hunil yn takyahthan
tin testamento hibicil tenil cen Jph pot u mehenen Ju.° pot u yalen Juana matu
lae bacacix cimil Yn cahe toh uol tin puksikal y tin nat uet sihci lae Bayxan uolah
mumucul Yn uinicil Yn uinicil Ychil yotoch Santa Yglesia lae Bayxan lic uoktic Ynba
ti ca pixanil yum padre cura ca u yalab hunpel missa cantado yokol Yn pixan lae uchebal Yantabal Yn pixan tu numYayl animas purgatorio tumen ca yumil ti d.s lae Bayxan
bin ɔabac u limosnayl oxpel tostones y capel tumin gelusalem lae—
 Bayxan hunpel tzimin potro utial Yn uatan Dominga Yam Bayxan hunpel Yeua utial
Yn mehen Sar.^{r} pot y hunpel silla kanche utial xan Bayxan hunpel yeua utial Yn uiɔin
pasq.la pot hunpel Yeua tzimin xan u tial Yn mam Andrez Juchim y gaspar Juchim Yn
mamob lae y hunpel silla ka[n]che lae—utial xan y heix solar yn cah lice mãntiali utial
ah chucob lae chen ɔan ten tumen Yn tzentic Ynba lae bay Yohelil Yn yum batab y Jus.^{as}
lae halili u xul Yn than tin testamento lae Bayxan cin uacuntic huntul almehen D^{n} gaspar canul aluasias lae lay bin tan oltic u katic missa ti yn pixan tu tan batab y Jus.^{as} lae ==

Jph pech a^{de}	D.^n Yg.^o tec	An^{tto} tec =
Diego may a^{de}	Batab	fran^o canul
	pablo tec ess^{no}	An^{tto} pech =
		pedro canul =
		Regi^{or}sob lae

Cantose esta missa y lo firme
  fr Juan de Hoyos

JOSEPH POOT DIED ON THE 17TH OF SEPTEMBER, 1766

In the name of God the Father, and God the Son, and God the Holy Spirit, three persons, one true God almighty, not many. It will be seen, the document of my final statement in my testament, as I who am Joseph Poot, the son of Juan Poot and the child of Juana Matu. Although I am dying, my heart and my understanding are sound, as it should be. Likewise, I wish my body buried in the home, the holy church. Likewise, I now supplicate our blessed lord, the Padre Curate, that he say one sung mass for my soul, empowered to aid my soul in the suffering of souls in purgatory, through our lord in God. Likewise, the fee will be given: three tostons and two tomins for Jerusalem.

Likewise, one colt for my wife, Dominga Yam. Likewise, one mare for my son, Salvador Poot, and one wooden chair for him, too. Likewise, one mare for my grandchild Pasquala Poot; one mare also for my grandson Andrés Huchim, and Gaspar Huchim—they're my grandsons—with one wooden chair. Also for them is a house plot where I am now living; it is property purchased from the Chucs, given to me only so that I may sustain myself, as my lord the batab and magistrates know. This is the truth, the end of my statement in my will. Likewise, I appoint one nobleman, don Gaspar Canul, as executor; he shall take care of requesting a mass for my soul. Before these the batab and magistrates:

Joseph Pech, alcalde	don Ignacio Tec	Antonio Tec
Diego May, alcalde	batab	Francisco Canul
	Pablo Tec, notary	Antonio Pech
		Pedro Canul
		regidors

This mass was sung and I signed it
  fray Juan de Hoyos

FOLS. 15V–16R DOCUMENT B33

WILL OF JOSEPH YAM
20 NOVEMBER 1766

CIMI JOSEPH YAM EN 20 DE NOE DE 1766 AÑ

tu kaba Dios yumbil y Dios mehenbil y Dios espiritu santo oxtul personas huntulil
Dios uchuc tumen tusinil maix pimobi lay bin Ylabac u hunil yn thakyahthan tin
testamento hibicil tenil cen Jph Yam u mehenen Mar.ⁿ Yam u yalen Bartolina ek ah
otochnalob uay tu mektan cahil ca cilich Yum ah bolon pixan Sabernaber lae bay bic
tan muc u payal yn cuxtal tumen ca yumil ti d.ˢ lae mamac bin u loh uba ti cimil lae ti
lic Yn kubic Ynba ti ca Yumil ti d.ˢ cilich nabil Yglesia bay bic layli U mektanma Yn
pixanobe ti lic Yn uoktic Ynba ti ca pixanil = yum padre cura ca u yal hunpe ɔ misa
kaybil yokol Yn pixan lae y ca u mansen tu payalchi Ychil u misa ca antabal Yn pixan
tu = numYayl animas purgatorio—Bayxan bin ɔabac u limosnayl lay missa oxper
tostones y capel tumin gelusalem lae—

Bayxan pat can yn cah tubal inba lae—Bayxan hunac Yn solal lae y chen lae conbil
yoklal lahunpis peso lae—lay pasgual Yam lay cubin manic lae hele lae cu kamic u parteob lae—ca capel pesso—u talobi lae—capel peso—Agus.ⁿ Yam—capel peso—An.
ᵗᵗᵒ Yam = capel peso ti Rogue Yam capel peso pasgual Yam—capel peso Mariaᵃ canᵈ
Yam—Bayxan hunpok tziminhunpel hol Na—V Vcpel y u hobonil cab y yikil utial
Agus.ⁿ Yam—Bayxan hunpok tzimin Yeua—y uucpay u cheyl cab Utial An.ᵗᵗᵒ Yam—
Bayxan cin ɔaic capel peso tin mehen Rogue Yam = y uucpay u hobonil cab—Bayxan
hunac solal cin ɔaic tin uixmehen Micolasa Yam y u chenil = y uucpay u cheel cab—y
hunpok capon tzimin utial xan y maria candelaria Yam—uucpay u cheel cab =
Bayxan hunac kax—utial yn mehen AGusⁿ Yam—y An.ᵗᵗᵒ Yam ~~catulpobi~~ canupobi u
tzayal lay kax lae—ti nohole pedro Juchim ti lakine ~~pedro~~ Diego pech = ti xaman—
Agusⁿ cante—lay kax lae ti ixuaytok yan lae—Bayxan hunac kax—cin ɔaic ti Rogue
Yam—y Clemente Yam canupobi lochchen yan lae he ti xamane Ju°chin pech ti
chikine—marcos pech—ti nohole Dⁿ cleᵗᵉ tec Bayxan lahucakal u chel cab lae—utial
yn uatan franᶜᵃ bas—Bayxan hunkal u chel cab Vtial yn mehen pasg.ˡ Yam = Bayxan
hunac kax utial xan u tzayale chikine sebas.ⁿ couoh—ti nohole layli sebasⁿ couoh lae
ti lakin Andrez canche—ti xamane—Agus.ⁿ Yam = Bayxan hunpel chen y sol[al]il u
pach utial yn mehenob—yan tu xaman cah lae—Agus.ⁿ yam—y An.ᵗᵗᵒ yam—y Rogue
Yam—y hunpel yeua tzimin utial yn uixmehen—maᵃ can.ᵃ yam halili u x[ul] yn than
tin testamento cin uacuntic catul almehenob albasiasob pe.° mis—y Sebas.ⁿ Yam—lay
bin tan oltic u katicob missa yokol yn pixan tu tan batab y Jusᵃˢ lae
[fol. 16r]

Jph pech aᵈᵉ	Capⁿ D.ⁿ Yg.° tec	Anᵗᵗᵒ tec
Diego may aᵈᵉ	Batab	fran° canul
pe.° miss	pablo tec essⁿᵒ	Anᵗᵗᵒ pech
y sebasⁿ Yam		pedro canul

albasias lae   Regidoresob lae

fr. Sebastián Suares

JOSEPH YAM DIED ON THE 20TH OF NOVEMBER, 1766

In the name of God the Father, and God the Son, and God the Holy Spirit, three persons, one almighty God, not many. It will be seen, the document of my final statement in my testament, as I am Joseph Yam, the son of Martín Yam and the child of Bartolina Ek, householders here in the cah governed by our holy lord the blessed San Bernabé. As I understand that when my life is called by our lord in God, nobody shall redeem himself from death, I now deliver myself to our lord in God and the holy mother church. As he has governed my soul, I now supplicate our blessed lord, the Padre Curate, that he say one sung mass for my soul and that he send up for me a prayer in the mass, to aid my soul in the sufferings of purgatory. Likewise, the fee will be given for this mass: three tostons and two tomins for Jerusalem.

Likewise, I am declaring the settlement of my household goods. Likewise, one house plot with its well, to be sold for ten pesos. Pasqual Yam here is to buy it; he will get his shares today, as two pesos is coming to him—two pesos [to] Agustín Yam, two pesos [to] Antonio Yam, two pesos to Roque Yam, two pesos [to] Pasqual Yam, two pesos to María Candelaria Yam. Likewise, one horse, one house beam, and seven beehives with honey, for Agustín Yam. Likewise, one mare and seven wooden beehives for Antonio Yam. Likewise, I give two pesos to my son, Roque Yam, with seven beehives. Likewise, one house plot I give to my daughter, Nicolasa Yam, with its well, and seven wooden beehives, and one gelding also for her and María Candelaria Yam—[with] seven wooden beehives. Likewise, one forest for my son, Agustín Yam, and Antonio Yam, both together. The neighbors of this forest are, to the south, Pedro Huchim; to the east, Diego Pech; to the north, Agustín Cante; this forest is at Ixuaytok. Likewise, one forest, which I give to Roque Yam, with Clemente Yam, both together, is at Lochchen; to the north is Joaquin Pech; to the west, Marcos Pech; to the south, don Clemente Tec. Likewise, thirty wooden beehives are for my wife, Francisca Bas. Likewise, twenty wooden beehives are for my son, Pasqual Yam. Likewise, one forest, also for him. Its neighbors: west, Sebastián Couoh; to the south, the same Sebastián Couoh; to the east, Andrés Canche; to the north, Agustín Yam. Likewise, one well and the house plot that goes with it, for my sons—it is to the north of the cah—Agustín Yam and Antonio Yam and Roque Yam. And one mare for my daughter, María Candelaria Yam. This is the truth, the end of my statement in my will. I appoint two noblemen as executors, Pedro Mis and Sebastián Yam. They shall take care to request mass for my soul. Before the batab and magistrates here:

[fol. 16r]

Joseph Pech, alcalde   captain don Ignacio Tec   Antonio Tec

Diego May, alcalde	batab
	Pablo Tec, notary
Pedro Mis and Sebastián Yam, executors	
fray Sebastián Suárez	

Francisco Canul

Antonio Pech

Pedro Canul

regidors

FOL. 16R DOCUMENT B34

WILL OF MARTHA CHAN

8 NOVEMBER 1766

CIMI MARTHA CHAN EN 8 DE NOBᵉ DE 1766 AÑ

tu kaba Dios yumbil y̱ Dios mehenbil y̱ Dios espiritu santo oxtul personas huntulil
Dios uchuc tumen tusinil Maix pimobi lay bin ylabac u hunil yn testamento bicil
tenil Martha chan u Yixmehen thomas chan u yalen pedrona coba ah cahalnalen
Vay ti cah Yxil lae Bayxan Volah mucul yn uinicil ychil Santa nabil Yglesia lae
Bayxan heix yn pixan yn kubic tu kab Ca Yumil ti d.ˢ lae—Bayxane cin uoktic
ynba ti ca pixanil yum padre cura ca u yalab hunpeɔ misa Yoklal Yn pixan ca ix V
mansen tu payalchi Ychil u misa lae uchebal Vantabal Yn pixan tu numiayl animas
purgatorio lae—bin ix ɔabac u limosnayl lay misa lae uacpel tumin y̱ hunpel tumin
helusalem lae

Bayxan cin patic solal y̱ chen tukab yn ualob Uhenio tec y̱ lix hecen ah chimob yn
ualimulae hel[. . .] bin culacob utialob bay bin in matan ychil u testamento yn yum
lae—halili V xul Yn than tin testamento lae cin uacuntic huntul almehen Jasinto pech
albasias lae—lay bin tan oltic u katic missa Yokol yn pixan tuta[n ba]tab y̱ Jusas—lae =

Jph pech alc	Dn Ygº tec	Anᵗᵗᵒ tec
Diego may alc	Batab	franᶜᵒ canul
	pablo tec essⁿᵒ	Anttº pech
		pedro canul
		Regidor[esob]

7 rrˢ

Dijose esta missa resada y lo firme—

fr Juan de Hoyos

MARTHA CHAN DIED ON THE 8TH OF NOVEMBER, 1766

In the name of God the Father, and God the Son, and God the Holy Spirit, three
persons, one almighty God, not many. It will be seen the paper of my testament,
as I am Marta Chan, the daughter of Tomás Chan and the child of Petrona Coba,

resident here in the cah of Ixil. Likewise, I wish the burial of my body to be in the holy house, the church. Likewise, hereby, my soul I deliver into the hands of our lord in God. Likewise, I supplicate our blessed lord, the Padre Curate, that he say one mass for my soul; also that he send up for me a prayer in the mass, empowered to aid my soul in the sufferings of purgatory. Also the fee will be given for this mass: six tomins and one tomin for Jerusalem. Likewise, I leave a house plot with well in the hands of my children, Eugenio Tec, together with the Chims, jointly my children; this shall be joint property established for them; it was given to me in my father's will. This is the truth, the end of my statement in my will. I designate one noble, Jacinto Pech, as executor; he shall take care to request mass for my soul. Before the batab and magistrates:

Joseph Pech, alcalde	don Ignacio Tec	Antonio Tec
Diego May, alcalde	batab	Francisco Canul
	Pablo Tec, notary	Antonio Pech
		Pedro Canul
		regidors

7 reales
This recited mass was said and I signed it
    fray Juan de Hoyos

FOL. 16V DOCUMENT B35

WILL OF FRANCISCO COUOH

23 DECEMBER 1766

CIMI FRAN^{co} COUOH EN 23 D^c DE 1766 AÑ ==

Tu kaba Dios yumbil y Dios mehenbil y Dios espiritu santo oxtul personas huntulil hahal Dios uchuc tumen tusinil maix pimobi lay bin ylabac u hunil yn testamento hibicil tenil cen fran^{co} couoh u mehenen marcos couoh V Yalen martha coba ah cahnalen Vay ti cah Yxil = lae bacacix cimil yn cah lae toh uol tin pucsikal y tin nat uet sihci lae ti ualac Yn nucticcilae maix mac bin u loh uba ti cimil lae heix ua tu yoltah ca Yumil ti Dios V xules Yn cuxtal Uay Yokol cab lae—Volah mucul Yn uinicil Ychil Yotoch santa nabil Yglesia lae—Bayxan licix uoktic ynba ti ca pixanil yum padre guar.^{an} ca u yalab hunpeɔ missa Resada yokol yn pixan y ca ix u masen tu payalchi Ychil u missa ca sebac V manel Yn pixan tu nunYayl animas purgatorio Bayxan bin ɔabac u limos oxpel nayl uacpel missa lae tumin y hunpel tumin Jelusalem lae—

    Bayxan heix yn parte chen —y solal lae cin patic tukab yn palillob lae Ju° caras couoh = y ylaria couoh—y lay yoman tumen yn uatan Maria Juchim lae—y hunpok YeVa tzimin y hunpay caha—Vtial yn uatan y yn paliloblob [sic] lae mamac bin luksictiob Yn Yum bin u kubtiob lae Bayxan cin uacuntic huntul almehen Jasinto pech albasias lay bin tan oltic u katic misa yokol in pixan tu tan Batab y Jus^{as} lae—

Jph pech a^{de}	D.^{n} Yg.° tec	= An^{tto} tec =
Diego may a^{de}	Batab	= fran° canul =
	pablo tec ess^{no}	= An^{tto} pech =
		pedro canul =
		Regid^{or}ob lae

7 rr^{s}
Dijose esta missa resada y lo firme
    fr Juan de Hoyos

FRANCISCO COUOH DIED ON THE 23RD OF DECEMBER, 1766

In the name of God the Father, and God the Son, and God the Holy Spirit, three persons, one true God almighty, not many. This will be made public, the document of testament, inasmuch as I who am Francisco Couoh, the son of Marcos Couoh and the child of Marta Coba, resident here in the cah of Ixil. Although I am dying, my heart and my understanding are sound, as it should be. It is my understanding that nobody shall redeem himself from death. As it is the wish of our lord in God to end my life here on this earth, I wish my body buried in the home, the holy house, the church. Likewise, I supplicate our blessed father, the guardian priest, that he say one recited mass for my soul, and also that he send up for me a prayer in the mass so my soul will pass quickly through the suffering of souls in purgatory. Likewise, the fee will be given: [deleted: three] six tomins for that mass and one tomin for Jerusalem.

Likewise, here is my share of a well, with house plot, which I leave in the hands of these my children—Juan Carlos Couoh and Hilaria Couoh, whom I begat through my wife, María Huchim; and one mare and one chest for my wife and my children. Nobody is to take it from them. My father will deliver it to them. Likewise, I designate one nobleman, Jacinto Pech, as executor; he will take care to ask for a mass for my soul. Before these the batab and magistrates:

Joseph Pech, alcalde	don Ignacio Tec	Antonio Tec
Diego May, alcalde	batab	Francisco Canul
	Pablo Tec, notary	Antonio Pech
		Pedro Canul
		regidors

7 reales
This recited mass was said and I signed it
    fray Juan de Hoyos

FOL. 16V DOCUMENT B35A

RECEIPT BY MARÍA HUCHIM

1 MARCH 1773

ten cen maria Juchi [*sic*] chicanpahen tu tan yn yum Batab y̱ Justiasob y̱ regrsob y̱
essno uay ti audensia lae utial in kame hunpok lleua tzim tu kab Ben^{ra} couoh Bia bicili
ɔaan ten tumen in uicham fran^{co} couoh cat cimi lae ychil u testamen^{to} y̱ in ualob ylaria
couoh lae lay tun cin kami chelel lae minan in than ti Ben^{ra} couoh y̱ u nataelel lae lay
u hahil yanil lay firma cabal hele en primero marzo de 1773 āñōs yetel hunpay caha in
kama xan lae

gaspar yam—Barme pech—	Cap^{n} D^{n} Joseph Cob	Gaspar pech
saruador cante Joseph pech—	Batab	pe^{o} canul
legidoresob lae =	Diego chim ess^{no}	alcaldesob lae

I who am María Huchim appear before my lord the batab and magistrates and
regidors and notary here in this courthouse, regarding my receipt of one mare from
the hands of Ventura Couoh. Note that it was given me by my husband, Francisco
Couoh, when he died, in his will, with my child, Hilaria Couoh. Now then I finally
receive it! I have nothing to say to Ventura Couoh and he understands this. This is
the truth. The signatures are placed below, on today the first of March of 1773. With
one chest, which I also receive.

Gaspar Yam, Bartolome Pech	captain don Joseph Cob	Gaspar Pech
Salvador Cante, Joseph Pech	batab	Pedro Canul
regidors	Diego Chim, notary	alcaldes

FOL. 17R DOCUMENT B36

WILL OF JUAN DE LA CRUZ COBA

12 NOVEMBER 1766

CIMI JU^{o} DE LA CRUZ COBA V YAL CATALINA COBA EN 12 DE NO DE 1766 A
tukaba Dios yumbil y̱ Dios mehenbil y̱ Dios espiritu santo oxtul ᵱelsonas—huntulil
Dios uchuc tumen tusinil maix pimobi lay bin ylabac u hunil yn tak—yah than tin
testamento hibicil tenil cen Ju^{o} de z coba u yal en catalina coba bacacix cimil yn cah
lae toh uol tin ᵱucsikal—y̱ tin nat uet sihci lae uolah—mucul yn uinicil ychil san.^{ta}
yglesia lae—Bayxan lic uoktic ynba ti ca pixanil yum pa.^{e} guar.^{n} ca yalab hunpel missa
Resada y̱ ca u masen tu payalchi tu missa uchebal u yantah yn pixan tumen ca yumil
ti Dios tumen yayl Animas pur—gatorio lae—Bayxan bin ɔabac u limosnayl missa
uacᵱel tumin—y̱ caᵱel tumin gelusalem lae—
    Bayxan hun xeth solal y̱ u chenil cin patic tu kab—in uixmehen pasq.^{la} coba—bay
bic yn matan ti yn Na Catalina coba lae—Bayxan hun xeth kax y̱ hunᵱel chen yan

ychil lae tu xaman cah yan—lae cuɔila u kaba—utial pasq.ᵗᵃ coba—y̶ in uiɔin Nicolas
couoh—Bayxan heix u lak hun xeth kax lae utial yn uiɔin phelipe coba—y̶ yn tillo
Agus.ⁿ coba—Bayxan heix in mul matan kax ti in Na catalina coba—yan tu xaman
tix culix lae—cin patic tu kab yn uixmehen pasqᵗᵃ coba y̶ yn uiɔinob phelipe coba—y̶
Nicolas couoh—y̶ in tillo Agusⁿ coba—u matanob tu cantuliloblae—u tzayal kax ti
nohole Agusⁿ ake—ti xam mane—Juᵒ matu t[i] lakine Nicolas coba tu xaman cah
yan lae ti nohol Dⁿ Jph pech u ca tzay lae ti noholae Bayxan hunpel mesa y̶ ca cilich
colebil y̶ u tabernacula—utial Nicolas couoh—Bayxan uucpay u che cab utial yn
uatan y̶ huncul Ya—hecabin yanac u uiche[c] ab yn tzenpal marcela coba—halilil
u xul yn than tin tes tamento lai—cin uacuntic huntul almehen pedro pot y̶ Diego
pech albasiasoblae lay bin tan oltic u katicob missa yn pixan tu tan batab y̶ Jus.ᵃˢ
lae—8 r—

Jph pech alde	Dⁿ Yg̶ᵒ tec batab	Anᵗᵗᵒ tec
Diego may alde	pablo tec ess.no pu.co	franᶜᵒ canul
		Anttᵒ pech
		pedro canul
		Regidoresob

8 rrˢ Dijose esta missa y lo firme
fr Juan de Hoyos

JUAN DE LA CRUZ COBA, CHILD OF CATALINA COBA, DIED ON THE 12TH OF NOVEMBER, 1766

In the name of God the Father, and God the Son, and God the Holy Spirit, three
persons, one almighty God, not many. This will be made public, the document of my
final statement in my will, inasmuch as I who am Juan de la Cruz Coba, I the child of
Catalina Coba, although I am dying, my heart and my understanding are sound, as it
should be, I wish my body to be buried there in the holy church. Likewise, I supplicate our blessed lord, the guardian priest, that he say one said mass and that he send
up for me a prayer in the mass so that my soul be aided by our lord in God through
the suffering of souls in purgatory. Likewise, the mass fee of six tomins will be given,
with two tomins for Jerusalem.

Likewise, one house plot share with its well I leave in the name of my daughter,
Pasquala Coba, as it was my inheritance from my mother, Catalina Coba. Likewise,
one share of a forest with one well inside it; the cah is to its north; it is called Cudzila;
[it is] for Pasquala Coba and my grandson Nicolás Couoh. Likewise, here is the other
portion of the forest, which is for my younger cousin Felipe Coba and my uncle
Agustín Coba. Likewise, here is my forest jointly inherited from my mother, Catalina
Coba; Tixculix is to its north; I leave it in the name of my daughter, Pasquala Coba,
with my younger cousin Felipe Coba, and Nicolás Couoh, and my uncle Agustín
Coba, their inheritance, the four of them together; the adjacent forest to the south

is Agustín Ake['s], to the north Juan Matu, to the east Nicolás Coba; to the north is the cah, which is adjacent on its south side to don Joseph Pech. Likewise, one table with Our Holy Lady and her tabernacle, for Nicolás Couoh. Likewise, seven beehives for my wife and one sapling sapote tree—the beehives will go to my infant, Marcela Coba. This is the truth, the end of my statement in my will. I designate one noble, Pedro Pot, and Diego Pech, as executors; they will request my wish for a mass for my soul. Before these the batab and magistrates: 8 reales

Joseph Pech, alcalde	don Ignacio Tec	Antonio Tec
Diego May, alcalde	batab	Francisco Canul
	Pablo Tec, public notary	Antonio Pech
		Pedro Canul
		regidors

8 reales; this recited mass was said and I signed it
    fray Juan de Hoyos

FOL. 17V DOCUMENT B37

WILL OF ANTONIO HUCHIM

20 DECEMBER 1766

CIMI ANTT.° JUCHIM EN 20 DIC^e DE 1766 AN^{os}

tu kaba Dios yumbil y Dios mehenbil y Dios esspiritu santo oxtul per sonas huntulili Dios uchuc tumen tusinil maix pimobi lay bin ylabac u hunil yn takyahthan tin testamento hibicil tenil cen Antt.° Juchim u Mehenen pedro Juchim u yalen Madalena coba u bacacix cimil yn cah tin cucutil lae toh uol tin pucsikal y tin nat uet sihci lae ti ualac yn nuctic cimi lae bay bic tan muc u pay cen ca yumil ti d.^s lae mamac bin u loh u ba ti cimil lae—Bayxan cin uoktic ynba ti ca pixanil yum padre cura ca u yalab hunpe ɔ missa utial yn pixan yetel ca u masen tu payalchi Ychil u missa uchebal u yantal yn pixan tu numyayl animas purgatorio lae Bayxan bin ɔabac U limosnayl missa oxpel tostones y capel tumin Gielusalem lae—14 rr^s

    Bayxan hunpel solar y u chenil yn matan tin yum lae cin patic tukab yn mehenob catulob ming.^l Juchim—y fran^{co} Juchim canupobi Bayxan Junpet kax yan tu xaman tan cin ɔayc tin mehen ming.^l Juchim Juan couoh ti nohor ti lakin Man.^l pech Bayxan Junper horNa y Junpay caha y Ju ɔit cuchala takin y Junpet kax yan ti xtucirNa utial yn meJen fran^{co} Juchim V tzayallob rae ti nohor Dⁿ Juan pech xtouar pech y Bartasar pech ti xaman Bayxan Junper chen solal cotan u pach cin ɔayc tin uixmehenob rae Martha Juchim y Bartolina Juchim canupobi Junpel kax yan ber Xku utial yn uixmehenob Martha Juchim y Bart.^{na} Juchim V tzayar kax ti laki[n] pasq.^l canche Andres tec ti xaman Bayxan Junper u hor Na utial yn Vixmehen luissa Juchim tu Junar Bayxan Junper che[n] yl u solalil u pach cin patic tin Mehen fran.^{co} Juchim yl u cic luissa Juchim = canupobi yn matan tin uixJan Juana pech Bayxan Junpet u matan kax tu chich Juana pech cu patar tu kab tu Junar lae fran.^{co} Juchim Jalili V xul yn than testamento cin uacutic catur almehenob Joseph Mis y gregolio pech lay bin tan ortic V katic missa yoklal yn pixan = bin ɔabac V limosnayl tumen yalabb otzil christianob rae 12 r^s y 2 r^s gielusalem

Capp^n D.^{n} ygn.^{o} tec Batab Andres tec then^e Diego coot alcardes gaspar yam alcardes gaspar chan gaspar ek Sebas.^{n} chim Regidorlessob Marcos pot ess^{no} cantose esta missa y lo firme

fr Juan de Hoyos

Antonio Huchim died on the 20th of December, 1766

In the name of God the Father, God the Son, God the Holy Spirit, three persons, one almighty God, not many. The paper of my final statement in my testament shall be seen, inasmuch as I who am Antonio Huchim, the son of Pedro Huchim and the child of Magdalena Coba. Although my body is dying, my heart and my understanding are sound, as it should be. At this time I understand that nobody shall free himself from death when our lord God calls me. Therefore I supplicate our blessed lord, the Padre Curate, that he say one mass for my soul and that he send up for me a prayer in the mass empowered to help my soul in the suffering of souls in purgatory. Likewise, the mass fee will be given: three tostons and two tomins for that Jerusalem—14 reales.

Likewise, one house plot with its well given me by my father, which I leave in the hands of my sons, Miguel Huchim and Francisco Huchim, both together. Likewise, one forest, to the north, in the middle, I give to my son, Miguel Huchim; Juan Couoh [is] to the south, Manuel Pech to the east. Likewise, one house beam and one chest and one silver spoon and one forest at Xtucilna for my son, Francisco Huchim; its neighbors are, to the south, don Juan Pech [and] Cristóbal Pech, with Baltasar Pech to the north. Likewise, one well and the stony plot that goes with it, I give to my daughters, Martha Huchim and Bartolina Huchim, both together. One forest on the road to Xku for my daughters Martha Huchim and Bartlina Huchim; its neighboring forests are Pasqual Canche['s] to the east [and] Andrés Tec['s] to the north. Likewise, one house beam for my daughter, Luisa Huchim, alone. Likewise, one well with the house plot that goes with it, I leave to my son, Francisco Huchim, with his older sister, Luisa Huchim, both of them together; [it was] my inheritance from my mother-in-law, Juana Pech. Likewise, one inherited forest that Francisco Huchim's maternal grandmother, Juana Pech, left in his hands alone. This is the truth, the end of my testament statement. I designate two noblemen, Joseph Mis and Gregorio Pech, to take care to request a mass for my soul; the fee shall be given, as we are believing Christians here—12 reales with two reales [for] Jerusalem.

Captain don Ignacio Tec, batab; Andrés Tec, lieutenant; Marcos Poot, notary; Diego Coot, Gaspar Yam, alcaldes; Gaspar Chan, Gaspar Ek, Sebastián Chim, regidors.

This mass was sung and I signed it
fray Juan de Hoyos

FOL. 18R DOCUMENT B38

WILL OF MARTHA COBA

3 DECEMBER 1766

CIMI MARTHA COBA EN 3 DE D.Z. DE 1766 Ã

V yixmehen Nico las Coba V yar magdalena cetz ah caharnalob Vay ti cah yxil tu
kaba D.s yumbir y D.s mehenbir y D.s espilitu santo oxtul personas Juntulili JaJar D.s
uchuc tumen tusinir mayx pimobi lay bin ylabac u Junir yn takyahthan Jibicir tenir
cen Marta coba Vyixmehen Nicolas Coba u yalen mag^{na} Cetz ah caharnalob Vay ti
cah yxil Bayxan cin tzolil yn than tin testamento lae Bayxan cin uoktic ynba ti ca pixanir yum pe cula ca yalab Junpeɔ missa Rezar yoklal yn pixan bin ɔabac V limosNayl
tumen yalab otzil christianob rae uacper tumin y Junper tumin gielusalen

Jalili u xur yn than tin testamento cin Vacuntic albasseas Andres tec =

Andres tec then^c	Capp^n d^n yg^o tec	Gaspar chan gaspar ek
Diego cot gaspar yam alcar	Batab	sebas^n. chim Regidoles
dessob rae	pabro tec ess^{no} pubrico	ob rae
	Marcos poot ess^{no}	

7 rr^s Dijose esta missa resada y lo firme
fr Juan de Hoyos

MARTHA COBA DIED ON THE 3RD OF DECEMBER, 1766

The daughter of Nicolás Coba and the child of Magdalena Cetz, residents here in
the cah of Ixil. In the name of God the Father, and God the Son, and God the Holy
Spirit, three persons, one true God almighty, not many. It will be seen, the document
of my final statement, inasmuch as I who am Marta Coba, the daughter of Nicolás
Coba and the child of Magdalena Cetz, residents here in the cah of Ixil. Likewise,
I order my statement in my will. Likewise, I supplicate our blessed lord, the Padre
Curate, that he say one said mass for my soul. The fee shall be given, for we are believ-
ing Christians: six tomins and one tomin for that Jerusalem.

This is the truth, the end of my statement in my will. I appoint as executor
Andrés Tec.

Andrés Tec, lieutenant	captain don Ignacio Tec	Gaspar Chan, Gaspar Ek
Diego Coot, Gaspar Yam	batab	Sebastián Chim
alcaldes	Pablo Tec, notary public	regidors

Marcos Poot, notary

7 reales; this mass was sung and I signed it
fray Juan de Hoyos

FOLS. 18R–18V DOCUMENT B39

WILL OF DIEGO COBA

14 JANUARY 1767

CIMI DIEGO COBA EN 14 DE ENERO DE 1767 Ā

tu kaba Ds yumbil y̠ Dios mehenbil y̠ Dios espiritu santo oxtul personas huntulil d^s
uchuc tumen tusinil maix pimobi lay bin ylabac tenil cen Diego coba u mehen Agus^n
coba u yalen Nicolasa pech ah canalob uay ti cah Yxil lae—ti lic in nuctic cimil Uolah
mucul ychil santa yglesia lae Bayxan cin uoktic ynba ti ca pixanil yum padre cura ca
yalab hunpe ɔ missa Resada yokol yn pixan bin ix ɔabac u limosnayl uacp̣er tumin xan
uchebal u yantal yn pixan tu numyayl animas purgatorio lae—

Bayxan heix hunpel chen solal minan u chenil yn mul matan y̠ yn tillo sebas.^{n} coba
lae cin patic tu kab yn mehen minguel coba y̠ hun ɔit ba[t] y̠ hun ɔit machete y̠ hun-
p̣el tirma tzutz utial xan—lae halili u xul yn than tin testamento cin uacuntic huntul
almehen Jacinto pech aluasias lay bin tan oltic u katic missa tu tan Batab y̠ Juss^{as} lae
[fol. 18v]

Diego cot alde	Capp^n d^n yg^o tec	Gaspar chan
Gaspar Yam alde	Batab	gaspar ek
		sebas^n. chim
	Marcos poot ess^{no} pu^{co}	xp.uar Na
		Regidresob lae

Dijose esta missa resada y lo firme
fr Juan de Hoyos

DIEGO COBA DIED ON THE 14TH OF JANUARY, 1767

In the name of God the Father, and God the Son, and God the Holy Spirit, three persons, one almighty God, not many. It shall be seen, I who am Diego Coba, the son of
Agustín Coba and the child of Nicolasa Pech, residents here in the cah of Ixil. Now
that I face death, I wish to be buried in the holy church. Likewise, I supplicate our
blessed lord, the Padre Curate, that he say one said mass for my soul. Also the mass
fee of six tomins shall be given, the wherewithal to aid my soul through the suffering
of souls in purgatory.

Likewise, here is one house plot only, without its well, given me jointly with my
uncle, Sebastián Coba. I leave [it] in the hands of my son, Miguel Coba, with one axe

and one machete and one closeable cloak also for him. This is the truth, the end of my statement in my will. I designate one noble, Jacinto Pech, executor; he shall take care to ask for a mass. Before the batab and magistrates:

[fol. 18v]

Diego Coot, alcalde	captain don Ignacio Tec	Gaspar Chan
Gaspar Yam, alcalde	batab	Gaspar Ek
	Marcos Poot, public notary	Sebastián Chim
		Cristóbal Na
		regidors

This recited mass was said and I signed it
  fray Juan de Hoyos

FOL. 18V DOCUMENT B40

WILL OF SEBASTIAN UH

10 JANUARY 1767

CIMI SEBAS.[n] UH EN 10 DE ENERO DE 1767 AÑ—

tu kaba Dios yumbil y Dios mehenbil y Dios esspiritu santo oxtul per sonas huntulil Dios uchuc tumen tusinil maix pimobi lay bin ylabac u hunil tin testamento hibicil tenil cen sebas.n Uh u mehenen Apa° Uh u yalen Micaela coba ah cahnalob uay ti cah Yxil lae Bayxan bacacix cimil yn cah lae toh uol tin puksikal y tin nat uet sihci lae ti lic u payal yn cuxtal tumen ca yumil ti d[s] lae Uolah mucul yn uinicil ychil cilich nabil Yglesia lae Bayxan ti lic yn uoktic ynba ti ca pixnan yum padre cura ca u yalab hunpeɔ missa yokol yn pixan y ca u mansen tu payalchi ychil u missa Bayxan bin ix ɔabac u limosnayl oxper tostones y hunpel tumin Jelusalem lae—

Bayxan hunpel chen y u solaril u pach yn cah lic lic lae ɔaic tin mehen mar.n Uh—y u yiɔin Ju°na Uh lae—y u lak hunpel chen y tanbuh u solaril u pach lae cin patic tukab yn uixmehenob catulob yokol lae—martha Uh—y pasquala Uh—u multialoblae Bayxan hunpet kax—yan ti xku lae cin patic tu kab yn mehen Mar.n uh lae Mul kax utial ah Uhil uinicob lae—u tzayal kax lae—Sebas.n Un chikin lae he ti xan mane—ygnasio coba—y hunpet solar yan capel chen ychil yan tu xan man cah lae cin patic tu kab yn mehen y yn uixmehenob lae mar.n uh marta Uh—y pas.[la] uh—y Ju°na lae halilil u xul yn than tin testamento lae cin uacuntic huntul almehen Jasin.[to] pech alba sias lae lay bin tan oltic u katic missa tin pixan tu tan ca yum batab y ca yum Jus.[as] lae—

Diego Cot alcar[s]	Capp.[n] D.[n] ygn.° tec	gaspar chan Sebas.[n] chim
gaspar yam alcar[s]ob lae	Batab	gaspar ek xtouar na
	Marcos pot css[no]	Regidoresob rae

Cantose esta missa y lo firme
   fr Juan de Hoyos

SEBASTIÁN UH DIED ON THE 10TH OF JANUARY, 1767

In the name of God the Father, and God the Son, and God the Holy Spirit, three
persons, one almighty God, not many. It will be seen, the paper of my will, inasmuch as
I who am Sebastián Uh, the son of Aparicio Uh and child of Micaela Coba, residents
here in the town of Ixil. Likewise, although I am dying, my heart and my understanding are sound, as they should be. When our lord God calls my life, I wish my body to
be buried inside the holy mother church. Likewise, I supplicate our blessed father, the
curate priest, that he say one mass for my soul and that he say a prayer for me in that
mass. Likewise, it will be given in alms three tostons and one tomin for Jerusalem.

Likewise, one well and its accompanying house plot, I am now giving this to my
son, Martín Uh, with his younger sister, Juana Uh; and the other well and accompanying half of a house plot I leave in the hands of both my daughters, Marta Uh and
Pasquala Uh, together. Likewise, one forest plot, which is at Xku, I leave in the name
of my son, Martín Uh; this joint forest is for the Uh men; its neighboring forests
are Sebastián Un['s] to the west [and] here to the north, Ignacio Coba['s]. And one
house plot, within which there are two wells, [and] which is to the north of the cah, I
leave in the hands of my son and my daughters, Martín Uh, Marta Uh, and Pasquala
Uh, and Juana Uh. This is the truth, the end of my statement in my will. I designate
one nobleman, Jacinto Pech, as executor. He shall take care to request a mass for my
soul. Before our lord batab and our lord[s] the magistrates.

Diego Coot, alcalde	captain don Ignacio Tec	Gaspar Chan, Sebastián Chim
Gaspar Yam, alcalde	batab	Gaspar Ek, Cristóbal Na
	Marcos Poot, notary	regidors

This mass was sung and I signed it
   fray Juan de Hoyos

FOL. 19R DOCUMENT B40A
STATEMENT BY THE CABILDO OF IXIL
13 NOVEMBER 1777

toon con Batab y then[e] y Jus[as] Reg[or]lessob y ess[no] t chicanpahon tu solal sebas.[n] Uh
utial capis yl u chenil utial ca u kam u parte sollalillob hebix cu yalic V testamento
sebasn Uh cimi lae lay tumen t chicanpahoon utial capi[s] lae ɔoci V man Bala lae
takpayah Juan mis y yatan Juana Uh y Andrea Uh ca ɔayccob V hahil V thanob Uay
[ti] audiensia bicil cu kubiccob lay tanbuh solal yan tu nohor chen tac kamic fran.[co]
canche y thomas canche catullob y ca utzil olal ca kubic tiob lae mantzil lob yarlob
Marta Uh = Junpel gilon u xether V cah lic lay fran.[co] canche lay yanil lay chen lae

Bayxan V chun u pakal guiob lae lahucakal—ti fran.co canche 30 la hucakal utial thomas canche—30 lay u hahil yanil ca firma en 13 de Nou.ᶜ de 1777 ã =

gaspar yam	capp.ⁿ D.ⁿ Jose cob	Diego tun Diego pot pasqⁱ
Nicolas Ytza	Batab phelipe can	yam Bar.ᵐᵉ matu leg.ᵒʳless
alcarrsob	che thenᵉ	Marcos pot essⁿᵒ

We who are the batab and lieutenant and magistrates, regidors and notary, we gather in judgment at the house plot of Sebastián Uh, in order to verify its well in regard to the receipt of the house plot shares that the deceased, Sebastián Uh, mentioned in his will. This is why we gather in judgment in order to verify that the purchase has just been made, with which were compensated Juan Mis and his wife, Juana Uh, and Andrea Uh. We are providing a truthful statement here in the court, on how we deliver this half house plot that is to the north of the well, to be received by Francisco Canche and Tomás Canche together, and it is our just wish that it be delivered to them. The purchasers are the children of Marta Uh. One portion—it now being divided—this [half] where the well is, for Francisco Canche. Likewise, an orchard of thirty henequen plants from Francisco Canche: 30; thirty [also] from Tomás Canche: 30. This is the truth. There are [below] our signatures, on the 13the of November of 1777:

Gaspar Yam	captain don José Cob	Diego Tun, Diego Poot
Nicolás Itza	batab	Pasqual Yam, Bartolomé Matu
alcaldes	Phelip Canche, lieutenant	regidors
	Marcos Poot, notary	

FOL. 19V DOCUMENT B40B

STATEMENT BY JUAN MIS, JUANA UH, AND ANDREA UH

13 NOVEMBER 1777

JAJARTHAN

te[n] cen Juan Mis y̱ yn uatan Juana Uh y̱ Andrea Uh t chicanpahoon tu tanil yn yum Batab y̱ thenᵉ y̱ Jusᵃˢ Reg.ᵒʳlessob y̱ es.ⁿᵒ ti audiensia utial ca kub hunpel gilon hun xe solal u tzayan lay ti fran.ᶜᵒ canche yan tu la[k u] mamtzil yar pasq.ʳᵃ Uh y̱ yixmehen sebasⁿ Uh lay tunun t chicanpahi yn yum Batab y̱ Jusᵃˢsob lae Vtial capisic lae u xether lay solal lae lay V hahil yanil ca pilma cabal helen 13 de Nou.ᶜ de 1777 =

gaspar yam	capp.ⁿ D.ⁿ Jose cob	Diego tun Diego poot
Nicolas Itza	Batab phelipe	pasq.ⁱ yam Barᵐᵉ matu
alcarsob	canche thenᵉ	Reg.ᵒʳlessoblae
	Marcos pot essⁿᵒ	

A TRUE STATEMENT

I who am Juan Mis, and my wife, Juana Uh, and Andrea Uh; we appear before my lord the batab and lieutenant and magistrates, regidors and notary, in the courthouse, in order to deliver one portion of a divided house plot that had been joined, to Francisco Canche, the other purchaser, the child of Pasquala Uh, Sebastián Uh's daughter. Therefore my lord batab and the magistrates appear in judgment in order to verify the above division of this house plot. This is the truth; our signatures are below; today, the 13th of November of 1777.

Gaspar Yam	captain don José Cob	Diego Tun, Diego Poot
Nicolás Itza	batab	Pasqual Yam, Bartolomé Matu
alcaldes	Phelip Canche, lieutenant	regidors
	Marcos Poot, notary	

FOL. 20R DOCUMENT B41

WILL OF MATEO CANCHE

26 NOVEMBER 1766

CIMI MATHE.° CANCHE EN 26 DE NOBIEM.ᶜ DE 1766 Ã

tu kaba D.ˢ yumbil y̱ D.ˢ mehenbil y̱ D.ˢ esspilitu santo oxtur perzonas huntulili hahar D.ˢ Vchuc tumen tusinil mayx pimobi lay bin ylabac V Junil yn thakyahthan tin testamento hibicil tenil cen mathe.° canche V meheNen franᶜᵒ canche V yalen Malia tec ah caharnalob Vay ti cah yxil lae Bayxan cin uoktic ynba ti ca pixanil yum p.ᶜ Van xul in Cuxtar uay yokol cab rae Volah mucul yn cucutil ti santa ygressia y̱ ca ya lab Junpeɔ missa Rezada bin ɔabac V limosnayl uacp̱er tumin y̱ hunper tumin gielusalem = y̱ ca u mansen tu payalchi ychil u missa antabar yn pixan tu nuMiayl purgatorliol =

Bayxan Junpet kax yan tu hor cah t lub be ber chicxulub mul kax yan tu tzayar potoob yn partelae cin patic tu kab yn uixmehenob rae luissa canche y̱ Martha canche Bayxan hunper caha utial yn uix mehe luissa canche Bayxan caɔit machete y̱ Junɔit cuchio Vtial [y̱]n uixmehen martha canche = halili V xul yn than kah ten xan hunpet kax yn con ma ti Joseph canul yan tixcacar lae Bay tun lae tin uaskahsah oxper tostones ti marn canul V mehen Joseph canul bay bic tun puɔan Marⁿ canul lae hebikin bin chicanac Marⁿ canul lae ca uɔoc uaskes u taknil tres pesso lay luiss canche y̱ martha canche catun culac lay kax tu kab bob yn uixmehenob rae halili u xul yn thak yah than tin testamento cin uaCuntic Juntul almehen Jassinto pech albasseas = 6 rrˢ y̱ gielusalem 1 rˢ

Diego coot alcarᵈ	D.ⁿ ygn.° tec Batab	gaspar chan gaspar ek
gaspar yam alcarᵈ	Andres tec thenᵉ	Sebas.ⁿ chim xtouar [Na]
	Marcos pot essno	Regidorlessob rae

Dijose esta missa resada y lo firme
    fr Juan de Hoyos

In the name of God the Father and God the Son and God the Holy Spirit, three persons, one true God almighty, not many. The document of my last will and testament will be made public, inasmuch as I am Mateo Canche, the son of Francisco Canche and the child of María Tec, householders here of the cah of Ixil. Wherefore I supplicate our blessed lord the Padre that when my life here on this earth ends, I wish my body to be buried in the holy church; and that one low mass be said, the fee for which will be given, six tomins, and one tomin for Jerusalem; and that a prayer be said for me in the mass so that my soul be helped in the suffering of purgatory.

Likewise, there is a forest at the entrance to the cah, a league along the Chicxulub road, adjacent to the forest of the Poot family, my share of which I leave in the hands of my daughters, Luisa Canche and Marta Canche; likewise, one chest for my daughter Luisa Canche; likewise, two machetes and one spoon for my daughter Marta Canche. This is the truth, the end of my statement—also I remember a forest. I sold it to Joseph Canul. It is at Tixcacal. However, I returned three tostones to Joseph Canul's son, Martín Canul. Then that Martín Canul ran away. On this day let it be recorded that when Luisa Canche and Marta Canche have fully returned his money, the three pesos, to the aforementioned Martín Canul, then this forest will be placed in the hands of these daughters of mine. This is the truth, the end of my final statement in my testament. I appoint a nobleman, Jacinto Pech, as executor. Six reales, with one real for Jerusalem.

Diego Coot, alcalde	don Ignacio Tec, batab	Gaspar Chan, Gaspar Ek
Gaspar Yam, alcalde	Andrés Tec, lieutenant	Sebastián Chim, Cristóbal Na
	Marcos Poot, public notary	regidors

This recited mass was said and I signed it
    fray Juan de Hoyos

FOL. 21R DOCUMENT B42

WILL OF PASQUAL HUCHIM
11 FEBRUARY 1767

CIMI PASG[1] JUCHIM EN 11 PIRMERO DE 1767 Ā—

tu kaba D.ˢ yumbil y D.ˢ mehenbil y D.ˢ esspilitu santo oxtul perzonas huntulili hahar D.ˢ uchuc tumen tuzinil maix pimobi lay bin ylabac u hunil yn takyahthan tin testamento hibicil tenil cen pasguar Juchim u mehenen ming.[1] Juchim V yalen Micolassa yam ah caharnalob uay ti cah yxil lae Bayxan cin tzolic yn than tin testamento Bayxan Uan tu yortah ca yumil ti D.ˢ u xuller yn cuxtar Vay yokol cab lae Uolah mucur yn cucutir ychil santa ygressia Bayxan cin uoktic ynba ti ca pixan nir yum pᶜ uardia ca yalab Junpeɔ missa Rezada Bin ɔabac u limosnayl tumen yalab otzil christianob rae uacper tumin =

Bayxan cin patin yn palillob tu kab yn yum y̱ yn na utiall u yilabbob bix bin
manebarl u cuxtar yokol cab tumen patin cah yokol cab rae Bayxan hunper yn pax
gerga cin patic tukab yn yum uɔoc bote oxper pesso ubiner ɔoc yn botic caper
pessoˢ y̱ Bayxan hunper sarga utial yn mehen thomas Juchim = hun ɔit baat utial
yn uixmehen martha Juchim y̱ hun ɔit machete utial yn uixmehen teressa Juchim y̱
Junpay cama utial yn uatan halili u xul yn than tin testamento cin ua Cuntic albasseas Mathe.° Canul =

Diego coot alcardes	D.ⁿ ygn.° tec Batab	gaspar chan gaspar
gaspar yam alcarˢ	Andres tec thenᵉ	ek Sebas.ⁿ chim x
	Marcos pot essⁿᵒ puᶜᵒ	touar Na Re
		gᵒʳlessob rae

Dijose esta missa resada y lo firme
   fr Juan de Hoyos
tin kamah lisa Misa Cen [. . .]

PASQUAL HUCHIM DIED ON THE 11TH OF FEBRUARY, 1767

In the name of God the Father, and God the Son, and God the Holy Spirit, three
persons, one true God almighty, not many. It will be seen, the paper of final statement in my will, inasmuch as I who am Pasqual Huchim, the son of Miguel Huchim,
the child of Nicolasa Yam, residents here in the cah of Ixil. Likewise, I order my
statement in my will. Likewise, as our lord in God wishes to end my life here on this
earth, I wish my body to be buried in the holy church. Likewise, I now supplicate our
blessed lord, the guardian priest, that he say one said mass. The fee will be given, for
we are believing Christians: six tomins.

Likewise, I leave my children in the hands of my father and my mother, who will
see to them. There is nothing for me of life in this world, for I am leaving this world.
And so my one cloth-debt I leave in my father's hands; he must pay three pesos to end
it; I've paid two pesos [so far]. Likewise, one blanket for my son, Tomás Huchim;
one axe for my daughter, Marta Huchim, and one machete for my daughter, Teresa
Huchim, and one bed for my wife. This is the truth, the end of my statement in my
will. I designate Mateo Canul as executor.

Diego Coot, alcalde	don Ignacio Tec, batab	Gaspar Chan, Gaspar Ek
Gaspar Yam, alcalde	Andrés Tec, lieutenant	Sebastián Chim, Cristóbal Na
	Marcos Poot, public notary	regidors

This recited mass was said and I signed it
   fray Juan de Hoyos
I received the fee for this mass, I [. . .][8]

FOL. 21V DOCUMENT B43

WILL OF DIEGO CANUL

30 FEBRUARY 1767

CIMI DIEGO CANUL EN 30 DE PE^cLO DE 1767 Ã

tukaba [D]s yumbil y̱ D.ˢ mehenbil y̱ D.ˢ espilitu santo oxtul personas huntulili hahar D.ˢ Vchuctumen tusinil mayx pinmobi lay bin ylabac u hunil yn thakyahthan tin testamento hibicil tenir cen Diego canul V mehenen Domingo canul U yalen malia mukul ah caharnalob Vay ti cah Yxil Bayxan cin uoktic yn ba ti ca pixnan yum pᶜ Vardian ca yalab hunpeɔ missa Resada Vtial yn pixan bin ɔabac V limosnayl tumen yalab otzil christianob rae uacper tumin—Bayxan hunac cħen y̱ solalil V pach cin ɔayc tin uixmehen Ysaber canul y̱ hunac kax yan ber ɔemul utial lay yn Vixmehen ysaber canul V tzayal kax lae ti lakin Joseph pech ti xaman phelipe pech ti nohol gaspar piste—y̱ Jun ɔit machete y̱ Jun ɔit baat y̱ Junper Xul mascab halili U xul yn takyahthan tin testamento cin Vacuntic huntur almehen yn albasseas Bentula coba—

Diego coot alcarˢ	D.ⁿ ygn.º tec Batab	gaspar chan gaspar ek
gaspar yam alcarˢ	Andres tec thenᶜ	Sebas.ⁿ chim xtouar
	Marcos pot essⁿᵒ	Na Regºʳlessob rae

6 rrˢ
Dijose esta missa resada y lo firme
    fr Juan de Hoyos

DIEGO CANUL DIED ON THE 30TH OF FEBRUARY, 1767

In the name of [God] the Father, and God the Son, and God the Holy Spirit, three persons, one true God almighty, not many It will be seen, the document of my final statement in my will, inasmuch as I who am Diego Canul, the son of Domingo Canul and the child of María Mukul, residents here in the cah of Ixil. Likewise, I supplicate our blessed lord, the guardian priest, that he say one said mass for my soul. The fee will be given, for we are believing Christians: six tomins.

Likewise, one well with accompanying house plot I give to my daughter, Isabel Canul, with one forest plot that is on the road to Dzemul; this is for my daughter, Isabel Canul. Its neighboring forest[s are], to the east, Joseph Pech; to the north, Felipe Pech; to the south, Gaspar Piste. And one machete, one axe, and one iron tool [for Isabel]. This is the truth, the end of my statement in my testament. I designate one nobleman as my executor, Ventura Coba.

Diego Coot, alcalde	don Ignacio Tec, batab	Gaspar Chan, Gaspar Ek
Gaspar Yam, alcalde	Andrés Tec, lieutenant	Sebastián Chim, Cristóbal Na
	Marcos Poot, notary	regidors

6 reales

This recited mass was said and I signed it

fray Juan de Hoyos

FOL. 22R DOCUMENT B44

WILL OF PASQUALA BALAM

5 MAY 1767

CIMI PASG^{ra} BALAM EN 5 DE MAYO DE 1767 Ã

tukaba D.ˢ yumbil y̱ D.ˢ mehenbir y̱ D.ˢ esspilitu san oxtur personas huntulili hahar
D.ˢ uchuc tumen tusinir mayx pimobi lay bin ylabac u hunil yn thakyahthan tin testamento hibicir tenil cen pasg^{ra} balam U yixmehenen D.ⁿ Juan balam u yalen pasgra
Cutz Bayxan uan tu yortah ca yumir ti D.ˢ u xul yn cuxtar Vay yokol cab rae Volah
mucur yn CuCutir ychir Santa ygressia Bayxan cin uoktic ynba ti ca pixanir yum pe
Cula ca yalab hunpe ɔ missa Resar yl ix ca u mansen tu payyarchi ychirl u missa mahebarl u xantar yn Pixan tu numiayl purgatolio bin ɔabac u limosnayl tumen yalab otzil
christianob rae uacper tumin y̱ caper tumin gielusalem—6 rrs // 2 rrs

halili V xul yn than tin testamento manbar yan ten lae cin uacuntic yalab otzil
Christianno tan ortic u ka[tic] miss yokol yn Pixan tu tan batab y̱ Justissiassob rae

Joseph mis al[b]asseas =

Diego coot alcardes	Capp̱ⁿ D.ⁿ ygn.º tec Batab	gaspar chan
gaspar yam alcardes	Andres tec then^c=	gaspar ek Sebas.ⁿ
	Marcos pot ess^{no}	chim xtouar
		Na Regidorles
		sob rae

Son 8 rrˢ =

Dijose esta missa rezada y lo firme

fr Juan de Hoyos

PASQUALA BALAM DIED ON THE 5TH OF MAY, 1767

In the name of God the Father, and God the Son, and God the Holy Spirit, three
persons, one true God almighty, not many. It will be seen, the document of my final
statement in my will, inasmuch as I who am Pasquala Balam, the daughter of don
Juan Balam and the child of Pasquala Cutz. Likewise, as it is the wish of our lord God
that my life on this earth end, I want my body buried in the holy church. Likewise, I
supplicate our blessed lord, the Padre Curate, that he say one said mass and also that
he send a prayer up in the mass to help speed my soul through the sufferings of purgatory. The fee will be given, for we are believing Christians: six tomins and two tomins
for Jerusalem: 6 reales; 2 reales.

This is the truth, the end of my statement in my will. I have nothing. I appoint a believing Christian to take care of requesting a mass for my soul. Before the batab and these magistrates;

Joseph Mis, executor.

Diego Coot, alcalde	captain don Ignacio Tec, batab	Gaspar Chan,
Gaspar Yam, alcalde	Andrés Tec, lieutenant	Gaspar Ek, Sebastián Chim
	Marcos Poot, notary	Cristóbal Na
		regidors

They are 8 reales.
This recited mass was said and I signed it
fray Juan de Hoyos

FOL. 22V DOCUMENT B45

SETTLING OF THE ESTATE OF JOSEPH CAB

30 MAY 1767

TESTIMONIO Vtial = JOSEPH CAB = cimi en 30 de mayo de 1767 ā
Ma tu yalah u than lae = cimi tiJoo = toon con Batab y then⁣ᶜ = y Jus.ᵃˢ Reg.ᵒʳlessob
rae y essⁿᵒ ti audiensia lae lic Mul tum tic titula calon yoklal lay solal yl u chenil lic
kubic tu palillob Joseph cab y ti yi ɔinob ti u palilob tulacar y yixmehen Marcos cab
u yumob tumen cimi Marcos cab minan u testamento cimi u mehen xan matu yalah
u than xan lay Joseph cab Bay tun lae ɔoc ylic u testamento u kilacabillob rae yoklal
lay solal lae tu testamento Joseph cab cimi tu habil [1] 726 ā u kila cabillob rae u
yummob tumen max bin tuc lic Uan bar ma u tzil lae ca ylac u testamento Joseph cab
rae he u yarl u mehennob = lic oc lic ychil lay solal tulacarlob = Dominga cab y malia
cab—franᶜᵃ cab lossa cab y franᶜᵒ cab = y yixmehenob Joseph cab cimi lae ysidro cab
Anna cab y Simona cab = Bayxan hunper baat y sarga y hunper [ma]chete y Junper
camissa y Junper ex y kaxnak utial ysidro cab = lay u hahil ɔoc tzoli tulacar toon
Batab y Jusᵃˢ Reg.ᵒʳlessob y essⁿᵒ heren 30 de mayo de 1767 ā

Diego cot alcardes	Capp.ⁿ D.ⁿ ygn.ᵒ tec Batab	gaspar chan gaspar
gaspar yam alcarᵉ	Andres tec thenᵉ	ek Sebas.ⁿ chim xtoua
	Marcos pot essno	r Na Reg.ᵒʳlessob rae

Joseph mis cuch cab
[different hand:] Bayxan lay solara lae ɔoc yn comic minan yn yoklal lay tunenel tin
conah ti theodoro coba yoklal holhunpis pˢ

Testimony regarding Joseph Cab, [who] died
on the 30th of May, 1767

He had not made his statement. He died in Tiho. We who are the batab, lieutenant, magistrates, regidors, and notary are now gathered together in court, all of us, in order to deliver this solar with its well to the children of Joseph Cab and to his younger siblings; to all his children and the daughters of Marcos Cab, as their fathers are dead. Marcos Cab had no testament. His son, this Joseph Cab, also died without making his statement. Therefore, we have just seen the will of their ancestors with respect to this solar, in the testament of Joseph Cab, who died in the year 1726, that it belonged to their ancestors, their fathers. For whosoever thinks this is not good, let them see Joseph Cab's will. His children will affirm it. All of them use this solar: Dominga Cab and María Cab, Francisca Cab, Rosa Cab, and Francisco Cab, and the daughters of this deceased Joseph Cab—Isidro Cab, Ana Cab, and Simona Cab. Likewise, one axe and blanket, and one machete, and one shirt, and one pair of trousers and belt, for Isidro Cab. This is the truth, the end of the arrangement of everything by us, the batab, magistrates, regidors, and notary, today, the 30th of May of 1767.

Diego Coot, alcalde	captain don Ignacio Tec, batab	Gaspar Chan,
Gaspar Yam, alcalde	Andrés Tec, lieutenant	Gaspar Ek, Sebastián Chim
	Marcos Poot, notary	Cristóbal Na
		regidors

Josef Mis, ah cuch cab[9]

Likewise, I have just sold that house plot; it has nothing to do with me, for I sold it to Teodoro Coba for fifteen pesos.

FOL. 23R DOCUMENT B46

WILL OF TOMASA TEC
9 JUNE 1767

Cimi thomassa tec en 9 de Junio 1767 ā—

tu kaba D.ˢ yumbil y D.ˢ mehenbil y D.ˢ espilitu santo oxtur personas huntulil hahar D.ˢ uchuc tumen tusinil mayx pimobi lay bin ylabac V hunil yn takyahthan tin testamento hibiguil tenil cen thomassa tec V yixmehen Pran^co tec V yalen Rorensa coba ah otochnalob Vay ti cah Yxil Bayxan Van xul yn cuxtar Vay yokol cab rae Volah mucur yn CuCutil ychil santa ygressia Bayxan licix yn Voktic ynba ti ca Pixanil yum pᵉ uardia ca yalab Junpeɔ missa Ressa yoklal yn Pixan y ca u mansen tu payarchi ychill u missa antabar yn pixan tu numiayl purgatolio—bin ɔabac V limosnayl tumen yalabb oztil christianob rae 6 rrˢ y 2 rrˢ gielusalem = —

Bayxan hunper boch y Jun ɔam tup Vtial yn uar pabia Na Mis = Jalili u xul yn than tin testamento cin uacu ntic Juntul almehen Jos Mis lay bin tan oltic V katic misse yoklal yn bixan [*sic*] tu tan batab y Jus^as

Diego coot alcar^s	Capp.^n D.^n ygn.^o tec Batab	gaspar chan Sebas.^n chi
gaspar yam alcar^s	Marcos pot ess^no	m gaspar ek xtouar
		Na Reg.^or lessob rae

8 rr^s
Dijose esta Missa y lo firme
  Fray Avila

Tomasa Tec died on the 9th of June, 1767

In the name of God the Father, God the Son, God the Holy Spirit, three persons, one true God, not many. It will be seen, the document of my final statement in my will, inasmuch as I who am Tomasa Tec, the daughter of Francisco Tec and the child of Lorensa Coba, householders here in the cah of Ixil. Likewise, as my life is ending here on this earth, I wish my body to be buried in the holy church. Likewise, I now also supplicate our blessed lord, the guardian priest, that he say one said mass for my soul and that he send up for me a prayer in the mass to aid my soul in the suffering of purgatory. The fee will be given, for we are believing Christians: 6 reales and 2 reales for Jerusalem.

Likewise, one shawl and a pair of earrings for my child Fabiana Mis. This is the truth, the end of my statement in my will. I designate one nobleman, Joseph Mis; he shall be responsible for requesting mass for my soul. Before the batab and magistrates:

Diego Coot, alcalde	captain don Ignacio Tec, batab	Gaspar Chan,
Gaspar Yam, alcalde	Marcos Poot, notary	Gaspar Ek, Sebastián Chim
		Cristóbal Na
		regidors

8 reales
This recited mass was said and I signed it
  fray Ávila

FOL. 23V DOCUMENT B47

WILL OF JUANA MO
9 JUNE 1767

Cimi Juana mo en 9 de Junio 767 ã—

tu kaba Dios yumbil D.^s mehenbil Dios espilitu santo oxtur personas huntulili hahar D.^s uchuc tumen tusinil mayx pimobi lay bin ylabac u hunil yn thakyahthan tin testamento hibiguil tenil cen Juana mo V yixmehen Andres mo V yalen Agus^na balam ah otochnalob uay ti cah yxil lae Bayxan cin katic tin pixanil yum p^e uardian

ca yalab Junpeɔ missa Ressada yoklal yn pixan bi ɔabac u limosnayl tumen yalab oztil
christianob uacper tu min y caper tumin giᶜlusalem =

halili u xul yn than tin testamento cin uacCuntic almehen albasias Joseph mis lay
bin tan oltic u katic missa tin pixan =

Diego Coot alcardes	Cap̲p̲.ⁿ D.ⁿ ygn.º tec Batab	gaspar chan
gaspar yam alcardes		gaspar ek Sebas
		ⁿ chim xtouar
Marcos pot essⁿᵒ		Na Reg.ᵒʳlessob rae

8 rrˢ
Dijose esta Missa y lo firme,
  Fray Avila

JUANA MO DIED ON THE 9TH OF JUNE, 1767

In the name of God the Father, God the Son, God the Holy Spirit, three persons, one
true God almighty, not many. It will be seen, the document of my final statement in
my will, inasmuch as I who am Juana Mo, the daughter of Andrés Mo and the child
of Agustina Balam, householders here in the cah of Ixil. Likewise, I ask my blessed
lord, the guardian priest, to say one said mass for my soul. The fee will be given, for
we are believing Christians: six tomins and two tomins for Jerusalem.

This is the truth, the end of my statement in my will. I appoint a nobleman as
executor—Joseph Mis; he shall take care to request a mass for my soul.

Diego Coot, alcalde	captain don Ignacio Tec, batab	Gaspar Chan
Gaspar Yam, alcalde		Gaspar Ek, Sebastián Chim
		Cristóbal Na
Marcos Poot, notary		regidors

8 reales
This recited mass was said and I signed it
  fray Ávila

FOL. 23V DOCUMENT B48

WILL OF JUANA TUN
1[. . .] JULY 1767

TESTAMENTO UTIAL JUANA TUN CIMI EN 1[. . .] DE JULIO 1767 Ā
tu kaba D.ˢ yumbil y D.ˢ mehenbil y D.ˢ esspilitu santo Amen Bayxan V yixmehenen
Simon tun V yalen Martha ytza ah otochnalob uay ti cah yxil lae Bayxan Volah mucur
yn CuCutil ychil Santa ygressia y ca u mansen tu payarchill ychil u missa Antabar
yn pixan tu numiayl pulgatolio bin ɔabac u limosna yl uacper tumin y caper tumin
gielusalem =

Bayxan cin ɔayc oxper camissa y̱ oxper ex y̱ oxper kaxnak y̱ catzill u hebar nok
Bayxan hunper boch utial yn ualob Juana chim = Bayxan Junper ypil y̱ Junper pic
Vtial ger^{na} Ytza = halili u xul yn than tin testamento cin uacuntic almehen Jasinto
pech albassias =

Diego Coot alcar^s	Capp.ⁿ D.ⁿ ygn.^o tec Batab	gaspar ch
gaspar yam alcar^s	Andres tec then^e	an Sebasⁿ chim xtouar
Marcos pot ess^{no}		Na legidorlessob rae

8 rrs Juana
   tun—fr. Mendez

Testament for Juana Tun, who died on the 1[. . .] of July, 1767

In the name of God the Father, and God the Son, and God the Holy Spirit, Amen.
Likewise, [she is] the daughter of Simon Tun, the child of Marta Itza, householders
here in the cah of Ixil. Likewise, I wish my body to be buried in the holy church. And
[I request] that he [the Padre] send up a prayer in the mass to aid my soul through the
sufferings of purgatory. The fee will be given: six tomins and two tomins for Jerusalem.

Likewise, I give three shirts and three pairs of trousers and three sashes and two
lengths of cloth, also one shawl, for my child Juana Chim. Likewise, one huipil and
one petticoat for Gerónima Itza. This is the truth, the end of my statement in my will.
I designate the nobleman Jacinto Pech as executor.

Diego Coot, alcalde	captain don Ignacio Tec, batab	Gaspar Chan
Gaspar Yam, alcalde	Andrés Tec, lieutenant	Gaspar Ek, Sebastián Chim
Marcos Poot, notary		Cristóbal Na
		regidors

8 reales
   Juana Tun; fray Méndez

FOL. 24R DOCUMENT B49

WILL OF SALVADOR POOT

24 JUNE 1767

Cimi Sarua^{or} pot en 24 de Junio 1767 ā—

tukaba D^s. yumbil y̱ D^s. mehenbil D^s. espilitu santo oxtul personas huntulil hahar D^s.
uchuc tumen tusinil maix pimobi lay bin ylabac u hunil yn thakyahthan tin testa-
mento hibiguil tenil cen sarua^{or} po u mehenen Joseph pot u yalen Dominga yam ah
caharnalob Uay ti cah Yxil lae Bayxan cin uoktic ynba ti ca pixnan yum p^e uardian
ca yalab Junpe ɔ missa Resada yokol yn pixan y̱ ca u mansen tu payarchi y̱ u missa ca
antabar yn pixan tu numiayl purgatolio lae bin ɔabac u limosnayl tumen yalab otzil
christianob rae uacper tumin

Bayxan Junper yn Matan solal yl u chenil tin Mam Joseph yam yn Mul Matan y
Joseph canche y yi ɔinob rae yn parte lae cin patic tu kab yn uixme hen Malia pot y
Junper caha y Junpok yeua tzimin cin patic tin uatan Juana Uh cu yalan car ca u ɔab
tin uixmehen Malia pot y Junper sia kanche utial yn uixmehen lay chichan Malia pot
y Bayxan Junper kax yn matan tin Mam cin ɔayc tin Sobrinob rae Andres Juchim y
gaspar Juchi M lay kax lae ti an xValahtun lae halili u xul yn than tin testamento cin
uaCintic Junper almehen Dⁿ gaspar canul albassias lay bin tan ortic V katic missa
yoko[l y]n pixan tu tan batab y Jusᵃˢ—

Diego cot alcarᵉ	Capp.ⁿ D.ⁿ ygn.º tec Batab	gaspar chan gaspar ek
gaspar yam alcarᵉ	Marcos pot essno	xtouar na Sebas.ⁿ chim
D.n gaspar canul aluasias		Reg.ºʳlessob rae

6 rrˢ Salvador Poot Fr. Mendez

SALVADOR POOT DIED ON THE 24TH OF JUNE, 1767

In the name of God the Father, God the Son, God the Holy Spirit, three persons,
one true God, not many. It will be seen, the paper of my final statement in my will,
inasmuch as I who am Salvador Poot, the son of Joseph Poot and child of Dominga
Yam, householders here in the town of Ixil. Likewise, I supplicate our blessed lord,
the guardian priest, that he say one said mass for my soul and that he send up for me
a prayer with the mass to aid my soul through the suffering of purgatory. The fee will
be given, for we are believing Christians: six tomins.

Likewise, my one house plot, with its well, inherited from my maternal grandfather,
Joseph Yam. I inherited it jointly with Joseph Canche and his younger siblings. I leave
my share in the hands of my daughter, María Poot. Also one chest and one mare I leave
in the hands of my wife, Juana Uh, who gave life to my daughter, María Poot; and one
wooden chair for my daughter, this little María Poot. And likewise, one forest, my
inheritance from my maternal grandfather, which I give to these nephews of mine—
Andrés Huchim and Gaspar Huchim. This forest is near Xualahtun. This is the truth,
the end of my statement in my will. I designate one noble, don Gaspar Canul, as executor. He shall take care to request mass for my soul. Before the batab and magistrates:

Diego Coot, alcalde	captain don Ignacio Tec, batab	Gaspar Chan, Gaspar Ek
Gaspar Yam, alcalde	Marcos Poot, notary	Cristóbal Na, Sebastián Chim
don Gaspar Canul, executor		regidors

6 reales; Salvador Poot; fray Méndez

FOL. 24V DOCUMENT B50

WILL OF LORENSA YAM

10 JULY 1767

CIMI RORENSA YAM—EN 10 DE JULIO DE 1767 Ã

tukaba Dˢ. yumbil Dˢ. mehenbil Dˢ. espilitu santo oxtur personas huntulil hahar Dˢ.
uchuc tumen tusinil maix pimobi lay bin ylabac V hunil yn thakyahthan tin testamento hibiguil tenil cen lorensa yam V uixmehenen Anᵗᵗᵒ yam V yalen petrona yam
ah caharnalob uay ti cah yxil lae Bayxan Van cu yortic ca yumil ti Dˢ. u xul yn cuxtar
uay yokol cab rae Bayxan cin uoktic ynba ti ca pixanil yum pᵉ Vardian ca yalab Junpeɔ
missa Resar Missa ylix ca u mansen tu payarchi ychill u missa antabar yn pixan tu
numiayl purgatolio lae bin ɔabac V limosnayl tumen yalabbotzil christianob rae 6 rrˢ
// y—2 rrˢ gielusalem—

　　Bayxan Junper caha y Junper ypil y Junper pic y Junpach u Colalles V kal yn uar
Malia Canul = Bayxan catzill u hebar Nok utial yn uar Man.ⁱ canul y Juntzi[l] utial
yn uar franᶜᵒ canul halili U xul yn than tin testamento cin uacuntic huntur almehen
Agus.ⁿ Cante albasiasob rae [lay] bin tan ortic u katic missa yoklal yn pixan tu tan
batab y Jusab rae—

Diego Coot alcarˢ　　Cappⁿ D.ⁿ ygn.º tec Batab　　gaspar chan Sebas.ⁿ [chim]

gaspar yam alcarˢ　　Marcos pot essⁿᵒ　　gaspar ek xtouarᵒʳ

　　　　　　　　　　　　　　　　　　　　Na Regᵒʳlessob rae

8 rrˢ Lorenza Yam, Fr. Mendez

LORENSA YAM DIED ON THE 10TH OF JULY, 1767.

In the name of God the Father, God the Son, God the Holy Spirit, three persons, one
true God, not many. It will be seen, the paper of my final statement in my will, inasmuch as I who am Lorensa Yam, the daughter of Antonio Yam and child of Petrona
Yam, householders here in the town of Ixil. Alas, our lord in God wishes to end my
life here on this earth! Therefore, I supplicate our blessed lord, the guardian priest,
that he say one mass, a said mass, and also that he send up for me a prayer in the mass
to aid my soul through the suffering of purgatory. The fee will be given, for we are
believing Christians: six reales, and two reales for Jerusalem.

　　Likewise, one chest and one huipil and one petticoat and one necklace of twenty
coral beads [for] my child, María Canul. Likewise, two lengths of cloth for my child
María Canul, and one for my child Francisco Canul. This is the truth, the end of my
statement in my will. I designate one noble, Agustín Cante, as executor; he shall take
care to request a mass for my soul. Before these the batab and magistrates:

Diego Coot, alcalde　　captain don Ignacio Tec, batab　　Gaspar Chan, Sebastián Chim

Gaspar Yam, alcalde　　Marcos Poot, notary　　Gaspar Ek, Cristóbal Na

regidors

8 reales; Lorensa Yam; fray Méndez

FOL. 25R DOCUMENT B51

WILL OF PASQUALA TEC

18 JULY 1767

CIMI PASGUALA TEC—EN 18 DE JULIO DE 1767 Ã—

tukaba D.ˢ yumbil Dˢ. mehenbil Dˢ. espilitu santo oxtur personas huntulil hahar Dˢ.
uchuc tumen tusinil maix pimobi lay bin ylabac V hunil yn thakyahthan tin testamento hibiguil tenil cen pasguala tec V uixmehenen pasg.ⁱ tec V yalen pasguala chim
ah otochnarlob Vay ti cah yxil Bayxan uan tu yortah ca yumil ti Dˢ. u xul yn cuxtal uay
yokol cab lae Volah mucur yn cucutir ychil santa ygressia Bayxan cin uoktic ynba ti ca
pixanil yum p.ᶜ uardia ca yalab Junpeɔ missa Ressada y ca u masen tu payarchi ychill
u missa la ca antabac yn pixan tu numiayl purgatolio bin ɔabac V limosnayl tumen
yalab otzil christianob rae uacper tumin y caper tumin gielusalem ===
    Bayxan Junac solal yl u chenil cin patic tu kab yn uarlob cre.ᵗᵉ cante y Ambronsio
cante y Sarua.ᵒʳ cante y pasq.ʳᵃ cante y pabiana cante y Ulsula cant[e] = y maᵃ candelalia cante uuctulob yoklal lay solal lae Bayxan hunper sia kanche y hunper bronso
licill u pabar tunich u multial yn uarlob rae Bayxan hunper boch tu ma nah yn uar
Ambrosi[o ca]nte utial yn uar Ulsula cante ɔocic u ber y hunper u lak boch tu [ma]
nah yn Uar Ambronsio cante utial ɔoc barl u ber yiɔin Ma.ᵃ candelalia Cante yl u lak
boch tu manah yn Uar Ambronsio cante ɔocic u ber yiɔin lipansia cante = Bayxan
hunpay caha Vtial yn uar Ambronsio cante = Bayxan hunperl u hol Na yl u marcoyl
cin patic tukab yn uar Ambronsio cante catun uɔaab uacper tumin yn uar Ambronsio
cante utiall u parte u lakob Bayxan ten clemente cante cin ualic minan yn than ti lay
u hor na cu cutar tu kab yn uiɔin Ambronsio cante lae Bayxan ten Agus.ⁿ cante helay
u hor na lae cin ualic u hahil yn than minan yn than y hele lae tumen yn Mul matan y
yn sucun gaspar cante cachi tu ɔah ten yn Sucun gaspar cante yn parte lae yoklal lay u
hor na lae halili u xul yn than tin testamento cin uaCuntic yalab botzil christiano lae
Juan chale albasias Bayxan hunper colil utial sarua.ʳ cante

Diego Coot alcarˢ	Capp.ⁿ D.ⁿ ygn.ᵒ tec Batab	gaspar chan gaspar ek
gaspar yam alcarˢ	Andres tec thenᶜ	Sebas.ⁿ chim xtouar na
Marcos pot essno—		Regidorlessob rae

8 rrˢ Pasquala Tec Fr. Mendez

PASQUALA TEC DIED ON THE 18TH OF JULY, 1767

In the name of God the Father, God the Son, God the Holy Spirit, three persons, one
true God, not many. It will be seen, the paper of my final statement in my will, as I

who am Pasquala Tec, the daughter of Pasqual Tec and the child of Pasquala Chim, householders here in the cah of Ixil. Likewise, as our lord in God wishes to end my life here on this earth, I wish my body to be buried in the holy church. Likewise, [I] supplicate our blessed lord, the guardian priest, that he say one said mass and that he send up for me a prayer in the mass to aid my soul through the suffering of purgatory. The fee will be given, for we are believing Christians: six reales, and two reales for Jerusalem.

Likewise, one house plot with its well, I leave in the hands of my children, Clemente Cante and Ambrosio Cante and Salvador Cante and Pasquala Cante and Fabiana Cante and Ursula Cante and María Candelaria Cante; this house plot is for all seven of them. Likewise, one wooden chair and one broken bronze-tipped digging-stick, to be the joint property of my children. Likewise, one shawl, bought by my child Ambrosio Cante, has just gone to my child Ursula Cante, and another shawl, bought by my child Ambrosio Cante, it has just gone to his younger sister, María Candelaria Cante; also another shawl, bought by my child Ambrosio Cante, has just gone to his younger sister, Lipansia Cante. Likewise, one chest for my child Ambrosio Cante. Likewise, one house beam with its frame [I] leave in the hands of my child Ambrosio Cante, who has given six tomins (has my child Ambrosio Cante) for the other share. Likewise, I, Clemente Cante, I declare that I have nothing to say regarding this house beam, that from now on it is in the hands of my younger brother, Ambrosio Cante. Likewise, I, Agustín Cante, I declare truthfully with regard to this house beam; that I have nothing to say about it today, for it was my joint inheritance with my older brother, Gaspar Cante; my share of this house beam had been given to me with my older brother, Gaspar Cante. This is the truth, the end of my statement in my will. I appoint this believing Christian, Juan Chale, as executor. Likewise, one field for Salvador Cante.

Diego Coot, alcalde	captain don Ignacio Tec, batab	Gaspar Chan, Gaspar Ek
Gaspar Yam, alcalde	Andrés Tec, lieutenant	Sebastián Chim, Cristóbal Na
Marcos Poot, notary		regidors
8 reales; Pasquala Tec; fray Méndez		

FOL. 25V DOCUMENT B52

WILL OF MICAELA TEC

9 AUGUST 1767

CIMI MICAELA TEC EN 9 DE AGOSTO 1767 Ã—

tukaba D^s. yumbil D^s. mehenbil D^s. esspilitu santo oxtur personas huntulili hahar D^s. V chuc tumen tusinil mayx pimobi lay bin ylabac V hunil yn thakyahthan tin testamento hibiguil tenil cen Micaela tec V yixmehene n sebas.^{n} tec V yalem Ber.^{na} pistec ah otochnarlob Vay ti cah yxil lae Bayxan Van tu yortah ca yumil ti D^s. u xul

yn cuxtal Vay yokol cab rae Volah mucur yn cucutir ychil santa ygressia Bayxan cin
uoktic ynba ti ca pixanil yum p.ᶜ uardian ca yalab Junpeꜟ missa Resar yoklal yn pixan
ꝡl ix ca u masen tu payarchil ichill u missa bin ꜟabac V limosna yl tumen yalab otzil
christianob rae uacper tumin ꝡ caper tumin gielusalem ==

Bayxan caac V mul matan kax yn yum ti u yum u par yn yum sebas.ⁿ tec yn parte
ten micaela tec lae cin patic tu kab yn uarlob rae = Man.ⁱ chan = thomassa chan
[=] oxtur yn uarlob lay kat lae ti an x tohil lae = halili yn than [t]in testamento cin
uacuntic huntur almehen Jasintho pech albassias lay bin ta ortic V katic Missa yokol
yn pixan tu tan Batab ꝡ Jusᵃˢsobrae—

Diego Coot alcardes	Capp.ⁿ D.ⁿ ygn.º tec	gaspar chan Sebas.ⁿ
gaspar yam alcardes	Batab	chim gaspar ek
	Andres tec thene	xtouar Na Re
MarCos poot essno		g.ᵒʳlessob rae

7 rrˢ Recivi de Michaela Tec siete rrˢ y lo firme
    Fr. Mendez

MICAELA TEC DIED ON THE 9TH OF AUGUST, 1767

In the name of God the Father, God the Son, God the Holy Spirit, three persons,
one true God, not many. It will be seen, the paper of my final statement in my will,
inasmuch as I who am Micaela Tec, the daughter of Sebastián Tec and the child of
Bernardina Piste, householders here in the cah of Ixil. Likewise, as our lord in God
wishes to end my life here on this earth, I wish my body to be buried in the holy
church. Likewise, I supplicate our blessed lord, the guardian priest, that he say one
said mass for my soul and also that he send up for me a prayer in the mass. The fee
will be given, for we are believing Christians: six reales, and two reales for Jerusalem.
Likewise, the forest that was jointly inherited by my father from his father, whose son
was Sebastián Tec, my father—I, Micaela Tec, leave my share in the hands of these
my children, Manuel Chan, Tomasa Chan; ask my three children if this is not just!
This is the truth, my statement in my will. I designate one nobleman, Jacinto Pech,
as executor; he shall take care to request a mass for my soul. Before the batab and
magistrates:

Diego Coot, alcalde	captain don Ignacio Tec, batab	Gaspar Chan, Sebastián Chim
Gaspar Yam, alcalde	Andrés Tec, lieutenant	Gaspar Ek, Cristóbal Na
Marcos Poot, notary		regidors

7 reales; I received from Micaela Tec seven reales and I signed it
    fray Méndez

FOL. 26R DOCUMENT B53

WILL OF PASQUAL COBA

20 SEPTEMBER 1767

CIMI PASGUAR COBA EN 20 DE SEPH.ᶜ DE 1767 Ã—

tukaba Dˢ. yumbil Dˢ. mehenbil Dˢ. esspilitu santo oxtur personas huntulili Dˢ. V chuc
tumen tusinil mayx pimobi lay bin ylabac V hunil yn thakyahthan tin testamento
hibiguil tenir cen pasguar coba V mehenen sebas.ⁿ coba V yalen Malia Candelalia yam
ah otochnalob Vay ti cah yxil lae bacacix cimill in cah lae thoh Vor tin pucsikal Bayxan
Van tu yortah ca yumil ti Dˢ. V xul yn cuxtar yokol cab lae Bayxan cin uoktic ynba ti ca
pixanil yum p.ᶜ uardian ca yalab Junpeɔ missa Resada tin pixan bin ɔabac V limosnayl
tumen yalab otzil christianob rae uacꝑer tumin y caꝑer tumin gielusalem =

Bayxan hunpok yn uixmehen Manʳᵃ coba yn Mul matan solal y yn tio Diego
Coba cin patic tu kab yn Vuixmehen manʳᵃ coba yn parte lae y hunpay caha Vtial yn
Vixmehen manʳᵃ coba = halili u xul yn than tin testamento cin uacuntic catur alme-
hen yalab otzi christianob rae caturlob gaspar coba y Agus.ⁿ cante albassiassob rae =

Diego Coot alcarˢ	D.ⁿ ygn.º tec Batab	gaspar chan sebas.ⁿ chim gaspar
gaspar yam alcarˢ	Andres tec thenᶜ	ek xtouar Na Reg.ºʳlessob
	Marcos pot essⁿº	lae

8 rrˢ

Recivi 8 rrs de Pasqual Coba y porque conste lo firme

Fr. Mendez

PASQUAL COBA DIED ON THE 20TH OF SEPTEMBER, 1767

In the name of God the Father, God the Son, God the Holy Spirit, three persons, one
God, not many. It will be seen, the paper of my final statement in my will, inas-
much as I who am Pasqual Coba, the son of Sebastián Coba and the child of María
Candelaria Yam, householders here in the cah of Ixil. Although I am dying, content is
my heart. Likewise, as our lord in God wishes to end my life on this earth, I therefore
supplicate our blessed lord, the guardian priest, that he say one said mass for my soul.
The fee will be given, for we are believing Christians: six reales, and two reales for
Jerusalem.

Likewise, [for] my one daughter, Manuela Coba, my house plot, jointly inherited
with my uncle, Diego Coba; I leave in the hands of my daughter, Manuela Coba,
my share of it, with one chest for my daughter, Manuela Coba. This is the truth, the
end of my statement in my testament. I designate two nobles who are both believing
Christians, Gaspar Coba and Agustín Cante, as executors.

Diego Coot, alcalde	captain don Ignacio Tec, batab	Gaspar Chan, Sebastián Chim
Gaspar Yam, alcalde	Andrés Tec, lieutenant	Gaspar Ek, Cristóbal Na

Marcos Poot, notary   regidors

8 reales

I received eight reales from Pasqual Coba and I signed, fray Méndez

FOL. 26V DOCUMENT B54

SETTLING OF THE ESTATE OF PASQUAL KU
8 OCTOBER 1767

TESTIMONIO CIMI PASG.¹ KU EN 8 DE OCTᵉ DE 1767 Ã

Batab y Justissias Leg.ᵒʳ—toon coon Justissias Y Regᵒʳ y essⁿᵒ tu kaba Dˢ yumbil Dˢ mehenbil Dˢ espiritu Santo oxtur personnas huntulili hahar Dˢ Vchuc tumen tusinil mayx pimobi = bay bic ɔoc V payarl u cuxtar lay almehen pasq.¹ Ku tumen ca yumil ti Ds ten Batab y Jusᵃˢ Regᵒʳlesob y essⁿᵒ lic ca mentic V testamento lae—pasq.¹ Ku Vmehen Rorenso Ku Vyal micaela cante V tulul missa lae uacper tum[in] Ressae Missa =

Bayxan hunper cuchala de prata conbil Vtiall u tulul missa lae = Bayxan hunac solal yl u chenil Vmultial yn palilob xibra y chuplallob Rorenso Ku y essteban Ku y pasqra Ku y petrona Ku y u mehen pelipe Ku Juan Ku u kaba u multiallob ray solob rae y tanbuh solal u multiallob xan Rossa Ku y Martha Ku = tulacar yn palillob V multiallobrae = y hunac kax yan XJualahtun V multiallob xan V tzayar kax lae ti nohor Fran.ᶜᵒ canul ti lakin Man.¹ cutz ti chim Matheᵒ pech ti xaman pasq.¹ canche = y huper V marco yl y u puerta y u hor na V multiallob xan y Junpay caha V multiallob xan y hunpay chichan messa V multiallob xan y Junpay chichan batella Vtial yn uatan simona chan y Junpay Vbancoyl Juch Vtial yn ua[ta]n simona chan = y hun ɔit baat y Jun ɔit machete Vtial esteban Ku y hupe[r] tzotz y hunpay kaxnak Vtial esteban Ku = Bayxan lahuyoxkal u chun prantanos [. . .] Vtial yn uatan simona chan halili be ɔoc tzolic y tulacar hebix Vchi V ɔayc ca [yum]il ti Ds t pucsikal lae—Bayxan helay cuchala cu bin conbil cachi lae ma u chahi cucutal tu kab esteban Ku =

Diego coot alcarˢ	Capp.ⁿ D.ⁿ ygn.ᵒ tec Batab	gaspar chan gaspar ek
gaspar yam alcarˢ	Andres tec thenᵉ	Sebas.ⁿ chim xtoual na
	Marcos pot essⁿᵒ	Regidorlessob rae

6 rrˢ recivi de Pasqual Ku seis rrˢ y lo firme
Fr. Mendez

TESTIMONY: PASQUAL KU DIED ON THE 8TH OF OCTOBER, 1767

The batab, magistrates, regidors; we who are the magistrates, regidors, and notary. In the name of God the Father, God the Son, God the Holy Spirit, three persons, one true God almighty, not many. Thus will end a prayer for the soul of this noble, Pasqual Ku, through our lord in God. I, batab, and the magistrates, regidors, and notary, now draw up the testament of Pasqual Ku, the son of Lorenso Ku, the child of Micaela Cante. He pays for his mass; six tomins for a said mass. Likewise, one silver spoon, sold to pay for that mass.

Likewise, one house plot with its well, for my children—boys and girls—Lorenso Ku and Esteban Ku and Pasquala Ku and Petrona Ku and Felipe Ku's son, Juan Ku; in their hands together, these house posts with a half plot, also together with Rosa Ku and Marta Ku—all my children together—and one forest at Xjualahtun, also theirs together. Its neighboring forest[s] are, to the south, Francisco Canul; to the east, Manuel Cutz; to the west, Mateo Canche; to the north, Pasqual Canche; and one frame with its beam, with its house beam, also theirs together; and one chest, also theirs together; and one small table, also theirs together; and one small dish for my wife, Simona Chan, with one polished bench for my wife, Simona Chan; with one axe and one machete for Esteban Ku, with one fur blanket and one belt for Esteban Ku. Likewise, fifty banana trees . . . for my wife, Simona Chan. This is the truth; everything has just been arranged, according to the wish formerly given by our lord in God. Likewise, this spoon shall be sold; it has not been broken or lost its shine; from now on in the hands of Esteban Ku.

Diego Coot, alcalde	captain don Ignacio Tec, batab	Gaspar Chan, Gaspar Ek
Gaspar Yam, alcalde	Andrés Tec, lieutenant	Sebastián Chim, Cristóbal Na
	Marcos Poot, notary	regidors

6 reales
I received from Pasqual Ku six reales and I signed it
    fray Méndez

FOL. 27R DOCUMENT B55

WILL OF ANTONIA COBA

21 OCTOBER 1767

AN^{tta} COBA CIMI EN 21 DE OCTU^e DE 1767 Ã TU KABA

Dios yumbil y Dˢ. mehenbil Dˢ. espilitu santo oxtur personas huntulili hahar Dˢ. u chuc tumen tusinil mayx pimobi lay bin ylabac V hunil yn thakyahthan tin testamento hibigˡ. tenil cen an^{tta} coba U yixmehenen Ber^{no} coba V yalen Martha chim ah otochnarlob Vay ti cah yxil lae Bayxan uan tu yoltah ca yumil ti Dˢ. V xul yn cuxtar yokol cab rae uolah mucul yn cucutil ychil Santa ygressia lae yl ix cin katic ti ca pixanil yum p.ᶜ uardian ca yalab Junpeɔ missa Kaybil yoklal yn pixan ca yx u mansen tu payalchi ychill u missa lae mahebarl u xantar yn pixan tu nummiayl pulgatolio lae bin ɔabac V limosnayl tumen yalab botzil christianossob rae oxᴘer tostones y hunᴘer tumin gielusalem

Bayxan hunac yn matan kax yan tu hor cah ber ɔemul utial yn uallob tulacallob yn matan tu testamento yn yum Ber.^{no} coba cimi lae = Agusⁿ pot y Bar.^{me} pot y lorenso

pot y̨ pasquala pot y̨ thomassa pot y̨ andrea pot y̨ An.ᵗᵗᵃ pot y̨ leornarda pot y̨ malia
crus pot tulacar yn ualob = Bayxan hunp̨er ypil y̨ hunp̨er pic y̨ hunpach V colales
Vtial yn uar Malia Crus pot tu hunar lae halili yn than testamento cin uacuntic allab
otzil christiano Jo[sep]h mis lay bin tan ortic Vkatic missa tin pixan tu tan batab y̨
J[usᵃ]sob rae—

Diego coot alcarˢ   D.ⁿ ygn.° tec Batab   gaspar chan, gaspar ek

gaspar yam alcarˢ   Andres tec thenᵉ   Sebas.ⁿ chim xtoual na

Marcos pot essⁿᵒ=   Regidorlessob rae

13 rr
cantose esta missa y lo firme
    fray Avila

ANTONIA COBA DIED ON THE 21ST OF OCTOBER, 1767

In the name of God the Father, God the Son, God the Holy Spirit, three persons,
one true God almighty, not many. It will be seen, the paper of my final statement in
my will, inasmuch as I who am Antonia Coba, the daughter of Bernardino Coba
and the child of Marta Chim, householders here in the cah of Ixil. Likewise, as our
lord in God wishes to end my life on this earth, I wish my body to be buried in the
holy church, and also I ask our blessed lord, the guardian priest, that he say one sung
mass for my soul, also that he send up for me a prayer in the mass to aid and assist my
soul through the sufferings of purgatory. The fee will be given, for we are believing
Christians: three tostons and one tomin for Jerusalem.

Likewise, my one inherited forest, which is at the entrance to the cah on the road
to Dzemul, for all my children—I inherited it in the will of my father, Bernardino
Coba, now deceased—Agustín Poot and Bartolomé Poot and Lorenso Poot and
Pasquala Poot and Tomasa Poot and Andrea Poot and Antonia Poot and Leonarda
Poot and María Cruz Poot; all my children. Likewise, one huipil and one petticoat
and one necklace of coral beads for my child María Cruz Poot, for her alone. This is
my true testamentary statement. I appoint the believing Christian Joseph Mis to take
care to request a mass for my soul. Before the batab and these the magistrates:

Diego Coot, alcalde   captain don Ignacio Tec, batab   Gaspar Chan, Gaspar Ek

Gaspar Yam, alcalde   Andrées Tec, lieutenant   Sebastián Chim, Cristóbal Na

                       Marcos Poot, notary   regidors

13 reales
This mass was sung and I signed it
    fray Ávila

FOL. 27V DOCUMENT B56

WILL OF LUISA TEC

2 NOVEMBER 1767

CIMI LUISSA TEC EN 2 DE NOU.ᶜ DE 1767 Ã

Dios yumbil Dˢ. mehenbil Dˢ. espilitu santo oxtul personas Juntulili hahar Dˢ. uchuc
tumen tusinil mayx pimobi lay bin ylabac V hunil yn thakyahthan tin testamento
hibiguil tenil cen luissa tec V yixmehenen Juan Ming.ⁱ tec V yalen Agus.ⁿᵃ ek ah
otochnalob Vay ti cah yxil lae Bacacix cimil yn cah lae toh uol tin pucsikal y ti naat Vet
sihgui lae Bayxan uan tu yoltah ca yumil ti Dˢ u xules yn cuxtal uay yokol cab lae uolah
mucul yn cucutil ychil Santa ygressia Bayxan licix yn uoktic ynba ti ca pixanil yum p.ᶜ
uardian ca u yalab Junpeɔ missa tin pixan Kaybil yl ix ca u mansen tu—payarchi ychill
u missa maheball u xantal yn pixan tu numiayl pulpulgatolio lae y cayx tac ca pixanil
yum p.ᶜ ucħaben y ca palic tun yn ɔayc hunpok pota otzin Vtial u tul V Missa lae
     Bayxan pat can yn cah tubal ynba hecen V ɔama ten ca yumil ti Dˢ yokol cab
lae Bayxan hunac solal y caac V cħenil Vtial ming.ⁱ tec y—Domingo tec catullobi y
hunpok mula y hunpok yeua tzimin y hunpay caha Vtial ming.ⁱ tec y hunper camissa
y caperl uakal kuch y hunper botihuela Vmatan ming.l tec tu hunar y hunperl u lak
botihuela Vtial Benʳᵃ tec y hunper sia tzimin Vtial ming.ⁱ tec y Junɔit chichan baleta y
hunper bronso Vtial ming.ⁱ tec y Junac kax yan ber xku utial min guer tec V tzayarlob
rae ti lakin Andres tec ti xaman Matheᵒ yam y l u lak kax yan ti culix Vtial Benʳᵃ tec
y Domingo tec catulob Vtza yal kax lae ti noh Dⁿ Juan pech ti xaman pasq.ⁱ pech
Bayxan hunpok macho utial Domingo tec y hunpay caha utial Benʳᵃ tec Bayxan helay
U sola yn yum lae yn parte lae cin patic tukab yn ual pablo tec V kahsicen yokol cab
lae Bay tun xan helay xanob rae yan ychil lay solal lae bolon lahun cu ti Ming.ⁱ tec y
hun cu ya Bay Domingo tec xan bolon lahun cul xan V tial xan y hun cul ya halili yn
than tin testamento cin uacuntic catul yalab otzil christiano lay bin yn helob yokol
cab rae Juan Matu y gaspar coba

Diego coot alcardes	Batab Capp.ⁿ D.ⁿ ygn.ᵒ tec	gaspar chan gaspar ek
gaspar yam alcardes	Andres tec thene	Sebas.ⁿ chim xtouar na
Marcos pot essⁿᵒ		Reg.dollessob rae

cantose esta Missa y lo firme
     fray Avila

LUISA TEC DIED ON THE 2ND OF NOVEMBER, 1767

In the name of God the Father, God the Son, God the Holy Spirit, three persons,
one true God, not many. The document of my final statement in my will shall be
seen, inasmuch as I who am Luisa Tec, the daughter of Juan Miguel Tec and child of
Agustina Ek, homeowners here in the cah of Ixil. Although I am dying, my heart and
my understanding are sound, as it should be. Likewise, when our lord in God ends
my life here on this earth, I wish my body buried in the holy church. Likewise, I now

supplicate our blessed lord, the guardian priest, to say one mass for my soul, a sung one, and also to send up for me a prayer in the mass so as not to detain my soul in the suffering of purgatory; and to empower our blessed lord Padre in this mediation I am giving one trussed cockerel to pay for that mass.

Likewise, I am declaring the settlement of my household goods brought together for me on this earth by our lord in God. Likewise, one house plot, with the well that is there, for Miguel Tec and Domingo Tec, both together; and one mule and one mare and one chest for Miguel Tec; and one shirt and two looms and one jar, the inheritance of Miguel Tec alone. The other jar is for Ventura Tec. And one saddle for Miguel Tec and one small iron tool and one bronze tool for Miguel Tec; and one forest on the road to Xku for Miguel Tec; its neighbors are, to the east, Andrés Tec, to the north, Mateo Yam; and the other forest is to be settled on Ventura Tec and Domingo Tec, both together; its neighboring forests are, to the south, don Juan Pech, and Pasqual Pech to the north. Likewise, one male mule for Domingo Tec; and one chest for Ventura Tec. Likewise, here is my father's house plot; my share of it I leave in the hands of my child, Pablo Tec; he remembered me on this earth. Also then here are the palm trees that are on that house plot: nineteen trees for Miguel Tec, with one sapote tree; Domingo Tec likewise gets nineteen palm trees and one sapote tree. This is my true statement in my will. I appoint two believing Christians to be my substitutes here on earth: Juan Matu and Gaspar Coba.

Diego Coot, alcalde	captain don Ignacio Tec, batab	Gaspar Chan, Gaspar Ek
Gaspar Yam, alcalde	Andrés Tec, lieutenant	Sebastián Chim, Cristóbal Na
Marcos Poot, notary		regidors

This mass was sung and I signed it
　fray Ávila

FOL. 28R DOCUMENT B57

WILL OF PEDRO HUCHIM

20 NOVEMBER 1767

CIMI Pº JUCHIM EN 20 DE NOUᵉ 767 Ã

tu kaba Dˢ. yumbil y Dˢ. mehenbil Dˢ. esspilitu santo oxtur personas huntulili hahar Dˢ. uchuc tumen tusinil mayx pimobi lay bin ylabac V hunil yn thakyahthan tin testamento hibigᴵ. tenil cen pº Juchim V mehenen Man.ᴵ Juchim V yalen mag.ⁿᵃ canul ah otochnalob Vay ti cah yxil lae Bayxan cin katic ti ca pixanil yum p.ᶜ uardian ca yalab Junpeɔ mis Ressada bin ɔabac V limosnayl uacᵖer tumin y caᵖer tumin gilusalem halili be—

Diego cot alcarˢ	D.ⁿ ygn.º tec Batab	gaspar chan gaspar ek
gaspar yam alcarˢ	Marcos pot essⁿᵒ	Sebas.ⁿ chim xtouar na

Regidorlessob rae

8 r
Resose esta Misa y lo firme
    fray Avila

PEDRO HUCHIM DIED ON THE 20TH OF NOVEMBER, 1767

In the name of God the Father, and God the Son, God the Holy Spirit, three persons,
one true God, not many. It will be seen, the document of my final statement in my
will, inasmuch as I who am Pedro Huchim, the son of Manuel Huchim and the child
of Magdalena Canul, householders here in the cah of Ixil. Likewise, I ask our blessed
lord, the guardian priest, that he say one said mass. The fee will be given: six tomins
and two tomins for Jerusalem.

Diego Coot, alcalde	captain don Ignacio Tec, batab	Gaspar Chan, Gaspar Ek
Gaspar Yam, alcalde	Marcos Poot, notary	Sebastián Chim, Cristóbal Na
		regidors

This recited mass was said and I signed it
    fray Ávila

FOL. 28R DOCUMENT B58

WILL OF ANTONIO COBA
11 NOVEMBER 1767

CIMI ANTT.° COBA EN 11 DE NOB.ᵉ DE 1767 AÑ

tu kaba Dios yumbil y Dios mehenbil y Dios esspiritu santo oxtul personas huntulili
Dios uchuc tumen tusinil mayx pimobi lay bin ylabac u hunil in testamento hibicil
tenil Antt.° coba U mehenen pasg.ˡ coba U yalen thomassa ma.tu bay bic tanmuc
u payal in cuxtal tumen ca yumil ti Dios lae ti lic in tzolic in than Uolah mucul in
uinicil Ychil Yotoch Cilich nabil Yglesia lae Bayxan lic uoktic ynba ti ca pixanil yum
padre guardian ca yalab hunpeɔ missa Resada utial in pixan lae Bayxan bin ɔabac u
limosnayl missa lae, uacpel tumin y capel tumin gelusalem lae—8 rrˢ

Bayxan hunpay caha utial in uixmehen Anttᵃ coba lae lay tumen cin uacuntic
huntul almehen Jasinto pech albasias lae—

Diego cot alˢ	D.ⁿ ygn.° tec	gaspar chan
gaspar yam alˢ	Batab	Sebas.ⁿ chim
	Marcos pot essⁿᵒ	gaspar ek
		xtouar Na
		Regidoresob rae

Resose esta Misa y lo firme
  fray Avila

ANTONIO COBA DIED ON THE 11TH OF NOVEMBER, 1767

In the name of God the Father, and God the Son, and God the Holy Spirit, three persons, one almighty God, not many. It will be seen, the document of my will, inasmuch as I am Antonio Coba, the son of Pasqual Coba and the child of Tomasa Matu. While, therefore, our lord in God summons my life, I now arrange my statement: I wish my body buried in the home, the holy mother church. Likewise, I supplicate our blessed lord, the guardian priest, that he say one said mass for my soul. Likewise, the mass fee will be given: six tomins and two tomins for Jerusalem. 8 reales.

Likewise, one chest for my daughter, Antonia Coba. Wherefore I designate one noble, Jacinto Pech, as executor.

Diego Coot, alcalde	captain don Ignacio Tec	Gaspar Chan
Gaspar Yam, alcalde	batab	Sebastián Chim
	Marcos Poot, notary	Gaspar Ek
		Cristóbal Na
		regidors

This recited mass was said and I signed it
  fray Ávila

FOL. 28V DOCUMENT B59

WILL OF MONICA NA

4 DECEMBER 1767

CIMI MONICA NA EN 4 DE DICSIEMBRE—

tu kaba Dios yumbil y̱ Dios mehenbil y̱ Dios esspiritu santo oxtul personas huntulili Dios uchuc tumen tusinil maix pimobi lay bin ylabac u hunil in thakyahthan tin testamento hibicil tenil monica Na u Yixmehenen—mathe.° Na U yalen Ana Juchim ah ochohnalob Uay ti cah Yxil lae—bay bic tanmuc u payal in cuxtal tumen ca yumil ti dios Uay yokol cab lae Uolah mucul in uinicil Ychil Cilich Nabil Yglesia lae—Bayxan ti lic in uoktic inBa ti ca pixanil Yum padre guardian ca Yalab hunpeɔ missa Resada utial in pixan bin ix ɔabac u limosNal missa uacpel tumin y̱ hunpel tumin Jelusalem lae—7 rrˢ

Diego cot alˢ	D.ⁿ ygn.° tec	gaspar chan gaspar ek
gaspar yam alˢ	Batab	Sebas.ⁿ chim xtouar Na
	Marcos pot essⁿᵒ	Regidoresob rae

Resose esta Misa y lo firme
  fray Avila

MONICA NA DIED ON THE 4TH OF DECEMBER

In the name of God the Father, and God the Son, and God the Holy Spirit, three persons, one almighty God, not many. It will be seen, the document of my final statement in my will, inasmuch as I am Monica Na, the daughter of Mateo Na and the child of Ana Huchim, householders here in the cah of Ixil. Seeing, therefore, that our lord in God summons my life here on this earth, I wish my body buried in the holy mother church. Likewise, I now supplicate our blessed lord, the guardian priest, that he say one said mass for my soul. Also the mass fee will be given: six tomins and one tomin for Jerusalem. 7 reales.

Diego Coot, alcalde	don Ignacio Tec	Gaspar Chan, Gaspar Ek
Gaspar Yam, alcalde	batab	Sebastián Chim, Cristóbal Na
	Marcos Poot, notary	regidors

This recited mass was said and I signed it
  fray Ávila

FOL. 28V DOCUMENT B60

WILL OF NICOLAS CHAN

N.D.

cimi Nicolas ch V gaspar chan V yal Nicolasa canul sote lo par U tulu missa uacpel tumin—

6 rr^s

Diego cot alcar^s	D.^{n} ygn.^{o} tec Batab	gaspar chan
Marcos pot ess^{no}—		Reg.^{or}

Resose esta Misa y lo firme Fray Avila

Nicolás Chan died; Gaspar Chan's; the child of Nicolasa Canul. He was a dropsied child. The mass payment is six tomins. 6 reales.

Diego Coot, alcalde	don Ignacio Tec, batab	Gaspar Chan
Marcos Poot, notary		regidors

This recited mass was said and I signed it, fray Ávila

FOL. 29R DOCUMENT B61

WILL OF JACINTO POOT
14 DECEMBER 1767

CIMI JASSINTO POT—EN 14 DE DIZ^e DE 1767 Ã

tu kaba D^s. yumbil D^s. mehenbil D^s. esspilitu santo oxtul personas Juntulili hahar D^s. uchuc tumen tusinil mayx pimobi lay bin ylabac V hunil yn thakyahthan tin testamento hibiguil tenil cen Jassinto pot V mehenen An^{tto} pot V yalen Malia chan ah otochnalob Vay ti cah yxil Bayxan tu yoltah ca yumil ti D^s u xul yn cuxtal uay yokol cab rae uolah mucul yn cucutil ychil Santa ygressia yl ix xan ca u mansen tu payalchi ychil u missa Antabar yn pixan tu numiayl pulgatolio Bin ɔabac V limosnayl uacper tumin y hunper tumin gieluSalem =

Bayxan Junac solal yn parte lae minan V chenil yn sucun marcos pot y yn mehenob bin V mul pot u chenil ca culac tu kab yn palillob rae—Sarua^{or} pot y ma[n].^l pot = y An^{tto} pot y Aug.^{na} pot cantullob V multiallob = Bayxan cantul tzimin cin patic tu kab yn uatan y yalob tu cantul[lo]b rae y hunperl u hol na V multial lob yl u nayl yn [. . .] lic lae Bayxan hunac kax yan tu xaman xlochchen V multial yn mehenob rae sarua^{or} pot y man.^l pot y An.^{tto} pot = V tzayal kax lae xaman ca yum D.ⁿ ygn.^o tec ti nohol Juanchim pech = Bayxan Junper sarga Vtial yn mehen sarua^{or} pot = y Junpay poyche Vtial yn uatan y yn palillob rae = halili u xul yn than tin testamento cin uacuntic huntul almehen fran^{co} coba albasseas

Diego cot alcar^{es}	Capp.ⁿ D.ⁿ ygn.^o tec	gaspar chan gaspar
gaspar yam alcar^{es}	Batab	ek Sebasⁿ chim xto
	Andres tec then^e	uar na Reg.^{or}sob rae

Marcos pot ess^{no}

Dijose esta missa y lo firme—
    fray Avila

JACINTO POOT DIED ON THE 14TH OF DECEMBER, 1767

In the name of God the Father, God the Son, God the Holy Spirit, three persons, one true God almighty, not many. The document of my final statement in my will shall be seen, inasmuch as I who am Jacinto Poot, the son of Antonio Poot and the child of María Chan, homeowners here in the cah of Ixil. Likewise, our lord in God ends my life here on this earth; I wish my body buried in the holy church. And also may he [the priest] also send a prayer up in the mass to protect my soul in the suffering of purgatory. The fee shall be given: six tomins and one tomin for Jerusalem.

Likewise, my share of a house plot; there is no well; my brother Marcos Poot and my sons shall share the Poot well that is settled in the hands of these my children: Salvador Poot and Manuel Poot and Antonio Poot and Agustina Poot, the four of them together. Likewise, I leave four horses in the hands of my wife and her four children, with one house beam, their joint property, with its house, which I [document damaged]. Likewise, one forest, which is to the north of Xlochchen, to go jointly to my sons, Salvador Poot and Manuel Poot and Antonio Poot. Its neighboring forests are, to the north, our lord don Ignacio Tec, to the south, Joaquin Pech. Likewise, one blanket for my son Salvador Poot, and one bed for my wife and my children. This is the truth, the end of my statement in my will. I appoint one nobleman, Francisco Coba, as executor.

Diego Coot, alcalde	captain don Ignacio Tec	Gaspar Chan, Gaspar Ek
Gaspar Yam, alcalde	batab	Sebastián Chim, Cristóbal Na
	Andrés Tec, lieutenant	regidors

Marcos Poot, notary

This mass was said and I signed it,
    fray Ávila

FOL. 29V DOCUMENT B62

WILL OF LORENSA CANUL

17 DECEMBER 1767

V testamen[to] Vtial Rorensa canul cimin en 27 de D.Z.[e] 1767 Ā tu kaba D[s]. yumbil D[s]. mehenbil D[s]. esspilitu santo oxtul personas Juntulili hahal D[s]. uchuc tumen tusinil mayx pimobi lay bin ylabac V hunil yn thakyahthan tin testamento hibiguil tenil cen Rorensa canul V yixmehenen elnardo canul ah caharnalob Vay ti cah yxil lae = Bayxan V yalen pabiana mas tu yoltah ca yumil ti D.[s] u xul yn cuxtal uay yokol cab rae Volah mucul yn cucutil y̱ = chil Santa ygressia y̱l ix yn uoktic ynba ti ca pixanil yum p.[e] uardian ca yalab Junpeɔ missa Rasada yoklal yn pixan y̱l ix ca u mansen tu payarchi ychill u missa Maheball u xantar yn pixan tu numiayl pulgatolio bin ɔabac V limosnayl y̱ gielusalem hunp̱er tumin—7 rr[s]
    halili yn than cin uacuntic almehen albasseas—

Diego cot alcar[s]	D.[n] ygn.[o] tec Batab	gaspar chan gaspar ek
gaspar yam alcar[s]	Andres tec then[e]	sebas[n] chim xtouar na
		Regidorlessob rae

Marcos pot ess[no]=

Resose esta Misa y̱ lo firme
    fray Avila

THE TESTAMENT OF LORENSA CANUL, WHO
DIED THE 27TH OF DECEMBER, 1767

In the name of God the Father, God the Son, God the Holy Spirit, three persons, one true God almighty, not many. The document of my final statement in my will shall be seen, inasmuch as I who am Lorensa Canul, the daughter of Leonardo Canul, residents here in the cah of Ixil. Likewise, Fabiana Mas's child. It is the wish of our lord in God to end my life here on this earth; I wish my body buried in the holy church. And also I supplicate our blessed lord, the guardian priest, that he say one recited mass for my soul and also that he send a prayer up in the mass so that my soul not tarry in the suffering of purgatory. The fee shall be given, with one tomin for Jerusalem. 7 reales.

My statement is true. I appoint one nobleman as executor.

Diego Coot, alcalde	captain don Ignacio Tec, batab	Gaspar Chan, Gaspar Ek
Gaspar Yam, alcalde	Andrés Tec, lieutenant	Sebastián Chim, Cristóbal Na
		regidors

Marcos Poot, notary

This recited mass was said and I signed it
fray Ávila

FOLS. 29V–30R DOCUMENT B63

WILL OF IGNACIA COBA

8 JANUARY 1768

CIMI—YGNASIA COBA EN 8 DE HENERO DE 176[8] AÑ

tu Kaba Dios yumbil y Dios menhenbil y Dios esspitu santo. oxtul personas huntulil Dios uchuc tumen tusinil maix pimobi lay bin ylabac u hunil yn takyahthan tin testamento hibicil tenil cen Yg.ª coba u yixmehenen Antt.º coba V yalen Juana canul ah otochnalob Vay ti cah Yxil = lae bacacix cimil yn cah tin cucutilae toh uol tin pucsikal y tin nat uet sihci lae mamac bin u loh uba ti cimil lae—Volah mucul yn uinicil ychil yotoch cilich Nabil Yglesia lae Bayxan cin uoktictic inba ti ca pixanil yum padre guardian ca yalab hunpeɔ missa Resada Bayxan bin ɔabac V limosnayl uacpel tumin y hunpel tumin Jelusalem lae y bin u masen tu payalchi ychil V missa ca manac in pixan tu numyayl purgatorio lae =

Bayxan hunpel pic utial Apolonia couoh y u lak pic utial marlia couoh y u lak pic hunpel xan utial—manˡᵃ couoh Bayxan hunpel toca utial Apolonia couoh—Bayxan hun ɔam colares V lae utial lay in chupul palalob lae—y capay sinta u multial in ualob xan Bayxan hunpel gergeta utial gregº couoh xan halili U xul yn than tin testamento cin uacuntic catul almeheno al albasiasob Dⁿ gaspar canul y pedro pot aluasisob lae [fol. 30r] lay bin tan oltic u katicob missa tu tan batab y Jusᵃˢ lae—

Sar.ᵒʳ coba alᵉ	Cappⁿ D.ⁿ ygn.º tec	Juan matu juº coba
Cle.ᵗᵉ cante alᵉ	Batab	franᶜᵒ Juchim
	pablo tec essⁿᵒ	Regiᵒʳsob rae

Resose esta misa y lo firme fray Avila

IGNACIA COBA DIED ON THE 8TH OF JANUARY, 176[8]

In the name of God the Father, and God the Son, and God the Holy Spirit, three persons, one almighty God, not many. The document of my final statement in my will shall be seen, inasmuch as I who am Ignacia Coba, the daughter of Antonio Coba and child of Juana Canul, householders here in the cah of Ixil. Although my body is dying, my heart and my understanding are sound, as it should be. Nobody shall redeem themselves from death; I wish my body buried in the home of the holy mother church. Likewise, I supplicate our blessed lord, the guardian priest, that he say one recited mass. Likewise, the fee shall be given: six tomins and one tomin for Jerusalem. And he shall send up a prayer in the mass so that my soul pass through the suffering of purgatory.

Likewise, one petticoat for Apolonia Couoh, and the other petticoat for María Couoh, and another petticoat also for Manuela Couoh. Likewise, one headscarf for Apolonia Couoh. Likewise, one [necklace] of coral beads to be the property of these my daughters, with two ribbons also jointly for my children. Likewise, also one rough blanket for Gregorio Couoh. This is the truth, the end of my statement in my will. I appoint two nobles as executors—don Gaspar Canul and Pedro Poot, executors—[fol. 30r] who shall take care to request mass. Before the batab and magistrates here:

Salvador Coba, alcalde	captain don Ignacio Tec, batab	Juan Matu, Juan Coba
Clemente Cante, alcalde		Francisco Huchim
	Pablo Tec, notary	regidors

This recited mass was said and I signed it, fray Ávila

FOL. 30R DOCUMENT B64

WILL OF MATEO YAM

15 NOVEMBER 1767

CIMI MATHE.° YAM EN 15 DE NOUE.ᶜ DE 1767 Ã

tu kaba D.ˢ yumbil D.s mehenbil D.ˢ espilitu santo huntulili hahar D.ˢ Vchuc tumen tusinil mayx pimobi lay bin ylabac V hunil yn takyahthan tin testamento hibicil tenil cen Mathe.° yam u mehenen gaspar yam V yalen Andrea canul ah otochnarlob Vuay ti cah Yxil lae Bayxan tu yortah ca yumil ti D.ˢ u xul yn cuxtal uay yokol cab rae Volah mucul yn CuCutil ychil santa ygressia liguix yn uoktic ynba ti ca pixanil yum p.ᶜ Vardian ca yalab Junpeɔ missa Resal mis yokol yn pixan y̱l ix ca u mansen tu payarchi ychill u missa mahebarl u xantar yn pixan tu numiayl pulgatolio bin ɔabac u limos-nayl tumen yalab otzil christianob rae uacꝑer tumin y̱ caꝑer tumin gielusalem—

Bayxan hunac cħen y̱ u sola[r u]pach yn mul matan y̱ yn sucun cremete yam yn parte lae cin patic tu kab yn uixmehen Dominga yam y̱ simona yam—Bayxan yl u yarlob yn tia martha canul Joseph cob y̱ marⁿ cob lic yocolob yokol lay cħen y̱ lay solal lae Bayxan hunac kax yan tay kulche tu lakin xaman tan kulche Vtial yn uixmehen

Dominga yam tu hunar lae u tza yallobe ti chikin Joseph pech ti nohol ming.[l] tec ti
lakin Joseph Mis ti xaman Sarua[or] coba Bayxan hunac kax yan tu nohor lochchen
mul kax yn parte lae cin patic tu kab yn uixmehen Dominga yam Bayxan hunper baat
Utial yn uixmehen Dominga yam halili u xul yn than tin testamento cin uacuntic
huntul almehen p.[o] pot albasseas lay bin tan ortic V katic missa yoklal yn pixan tu tan
batab y Jus[as]—

Diego cot alcar[s]	Capp[n] D.[n] ygn.[o] tec Batab	gaspar chan gaspar ek
gaspar yam alcar[s]	Andres tec then[e]	sebas.[n] chim xtouar na
Marcos pot ess[no]—8 rr[s]		Reg.dorlessob rae

8 rr[s] Resose esta misa y lo firme fray Avila

MATEO YAM DIED ON THE 15TH OF NOVEMBER, 1767

In the name of God the Father, God the Son, God the Holy Spirit, one true God
almighty, not many. It will be seen, the document of my final statement in my will,
inasmuch as I who am Mateo Yam, the son of Gaspar Yam and child of Andrea
Canul, householders here in the cah of Ixil. Likewise, as our lord in God wishes to
end my life here on this earth, I wish my body buried in the holy church. I now also
supplicate our blessed lord, the guardian priest, to say one mass, a recited mass, for
my soul, and also to send up a prayer for me in the mass, so nothing delays my soul in
the suffering of purgatory. The fee shall be given, for we are believing Christians: six
tomins and two tomins for Jerusalem.

Likewise, one well with the house plot that goes with it, which I inherited jointly
with my older brother, Clemente Yam; my share of it I leave in the hands of my
daughters, Dominga Yam and Simona Yam. Likewise, the children of my aunt, Marta
Canul—Joseph Cob and Martín Cob—who use this house plot and well. Likewise,
one forest plot, which is near Kulche, to the northeast toward Kulche, for my daughter, Dominga Yam, alone. Its neighbors are Joseph Pech to the west, to the south
Miguel Tec, to the east Joseph Mis, to the north Salvador Coba. Likewise, one forest
plot, which is to the south of Lochchen, a joint forest; my share of it I leave in the
hands of my daughter Dominga Yam. This is the truth, the end of my statement in
my will. I appoint a nobleman, Pedro Poot, as executor; he shall take care to request
mass for my soul. Before the batab and magistrates:

Diego Coot, alcalde	captain don Ignacio Tec, batab	Gaspar Chan, Gaspar Ek
Gaspar Yam, alcalde	Andrés Tec, lieutenant	Sebastián Chim, Cristóbal Na
Marcos Poot, notary—8 reales		regidors

8 reales; this recited mass was said and I signed it, fray Ávila

FOL. 30V DOCUMENT B65

WILL OF LUISA COUOH
13 JANUARY 1768

CIMI LUISSA COUOH EN 13 DE ENERO DE 1768 AN⁵ =

tu kaba Dios yumbil Dios espiritu santo oxtul personas huntulil Dios uchuc tumen
tusinil maix pimobi lay bin ylabac u hunil yn testamento hibicil tenil luissa couoh
u yixmehen Saluador couoh u Yalen pabiana Juchim ah otochnalob ua ti cah Yxile
bacacix cimil in cah toh uol tin pucsikal y tin naat uet sihci lae bayxan cin uoktic inba
ti ca pixanil yum padre gualdian ca yalab hunpeɔ missa Resada Bayxan bin ɔabac u
limosnayl uacpel tumin y lae y hunpel tumin Jelusalem lae—

   Bayxan hunpel caha cin ɔaic tin ual Berⁿᵃ Ytza y u lak hunpay caha utial in ual
Bartesara Ytza halili u xul Yn than in testamento lae uacuntic huntul almehen Dⁿ gaspar canul albasiaslae lay bin tan oltic u katicob misa tin pixan tu tan Batab y Jusᵃˢ lae

Sar.ᵒʳ coba alᵉ	Cappⁿ D.ⁿ ygn.º tec	juº matu
Cle.ᵗᵉ cante alᵉ	Batab	juº coba
	pablo tec essⁿᵒ	franco Juchim
		pasqual canche
		Regiᵒʳsob rae

[different hand:] Resose esta misa y lo firme fray Avila

LUISA COUOH DIED ON THE 13TH OF JANUARY, 1768

In the name of God the Father, God the Holy Spirit, three persons, one almighty God,
not many. The document of my testament will be seen, inasmuch as I am Luisa Couoh,
the daughter of Salvador Couoh and child of Fabiana Huchim, householders here in
the cah of Ixil. Although I am dying, my heart and my understanding are sound, as it
should be. Likewise, I supplicate our blessed lord, the guardian priest, to say one recited
mass. Likewise, the fee shall be given: six tomins, and with it one tomin for Jerusalem.

   Likewise, I give one chest to my child, Bernardina Itza, and the other chest is
for my child, Baltesara Itza. This is the truth, the end of my statement in my will. I
designate one nobleman, don Gaspar Canul, as executor. He shall take care to request
a mass for my soul. Before the batab and magistrates here:

Salvador Coba, alcalde	captain don Ignacio Tec, batab	Juan Matu
Clemente Cante, alcalde		Juan Coba
	Pablo Tec, notary	Francisco Huchim
		Pasqual Canche
		regidors

This recited mass was said and I signed it, fray Ávila

FOL. 19R DOCUMENT C1[10]

WILL OF VIVIANA PECH

4 JULY 1738

IXIL

CIMI BIBIANA PECH HELE EN 4 DE JULIO DE 1738 AÑOS

tu kab Dios yumbil y̱ Dios mehenbil y̱ Dios espir[itu sa]nto oxtul persona huntuli
Dios uchuc tumen tusinil Maix pinobi lay bin ylabac u hunil yn takyahthan tin testamento hebicilil tenil cen bibiana pech u yyxmehen Alonso pech u yalen usula cime
Ah otochnalon uay ti cah yxil le Bacix cimil yn cah ten tin cuttile toh uol tin pucsikal
y̱ tin nat uet sicey uolah mucul yn uiniccil lae Maixnac bin u loh uba ti cimi lae lay u
chun licilil yn tzolic yn than tin testamento enebal u cuch yn pixan tu tan ca yumil
ti Dios lae Bayxan ua tu yoltah u xul yn cuxtal uay yokol cab uolah mucul yn manhal
lumil ychil u yotoch ca kuna lae Bayxan lic yn uoktic ynba ti ca pixnal yum padre
guardian ca yab hunpec kaybil misa yokol yn pixan y̱ ca u mansen payalchi ychil u
misa Antebal yn pixan tu numyail purgatoriol hex bin yn hach nahahaltic bin ɔabac
limosnail oxpel toxt[ones] y̱ capel tumin helusale[m]

   Bayxan cin ɔaic uacpet kax ti yn ual pedro pech y̱ Felipe pech u multiallob lae—
Bayxan cin uaCuntic huntul Almehen felipe tec Aluasias lay bin tan oltic u katic misa
yokol yn pixan tu tan Batab y̱ Justisias lae

Ber.[no] coba	D[n] Fran[co] Pech	mingel tun
Ignasio pech	Batab	Matheo pech
Alcardesob	Juan cetz esno	Agustin yam
		Diego Euan
		Regidoresob

IXIL

VIVIANA PECH DIED TODAY, ON THE 4TH OF JULY, 1738

In the name of God the Father, and God the Son, and God the Holy Spirit, three
persons, one almighty God, not many. My final statement in my will shall be seen,
inasmuch as I who am Viviana Pech, the daughter of Alonso Pech, the child of Ursula
Cime; we are householders here in the cah of Ixil. Although I am dying with respect
to my body, my heart and my understanding are sound, as it should be. I wish my
body to be buried. Nobody shall redeem herself from death. This is the reason that
I now arrange my statement in my will—to lighten my soul before our lord in God.
Likewise, as he wishes to end my life here on this earth, I wish my body buried, to be
placed in the earth, in the home of our church. Likewise, I now supplicate our blessed
lord, the guardian priest, to say one sung mass to aid my soul in the suffering of
purgatory. Thus shall I be truly worthy. The fee shall be given: three tostons and two
tomin for Jerusalem.

Likewise, I give six forest plots to my children, Pedro Pech and Felipe Pech, as their joint property. Likewise, I appoint one nobleman, Felipe Tec, as executor; he shall take care to request mass for my soul. Before the batab and magistrates here:

Bernardino Coba	don Francisco Pech	Miguel Tun
Ignacio Pech	Batab	Mateo Pech
alcaldes	Juan Cetz, notary	Agustín Yam
		Diego Euan
		regidors

FOLS. 37R–37V DOCUMENT C2

WILL OF MARTA MIS
14 OCTOBER 1769

ten cen Batab yetel thi^{te} y Justisia yetel Regi^{or}sob yetel ess^{no} ti audensia tu mektan cahil Ah bolon pixan—san bernarbe Patron lae ti lic hoksic u hochol u testamiento marta mis cimi en 14 de octubre de 1769 anios—hebix u chic u tzolic ton Yum Juez tu noh Almahthan yum halach uinic lae—

tu kaba Dios yumbil y Dios mehenbil y Dios espiritu santo huntulili hahal Dios uchuc tumen tusinil maix pimobi lay bic ylabac u hunil tin testamiento hebicil ten cen marta mis u yixmehenen Nicolas mis u yalen Marta tun Ah cahnalen uay tumen tan cahil Ah bolon pixan san bernarbe Yxil lae Bayxan cin uoktic ynba ti ca pixanil Yum Padre Guardian Ca yalab hunpeɔ chichan misa Resada uacpel tumin y capel tumin Jelusalem Bayxan bin u mansen tu payalchi ychil u misa manhebal u xantal yn pixan tu numyail Purgatorio lae Bay cin thoxic hen cen ɔecbal yan tene—

Bayxan hunpel chen y u solarir u pach y mul man y in uichan Roque Yam bay licil Yn ɔaic ti in ualob Gaspar Yam y Nicolas Yam y Maria Yam Agustin Yam manuel yam multialob [. . .] Bayxan helay sebastian yam [. . .] solarar y u chen [. . .]ah [. . .] ti sebastian chim u matan tu hunac lae—Bayxan hunpay caJa cin ɔaic ti in ual Gaspar Yam Agustin Yam catulob yoklal lae—Bayxan cin ɔaic hunpel u hol Na ti in ual Nicolas Yam y Martin Yam canup yoklal—Bayxan hetun lay Yn Chupul Al Agustina Yam mabal tin ɔah ti tumenel ma tu mentah in quentail y yicham yohel Yn yum Batab y Justisia u ma subtalil lae Bayxan hunpel Pic cin ɔaic Yn uicham Roque Yam hunpel ypil cinpat ti yn uilib Antonia Couoh hunpel ypil cinpat tic ti in uilib Maria Pech—Bayxan Hunpel kax yan ti Tan cinpat tic yn ualob tu uactulilob in matan ti in Yum tu teztamento u multialob—Bonifasio cob y Josef mis chikin chritobal Juchim—xa[man] hunpel kax yal bel Baca cin patic tu kab yn ualob uactul-lob multiallil Pasqual coba ti lakin ti Nohol Josef mis [fol. 37v] chikin Diego Pech xaman Diego Pech y hunpel ca cilich colebil u matan Nicolas Yam halil u xul yn than tin teztamento cin ualcuntic huntul Almehen Josef cob Albasiasob lay bin tan oltic u katal misa yokol yn pixan tu tan yn yum Batab Justisia—cap^{n}D^n Ygnacio tec

Batab—Juan Pech Al^{de}—fran^{co} may Al^{de}—Pasqual Canche—Pasqual Na—Nicolas Euan—Antonio Kinil Regidoresob—Alonso cob es^{no}

lay u hahil ca firma ɔaic yoklal lay kax tu conah—Nicolas Yam ti Abronzio tun lae tu xaman cah yan u talel ti cahe sinco mil baras y̶ ochosientos baras lay u hahil Hochic u than lay testamento hebix tzolanil lae lay u hahil ca ɔaic ca firma yalan cabal hele en 8 de Julio de 1807 anias

Esteban tec	J^{n} de la crus cham th^{e}	Esteban cutz
Batab	pedro mis Ald^{es}	pablo chale
	pedro pan Ald^{es}	Ju^{n} Gaspal chan
		Marsel matu
		Regidoresob

I who am batab, with the lieutenant and magistrates and regidors and notary of the court in the cah governed by the blessed San Bernabé, patron here, now take a copy of the will of Marta Mis, who died on the 14th of October, 1769, so as to show its arrangement to our lord judge, our great commanding lord, the halach uinic.

In the name of God the Father, and God the Son, and God the Holy Spirit, one true God almighty, not many. It will be seen, the document of my testament, inasmuch as I who am Marta Mis, the daughter of Nicolás Mis and the child of Marta Tun, residents here beside the cah of the blessed San Bernabé of Ixil. Likewise, I supplicate our blessed lord, the guardian priest, that he say one small recited mass; six tomins and two tomins for Jerusalem. Likewise, he shall send up for me a prayer in the mass, so nothing delays my soul in the suffering of purgatory.

Thus I divide up the property that is mine. Likewise, one well with the house plot that goes with it, jointly inherited with my husband, Roque Yam; thus I now give it to my children, Gaspar Yam and Nicolás Yam and María Yam, Agustín Yam, Manuel Yam, their joint property. Likewise, as for Sebastián Yam, [document damaged] house plot with its well [document damaged] to Sebastián Chim, his inheritance forever. Likewise, one chest, which I give to my children Gaspar Yam and Agustín Yam; it is theirs both together. Likewise, I give one house beam to my children Nicolás Yam and Martín Yam; for them both together. Likewise, as for my daughter, Agustina Yam, I have left her nothing, because she and her husband do nothing on my behalf, as my lord the batab and magistrates know; she has no shame, that one. Likewise, I give one petticoat to my husband, Roque Yam; I leave one huipil to my daughter-in-law, Antonia Couoh; one huipil I leave to my daughter-in-law, María Pech. Likewise, one forest plot, which is at Tan, I leave to my children—all six together. I inherited it from my father, in his will; it was his joint property. Bonifacio Cob and Joseph Mis are to the west, Cristóbal Huchim to the north. One forest that is on the Baca road I leave in the hands of my children, the joint property of all six; Pasqual Coba is to the east, Joseph Mis to the north, [fol. 37v] Diego Pech to the west, Diego Pech to the north. And our Holy Lady is the inheritance of Nicolás Yam. No more; the end of my statement in my will. I appoint one nobleman, Joseph Cob, as executor; he shall take care of the mass request for my soul. Before my lord the batab and magistrates:

Captain don Ignacio Tec, batab; Juan Pech, alcalde; Francisco May, alcalde; Pasqual Canche, Pasqual Na, Nicolás Euan, Antonio Kinil, regidors; Alonso Cob, notary.

Our signatures affirm the truth regarding this forest that Nicolés Yam sold to Ambrocio Tun; it is to the north of the cah; on its approach to the cah, it is five thousand varas, by eight hundred varas; this is a true statement of measurement. This is the will as it was arranged. This is the truth; we give our signatures here below, today, the 8th of July, 1807.

Esteban Tec	Juan de la Cruz Chan, lieutenant	Esteban Cutz
batab	Pedro Mis, alcalde	Pablo Chale
	Pedro Pan, alcalde	Juan Gaspar Chan
		Marcelo Matu
		regidors

FOL. 19V DOCUMENT C3

WILL OF DON PEDRO PECH

25 MAY 1779

[. . .] PEDRO PECH EN 25 DE MAYO DE 1779 AÑOS

Bayxan im chahil testamento cuxan en onse de Abril layli habe 79 cuxanen yanil yn than tu kaba Dios yumbil y Dios mehenbil y Dios espirito santo oxtil personaob lae halil huntulili hahal Dios uchuc tumen tusimil maix pimobi lay bin ylabac yn thakyahthan tin testamento hibicilil tenil cen Cap^n D^n pedro pech u mehen Agustin pech u yalen bibiana pech Ah cahalnalon uay ti in mektan cahil ca yumilan A bollon pixan san Bernaber yxil Bacix cimil yn cah lae toh uol tin pucsikal y yn nat uethalae Bayxan lic uoktic ynba ti ca pixanil yum padre Cura ca yub hunpec misa Kaybil yokol yn pixan y ca u mansen tu payalchi Magebal u xantal yn pixan tu numyail pulgatorio bin ix ɔabac u limosnail tumen yalab otzil christiano

Bayxan hunac kax yan tan kulche tu ɔah ten yn tata D^n pedro pech ychil u testamento u tzayal lay kax lae ti lakine christobal pech ti xamane Diego cab ti chikine Martin cante ti nohol Fran^{co} pech lay yn testamento minchahilae tu tanil yn yuon ta[bal]

Diego Pech y Cap^n D^n Jose cab Batab y ca yum Alferes D^n Antonio Pech y ca yum D^n Manuel Pech Alferes y ca yum th^e D^n Pasqual Pech Bayxan cin uacuntil yn hel catul Almehenob Albasiasoblae Jph Pech y Diego pot

| sebastian chim | Felipe canche th^e | Fran^{co} may |

matheo uh	Domingo Ytza esno	pedro coba
Alcardeob lae		Gaspal cob
		felipe canul
		Regidoresob

[Don] Pedro Pech [died] on the 25th of May, 1779

Likewise, my diligent testament; being alive on April 11th of this year, '79; I am alive; my statement: In the name of God the Father, and God the Son, and God the Holy Spirit, three persons, no more, one true God almighty, not many. My final statement in my testament will be seen, inasmuch as I who am Captain don Pedro Pech, the son of Agustín Pech, the child of Viviana Pech; we are residents here in the cah governed by our lord the blessed San Bernabé of Ixil. Although I am dying, my heart and my understanding are sound, as it should be. Likewise, I now supplicate our blessed lord, the Padre Curate, to deliver one sung mass for my soul and to send up for me a prayer so nothing delays my soul in the suffering of purgatory. Also the fee shall be given, for I am a believing Christian.

Likewise, one forest plot, which is toward Kulche, given to me by my uncle, don Pedro Pech, in his will. The neighbors of this forest are Cristóbal Pech to the east, Diego Cab to the north, to the west Martín Cante, to the south Francisco Pech. This is my will. I have omitted nothing. Before my consanguineal relatives:

Diego Pech and Captain don José Cob, batab, and our lords don Antonio Pech and don Manuel Pech, alféreces, and our lord lieutenant don Pasqual Pech. Likewise, I appoint as my substitutes, two nobles as executors, Joseph Pech and Diego Poot.

Sebastián Chim	Felipe Canche, lieutenant	Francisco May
Mateo Uh	Domingo Itza, notary	Pedro Coba
alcaldes		Gaspar Cob
		Felipe Canul
		regidors

NOTES

1. The A corpus (or Christensen corpus) is in AHAY, "Oficios 1748–1749, 1801–1884," vol. 1.

2. Originally, we translated this as "house door," and indeed *hol na* is glossed and discussed in Restall (1995) and (1997) as if it referred to the door of a Maya home. However, Amara Solari (personal communication, August 2017) has persuaded us that *hol* was a term for a wooden beam and that *hol na* meant "house beam" or the central wooden beam that ran the length of the roof of a Maya house—certainly a valuable and enduring possession. In cases where the beam was specifically meant as a door beam, the Spanish term *puerta* was added (such instances only appear in the later wills: B19, B24, B30, B54). Note that Restall had originally translated another term, *bac*, as "beam," in its sole appearance in the wills (doc. B4); we have left it glossed thus, although we suspect it in fact refers to an item of men's clothing.

3. Cogolludo (1688: bk. 2, 661) places Tiz as part of the doctrina of Hunucma.

4. This phrase, "oxtul personas" (three people), was inserted in the left margin as a correction.

5. On the last few pages there are watermarks of a soldier on a horse, a crest on another.

6. This is the last page of the collection, and the next page of the will is missing.

7. The B corpus (or Restall corpus) is in CAIHY (see Restall 1995).

8. This notation appears in a Maya hand and differs from that of the notary, Marcos Poot.

9. Literally, "he who carries honey on his back," this was a Maya political office, noteworthy for its inclusion centuries after Spanish cabildo office titles were introduced; see the discussion in chapter 2.

10. The three documents that follow, C1, C2, and C3, are out of chronological sequence because they were not found in the two corpora of wills that are extant remnants of Ixil's original Book of Wills (the A corpus found by Christensen and the B corpus found by Restall); instead, these three were found by Restall in 1990 buried within land records in the volumes of the ANEY that were (as mentioned earlier) subsequently stolen, recovered, and eventually rearchived in the AGEY.

References

ARCHIVAL SOURCES AND ABBREVIATIONS

AGEY   Archivo General del Estado de Yucatán, Merida, Yucatan

AGI   Archivo General de Indias, Seville, Spain

AGN   Archivo General de la Nación, Mexico City

AHAY   Archivo Histórico del Arzobispado de Yucatán, Conkal, Yucatan—Visitas Pastorales

ANEY   Archivo Notarial del Estado de Yucatán, Merida, Yucatan

CAIHY   Centro de Apoyo a la Investigación Histórica de Yucatán, Merida, Yucatan

CS-1722   Bishop Gómez de Parada's 1722 synod (see Gómez de Parada 2008)

DM   Diccionario de Motul, manuscript Codex Ind 8 in the John Carter Brown Library, Providence, RI

DT   Documentos de Tekanto, originally in ANEY (reportedly now in AGEY)

FS-MY   "Mexico, Yucatan," Family Search (online database) https://www.familysearch .org/search/collection/location/1928711?region=Yucat%C3%A1n

GGMM   Garrett-Gates Mesoamerican Manuscripts, Princeton University Library, Princeton, NJ

LC   Library of Congress, Washington, DC

RLRI   *Recopilación de leyes de los reinos de las indias*, tomo III (Madrid: La viuda de D. Joaquín Ibarra, 1943)

TULAL   Tulane University Latin American Library, New Orleans, LA

DOI: 10.5876/9781607329220.c009

PUBLISHED SOURCES

Antochiw, Michel. 2006. *Milicia de Yucatán (siglos XVI y XVII) & la unión de armas de 1712*. Campeche, Mexico: Universidad Autónoma de Campeche.

Bourdin, Gabriel. 2008. "El cuerpo humano en el léxico del maya peninsular." *Ketzalcalli* 1: 47–68.

Bricker, Victoria R. 2015. "Where There's a Will, There's a Way: The Significance of Scribal Variation in Colonial Maya Testaments." *Ethnohistory* 62, no. 3: 421–44.

Bricker, Victoria R., and Rebecca E. Hill. 2009. "Climatic Signatures in Yucatecan Wills and Death Records," *Ethnohistory* 56, no. 2: 227–68.

Bricker, Victoria R., and Helga-Maria Miram, eds. and trans. 2002. *An Encounter of Two Worlds: The Book of Chilam Balam of Kaua*. New Orleans, LA: Tulane University Middle American Research Institute.

Burkhart, Louise M. 2004. "Death and the Colonial Nahua." In *Nahuatl Theatre: Death and Life in Colonial Nahua Mexico*, edited by Barry D. Sell and Louise M. Burkhart, 29–54. Norman: University of Oklahoma Press.

Burns, Kathryn. 2010. *Into the Archive: Writing and Power in Colonial Peru*. Durham, NC: Duke University Press.

Burns, Robert I. 2001. *Las Siete Partidas*. Vol. 5. Philadelphia: University of Pennsylvania Press.

Calderon Quijano, Jose Antonio. 1984. *Historia de la fortificaciones en Nueva España*. Madrid: Escuela de estudios hispanoamericanos.

Carillo y Ancona, Crescencio. 1883. *Vida del v. padre fray Manuel Martinez, celebre franciscano yucateco, o sea estudio historico sobre la extincion de la orden franciscana en yucatan y sobre sus consecuencias*. Merida: Gamboa Guzman y Hermano.

Caso Barrera, Laura. 2002. *Caminos en la selva: migración, comercio y Resistencia, mayas yucatecos e itzaes, siglos XVII–XIX*. Mexico City: El Colegio de México.

Caso Barrera, Laura. 2011. *Chilam Bilam de Ixil Facsmiliar y Estudio de un Libro Maya Inédito*. Mexico City: Artes de México.

Christensen, Mark Z. 2013. *Nahua and Maya Catholicisms: Texts and Religion in Colonial Central Mexico and Yucatan*. Stanford, CA: Stanford University Press.

Christensen, Mark Z. 2104. *Translated Christianities: Nahuatl and Maya Religious Texts*. State College: Pennsylvania State University Press.

Christensen, Mark Z. 2015. "The Spoils of the Pech Conquistadors." In *Native Wills from the Colonial Americas: Dead Giveaways in a New World*, edited by Mark Z. Christensen and Jonathan Truitt, 119–37. Salt Lake City: University of Utah Press.

Christensen, Mark Z. 2016. *The Teabo Manuscript: Maya Christian Copybooks, Chilam Balams, and Native Text Production in Yucatan*. Austin: University of Texas Press.

Christensen, Mark Z., and Matthew Restall. 2019. "Maya Militia: The Defense and Government of Colonial Ixil, Yucatan." *Colonial Latin American Review* 28, no. 1 (forthcoming).

Christensen, Mark Z., and Jonathan Truitt, eds. 2015. *Native Wills from the Colonial Americas: Dead Giveaways in a New World*. Salt Lake City: University of Utah Press.

Christenson, Allen J, trans. 2003. *Popol Vuh: The Sacred Book of the Maya: The Great Classic of Central American Spirituality*. Norman: University of Oklahoma Press.

Chuchiak, John F., IV. 2000. "The Indian Inquisition and the Extirpation of Idolatry: The Process of Punishment in the Provisorato de Indios of the Diocese of Yucatán, 1563–1812." PhD diss., Tulane University.

Chuchiak, John F., IV. 2002 "The Images Speak: The Survival and Production of Hieroglyphic Codices and Their Use in Post-Conquest Maya Religion, 1580–1720." In *Maya Religious Practices: Processes of Change and Adaptation*, edited by Daniel Graña Behrens, Nikolai Grube, Christian Prager, Frauke Sachse, Stefanie Teufel, and Elisabeth Wagner, 71–103. Acta Mesoamericana 14. Markt Schwaben, Germany: Verlag Anton Saurwein.

Chuchiak, John F., IV. 2004. "It Is Their Drinking That Hinders Them: *Balche* and the Use of Ritual Intoxicants among the Colonial Yucatec Maya, 1550–1780." *Estudios de cultura maya* 24: 137–71.

Chuchiak, John F., IV. 2007. "Forgotten Allies: The Origins and Roles of Native Mesoamerican Auxiliaries and Indios Conquistadores in the Conquest of Yucatan, 1526–1550." In *Indian Conquistadors: Indigenous Allies in the Conquest of Mesoamerica*, edited by Laura E. Matthew and Michel R. Oudijk, 175–226. Norman: University of Oklahoma Press.

Chuchiak, John F., IV. 2009. "'Ah Dzib Cahob yetel lay u katlilob lae': Maya Scribes, Colonial Literacy, and Maya Petitionary Forms in Colonial Yucatán." In *Text and Context: Yucatec Maya Literature in a Diachronic Perspective*, edited by Antje Gunsenheimer, Tsubasa Okoshi Harada, and John F. Chuchiak, 159–84. Aachen: Bonner Amerikanistische Studien.

Chuchiak, John F., IV. 2012. "Indigenous Sentries and Indios Flecheros, or How the Maya Saved the Port of Campeche: The Importance of Maya Indigenous Militias and Coastal Guards in the Defense of the Port of Campeche, 1550–1750." Paper presented at the American Society for Ethnohistory meeting, Springfield, IL.

Ciudad Real, fray Antonio de. 1976. *Tratado curioso y docto de las grandezas de la Nueva España*. Vol. 2. Mexico City: Universidad Nacional Autonoma de Mexico.

Cline, S. L. 1986. *Colonial Culhuacan, 1580–1600: A Social History of an Aztec Town*. Albuquerque: University of New Mexico Press.

Cline, S. L. 1998. "Fray Alonso de Molina's Model Testament and Antecedents to Indigenous Wills in Spanish America." In *Dead Giveaways: Indigenous Testaments of Colonial Mesoamerica and the Andes*, edited by Susan Kellogg and Matthew Restall, 13–33. Salt Lake City: University of Utah Press.

Cline, S. L., and Miguel León-Portilla, eds. 1984. *The Testaments of Culhuacan*. Los Angeles: UCLA Latin American Center Publications.

Cogolludo, Diego López de. 1688. *Historia de Yucatán*. Madrid: por Juan Garcia Infanzon.

Collins, Anne C. 1977. "The *Maestros Cantores* in Yucatán." In *Anthropology and History in Yucatán*, edited by Grant D. Jones, 233–47. Austin: University of Texas Press.

Cromwell, Jesse. 2009. "Life on the Margins: (Ex) Buccaneers and Spanish Subjects on the Campeche Logwood Periphery, 1660–1716." *Itinerario* 33, no. 3: 43–71.

Evans, Sterling. 2013. *Bound in Twine: The History and Ecology of the Henequen-Wheat Complex for Mexico and the American and Canadian Plains, 1880–1950*. College Station: Texas A&M University Press.

Farriss, Nancy. 1984. *Maya Society under Colonial Rule: The Collective Enterprise of Survival*. Princeton, NJ: Princeton University Press.

Fernández del Castillo, Francisco. 1914. *Libros y libreros en el siglo XVI*. Mexico: Tip. Guerrero hnos.

Fitzsimmons, James L. 2009. *Death and the Classic Maya Kings*. Austin: University of Texas Press.

Frederick, Jake. 2016. *Riot!: Tobacco, Reform, and Violence in Eighteenth-Century Papantla, Mexico*. Brighton, UK: Sussex Academic Press.

García Bernal, Manuela Cristina. 1972. *La sociedad de Yucatán, 1700–1750*. Seville: Escuela de Estudios Hispano-Americanos.

Gillpatrick, W. W. 1885. *The Navigation of the Caribbean Sea and Gulf of Mexico*. Vol. 2. Washington, DC: Government Printing Office.

Gómez de Parada, Juan. 2008. *Constituciones sinodales del obispado de Yucatán*. Edited by Gabriela Solís Robleda. Merida: Universidad Nacional Autónoma de México. Originally published 1722.

González Echevarría, Roberto. 1998. *Myth and Archive: A Theory of Latin American Narrative*. Durham, NC: Duke University Press.

Gosner, Kevin. 1992. *Soldiers of the Virgin: The Moral Economy of a Colonial Maya Rebellion*. Tucson: University of Arizona Press.

Greenleaf, Richard. 1969. "The Mexican Inquisition and the Masonic Movement: 1751–1820." *New Mexico Historical Review* 44, no. 2 (April): 93–118.

Gubler, Ruth, and David Bolles. 2000. *The Book of Chilam Balam of Na: Facsimile, Translation, and Edited Text*. Lancaster, CA: Labyrinthos.

Güereca Durán, Raquel Eréndira. 2013. "Las milicias de indios flecheros en la Nueva España, siglos XVI–XVII." Thesis, Universidad Nacional Autónoma de México.

Haskett, Robert Stephen. 1991. *Indigenous Rulers: An Ethnohistory of Town Government in Colonial Cuernavaca*. Albuquerque: University of New Mexico Press.

Hanks, William F. 2010. *Converting Words: Maya in the Age of the Cross*. Berkeley: University of California Press.

Hoggarth, Julie A., Matthew Restall, James W. Wood, and Douglas J. Kennett. 2017. "Drought and Its Demographic Effects in the Maya Lowlands." *Current Anthropology* 58, no. 1 (February): 82–113.

Hosselkus, Erika. 2011. "Death, Dying, and the Noble Nahuas of New Spain's Colonial Puebla-Tlaxcala Valley." In *Death and Dying in Colonial Latin America*, edited by Miruna Achim and Martina Will de Chaparro, 28–52. Tucson: University of Arizona Press.

Hsia, R. Po-chia. 2010. *A Jesuit in the Forbidden City: Matteo Ricci, 1552–1610*. New York: Oxford University Press.

Jones, Grant D., ed. 1977. *Anthropology and History in Yucatán*. Austin: University of Texas Press.

Jones, Grant D. 1998. *The Conquest of the Last Maya Kingdom*. Stanford, CA: Stanford University Press.

Kellogg, Susan, and Matthew Restall, eds. 1998. *Dead Giveaways: Indigenous Testaments of Colonial Mesoamerica and the Andes*. Salt Lake City: University of Utah Press.

Landa, Friar Diego de. 1937. *Yucatan before and after the Conquest*. Translated by William Gates. Baltimore, MD: Maya Society.

Lane, Kris. 1998. *Pillaging the Empire: Piracy in the Americas, 1500–1750*. Armonk, New York: M. E. Sharpe.

León, Fray Martín de. 1611. *Camino del cielo en lengua mexicana, con todos los requisitos necesarios para conseguir este fin*. Mexico City: Diego López Daualos.

León Pinelo, Antonio de. 1992. *Recopilación de leyes de Indias*. Vol. 2. Edited by Ismael Sánchez Bella. Mexico City: Editorial Porrúa.

Lentz, Mark W. 2013. "Batabs of the Barrio: Urban Maya Rulers, Mérida, Yucatan, 1670–1806." In *City Indians in Spain's American Empire: Urban Indigenous Society in Colonial Mesoamerica and Andean South America, 1530–1830*, edited by Dana Velasco Murillo, Mark Lentz, and Margarita R. Ochoa, 172–98. Portland, OR: Sussex Academic Press.

Lockhart, James. 1992. *The Nahuas after the Conquest: A Social and Cultural History of the Indians of Central Mexico, Sixteenth through Eighteenth Centuries*. Stanford, CA: Stanford University Press.

Martín de Guijo, Gregorio. 1952. *Diario, 1648–1664*. Vol. 2. Mexico City: Editorial Porrúa.

Matthews, Jennifer P. 2009. *Chicle: The Chewing Gum of the Americas from the Ancient Maya to William Wrigley.* Tucson: University of Arizona Press.

Melton-Villanueva, Miriam. 2016. *Aztecs at Independence: Nahua Culture Makers in Central Mexico, 1799–1832.* Tucson: University of Arizona Press.

Molina, fray Alonso de. 1984. *Confesionario mayor en la lengua mexicana y castellana (1569).* Introduction by Roberto Moreno. Mexico City: Instituto de Investigaciones Filológicas, Instituto de Investigaciones Históricas, Universidad Nacional Autónoma de México.

Molina Solís, Juan Francisco. 1904–10. *Historia de Yucatán durante la dominación española,* 2 vols. Merida: Imprenta de la lotería del estado.

Morales, Francisco. 1973. *Ethnic and Social Background of the Franciscan Friars in Seventeenth-Century Mexico.* Berkeley, CA: Academy of American Franciscan History.

Narváez Hernández, José Ramón. 2007. *Historia social del derecho y de la justicia.* Mexico City: Editorial Porrúa.

O'Callaghan, Joseph F. 1975. *A History of Medieval Spain.* Ithaca, NY: Cornell University Press.

Olko, Justyna, John Sullivan, and Jan Szemiński, eds. 2018. *Dialogue with Europe, Dialogue with the Past: Colonial Nahua and Quechua Elites in Their Own Words.* Louisville: University Press of Colorado.

Orilla Canche, Juan Francisco. 2005. *Crónicas de Ixil.* Merida: Ediciones PACMYC.

Patch, Robert W. 1993. *Maya and Spaniard in Yucatan, 1648–1812.* Stanford, CA: Stanford University Press.

Paxton, Frederick S. 1990. *Christianizing Death: The Creation of a Ritual Process in Early Medieval Europe.* Ithaca, NY: Cornell University Press.

Peniche Moreno, Paola. 2007. *Ámbitos del parentesco: la sociedad maya en tiempos de la Colonia.* Mexico City: CIESAS: Miguel Ángel Porrúa.

Peraza Guzmán, Marco Tulio. 2000. "La defensa y fortificación portuaria en el Yucatán virreinal." In *Arquitectura y urbanismo virreinal,* edited by Marco Tulio Peraza Guzmán, 94–107. Merida: Unidad de Posgrado e Investigación, Facultad de Arquitectura, Universidad Autónoma de Yucatán.

Pizzigoni, Caterina, ed. and trans. 2007. *Testaments of Toluca.* Stanford, CA: Stanford University Press.

Pizzigoni, Caterina. 2012. *The Life Within: Local Indigenous Society in Mexico's Toluca Valley, 1650–1800.* Stanford, CA: Stanford University Press.

Quezada, Sergio. 2014. *Maya Lords and Lordship: The Formation of Colonial Society in Yucatán, 1350–1600.* Translated by Terry Rugeley. Norman: University of Oklahoma Press.

Quezada, Sergio, and Tsubasa Okoshi Harada. 2001. *Papeles de los Xiu de Yaxá, Yucatán.* Mexico City: Universidad Nacional Autónoma de México.

Ramos, Gabriela. 2010. *Death and Conversion in the Andes: Lima and Cuzco, 1532–1670*. Notre Dame, IN: University of Notre Dame Press.

Ramos, Gabriela. 1873. *Relación breve y verdadera de algunas cosas de las muchas que sucedieron al padre fray Alonso Ponce en las provincias de la Nueva España*. Madrid: Imprenta de la viuda de Calero.

Recopilación de leyes. 1906. *Recopilación de leyes, decretos y providencias de los poderes legislativo y ejecutivo de la unión*. Vol. 78. Mexico City: Imprenta del gobierno federal.

Restall, Matthew. 1995. *Life and Death in a Maya Community: The Ixil Testaments of the 1760s*. Lancaster, CA: Labyrinthos.

Restall, Matthew. 1997. *The Maya World: Yucatec Culture and Society, 1550–1850*. Stanford, CA: Stanford University Press.

Restall, Matthew. 1998a. *Maya Conquistador*. Boston: Beacon Press.

Restall, Matthew. 1998b. "Interculturation and the Indigenous Testament in Colonial Yucatan." In *Dead Giveaways: Indigenous Testaments of Colonial Mesoamerica and the Andes*, edited by Susan Kellogg and Matthew Restall, 141–62. Salt Lake City: University of Utah Press.

Restall, Matthew. 2009. *The Black Middle: Africans, Mayas, and Spaniards in Colonial Yucatan*. Stanford, CA: Stanford University Press.

Restall, Matthew. 2014a. "Invasion: The Mayas at War, 1520s–1540s." In *Embattled Bodies, Embattled Places: Conflict, Conquest, and the Performance of War in Pre-Columbian America*, edited by Andrew K. Scherer and John W. Verano, 93–117. Washington, DC: Dumbarton Oaks.

Restall, Matthew. 2014b. "Crossing to Safety? Frontier Flight in Eighteenth-Century Belize and Yucatan." *Hispanic American Historical Review* 94, no. 3 (August): 381–419.

Restall, Matthew, Lisa Sousa, and Kevin Terraciano, eds. 2005. *Mesoamerican Voices: Native Language Writings from Colonial Mexico, Oaxaca, Yucatan, and Guatemala*. New York: Cambridge University Press.

Restall, Matthew, Amara Solari, John Chuchiak, and Traci Ardren. Forthcoming. *The Friar and the Maya: Diego de Landa's Account of the Things of Yucatan*. Louisville: University Press of Colorado.

Robles, Antonio de. 1946 [1665–1703]. *Diario de sucesos notables (1665–1703)*, vol. 2. Mexico City: Editorial Porrua.

Roys, Ralph L. 1939. *The Titles of Ebtun*. Washington, DC: Carnegie Institution of Washington.

Roys, Ralph L. 1957. *The Political Geography of the Yucatan Maya*. Washington, DC: Carnegie Institution of Washington.

Ruz, Fray Joaquin. 1847. *Catecismo y esposición de la doctrina Christiana*. Merida: José D. Espinosa.

Sahagún, Bernardino de. 1997. *Primeros memoriales*. Translated by Thelma D. Sullivan, edited and revised by H. B. Nicholson, Arthur J.O. Anderson, Charles E. Dibble, Eloise Quiñones Keber, and Wayne Ruwet. Norman: University of Oklahoma Press. Originally published ca. 1558–61.

Sanchez de Aguilar, Pedro. 1937. *Informe Contra Idolorum Cultores*. Merida: E. G. Triay. Originally published 1639.

Scherer, Andrew K. 2015. *Mortuary Landscapes of the Classic Maya: Rituals of Body and Soul*. Austin: University of Texas Press.

Sell, Barry D., and Louise M. Burkhart, eds. 2004. *Nahuatl Theatre: Death and Life in Colonial Mexico*. Norman: University of Oklahoma Press.

Socolow, Susan Migden. 2015. *The Women of Colonial Latin America*. 2nd ed. New York: Cambridge University Press.

Terraciano, Kevin. 1998. "Native Expressions of Piety in Mixtec Testaments." In *Dead Giveaways: Indigenous Testaments of Colonial Mesoamerica and the Andes*, edited by Susan Kellogg and Matthew Restall, 115–40. Salt Lake City: University of Utah Press.

Thompson, Philip C. 1999. *Tekanto, a Maya Town in Colonial Yucatan*. New Orleans, LA: Middle American Research Institute, Tulane University.

Tozzer, Alfred M. 1921. *A Maya Grammar*. Cambridge, MA: Peabody Museum of American Archaeology and Ethnology, Harvard University.

Victoria Ojeda, Jorge. 1995. *Mérida de Yucatán de las Indias: Piratería y estrategia defensiva*. Merida: Ayuntamiento de Mérida.

Victoria Ojeda, Jorge. 2000. "Las vigías en la defensa y el poblamiento de la costa yucateca: su diseño y representación cartográfica." In *Arquitectura y urbanismo virrenal*, edited by Marco Tulio Peraza Guzmán, 59–69. Merida: Unidad de Posgrado e Investigación, Facultad de Arquitectura, Universidad Autónoma de Yucatán.

Victoria Ojeda, Jorge. 2005. "Entre la historia y la literatura: versos testimoniales de Íñigo Escalante, un poeta del Yucatán colonial." *Mesoamérica* 47: 1–22.

Victoria Ojeda, Jorge. 2007. *Las torres de vigía en Yucatán: una manifestación histórica de la proyección hispana a ultramar*. Madrid: Ministerio de defensa instituto de historia y cultura naval.

Victoria Ojeda, Jorge. 2010. "Uso y abuso de los indígenas atalayeros en el Yucatán Novohispano." *Tzintzun*, no. 51: 61–82.

Vinson, Ben, III. 2002. *Bearing Arms for His Majesty: The Free-Colored Militia in Colonial Mexico*. Stanford, CA: Stanford University Press.

Will de Chaparro, Martina. 2007. *Death and Dying in New Mexico*. Albuquerque: University of New Mexico Press.

Index